ON SEEING FORMS

BOOKS BY
WILLIAM R. UTTAL

ON SEEING FORMS

William R. Uttal

Naval Ocean Systems Center
Hawaii Laboratory
Kaiula, Hawaii

 LAWRENCE ERLBAUM ASSOCIATES, PUBLISHERS
1988   Hillsdale, New Jersey   Hove and London

Lawrence Erlbaum Associates, Inc., Publishers
365 Broadway
Hillsdale, New Jersey 07642

Library of Congress Cataloging in Publication Data

Uttal, William R.
  On seeing forms.

  Bibliography: p.
  Includes indexes.
  1. Form perception. 2. Visual perception.
I. Title. [DNLM: 1. Form Perception. 2. Visual
Perception. WW 105 U93o]
BF241.U854 1988   152.1′423   88-421
ISBN 0-89859-994-6

Printed in the United States of America
10 9 8 7 6 5 4 3 2

For my favorite
- *Marine biologist*
- *Sociologist*
- *Atmospheric Physicist*
 and
- *Art Historian*

This is a world of form and structure and can only be properly understood as such.
—L.L. Whyte, 1968, p. xi

CONTENTS

PREFACE

Some years ago, I set myself the task of writing a series of books that would discuss the many levels of sensory and perceptual processing underlying our ability to acquire information and knowledge from the physical world of which we are a part. Figure P.1 depicts in a few words and a single drawing the general organization of this project. The first three books (previously completed) were intended to deal, respectively, with the peripheral neural coding mechanisms found in all of the senses (*The Psychobiology of Sensory Coding*, 1973), the central neural mechanisms of perception and other aspects of mind (*The Psychobiology of Mind*, 1978), and the immediate and automatic visual processes (*A Taxonomy of Visual Processes*, 1981). In the third volume, the "Taxonomy," I proposed a classification system of the visual processes based on six levels of "critical processes." However, that book dealt only with the first five of those six levels of processing, all of which could be considered to be more or less automatic and preattentive with regard to the involved mental activities. A detailed discussion of the sixth and highest level of processing (Level 5—attentive, active, cognitive processing) was omitted from that volume for some very practical reasons (the book had already grown into a large and expensive 1,100 pages by the time I finished discussing Levels 0 through 4), as well as some important theoretical reasons (attentive and preattentive processing exhibit critical differences in their nature that necessitate that they be handled separately).

Over the years that I have been working on this project, my interests have focused more sharply on visual processing, almost to the exclusion of the other senses, for some compelling reasons. First, there is simply too much data to

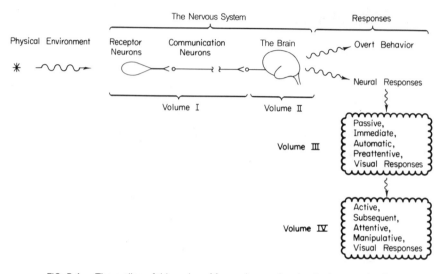

FIG. P.1.   The outline of this series of four volumes showing topics contained in each of the volumes (from Uttal, 1981).

allow anyone to be a global sensory and perceptual generalist anymore. Second, vision is so much like the other senses in terms of its general properties that it can serve as a model for the other modalities. Third, vision is the main gateway between the interpersonally shared "external" physical world and the intrapersonally private "internal" mental realm experienced by each individual in what we now appreciate is a profound solitude: It may be argued that "We" are connected to the external world and to others by frail and indirectly encoded neural threads. Our sense of intimacy with that world, this argument continues, is but a reconstructed illusion displaying many inconsistencies and discrepancies.

Therefore, concentrating on vision means attending to both the major means of information acquisition and the most complete answer to the epistemologist's quest. As the years have gone by, I have thus found myself becoming more and more constrained in the breadth of topics I attempt to cover in each of these volumes of what now constitutes a tetralogy. Whereas the first two dealt with all aspects of peripheral and central psychobiological processing respectively, the third had to be limited to only the preattentive aspects of vision. The forces compelling this narrowing continue; my original intent was to deal with the full range of attentive visual perception in this fourth volume, but I now appreciate that even this limited objective was too broad. After prolonged concern and a substantial amount of further study, simple prudence now demands that to try to cover even what I have called Level 5 would be overly ambitious. Therefore, this final volume in my tetralogy has been constrained to a much smaller range of topics. It is now my intent that this book deal only with the visual perception of *form*. This is the field of study that has increasingly become my major research interest in the last decade both in the laboratory and in the study. It is now clear to me that this topic is itself sufficiently expansive to fill the pages of a reasonably sized book and that to broaden the range further is likely to make this volume unmanageable from the mechanical, economic, and intellectual points of view.

My goal in this present volume remains, as it was in the "Taxonomy"; that is, to bring some degree of classificatory order to the enormous mass of knowledge that has accumulated in the archival literature concerning a major aspect of visual perception. In that earlier book the topic was the preattentive aspects of vision—here it is visual form perception, an area that, in large part, involves cognitive and attentive processes as well. A major difference, however, is that in this volume I plan to concentrate more on the relevant theories than on the empirical data. In doing so, I am also preparing both my readers and myself for a critical consideration of the current status and achievements of modern theories of form perception in the final chapter.

As I begin this part of the project I must note again my awareness of the fact that this role of a book-writing integrator and systemizer is not one that is universally held in high repute by all members of the visual science community—many students of vision value much more highly the explorations and measurements of the laboratory than the search for order through the already, or soon-to-be, dusty shelves of libraries: Indeed, many overtly eschew "books" as an appropriate medium of scientific expression. Be that as it may, I have found a great deal of personal satisfaction and understanding accruing from the task that I have set for myself.

Beyond that personal satisfaction and enlightenment, however, is an ever increasing conviction on my part that this type of endeavor, carried out by at least a few of us is not just worthwhile, but is essential for the progress of our science. The rich disorder of the empirical journals demands that a few visual scientists attend to the taxonomic tasks of classification, systemization, and categorization so that the rest of us can begin to see the kind of natural order that permeates this field of science, just as other kinds of order are natural to chemistry, physics, and the several other fields of biology.

It is also important that some of us continuously pay attention to the logical and philosophical foundations of our science so that we can collectively avoid the conceptual traps that so often can lead entire schools of thought astray. Nowhere is the possibility of such a trap better considered than in Elliot Valenstein's brilliant historical study (Valenstein, 1986) describing what happened to neurosurgery in the mid-20th century. The parallels to perceptual science are very close even if the perils of a conceptual misunderstanding are not so great in this field as in psychiatry.

At the risk of becoming a nagging gadfly (as opposed to just an ordinary one), I must reassert an opinion that I have already expressed in print several times previously: From my point of view, the main purpose of science is not to collect data or to test narrowly and precisely defined hypotheses, but rather to achieve global understanding of the natural world of which we are both a component part and an investigator. The function of the highly abstract and controllable tests of reality we call experiments is to provide us with a manageable level of complexity that, unlike full-scale reality, can be manipulated in the search for causal relations, or at the very least, correlations. For reasons that are predominantly practical and that were well understood in the 16th and 17th centuries, it is only in this manner that we can add to our understanding of nature as it is. However, no single datum, observation, or measurement is in itself important. In abstracting nature to a low level of complexity in the laboratory in order to carry out controlled experiments, we remove ourselves to some distance from the full blown reality of natural scenes and may pay a serious price — loss of the complex, yet essential, substance of what it is that we are studying. Indeed, the difference between the total amount of information contained in natural scenes and that represented in the idealized experiment is usually so great (particularly in the psychological sciences) that it sometimes seems as if the laboratory has nothing to say to the real world of ecologically significant perception.

Rest assured, I am not proposing discarding experimental science in the search for the chimera of some fantastic kind of "ecologically significant" methodology. To study visual perception only from such a point of view would emasculate the power of analytic methods to search for understanding of whatever kind of psychobiological reality actually exists. We must continue to use these "perceptual fruitflies" (i.e., reduced, abstract experiments) if we are to achieve the understanding toward which we quest. To do otherwise would leave visual science mired in the multivariate and controlled tangle in which it was embedded prior to Rene Descartes' and John Stuart Mill's assertion of the "method of detail." But, we must appreciate that we do so at a cost.

On the other hand, microscopic experimentation in which we do nothing more than manipulate abstractions of reality must not be the end all of science. We must ask "What does it all mean?" and we must try to "put it all together." It is this responsibility that I believe validates the effort that Jerry A. Fodor has called *speculative psychology*. My work here, and that of others elsewhere, are self-conscious efforts to go beyond the data and the data-bound microtheories in order to draw from them, to the extent that it is possible given the complexity of the situation and my own personal limits, some expression of the scientific community's present state of understanding of visual form perception after what is in fact a 2,500-year history of interest in this topic. Therefore, the most important part of this book, the part on which any success that it may enjoy will depend, will certainly be the last chapter that I write many months hence. That final chapter will be a statement of my view of the state of our perceptual science.

It is essential that I make another important point clear at the outset of this work. Whatever the conclusions, I am fully aware that it is all made possible because of the corpus of empirical data that currently exists. *Everything that is written here is made possible by what has been done in the laboratory by a group of specialists to whom all of us are deeply indebted.* It is also my earnest hope that I do not inadvertently offend some important contributor by an oversight of citation caused either by clumsy scholarship or by simple ignorance of the intellectual roots of a significant idea. I am a student and an intellectual creation of my times as have been all of my speculative predecessors. Neither the contemporary theoretical consequences, nor those existing at other times, are independent of the scientific milieu in which they are embedded. I hope that I understand my own intellectual roots well enough to acknowledge in a proper and timely manner, the sources that have exerted their influence on my thinking. I suppose, however, that in some instances some of the most important ideas have become such a fundamental part of the scientific community thinking that I may sometimes inadvertently take them as axiomatic.

Another fact about which I hope I have also the minimum amount of self-deception concerns the classification system that I propose here. Embodied in this book's table of contents is a specific taxonomic theory of the relation of the various perceptual phenomena and processes involved in our ability to "see" forms. Briefly, it assumes a hierarchical series of processes — detection, discrimination, and recognition — somewhere within which preattentive mechanisms are at least supplemented, if not supplanted, by attentive ones. Such a taxonomy, explicit or implicit, can never be unique nor final. Others may well have proposed a different classification system, and may find this system unsatisfying or incomplete. To those who differ with me, the challenge is simple. Join me in this endeavor; suggest and develop your own system. The field is wide open, indeed, given the small number of us working here. I am convinced that perceptual science, long a "garbage can" of taxonomically unrelated ideas, would greatly benefit from having others join in the search for order and classification.

In these prefatory remarks, I must also acknowledge that I have undergone a change in personal philosophy and perspective that a few years ago I would have thought highly improbable, if not impossible. In the past I have always looked to neurophysiology and to its attendant metaphysics — either cellular or network neuroreductionism — as the ultimate form of explanation and understanding in our search to unravel the problems of visual perception. As I worked on the "Taxonomy," however, I gradually became more convinced that the goal of a totally neuroreductionistic visual psychology (or, for that matter, any kind of psychology) is a totally unrealistic expectation. I have much more to say about this point later in this volume.

I must reiterate one essential point here, however, to avoid another dismal misunderstanding. The practical and combinatorial reasons for rejecting cellular or network neuroreductionism do not involve any disillusionment on my part with the fundamental metaphysical premise that all mental activity, including perception, is totally, completely, and absolutely, the result or equivalent of, or is identical to, physical processes in the nervous system. In other words, brain-language is sufficient, *in principle*, to explain mind-language. In terms of my basic view of mind-brain reality I thus remain a deeply committed physicalistic, materialistic, psychobiological, monist. That *the mind is nothing but a function or process of the brain* is still the primary premise of my personal scientific philosophy. The identity association between certain brain processes and mental processes that has been drawn by philosophers as Herbert Feigl (1958) or Mario Bunge (1980), among many others, still seems to me to be the best possible metaphysical stance to take with regard to the mind-brain problem.

This does not mean, of course, that the mind is any less "real" than when it is considered to be a separate kind of reality. Mind is a legitimate topic for research; mind can be measured; and thus mind as *process* is equally as real as brain *as matter*. Making mind a function, rather than an object, does not make it a "ghost in a machine" (in Gilbert Ryle's, 1949, terms), it simply means that it must be considered as an activity or process of a material thing rather than the material thing itself. Where to draw the line between process and mechanism is, of course, sometimes difficult to specify. Identity theory is, thus, not a panacea either.

However, this *in principle* material-process metaphysical monism is not easily (if at all) translated into an *in practice* epistemology or methodology. The very complexity of the myriad interconnections among the 10^{13} neurons of the brain makes it computationally *impossible*, from my point of view (and that of many mathematical computational theorists; e.g., Knuth, 1976; Pippenger, 1978; Stockmeyer & Chandra, 1979) to ever expect that there will be a complete neuroreductionism of even the relatively simple kind of visual processes with which this book is concerned.

I can be more specific about this point. The epistemological premise on which this book is based is exactly that *there is a fundamental limit to the explanatory power of neuroreductionism* for most perceptual processes. A corollary of this premise is that virtually *all of the phenomena and processes that are discussed in this book are beyond that limit*. Although a large number of physiologically oriented visual scientists have developed neuroreductionistic models of various kinds to explain various examples of form perception, I consider none of these models to be compelling or even acceptable as anything beyond remote process analogies reflecting superficial similarities between neural and psychophysical processes except when they deal with the communication aspects of the peripheral nervous system.

I thus explicitly abandon the neuroreductionistic philosophy that permeated the first two (and one half) volumes of this series and deal with the material in this fourth book in the only way I believe it can be properly considered. I describe, using both the words of English and a few of the words of mathematics, and I infer (to a modest degree) something about the general nature of the underlying processes. However, I plan no further use of the neural vocabulary (and its attendant conceptual superstructure) in this volume beyond expanded statements of my premises and brief critiques of what I believe are the fallacious foundations of some modern pseudoneurophysiological theories of form perception.

There are two other general ideas I personally hold that will necessarily guide and influence the intellectual development of this book. These two ideas also should be made explicit. First, the review of the literature and the laboratory studies I have conducted over the years have impressed on me the fact that stimuli alone do not directly "determine" perceptual responses. The perceptual response is, quite to the contrary, influenced by a host of properties of the neural network (which communicate and integrate the incident information) and by powerful and influential factors related to the previous experience and the current "set" of the observer (which themselves are only other manifestations of the current state of the neural network). This is the grand message of the study of illusions, one of the most superficially "understandable" topics in perception, yet a field that actually includes some of the least well understood phenomena (in terms of satisfying reductionistic explanations) in psychology. To assert that the psychological response is a direct function of the stimulus [i.e., $R = f(s)$] is the most common and yet probably the most incorrect trivialization of perceptual science. Much of what is to be said in this book is going to speak to this point.

Great dimensional and semantic differences between the stimulus and the perceptual response result from transformations that occur within the observers' visual system. The usual nonveridicality of our percepts in comparison with independent measures (i.e., other more direct and less complex percepts) of the stimulus is evidenced again and again throughout the history of perceptual science. It is only in the most abstract and simplest laboratory situations that simple graphs or mathematical functions relating some single dimension of the stimulus and some single dimension of the percept can be realized. Even then, the all important phrase "...*all other dimensions and influences being held constant*" is implicit in the results of any visual experiment purporting to show how the physical stimulus is related to the phenomenal response.

It is now known, for example, that there is not even any unique relationship between such "simple" and "directly" related parameters as perceived hue and stimulating wavelength (Land, 1977, 1983; Land & McCann, l971). Rather, virtually any hue can be associated with almost any wavelength if one is given control over the spatial and temporal environment of the stimulus. In short, the causal relationships between stimuli and visual responses must be considered to be very loose; at the very least, multidimensionally determined; at the very worst, only fortuitously correlated by the very complex processes underlying what we glibly call *illusion* and *perceptual construction*.

The second general idea constraining and guiding what I have to say concerns the range of topics to be surveyed in this volume. I have always found it terribly difficult to distinguish between studies of "thinking" and studies of "vision." It is, in virtually every case, an act of arbitrary judgment concerning whether a particular study should be included in a volume like this on visual perception or in one dealing, not with vision, but with some other level of cognition. The problem is that many, if not most, studies of problem solving or cognition involve visual presentations, and most studies of visual perception involve some kind of intellectual activity that goes beyond the automatic, passive, immediate processing carried out at lower levels of visual processing. In the final analysis, therefore, it can only be the emphasis that I place on the visual aspects of any given experiment that will determine whether or not it is to be considered relevant and includable or irrelevant and excludable. I know full well that others might make different judgments, but just as the processes of vision become less easily understood as one ascends the various levels of processing, so too the classification of the processes that are involved becomes less clear cut. Indeed, it is not really certain whether the words cognition and vision have separate denotations at this level, however clearly they connote different meanings. For this very reason, one that is intrinsic to the innate complexity of the subject matter, I expect that many readers will be more likely to find fault with my taxonomic judgments in this book than they did with the material considered in the earlier three volumes.

The field of form perception is not only enormous, but also so much less crisply defined than the earlier material about which I have written, that the trepidation I have felt upon embarking on each of these volumes looms over me even more intensely than previously. Students of "form" can be found among philosophers, engineers, psychologists, computer scientists, physicists, as well as among practitioners of less formidable technologies and even pursuits such as art and advertising. The task of processing forms has assumed great interest in recent years because of the increasing number of applications in many practical situations. What had hitherto been only curiosities and esoterica of interest only to parlor entertainers or perceptual theoreticians now have evolved into the sphere of interest of huge corporations and magnificently endowed government agencies. Thus, the basic research and theory of a subject matter that psychologists had previously considered to be their private domain has now become a part of the research and development efforts of many others operating in a wide variety of related fields of science, engineering, and public affairs. This interdisciplinary ferment has had a very positive effect; many new and quite different points of view have been introduced into perceptual theory. Unfortunately, communication among these diverse fields has not always been as good as one might have hoped. In particular, engineering efforts to simulate human form perception capabilities (i.e., the subfield of artifical intelligence—AI—called *computer vision*) have all too often gone on in isolation from the research done in human perceptual psychology. This is neither entirely unexpected nor entirely disadvantageous; indeed, it is an explicit goal of many AI researchers. For example, Yang and Kac (1986) after expressing the hope that AI would produce good psychological theory and successfully "simulate" the processes of Gestalt organization and stereo perception, go on to say:

> More recently, the attitude has been that while research must continue in simulating these human abilities, which appear to be guided by knowledge and driven by

expectation, we must in the meantime also look for purely engineering solutions
to the sensory feedback problems of robots. (p. 229)

Indeed, the two efforts, it must be appreciated, are not equivalent either in
goals or methods. AI research is specifically aimed at the mechanical reproduction of the *performance* of a preceiving organism by invoking *any* process or
mechanism that will work even if it is not the exact homologous replica of the
process going on within the human. To the AI researcher it is the outcome, not
the mechanism, that is essential. Theoretical psychology, however, is specifically aimed at understanding the internal mechanisms by means of which the *human*
processes visual form. However useful this book incidentially may be to the engineering practitioner, it is, by my intent, a work of theoretical psychology.

A lack of appreciation of the logical nonidentity of these two endeavors—the
applied field of artificial intelligence and theoretical psychology—has sometimes
led to a considerable misunderstanding. This is especially true when one is concerned with perceptual theories invoking possible mechanisms that can accomplish the same tasks as human vision. The fact that one can simulate or analogize
the performance or process of one system with any other device or mechanism
is not, repeat *not*, an existence proof that the particular mechanism used in the
analogy is, *ipso facto*, the same as the one to be found in the human perceptual
system.

Although it may be somewhat unusual in a preface, I would now like to summarize some of the main conclusions about theory to which I come as we progress
through this book. This may help the reader to understand some of the selections
that I have made and issues that I have considered. It also serves as a summary
of the some of the thoughts that have been presented in this preface. My main
conclusions are:

1. *Cognitive processes, including perception, can not be reduced to neurophysiological terms.* The totally bizarre, and—when closely examined—unsubstantiated, idea that single cells can represent complex experiences still permeates
much of the thinking of contemporary perceptual theory, but is, in my judgment,
almost certainly rejectable for both empirical and theoretical reasons. An alternative monistic and neuroreductionistic hypothesis, that mental states are encoded or represented by vast *networks* of neurons, is probably closer to some kind
of psychobiological "truth." Unfortunately, reduction from percept to neuronal
net is equally certain to be precluded by the complexity of the nerve nets according to theorems from combinatorial, chaos, and automata theories. Thus, although
many heuristics and enjoyable mathematical exercises may come from such studies
and even though they may be of interest in their own right, the idea of neuroreductionism is not likely to provide the kind of answers dreamt of by some of today's
theoreticians.

2. *Cognitive processes, including perception, can not be reduced to unique
underlying logical mechanisms.* Modern cognitive psychology strives to ana-

lyze mental processes into algorithmic processing steps that uniquely describe the underlying processing steps. Two difficulties arise here. The first is the awesome adaptability of the human brain. There is a terrible unreliability of even the empirical data in the literature of today's cognitive psychology. An enormous number of controversies characterize the field. The student of this science hunts, more often than not, without great success for the stable and universal rules of human perceptual performance. In a certain sense we know less now than we did a few years ago about how we, for example, recognize patterns—so many myths of only a few years ago having disappeared under the harsh light of replication. A probable reason for this is that the human has many alternative cognitive strategies available to solve any mental problem; even the slightest change in experimental protocol can stimulate the evocation of an alternative one.

The second difficulty is that psychological research is a form of input–output analysis and this "black box" approach is, by formal proof, prohibited from uniquely defining internal mechanisms. All of the chatter about "converging methods" is fiddle-faddle compared to this profound, and totally unappreciated, constraint on what cognitive psychology is about.

3. *Mathematical models, although powerful descriptors, are not useful as analytic engines.* Mathematics is so powerful that it is not always obvious that it does not say anything about internal implementation. The descriptive power of mathematics is great but in no way is a good description of the course of events in some perceptual process equivalent to a proof that any particular one of many equivalent analogous structures or mechanisms is involved. An associated difficulty is that whatever mathematics is available is all-too-often used to dictate theoretical explanations rather than the salient phenomenological or psychobiological facts, thus misleading the science in terms of the overall directions and points of view adopted.

4. *Artificial Intelligence models are not psychological theories.* Although, this judgment was never a part of my thinking at the outset of the project, I am now increasingly convinced (and many of my colleagues also seem to becoming convinced) that AI or computational vision algorithms *simulating* human visual processes are not, necessarily, or even in general, very good explanatory models of human form perception. Neither the needs of engineering nor the mathematical tools available have led to computer vision programs that unarguably operate in any way like the still obscure principles of human visual perception. The two fields interact, but the goals of each are so different that neither can depend on the other for final answers.

This is a terribly negative set of conclusions (or preview of conclusions) to which to expose my readers at the outset of this book. Be that as it may be, and however small a minority in which it may place me, these are the conclusions to which I have come during the course of this book. Perhaps, by alerting readers to the conclusions, they will better understand, even if they do not agree with, the route that I follow as I move through this volume.

All of this is not to say that this perceptual science is static or futile, but rather that we must appreciate that we are at a very primitive level of understanding about cognitive processes in general and perception in particular. Nevertheless, I am convinced that there are some useful and profitable lines of research to pursue, as well as some that are wasteful, a priori. This book is one contribution to a redirection of our research efforts in perceptual science.

ACKNOWLEDGMENTS

I would like to conclude this preface by thanking the people and organizations who made it possible for me to do this work. First and foremost, I have to thank Dr. John O'Hare of the Office of Naval Research and Dr. John Tangney of the Air Force Office of Scientific Research for their support. This book was written because of a document numbered N0001486WR24178AA, a formality that does not do justice to the intellectual as well as the financial support this project received from these two scholar-administrator-scientists. I am deeply grateful to them and to their respective organizations for their willingness to support this unusual venture.

I also had some other opportunities for reflection and learning that can not be overlooked. I would like to thank the staff of the Rockefeller Foundation's Villas Serbelloni in Bellagio, Italy for an incomparable month during which I had the opportunity to almost too peacefully contemplate the outline that this book was ultimately to take. Specifically, Susan Garfield of the New York Office and Robert Celli and Angela Barmetier of Bellagio made that gracious lifestyle a strong memory. Professor Tadasu Oyama also is remembered for inviting me to enjoy the privileges of a Japanese Society for the Promotion of Science visiting scholar and to see perceptual psychology from the point of view of another country.

I am eternally grateful to my publisher—Lawrence Erlbaum—for his continued support over many years. The existence of this tetralogy owes much to his enormous contribution to scientific psychology, a fact that has led many of us to acknowledge him a "man of psychology." His staff, in particular Arthur Lizza, Jr., has always made the publication experience a pleasant and painless one. Robin Weisberg also did a fine job as production editor on this book.

Robert Radcliffe, an undergraduate philosophy student with whom I had the pleasure of interacting while at the University of Michigan, also helped me to understand some of the subtleties of the rationalism–empiricism controversy and, in particular, the role of the enigmatic Kant. Cindy Welke and Vicki Emerson have helped enormously with various aspects of the editorial work on the manuscript. Professor Myron Braunstein, of the University of California at Irvine, added immeasurably to whatever success this book will have in communicating my ideas by technically reviewing and commenting on the entire manuscript. I am deeply indebted to him for what is always an onerous task. For all of the years that she has made my life far better than it would have otherwise have been, finally, I thank my dear wife May.

REFERENCES

Bunge, M. (1980). *The mind-body problem: A psychobiological approach*. Oxford: Pergamon Press.

Feigl, H. (1958). The mental and the physical. In H. Fiegl, (Ed.), *The Minnesota studies in the philosophy of science (Vol. II). Concepts, theories, and the mind-body problem*. Minneapolis: University of Minnesota Press.

Knuth, D. E. (1976). Mathematics and computer science: Coping with finiteness. *Science, 194*, 1235-1242.

Land, E. H. (1977). The retinex theory of color vision. *Scientific American, 237*, 108-128.

Land, E. H. (1983). Recent advances in retinex theory and some implications for cortical computations: Color vision and the natural image. *Proceedings of the National Academy of Science (USA), 80*, 5162-5169.

Land, E. H. & McCann, J. J. (1971). Lightness and retinex theory. *Journal of the Optical Society of America, 61*, 1-11.

Pippenger, N. (1978). Complexity theory. *Scientific American, 238*, 140-159.

Ryle, G. (1949). *The concept of mind*. New York: Barnes & Noble.

Stockmeyer, L. J., & Chandra, A. K. (1979). Intrinsically difficult problems. *Scientific American, 240*, 140-159.

Uttal, W. R. (1973). *The psychobiology of sensory coding*. New York: Harper & Row.

Uttal, W. R. (1978). *The psychobiology of mind*. Hillsdale, NJ: Lawrence Erlbaum Associates.

Uttal, W. R. (1981). *A taxonomy of visual processes*. Hillsdale, NJ: Lawrence Erlbaum Associates.

Valenstein, E. S. (1986). *Great and desperate cures*. New York: Basic Books.

Yang, H. S., & Kac, A. C. (1986). Determination of the identity, position, and orientation of the topmost object in a pile. *Computer Vision, Graphics, and Image Processing, 36*, 229-255.

I

INTRODUCTION AND PERSPECTIVE

A. GENERAL ORIENTATION

How do we see forms? This question has been asked by philosophers and scientists, each from their field's own perspective, for 2,500 years at the very least. And yet there are still so many intricacies and so many complexities that this brief five-word query is as perplexing now as it must have been when some Greek philosopher may have first formalized the issue. Nevertheless, in spite of its persistence, there have been many changes over the centuries in the way we approach the problem of form perception. Where previously the dominant approach to this problem involved philosophical speculation concerning some arcane epistemology, what had been a minor theme—the experimental analysis of visual perception—now dominates the search for answers to the question of how we see. However, as different as the *methods* of philosophy may seem to be from those of experimental psychology, one should not be misled into believing that their respective goals are also very different. They are not. Both philosophy and modern scientific psychology seek to answer virtually the same fundamental questions concerning the nature of knowledge acquisition through the visual modality. It is in terms of method, not substance, that they differ.

Indeed, a similar unity of goals exists between visual science and many other sciences. It is interesting to note that vision and physical optics are closely related in history just as are other aspects of physiology and electricity; the respective subdivision into distinct fields of endeavor of these pairs of sciences is only a fairly recent development. The reasons for the current separation and specialization are not difficult to discern. Biological, psychological, and physical stores of knowledge, respectively, have increased enormously since the 17th and 18th

1

century explosion of scientific enquiry. Simple mass, as well as complexity, of data would have inevitably led to both the differentiation of the sciences and the evermore narrowly circumscribed approach to understanding that each research scientist is now forced to follow. Each practitioner of each science delves deeper and deeper into a specialized corpus of ideas. The result is that each of us often sees less and less of the grander scheme into which our work fits.

It is, therefore, something of an anomalous role in this time of increased specialization for anyone to stand back and ask such broad questions as: How do we see forms? Such a query is of quite a different genre than, for example, the question: What is the effect of dark adaptation on the critical flicker- fusion threshold? Yet I am firmly convinced that a critical review asking expansive questions of a more general kind is not only important but necessary if our science is to progress and prosper. It is vital that at least a few of us attempt to determine the current state of the science of visual perception from a self-consciously broader perspective than that typically held by laboratory scientists. That is the purpose of my tetralogy on sensory and perceptual processes.

In the three preceding books in this tetralogy, I have tried to ask and, to a certain degree provide one contemporary set of answers, to three basic questions:

1. How is information communicated along the peripheral sensory nerves? (Uttal, 1973b)
2. How is information processed, stored, and modified in the central nervous system? (Uttal, 1978)
3. What are the immediate, preattentive, and automatic aspects of visual perception? (Uttal, 1981)

The purpose of this volume is to consider certain aspects of the next logical stage of visual processing, the stage that has to do with some (but certainly not all) of the more attentive, less automatic, and cognitive aspects of vision. Because the full range of visual cognition is so extensive, I have chosen to limit the range of issues with which I deal to only those involved in form perception—the detection, discrimination, and classification (or recognition) of visual stimuli. A further constraint is that I consider only those situations in which the major independent variable is the spatial geometry of the stimulus. Another major goal of this study is to determine if it is possible to more precisely specify the locus of the interface between attentive and preattentive visual processes.

The list of visual topics that I do not consider, or mention only briefly in passing, is thus much longer than those that are encompassed within these constraints. The reader looking for detailed information in this book on such problems (among others) as visual memory, illusions, subjective contours, stereopsis, hemispheric laterality, visual direction, persistence, movement, attention, or even picture perception and reading will have to look at some of the earlier books in this tetralogy or elsewhere.

The self-imposed circumscription of topics to be considered is a practical expedient, and delimits what otherwise could have been an unmanageable amount of data and theory to be analyzed and classified. Even more important than the very mass of material that would have had to be considered if I had done otherwise is the fact that such a constraint helps enormously to place the material that is to be covered into a kind of natural taxonomic order. As I stressed in the third volume of this tetralogy, some self-conscious effort to classify the findings of perceptual science is absolutely necessary if we are not to drown in the backwash of an empirical flood of unrelated observations and measurements.

B. A PERCEPTUAL CREDO

As with any other such metatheoretical effort, this book is biased and prejudiced by my own personal beliefs and premises about the nature of perceptual science, in particular, and of psychology and psychobiology, in general. To properly orient the reader, I believe it is appropriate for me to explicitly state the metaprinciples under whose influence I am now operating. To a very substantial degree this credo of metaprinciples is also the link between the conclusions of the previous book in this series (Uttal, 1981) and the premises of this present work. Indeed, some of those conclusions and these premises are virtually identical. I describe those that seem to me to be particularly relevant to the subject matter of this new volume in the following paragraphs.

I. Physical Realism

The external (to the perceiver) physical world is real and does not require that it be perceived to exist. The historical traces of the existence of physical reality prior to measurement or perception are ubiquitous in those measurements. This concept of physical reality is necessary because it serves as an essential anchor against which all other measurements must be standardized.

2. Psychobiological Monism
(Psychoneural Equivalence)

All mental processes, including those of perception, are the function of neurophysiological mechanisms occurring within the nervous system of the perceiver. There is no such thing as ''extrasensory'' perception or any other kind of disembodied mentation, a foolishness that is perpetuated among lay people for reasons that have nothing to do with scientific progress or understanding. Mind exists to the degree that there is a materialistic substrate present that is complex enough to encode and represent the semantic content of meaningful messages and ideas. At the present time, at least, the only known substrate capable of mentation is the organic brain. The best artificial systems are far less capable than the least intelligent human.

3. Methodological Dualism

In spite of the metaphysical primacy of the psychobiological monism to which I subscribe, practical considerations make it unlikely that we will *ever* be able to provide a full description of psychological events in a purely neurophysiological language. The limit is a practical one; the number of neurons involved in even the simplest sensory response of the vertebrate brain is so enormous that it is currently beyond, and will probably always be beyond, microscopic analysis or quantitative computability. For some specific cases this premise can be concluded from the axioms of computational theory (e.g., see my discussion of the important work of Moore, 1956, later in this book). It is, therefore, not a matter of speculative debate (for those cases), even though we may quibble over how far such proofs can be extrapolated from ideal automata to realistic neural systems. Nevertheless, this fact, this limit, this barrier does not seem to be fully accepted as a part of the contemporary perceptual science zeitgeist, and its rather substantial implications appear to me to be ignored in a flurry of totally unfounded and fanciful neuroreductionistic theory.

One major implication of this limit on neuroreductionistic theory is that we must maintain a non neuroreductionistic vocabulary and approach to perceptual science. This perspective must be framed in what once were called rationalist (and which now may better be designated as descriptive linguistic and mathematical) terminologies if we are to make any progress in understanding form perception. To attempt a totally neuroreductionistic explanation with today's technology would probably leave us forever mired in a morass of pseudoexplanation and often irrelevant electrophysiological data. Of course there are some visual processes that can best be explained in terms of photochemistry and neurophysiology; but, according to this premise, most of the interesting postretinally mediated phenomena cannot. From my point of view the phenomena and processes I discuss in this book are, for the most part, not currently neuroreducible in the sense to which I allude here. I should add that in my experience this conviction is one of the most controversial of those to be presented in this book. It has been more likely than any other contentious assertion I make to stir up an argument from neuroscientists. And well it should, for it challenges an idea fundamental to their science; it denies the usually unspoken hope many reductionistically oriented neuroscientists have that their studies of neurons and neuron networks will ultimately lead to theories of mind. But in principle, it seems clear that we are not likely to achieve a neuroreductionistic account of even a restricted view of most of the more intriguing aspects of form perception. Others who agreed with this premise (or prejudice) include von Neumann (1951), Knuth (1976), Stockmeyer and Chandra (1979), and Braunstein (1983). Those who disagree are too numerous to list here.

Braunstein (1987) raises an even more contentious question in a personal communication: Even if we could overcome the technical and combinatorial problems and learn all that is necessary about the neuronal circuits, would that be sufficient? He notes that the sequence of logical steps in a computer program is more important than the wiring of the circuitry used to instantiate a given step. Thus, at the very least, the difficulty of the problem will be elevated by being transformed from a three-dimensional spatial one to a four-dimensional spatial-temporal one. The question of the appropriate level of reductionistic analysis, therefore, is still not resolved. At the very worst, we simply may not be dealing with the critical logical events by considering the architecture of the neuronal net wherein many different circuits might accomplish the same function simultaneously.

4. The Invisibility of Internal Processes

There are two aspects of this fourth foundation premise. First, as I have noted, it is unlikely that any input–output analysis of the functioning of any system, and especially one of the complexity of the human brain, will ever give unique answers to the question of that system's internal structure or mechanisms. Engineers refer to this as the *black box limitation*. There are always many (and probably an infinite number of) possible analogous mechanisms capable of producing the same transformation between the input and the output. (See, for example, Moore, 1956, and Uttal, 1981.) Therefore, internal mechanisms are, in some fundamental way, invisible to the external observer. But this aspect of the problem is even more difficult than is suggested by the metaphor of a closed black box. Even in the unlikely event that some super neurophysiological investigator was able to open the cerebral black box and insert an adequately large array of electrodes, the system would remain functionally "invisible" simply because of the enormous complexity of the neural circuitry.

The second way in which the internal functions of the brain are invisible is with regard to the perceivers themselves. We are only aware of the end product—the percept—of all of the internal processes going on in our brains, never of the processes themselves. The mental constructions created in visual perception (see the following) are, with regard to the responsible internal mechanisms, as opaque to the introspective perceiver as they are to the external observer of the inputs and outputs alone.

5. The Existence of Multilevel Processing

This premise asserts that visual processing is the result of unperceived transformations that are executed by many levels of nervous activity. In this book I will be mainly concerned with examples from higher levels of attentive and not just those encoding preattentive information processing, even though some of the phenomena that are observed at higher levels are mimicked by those at other lower levels of processing.

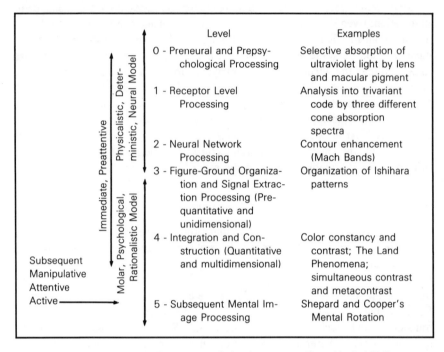

FIG. 1.1. A proposed taxonomy of visual processes (from Uttal, 1981).

This is not the place to go into the details of my proposed taxonomy of visual processes. The third volume in this tetralogy (Uttal, 1981) did so to a greater extent than it perhaps should have. However, Fig. 1.1 does sum up the classification scheme that was presented in the 1981 volume. The essential point in the present context is that there must be activity at all levels for a percept to occur, even though the *critical* transformation altering the *meaning* conveyed by the stimulus form to that of the perceptual experience may be attributable to only one or a few of the involved processing levels. Critical transformations are those that change the meaning, message, or information content of a stimulus, not those that just change the neurophysiological code or energetic medium in which it is represented.

The fact that this taxonomy is based upon a classification of processes rather than of phenomena is an important advantage. To the extent that processes and transformations (as opposed to phenomena) are emphasized, equivalences between different phenomena become more self-evident and our attention is more forcibly directed to understanding rather than merely to description.

6. The Composite Nature of Mind

Although it may be only a convenience, no definite proof of the composite nature of mind yet having been given, it is herein assumed to be axiomatic that mind is made up of a number of semi-independent processes. It is further assumed that these semi-independent processes can be assayed separately by judicious choice of experimental paradigms. Although I am not satisfied that the words we currently use are adequate to meet their semantic responsibilities (e.g., mind, process, perception, recognition, discrimination, emotion, attention, and so on) they do provide the framework of a preliminary model of a multifaceted mind. Part of my task here is to identify the particular semi-independent subprocesses involved in form perception to the extent that we can distinguish among them.

7. The Rule of Dimensional Nonisomorphism

Abundant evidence exists in the literature of sensory neurophysiology that there are virtually no limits with regard to which dimensions of the neural response can be used to encode either the dimensions of the physical stimulus or those of the psychophysical experience. In other words, virtually any dimension of the stimulus can be encoded by virtually any dimension of the neuronal response and virtually any dimension of the neuronal response is capable of creating the experience of virtually any dimension of perception. The important generalization that is emphasized by this neurophysiological and psychobiological principle is that there is no need for any kind of isomorphism between the dimensions of the code and the dimensions of the message. For example, the intensity or quantity of a stimulus may be conveyed by spatial, temporal, or even elaborate spatial-temporal patterns. Indeed, stimulus intensity may be encoded by either a decrease or an increase in activity.

This premise becomes immediately self-evident when one considers that such stimulus dimensions as the physical wavelength of light and its attendant percepts (chromatic responses) are not and cannot be dimensionally isomorphic, either with each other or with the neural response encoding physical wavelength and/or psychophysical chromaticity. Neither the high frequency oscillation of a photon nor the color of the experience need or can exhibit any dimensional isomorphism to the neurophysiological code being used within the sensory system. Indeed, this gentle caveat should be extended to a vigorous warning to psychobiological theorists: Simple dimensional similarities between codes and stimuli and responses, when they occur, do not imply that the one is necessarily the code for the other. False associations based upon such superficial isomorphisms have, in the last half century, led more psychobiologists astray than one would like to think. Teller (1984) has also discussed this same problem in her important paper on "linking hypotheses."

It is also important to appreciate that the concept of *dimensional isomorphism* used here is not exactly the same as the mathematical concept of *isomorphism*. In mathematics, isomorphism only means that there is a one-to-one correspondence between two sets. The concept of dimensional isomorphism used in this coding theory context requires that the neural codes be comparable dimensionally to the stimulus or perceptual response, as well. That is, space would encode space, time would encode time, and intensity would encode intensity, each with the same type of modulation. Though dimensionally isomorphic coding does occur some-times in the nervous system (e.g., in retinotopic maps of the spatial attributes of the stimulus scene) these instances are often peripheral or fortuitous. There are many more instances of dimensional nonisomorphism than of isomorphisms; for example, "greenness" is encoded by something as dimensionally nonisomor-phic as the *relative* frequency of firing among designated groups of neurons.

8. The Perceptual Indeterminacy of Stimuli: Perceptual Constructionism

The next metaprinciple of perceptual processing that I put forward is perhaps the one most germane to the content of this volume. It is now widely accepted among perceptual theorists that the traditional stimulus-response psychology, which asserted that the stimulus was the main determinant of the perceptual response, cannot be valid in a general way. Stimuli may, an alternative non–stimulus-response view propounds, trigger, clue, or cue responses; but, in fact, the veridicality that sometimes exists between our percepts and the outside world is far more the result of an *indirect* and *active* reconstruction of the outside world based on stimulus-borne hints than a *direct* result of *passive* processing of the attributes of the stimulus. The many intriguing classic examples of visual illu-sions that fill the perceptual literature and a plethora of new developments in cognitive research are ample reminders of the many influences on what we see that transcend the specific attributes of the physical stimulus. Our set, our preju-dices, our expectations, and our experiences all modulate the construction of the experiential model of physical reality away from the raw stimuli presented to us.

So, too, does the meaning or implied meaning conveyed by the stimulus dic-tate what we shall see. If the stimulus is ambiguous, then we tend to construct order where it did not physically exist by means of transformations occurring on several different levels of visual processing. Stimuli are incomplete, a point also made by Chomsky (1981) when he alluded to the "poverty of the stimulus." Indeed Chomsky deviates so far from stimulus determinism (and its antecedent, radical empiricism) that he virtually champions a modern-day rationalism com-plete with Kantian and sociobiological "innate ideas."

Nevertheless, I must stress that however deep my personal commitment and that of a few others to the premise of constructionism, it should not be miscon-strued as reflecting a contemporary consensus. I have not really counted noses, but in the review of old and new theories in chapter 2, it is clear that this dynamic, active view of perception is not universally accepted and, in fact, may currently be a minority stance, at least if one concentrates on what are arguably "simpler" forms of perception.

There have been and are two main approaches to theory in form perception science. One approach emphasizes direct stimulus determination of perceptual experience and passive processing by the perceptual mechanism. The other emphasizes the active role of the observer and the percepts. Both points of view are aggressively championed today by some very reasonable scholars indeed. Not surprisingly, both sets of champions may be right! Compromises and intermediate positions are probable and, if history is any guide, most likely. It is possible to imagine intermediate processes such as automatically applied inferential processes as well as the extremes of the automatic-inferential dichotomy.

9. Attentive and Preattentive Process

My next premise concerns a major distinction between two kinds of perception, that is, it is the dichotomy drawn between Levels 0–4 and Level 5 in the taxonomy presented in Fig. 1.1. This dichotomy differentiates between attentive and preattentive visual processing. A number of psychological theorists (including, among many others, J. Piaget, J. Fodor, B. Julesz, A. Triesman, and I. Rock) now believe that although many visual processes are more or less passive and automatic (in the mental, not the neurophysiological or the electrical, sense of the terms) others require a kind of selective attention or mental activity that is more active and effortful. The terms just used to distinguish between the two alternatives are, admittedly, vague and difficult to precisely define (just as are all other mental constructs) . Nevertheless, a consensus is emerging that two kinds of processes are, in fact, going on—one "active," or attentive, and one "passive," or preattentive. I maintain this distinction as a major premise of the present work. Some of the processes discussed fall into the former category; some into the latter. Some, undoubtedly, also fall between the ends of the continuum anchored by the dichotomy "attentive–preattentive."

10. The Complementarity of Rationalism and Empiricism as Fundamental Theories

Because of the nature of perception, and both the relative simplicity of the peripheral sensory communication systems and the relative complexity of the central nervous integration system, it is unlikely that either the empiricist or rationalist approaches will ever totally supplant the other. Both represent necessary approaches to understanding perceptual processes and are complementary in their explanatory powers.

These, then, are some of the premises or axioms of the perceptual philosophy that guide my thinking and must certainly affect the presentation of the material in this book. I present this set of premises or metaprinciples more in the form of a preliminary caveat characterizing my biases than as a set of rigorously validated laws. The reader of this book, as of any other, must keep these premises in mind if the origins of any idiosyncratic interpretation on my part are to be understood. This will not negate any disagreements, but at least it may indicate their origins, and arguments can then be directed at the essential rather than the superficial aspects of whatever controversies ensue.

C. SOME DEFINITIONS

Almost as important as the philosophical premises that underlie this work are the definitions of some of the key terms that are used as conceptual tools in this analysis of the mechanisms, processes, and phenomena of form perception. It is widely appreciated that it is extraordinarily difficult to satisfy everybody with definitions of most of the terms used in any field of psychology, even though we all use these words in ways that consensually communicate the necessary information.

It is not so widely appreciated that, in fact, satisfactory definition of mental terms may, in principle, always be unsatisfactory and that, in principle, we should be able to satisfy nobody. That is, satisfactory definitions should involve comparison with referents that are *inter*personally shared by members of an interacting community. The fundamental nature of mental acts, however, is one of *intra*personal privacy, so that the true referents of visual experience, if used in definitions, cannot be shared. Some logicians, philosophers, and psychologists, therefore, believe that definitions of such events can be, at best, metaphorical and/or circular, and thus never precise. (I should note in passing that what I have just said in words may be exactly equivalent to Moore's formal theorem discussed later in this chapter, as well as the teachings of our behaviorist predecessors.)

My past experience has led me to agree with this point of view, be it expressed in words or mathematical proofs. Every effort that I have made in my career to define mental terms has left me with a sense of at least partial and sometimes monumental frustration. At best, I now believe, definitions of psychological terms can help only to narrow the intended general *connotation* of these words, but they will always leave us floundering with regard to their specific *denotation*. How many psychological debates have we all been involved in that have ended when the debaters agreed that they were, in fact, talking about different things, but inadvertently using the same ill-defined vocabulary?

Neither should it be overlooked that there has also been a great deal of needless controversy generated in the dialogues of this science because different speakers were connoting similar ideas while using different words, or vice versa. Some of the most fundamentally important words in psychology are definitionally imprecise in exactly this way.

For example, at the University of Michigan several of us taught a course with the same title—"Perception." It is an illuminating experience to see the wide range of orientations and approaches taken and, for that matter, the variability of the content matter taught by each of us Some approached the problem from a biological, passive, neuroreductionistic point of view, whereas others approached it from a holistic, cognitive, active point of view. The strategic philosophy could vary within the microcosm of this single course from one instructor to the next even though it was nominally the same topic. Some instructors concentrated on using the microscopic neuron as a foundation and built upward. Others preferred to think and talk in terms of molar psychological processes and work down to the mechanisms and processes that they believed may plausibly be invoked to account for them.

Shorthand expressions for this difference in approach has come into common parlance: Cognitive types invoking the application of semantic knowledge are *top-down* analysts, whereas the neuroreductionists and others who would apply automatic, algorithmic processes to the stimulus are approaching the issue from the *bottom up*. (In spite of their fundamental reductionistic philosophy, it seems they should, more properly, be considered to be bottom-up *synthesists* rather than analysts, at least with regard to the psychological implications of their work.) Top and bottom, in this case, are roughly quantified in terms of the complexity of the neural systems involved in the percept, but the concept is more general than simply neuroreductionistic. Computational vision researchers such as Marr (1982) and Ullman (1979) are also theorists of the bottom-up genre, from my perspective.

Another manifestation of the *bottom-up* and *top-down* dichotomy can be observed in the two major schools of thought concerning how one should study vision and even in the professional associations in which the practitioners of each approach congregate. The annual meeting of the Association for Research in Vision and Ophthalmology (ARVO) emphasizes the biological foundations and is, therefore, predominantly populated with bottom-up types. The Psychonomics Society, however, gathers together at its annual meeting scientists who emphasize human information processing in a way that is clearly top down. The adjectives *top-down* and *bottom-up* also can be used to describe the actual organization of the perceptual mechanisms as well as the orientation of the theorist. Figure 1.2 graphically depicts the difference in approach in each case.

The point is that it is not always clear exactly what is meant by a course in "perception" or what many of the other psychologese words mean in common usage. This book, directed as it is to one aspect of perception, uses words in a way that it is hoped is consistent. Because of the intrinsic difficulty in defining terms, however, I depend on some common sense appreciation of what it is that is being discussed. Nevertheless, understanding of much of what has to be said may be expedited if I take a moment now (and at many other points in this book) to clarify my personal use of some of these words. The following list is not inclusive but it does deal with some of the most-often-confused terms.

I. Perception

Having already spent some considerable effort (Uttal, 1981, pp. 9–14) striving toward a specific definition of perception, I simply quote myself here:

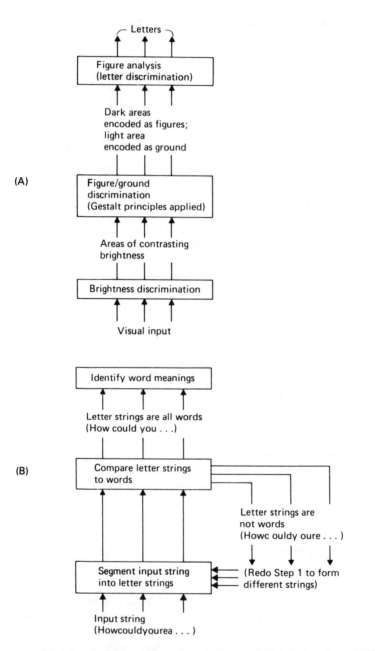

FIG. 1.2.   (A) Flow chart illustrating a bottom-up model of perception, specific in this case to letter recognition. (B) Flow chart illustrating a top-down model of understanding the sentence "Howcouldyoureadthissentence" (both figures are from Glass, Holyoak, & Santa, 1979).

Perception is the relatively immediate, intrapersonal, mental response evoked as a partial, but not exclusive, result of impinging multidimensional stimuli, as modulated by the transforms imposed by the neural communication system, previous experience, and contextual reasonableness. Each percept is the conscious end product of both simple computational transformations and more complex constructionistic 'interpretations.' However, the underlying neural and symbolic processes are not part of the observer's awareness. (pp. 13–14)

Visual perception, in particular, specifies those mental responses associated generally, but not exclusively, with photic stimulation. (Nonphotic visual experiences may be either phosphenes—vision elicited by nonadequate electrical, mechanical, or chemical stimulation of the visual system; recalled memorial images—vision associated with previous stimuli; or totally endogenous experiences we call hallucinations or imaginations.)

The word *seeing* is synonymous with the term *visual perception* and includes both kinds of classic *sensory* and *perceptual* experiences, These latter two terms are not currently distinguished in my lexicon, and their continued separate usage, I believe, merely reflects what was only a differing methodological emphasis in the past. There is no basis for distinguishing between a "percept" and a "sensum" in scientific psychology beyond a rough measure of: (a) the simplicity of the stimulus scene selected by the experimenter; and (b) the fact that "sensory" experiences are more likely to be discussed in neuroreductionistic terms than are perceptual experiences.

This general definition of perception, as the reader must certainly realize, has been influenced by many of the metaprinciples that were enunciated in the previous section. It is also clear that this definition is extraordinarily broad, and as a result is virtually useless in an operational sense. It is probably not possible to consider studying such a process in its entirety. Fortunately, according to another premise, perception as defined is probably made up of a large number of quasi-independent subprocesses, not all of which have yet been fully defined or understood, but that are, nevertheless, the stuff of manageable research projects. Students of perception are usually found to be using experimental paradigms that are intentionally designed to tease out such subprocesses as, for example, "*detection*."

2. Detection

One of the perceptual responses that must be invoked early on in the sequence is *detection*. Logically the presence of the stimulus must be encoded and its presence signified phenomenologically in some way before anything else can be done to or with it. This phenomenological signification need not be "conscious." In some situations we respond as if we were processing some attribute of a stimulus' presence before we actually report awareness of its presence. Such a paradoxical situation occurs, for example, in the phenomenon of apparent motion in which the direction (toward the second light) of the apparently moving light is determined prior to the awareness of the second light, as has been pointed out by Kaufman (1974).

Operationally, detection experiments may be defined as those in which the presence of a stimulus form must be discriminated from the nonpresence of the stimulus.[1] Signal-in-noise types of tasks are examples of the application of detection-measuring paradigms. Signal-detection theory (see Green & Swets, 1966) is an excellent formal model of this process and helps us to distinguish between sensory and criterion factors in performance. In general, as we see in chapter 3, detection experiments require degraded stimuli because detection is usually so effortless as to seem to be an intrinsic part of other perceptual processes.

3. Discrimination

The perceptual subprocess of discrimination requires that a sufficiently high level of perceptual awareness exists such that an observer can report whether two stimuli are the same or different. Logically, discrimination is dependent on detection, a subprocess that might have been defined as the discrimination of a stimulus from a nonstimulus.[2] The behavioral correlate of appropriately responsive discrimination behavior would be a correct answer to a question concerning the sameness or difference or similarity of two stimuli. It is an assumption of this work that discrimination does not necessarily require classification or recognition of the object, only a sense of the degree of identity or nonidentity. It would, furthermore, be implausible to consider either recognition or discrimination to be occurring without some kind of detection. However, phenomena such as apparent motion, as described earlier, make what seems to be simple, very complex, and the implausible, plausible.

4. Organization

Even though it failed to explain much, Gestalt psychology left us with many important phenomenological concepts, not the least of which is the idea that the organization of the visual stimulus into a coherent percept is very much a function of both the perceiving organism and the stimulus. Bequeathed to us along with this concept was set of specific rules of organization and grouping that characterizes the observer's active construction of perceptual forms that may have

---

[1] However, in some experimental paradigms discrimination can seemingly occur at a lower stimulus level than detection (Diener, 1981; Doehrman, 1974). This is usually due to partial information being acquired in a failed detection trial that allows the discrimination to be based on a partial match.

[2] In this sense, detection becomes a variant of discrimination itself, a process that may be considered to be a variant of recognition. This is an acceptable, but different, taxonomy than the one I propose here.

been present in the actual physical stimulus only by implication. The behavioral correlates of these organizational subprocesses include, for example, reports of perceived grouping or texture in appropriately designed experiments.

5. Recognition

The term *recognition* has taken on such an enormous range of meanings to so many interested parties that it is no longer clear that a simple definition of it can be given. The way that I use it in this book connotes the idea of the association of a given stimulus pattern with a particular category of ideas, a name, or some concept. Recognition thus denotes naming and/or concept categorization such that one appropriate response (from among a larger set of alternatives) is made to the stimulus. It certainly requires detection and possibly requires discrimination (of the specific stimulus from other possible stimuli) as prerequisite processing steps. The behavioral correlate of recognition is the ascription of a name of the class of items to which the stimulus belongs or the selection of some other kind of motor response appropriate to the stimulus. Nonverbal—or even preverbal—motor signified recognitions are, therefore, perfectly acceptable considerations.

6. Scaling or Quantification

A perceptual process of considerable importance, but often overlooked or relegated to some dark corner of methodological concern, is *scaling*. The quantification of stimuli and, in particular, the judgments that go into the comparison of the magnitude, quality, or position of some object or the value of some dimension relative to some other object or value is as much a perceptual process as is recognition. The logic and the detailed psychophysics of scaling, and the relationship of psychological scales to mathematics, is well presented in the milestone chapter by S.S. Stevens (1951) in the now classic *Handbook of Experimental Psychology*.

7. Searching, Sorting, Reading, and Other Processes

Terms like these refer to several different kinds of visually guided processes all of which are best considered to be composites of detection, discrimination, and recognition subprocesses. Currently these composites are mainly measured with recognition paradigms. All require that these primarily visual processes be mixed with cognitive and effector responses in a way that involves much more complex and effortful mental activity than merely the detection, discrimination, or recognition of a stimulus. The imputation of meaning or order to the percept is a major part of all of these processes.

8. Image Manipulation

Another visual process of great current interest is the attentive and effortful manipulation of spatial images that may have been recalled from memory or briefly stored after some initial stimulus presentation. Imagery is a compelling kind of evidence that the immediate stimulus and the perceptual response may be disassociated from each other in a profound way. During imagery, complex constructions or transformations of the perceptual experience are carried out and extrapolations from the stimulus-defined information computed. A fundamental question is thereby generated: How closely related are the stimulus and the percept when the latter can exist without the former? The fact that illusions of completion or closure occur, even when stimuli are fragmentary, absent, or brief, links illusions together with images as members of a common class of constructed mental events. This line of logic also does severe damage to any simple theory in which stimuli lead directly to perceptual responses.

9. Understanding

The next entry in this little glossary of perceptually relevant processes is *understanding*. To achieve understanding of the term *understanding* is as formidable a task of definition as one could undertake. A typical dictionary definition of understanding is that to understand is to "get or appreciate the meaning" of something or to "grasp what is meant" by something (*Webster's New World Dictionary*, 1976, p. 1548). Thus, understanding goes beyond the perception of the simple physical geometry of the stimulus (and even beyond the syntactic relationships within the stimulus) to the ideas or semantic content it may be encoding. To understand is to *apprehend* (unfortunately, another vaguely defined term) the message or meaning that is conveyed by the objects and their relationships in their role as symbols of that message. We are less concerned, if studying *understanding*, with the physical aspects of the symbols or the rules of using the symbols and more with the message that they convey.

A more restricted definition of the term *understanding* is offered by artificial intelligence researchers. To them, understanding is the ability to construct a model or a computer program description of objects and the scenes into which they are arranged that is sufficiently complete to allow meaningful and appropriate responses to reasonably relevant commands. (The reader interested in a more complete definition of what is meant by understanding in this field is directed to chapter 13 of Cohen & Fiegenbaum, 1982.) A typical example of an "understanding" artificial intelligence computer program is, according to them, one capable of examining the elements of some small world (such as an array of simple three-dimensional objects) and then, on the basis of this inspection, to respond appropriately to such directions as "place the red pyramid on top of the green cube." To do so without destroying or displacing other unmentioned objects that coexist in the scene is tantamount to "understanding" the scene in the artificial intelligence community. Of course, this miniature microcosm of cubes and pyramids is not a complete world and such a program is probably not "understanding" in the sense that a human might; nonetheless, it is a model that helps to clarify the meaning of *understanding* just as any other abstraction helps to clarify other overly complex words and ideas.

Gibson (1950) also tackled the idea of "understanding and came up with the somewhat cryptic idea of *affordance. Understanding* to him was defined in terms of what an object or scene "affords" to the observer. My personal view is that this concept is not theoretically or empirically useful, but merely an equally undefinable synonym—a metaphor—as was so much of the elegant poetry of this very important psychologist.

10. Form

The list presented so far comprises some of the subprocesses making up that part of our minds activity called *visual perception*. There are some other terms that, although not denoting mental processes themselves, are, nevertheless, so closely related to the context of this book that I must also attempt to devise a definition or them in this minilexicon. These additional words deal with the particular dimension of a stimulus—form—that is the main concern of this book. What exactly is meant by the word *form*?

At first glance, it is a surprising fact that in spite of the enormous past and current interest in "form" perception, there has been remarkably little success in precisely defining *form*. Some of the attempts to designate *form* have been downright fanciful. For example, in one of the first attempts to apply communication ideas to psychology, Cherry (1957) makes an absolutely true, exquisitely elegant, but totally useless statement when he asserts:

> The concept of form is one of those rare bridges between science and art. It is a name we may give to the source of aesthetic delight we sometimes experience when we have found a 'neat' mathematical solution or when we suddenly 'see' broad relationships in what has hitherto been a mass of isolated facts. Form essentially emerges from the continual play of governing conditions or 'laws.' An artistic mode of expression, such as music, painting, sculpture, represents a 'language'; through this means the artist instills ideas into us. His creation has form inasmuch as it represents a continuity of his past experience and that of others of his time, so long as it obeys some of the 'rules.' It has meaning for us if it represents a continuity and extension of our own experience. (p. 71)

Even when one reads those few books that are fully dedicated to the problem of form—some of the most notable among these are the pioneering biomathematical work by Thompson (1917) on growth and form, Whyte's (1951) edited collection, Zusne's (1970) comprehensive review of the field, Dodwell's (1970) fine analysis, and the extremely thoughtful and recent collection of papers edited by Kubovy and Pomerantz (1981)—it becomes clear that we, as a scientific community, have not yet succeeded in precisely defining what it is that we mean by the word *form*. We have progressed only modestly beyond the Gestalt notion that a form is "any segregated whole or unit." Even the great D'Arcy Thompson, whose union of mathematics and morphology was one of the notable intellectual contributions of this century, equivocates (along with lesser savants) by analogizing spatial form with physical forces when he defines *form* in the following way in the newest edition of his 1977 work:

> The form, then, of any portion of matter, whether it be living or dead, and the changes of form which are apparent in its movements and in its growth, may in all cases alike be described as due to the action of force. In short, the form of an object is a 'diagram of forces,' in this sense, at least, that from it we can judge of or deduce the forces that are acting or have acted upon it: in this strict and particular sense, it is a diagram—in the case of a solid, of the forces which *have* been impressed upon it when its conformation was produced, together with those which enable it to retain its conformation; in the case of a liquid (or of a gas) of the forces which are for the moment acting on it to restrain or balance its own inherent mobility. (p. 11)

Thompson also obviously appreciates the difficulty in defining *form* in words and specifically turns to mathematics for precision, to wit:

> The study of form may be descriptive merely, or it may become analytical. We begin by describing the shape of an object in the simple words of common speech; we end by defining it in the precise language of mathematics; and the one method tends to follow the other in strict scientific order and historical continuity. Thus, for instance, the form of the earth, of a raindrop or a rainbow, the shape of the hanging chain, or the path of a stone thrown up into the air, may all be described, however inadequately, in common words; but when we have learned to comprehend and to define the sphere, the catenary, or the parabola, we have made a wonderful and perhaps a manifold advance. The mathematical definition of a 'form' has a quality of precision which was quite lacking in our earlier stage of mere description; it is expressed in few words or in still briefer symbols, and these words or symbols are so pregnant with meaning that thought itself is economized; we are brought by means of it in touch with Galileo's aphorism (as old as Plato, as old as Pythagoras, as old perhaps as the wisdom of the Egyptians) that 'the Book of Nature is written in characters of Geometry.' (p. 269)

Obviously, Thompson is evading the specific issue in alluding only to the forces or the formulae defining and producing form as a genus, in spite of the fact (which he obviously realizes) that the word is the essence of everything of which he writes. Equally obvious is the fact that the approach to a definition of form is inadequate: Many forms are not represented in a nontrivial way by mathematical formulas. Consider the form of a face, a cow, or a book. Even the new formality called the *mathematics of fractals* (Mandelbrot, 1983) is not able to represent the "form" of such highly structured objects. We do well with hyperbolic paraboloids; we do poorly with trees or spouses.

It should also be noted that although it is possible to represent any form with a mapped representation (e.g., a pixel or bit map on a CRT screen or in a computer memory, or by an exhaustive listing of all parts of the form) such a procedure does not condense the form in the practical sense that an equation does. That is, if the number of degrees of freedom in a mapped representation are as great as that of the original picture itself, then no progress has been made.

Other mathematicians have done somewhat better, at least, in formalizing what is meant by them to be a geometric form. For example, Duff (1969) has suggested two general definitions (using the word *pattern* in the way I would use the word *form*) as follows:

> 1. A pattern (form) is any arbitrary ordered set of numbers, each representing particular values of a finite number of variables.... Each arbitrary set is given a label which thereby defines its class, with the result that two such sets might be associated within a particular class, although there may be no obvious similarity between the two sets.

> 2. A pattern (form) is an ordered set of numbers, each representing particular values of a finite number of variables, in which there are certain definable relationships between the numbers in the set, involving both the values of the numbers and their positions in the set. Two such sets would only be given the same classifying label if they are observed to conform to the same definable relationships. (p. 134)

Duff goes on to break these two definitions up into five subclasses, the first of which is the same as his first definition, whereas the latter four further specify the second definition:

> (a) *Random Patterns* (Forms), being patterns of the type described in the first definition.
> (b) *Point Patterns* (Forms), in which the essential quality of the pattern could be represented by a set of points distributed with a particular relative orientation in the input field.
> (c) *Texture Patterns* (Forms), in which there is a repetition of well-defined groups across the input field (although the group itself may be a random pattern; it is the presence of repetition which is significant here).
> (d) *Line Patterns* (Forms), figures in which the essential quality of the pattern could be represented by a system of zero-width lines (connected points).
> (e) *Area Patterns* (Forms), figures in which the essential quality of the pattern could be represented by a system of areas. (For example, note that a circle is obviously a line pattern, as is, perhaps, an annulus of finite width, but a disc must be regarded as an area pattern if confusion with a circle is to be avoided.) (p. 135)

Although interesting and precise to a degree, such a definition still does not help the psychologist to manipulate forms in a controlled manner. These definitions are in fact no better than such words as *dot pattern* or *texture* although they do help to clarify the formal distinctions between different classes of forms.

For an eclectic group of points of view, I turned to Whyte's (1951, 1968) fascinating collection of papers by students of form from many disciplines. Is it possible that *form* is satisfactorily defined by this interdisciplinary effort? Here are some entries in this enjoyable and insightful book:

> The word 'form' has many meanings, such as shape, configuration, structure, pattern, organization, and system of relations. . . . Common to the ideas of form, configuration, pattern, and structure, is the notion of an ordered complexity, a multiplicity which is governed by some unifying principle. . . . But 'form' includes development and transformation. Indeed we can regard 'matter' as that which persists, and 'form' as that which changes, for no form is eternal. And form, like change itself, is in many fields still obscure. (L.L. Whyte, 1951, p. 2)

> The word 'form' in this article will refer to the shapes of material objects, the arrangement in space of groups of them, and the arrangement in space of their component parts. (S.P.F. Humphreys-Owens, 1951, p. 8)

> If we understand by *form* something more than mere *shape*, if we mean by form all that can be known about the object with all the aids that science can provide, then it is to be expected that there will be systems of classification according to the various modes of apprehending the object. (C.C.L. Gregory, 1951, p. 23)

> In any definite situation offered by a real system, we have still the right to consider that its material and energetic elements can be combined in numerous ways (Power) , but that a certain set of definite relations has been adopted (Form), resulting in the actual situation (Act). (A.M. Dalcq, 1951, p. 92)

Peter Dodwell (1970), a psychologist, offers the following highly specialized and, to me, most unsatisfactory definition of form (pattern): "By a visual pattern I shall mean a collection of contours or edges, which in turn are defined as regions of sharp change in the level of a physical property of light (usually intensity) impinging on the retina" (p. 2). The problem with this definition is the linkage Dodwell makes between the aggregate organization (what he refers to as "pattern") and the specialized contour attributes. Certainly forms or patterns could exist without lines or contours of any kind: A dot pattern is one obvious example. I believe this erroneous linkage of form and a particular kind of feature is a reflection of the selective attention that neurophysiologists were giving to "line detectors" in the early 1970s. Such a misdirection illustrates the strong hold on even the words of our scientific vocabulary that can be exerted by the contemporary zeitgeist.

In a book devoted to the topic of perceptual organization (Kubovy & Pomerantz, 1981), two other prominent psychologists finesse the issue entirely. The words *form*, *pattern*, and *Gestalt* simply do not appear in the index nor are they defined, to my knowledge, by any of the contributing authors anywhere in the book.

The distinguished psychologist of art, Rudolf Arnheim (1974), offers the following:

The words 'shape' and 'form' are often used as though they meant the same thing. Even in this book I am sometimes taking advantage of this opportunity to vary our language. Actually there is a useful difference of meaning between the two terms. The preceding chapter dealt with shape—that is, with the spatial aspects of appearance. But no visual pattern is only itself. It always represents something beyond its own individual existence—which is like saying that all shape is the form of some content.

Content, of course, is not identical with subject matter, because in the arts subject matter itself serves only as form for some content. But the representation of objects by visual pattern is one of the form problems encountered by most artists. Representation involves a comparison between the model object and its image. (p. 82)

This discourse, although poetic and interesting, is also totally useless in helping us manipulate form as a variable in experimental research.

Another place in which the question what is form? is specifically asked is to be found in a personally distributed monograph by Liam (1973). Noting that the word is used in many ways and that "it may still be difficult to specify one meaning of form" (p. 257), a caveat that is, incidentally, ubiquitous throughout this literature, Liam goes on to discuss various uses of form as an attribute of a stimulus in psychological research. One attribute of a form Liam specifically designates as being inappropriate to defining the form is its congruence with another form (i.e., a template matching process). With this point, I heartily agree.

This absence of a precise formal definition of the word does not mean that *form* is totally without a consensual connotation. Many authors behave as if the word's meaning is self-evident: "Form is the arrangement of the parts" is a recurrent, though from my point of view circular, definition often used by form theorists. It is, however, quite possibly the best that we can do.

Form is more often defined operationally by psychologists in terms of the particular experiment in which they are currently involved. Typically, a small set of forms that differ in some arbitrary, but specific, fashion is used with no effort to define the general concept or even the prototype from which they are modified. When precision of definition has been explicitly sought by psychologists, the concept of "form," more often than not, has been embodied in terms of certain *classes of form* rather than a specific form. Indeed, some of the approximations to a precise specification of form used in the psychological literature have been only statistical in nature and do not and cannot uniquely define particular forms in the manner achieved by the mathematical equations so dear to Thompson.

Consider, for example, the classic Attneave and Arnoult (1956) patterns or the "random histograms" of Fitts and Leonard (1957). Each of these statistical devices was intended to generate a family of stimulus forms that share some common statistical attribute rather than to generate a specific form. Each does, in a statistical sense, accomplish that goal. However, this kind of statistical specification is not adequate if one wishes to control form as an independent variable in a psychophysical experiment. Two forms having very similar statistics may be perceived to be quite different because of global organizational factors that are not distinguished by the statistical generating rule that gave rise to them. This may occur for the simplest of reasons: the nervous system may not be sensitive to the statistical dimension being manipulated. To the contrary, it may be sensitive to some aspect not measured by such a statistic. Indeed, it seems more likely that our nervous systems may be sensitive to variations in the spatial or topological domains to a more profound degree than they are to statistical properties in the case of spatial forms. Thus, statistical descriptions of form fail in two ways. First, they do not define unique exemplars of form. Second, they often metricize a variable to which the human nervous system is not particularly sensitive and ignore others on which we are very dependent.

I believe that the criticism of nonuniqueness can also be applied to the form "equation" work of Leeuwenberg (1971), as well as to that of Rogers and Trofanenko (1979). The latter workers use spatial entropy (another statistical type of measure) to characterize the complexity of a shape, whereas Leeuwenberg has developed a new spatial-notation system. Neither model appears to uniquely define a particular shape; they only provide measures or descriptors of classes of shapes that are similar in certain aspects. Other more familiar systems have also been used. For example, within very limited classes of form, such as those that can be represented by the formulae of plane or solid geometry, continuous transformations over a range of related forms can be produced. Thompson's (1917, 1977) work is of this genre as is my own (Uttal, 1985, 1987; see also chapter 3 of the present work on the detection of nonplanar signal surfaces in visual noise). However, these useful artifices do not solve the problem of precisely defining particular examples of interestingly large classes of realistic forms.

Other global attributes of form, closely related but very vaguely defined, were the foundations on which the Gestalt theoretical approach was based. Scholar-scientists such as Max Wertheimer (1880–1943), Kurt Koffka (1886–1941), and Wolfgang Köhler (1887–1967) appreciated that forms possessed attributes that were neither precisely quantified nor easily defined qualitatively (e.g., *prägnanz* and goodness). Indeed, they built their entire scientific system around these unquantified and ill-defined concepts of organization and form.

It is only recently that the depth of the word *prägnanz* has been plumbed by Kanizsa and Luccio (1987). They note two separate meanings for this ambiguous term. One meaning may be synonymous with phenomenal singularity or uniqueness; the other with simplicity, stability, or regularity. A form may be, according to Kanizsa and Luccio, singular even though it is not regular.

The Gestalt psychologists' inability to precisely specify what they meant by a form and to quantify this all-too-complex attribute of a stimulus was the major factor leading to the collapse of what otherwise was their important and, I think, fundamentally correct holistic and descriptive approach to perceptual science. (Their total failure in an ill-advised attempt to develop a plausible neurophysiological foundation for their ideas did not help either, of course.) In the absence of quantitative measures of their dependent variables, definitions of key concepts, and an efficient methodology, they simply could not carry out the crucial experiments necessary to develop a psychophysics of form. As a result, their approach, however correct in principle, was infertile in practice, and like all such fruitless approaches quite properly was abandoned by scientific psychology.

In recent years there have been continued efforts to develop nomenclature systems that can specifically define a unique form. But the problem remains refractory. Zusne (1970), in his exhaustive and excellent search of the literature of visual form, refers to the influence on psychophysical responses of "variables of the distal stimulus." I share with him the belief that our key word—form—has not yet been adequately quantified. He proposes the following interim definition: "form may be considered both a one-dimensional emergent of its physical dimensions and a multidimensional variable" (p. 175). This kind of language merely hints at a future definition, but does not constitute one.

Form, Zusne asserts elsewhere in this same work, can mean all of the following things to psychologists:

(a) the corporeal quality of an object in three-dimensional space;
(b) the projection of such an object on a two-dimensional surface;
(c) a flat, two-dimensional pictorial representation;
(d a nonrepresentational distribution of contours in a plane; or
(e) the values of coordinates in Euclidean space. (p. 1)

None of which satisfies the need for a general definition of the word.

Zusne (1970) then also turns, unsatisfyingly, I am sure, to him as well as to me, to discussions of statistical generating rules (pp. 176–189) as the prototypes of experimental forms. For usable descriptions of individual stimuli, he points out that psychologists often invoke such multidimensional "factors" as compactness, jaggedness, or skewness (e.g., Brown & Owen, 1967), which do not, by themselves, quantify or define the specific "arrangement of the parts," even though they do describe the general global nature of the form.

Precise definitions and specific quantitative measures of whatever it is that we mean by *form* thus seem to be continuously elusive to psychologists. Hochberg and McAlister's (1953) well known, but seriously mistitled, paper ("A Quantitative Approach to Figural Goodness") is another example that makes this argument clear. Their "quantitative" measures of goodness (an aspect of form) were nothing more than counts of the numbers of line segments, angles, or points of intersection—properties that themselves in no way define the arrangement or the form of a visual stimulus, only the first-order statistics (numerosity) of its component parts.

Recent attempts to quantify form on the basis of two-dimensional Fourier analyses have been offered as another alternative, but this approach suffers from the safe kind of difficulty as does the statistical one. Form, from this point of view, is to be represented in terms of the sum or superposition of the spatial-frequency components that can be analyzed out of the stimulus scene. So far this technique has proven to be extremely useful if one uses stimuli that are grating- or spatial-frequency-like in their global appearance. If, on the other hand, the spatial-frequency model is used for nongrating stimuli (such as block letters), the analysis does not work well in predicting the outcome of psychophysical experiments (e.g., Coffin, 1978). There is obviously something more to a form than its constituent ensemble of spatial frequency features.

Incidentally, the unarguable utility of the Fourier approach in defining stimuli and quantifying responses does not necessarily mean, as many of my colleagues seem to think it does, that there must also exist neuroanatomically real spatial frequency "channels" in the nervous system. But this is another contentious matter, and for a more complete critique of this issue, I refer my readers both to my earlier work (Uttal, 1981) and to subsequent discussions in this book.

Another difficulty arises from the confusion of the two words *form* and *pattern*. There is a subtle distinction here that should constrain injudicious use of the term *pattern*. *Pattern*, according to my dictionary, carries the connotation of a prototype or model from which replicas or repetitions are produced. The connotation is different from that of the term *form*, which specifically speaks to the attributes of shape or arrangement. The distinction to which I allude may be fine but may have, in fact, already had a profound theoretical outcome: *Pattern perception* is often used as a synonym for *form perception* in a way that leads directly to a particular kind of theoretical construct that, in fact, is physiologically, logically, and psychologically unlikely to be found in the vertebrate brain—a template-matching process. This is why definitions are so important and why this section of this chapter is so necessary—a single misdefinition early on can lead directly to the subsequent acceptance of an implausible and unrealistic theoretical outcome; in other words, it is all too easy to beg the theoretical question with definitional premises.

In summary, there are no formal definitions of what is meant by the word *form* that come close to satisfying the needs of perceptual researchers to manipulate form in the same way that the monochromator satisfies the need for a tool to manipulate wavelength. Perhaps because of its multidimensional nature, form is intrinsically difficult or even impossible to define and to quantify. At best we manipulate something as simple as the height–width ratio of a rectangle and thus reduce the problem to a level at which the essence of form is ignored; at worst we utilize complex stimulus scenes, so superloaded with symbolic meaning that they tap high-level cognitive and symbolic processes quite different from the simpler form-perception processes with which this book is mainly concerned.

All of this, finally, leads me back to the working definition of the word *form* that I have come to use most often: *Form, in some ill-defined manner, is the arrangement of the parts.* The preceding paragraphs should help to clarify some of the special uses I make of vocabulary items with slightly different general meanings even though I, too, cannot produce anything more satisfactory than this simple capsule definition of the elusive word *form*.

The next matter with which I deal concerns the questions that students of form perception ask. To what end are the sophisticated methods and concepts of this science directed? Answering this metaquestion is the main goal of the next section.

D. THE ISSUES

In this section, I want to accomplish two goals. The first is to tabulate what I believe to be the intellectual questions that guide form-perception research in perceptual science. Some of these questions will be very general, very broad, and very speculative, but as we pass through the list of issues and queries they become increasingly specific.

The second goal of this section is to partially answer some of these questions, by way of further clarifying exactly what my personal biases are concerning the sometimes abstruse perplexities of the form-perception field. There should be no doubts about this matter; many of these questions *are* refractory as well as esoteric and as far from being answered as they are from practical utility. Indeed, most visual scientists do not explicitly concern themselves with most of the questions I pose in this section. At best, some of these matters are only implicit in their work and represent the broad, invisible (in their publications) set of philosophies, premises, and intellectual goals that underlie the specific, narrow, and visible reasons for which researchers in this field carry out their empirical studies. Perhaps these issues were once considered in graduate school but, like old textbooks, they have been put away out of sight and mind. It is profoundly regrettable that most visual scientists today work at the level of much more specific empirical questions such as: What is the effect of stimulus dimension x on response domain y? or test specific microtheoretical concepts. This sad generality is, of course, less and less true the higher one ascends the cognitive ladder, but even at the most elevated and global levels of psychological research most experimentation is mainly motivated (perhaps as it must necessarily be in today's highly specialized world) by ultraspecific questions, many conceptual levels down from the great philosophical issues with which this discussion begins.

There are four broad classes of question to be considered in this tabulation of motivating issues that are best kept distinct from each other. The first class has to do with the great metaphysical and epistemological questions that have been omnipresent in human thinking throughout history. The second class deals with a closely related, but rather special scientific issue: the mind-brain problem.[3]

---

[3] I assert the mind-brain problem is now a scientific issue. In the past, certainly, it was the stuff of philosophy and was better known as the mind-body problem. The central issue is the same, however: How do the mind and the brain interact? (Or, in more modern terms: How does the brain influence behavior?) Indeed, recent conversations with theologians such as Maurice Wiles of Oxford University and W.C. Davies of Texas Christian University have convinced me that the same matter is also of active concern in their field. Surprisingly, the tentative answers to which at least some theologians and at least some psychobiologists have come are not too different. It is only when we compare the most basic premises concerning *why* such answers emerge in each field that we part ways.

Herein is studied the relation between the neural substrate and the mental process, the latter only partially reflected in performance scores. This is the arena
in which psychobiologists have worked for many years. Nevertheless, the restate-
ment of this classic speculative issue in contemporary neuroreductionistic terms
may be useful. Though the mind-brain issue in its modern context is omnipresent
(even though unspoken), as I have already noted, a premise of my current perceptual credo is that in only relatively rare instances is the physiological approach
likely to be useful in explaining perceptual processes or phenomena. Most are
simply too complex for such an analysis.

The third class of questions concerns the general nature of perception—what
it is and what are its attributes. The fourth class of issues includes related matters, but concentrates on those in which particular attention is paid to the nature
of the subprocesses involved in the perception of form. This category also includes queries that deal with the specific phenomena (as opposed to the underlying processes) of form perception. This is the practical level at which most experimental scientists frame their day-by-day, nitty-gritty activities in the laboratory.
As we see, these four classes of questions range from the most profound,
philosophical, and refractory to the most elemental, empirical, and answerable.
In some case where an answer is not available, our unsubstantiated biases and
prejudices must stand in the place of a valid, substantiated answer. My personal
perspective has already been exposed in the "credo" presented in the section
entitled A Perceptual Credo.

I. The Great Philosophical Issues

Throughout history the common experience of all humans has led them to repeatedly ask many of the same questions concerning the nature of both their environment and themselves and how the two interact. My concern in this section is with
these nearly universally asked questions that deal particularly with the fundamental
nature of reality, both in terms of the external context of the physical environment and in terms of the internal mental aspects of our existence. It is *self-evident*
in the most immediate sense of the term that we are sentient and conscious beings. That is, we ourselves are aware of both the external environment in which
we are embedded and of our own (and only our own) personal mental experiences.
It seems likely that this universal human attribute—awareness of both an internal
self and of an external world—is, perhaps, the critical influence that leads directly to universally asked questions of the following genre. From awareness of self
and nonself comes doubt and curiosity concerning life, consciousness, death, mor-
tality, knowledge, and the nature of reality. From these doubts and concerns come
both science and religion.

a. *What Is the Fundamental Nature of the External World?*   This is the
foundation question concerning the attributes, characteristics, and properties of

the physical universe. What is the nature of physical reality? On what does its existence depend? From primitive animists to elaborate theologies to quantum chromodynamicists and superstring theorists, the foundation questions are very much the same, even though there may be great differences in the specific jargon or strategy used to obtain answers. The traditional opposing positions concerning the "real" nature of the external world have been called *realism* and *idealism* respectively. Idealism gives priority to the mental representation of external objects and events, whereas realism asserts the primacy of the external physical world itself.

Today virtually all psychobiological scientists anchor their models, theories, and explanations of all aspects of both mind and behavior by attesting to some version of a radical realism. That is, most scientists believe that the world is real, it truly has existed, it currently exists "out there," and that it has certain properties constantly exerting physical forces independent of our (or any sentient) awareness. Sensory and perceptual psychology, and in particular psychophysics, is founded on adherence to such a radical realism. The physical stimulus world, no matter how thoroughly it may be transformed and processed by neural mechanisms of greater or lesser complexity, is the reference against which all perceptual experiences must be anchored or referenced. To the extent that they are not so anchored, as in the loftier reaches of cognitive and personality theories, a vagueness and nebulosity begins to permeate the theories and language of psychology.

So far, our most potent means of learning about the nature of the perceiving mind has been to study the transformations between physical stimuli and mental responses by inferring mind from behavior. The power and precision of psychophysical science is directly associated with the extent that percepts are so referenced and that the discrepancies or correspondences between stimuli and percepts can be shown to exist. To not so reference our perceptual experiments would be tantamount to forcing this science to exist in a kind of floating, vague, unanchored state that would neither permit the progressive development of ideas much beyond primitive mysticisms and intangible theologies nor allow results obtained in different laboratories to be compared. Thus, although immaterialists or idealists are still to be found among a small minority of contemporary scientists (surprisingly, even among basic particle physicists and quantum mechanists; see, for example, d'Espagnet, 1979), most biological, behavioral, and physical scientists today are implicitly, at least, radical realists with regard to the external world. I explicitly include myself among them.

b. What Is the Fundamental Nature of the Internal Mind?   There is perhaps no word as difficult to define as *mind*. It, and a host of synonyms and near synonyms, have defied precise definition throughout all of history up to and including this present effort at lexicographic elaboration. In general, we all know what *we* as individuals mean by the term, although there may be as many special meanings of the word as there are individuals. Most certainly, however, different professions use different words to convey the same meaning. Theologians probably mean the same thing when they refer to the soul. But, the dualistic connotation of *mind* as a separate level of reality in their domain is quite different from the monistic, process-oriented use I make of the word. Other specialized words have become almost synonymous with *mind*. Experimental psychologists now study *selective attention* as they probe the mechanics of the mind, whereas anesthetists and sleep researchers believe they are also manipulating some aspect of mind when they allow (or force) a subject to pass into different *levels of consciousness*.

These latter workers have raised the corollary question of whether or not consciousness is a necessary adjunct of mind. But this question can only be answered in the presence of a precise definition of *mind*, a definition that might as easily include consciousness as exclude it. *Mind*, to the psychoanalyst, for example, is the sum total of all mental processes, whether they be conscious or unconscious. Behaviorists, on the other hand, have rejected both mind and consciousness as valid objects of inquiry just as their metaphysical bedfellows—the logical positivists—have asserted that the very question I ask here is a "bad question." However, it is a rare individual who rejects the existence or special significance of his or her own mind.

Mind's nature will always probably be mysterious to some currently unknown degree because it must always be measured through the mediation of behavior, there being no direct mental communication possible except in the fantasies of the ascientific, lunatic fringes of parascience. This is so, not because mind is itself intrinsically mysterious or unreal, but, rather, because the incredible complexity of the measurable physical reality—the great neural networks of the brain—to which we must anchor mind, will probably guarantee that mind will always be intrapersonally private.

The answer to the question What is mind? as a result, remains both well known to each of us in a private way and, in my judgment, mainly opaque to all of the tools of science. I can only reassert my belief that mind is not, as Gilbert Ryle (1949) argued, a linguistic illusion or an unreal "ghost in the machine." Rather, it is real in the same sense as the *function* of any other physical entity. The best guide I can give to a practical and usable definition of the mind is to note that I use the word *mind* to denote one operational aspect of the brain. That aspect is best understood as a process or function of the material substrate—it is something the brain does—and thus it is inseparable from that substrate (or another one that is process equivalent). That, in a nutshell, is the outcome of an entire chapter I devoted to this problem in what I now realize was but another unsuccessful attempt to answer this question earlier (see Uttal, 1978, pp. 196–246).

In summary, my philosophical bias concerning mind is realistic and materialistic. Mind is as real as the brain or any kind of matter, but it is a process rather than a thing. It is a process of a material mechanism, and thus that mechanism is, in a sense, primary. A mechanism can exist without functioning, but a function cannot exist without the mechanism. Therefore, to disembody the mind is to destroy it: but, to lose consciousness has little effect on the tangible physical reality of the brain other than to place it in another process state.

Both this and the preceding questions constitute the subject matter of technical metaphysics. Both ask What is the nature of reality? One does so for the intrapersonal mental world and one does so for the external interpersonal material world we all share.

c. ***How Is Knowledge Communicated from the External World to the Mind?*** This query, of course, is the great perplexity studied by technical epistemologists, who in somewhat different words, ask What is the basis of knowing? Given that there is an external world and that there is an internal self-awareness, they are concerned with the question How does this intrapersonal mind "know" the outside world? (Parenthetically, I must acknowledge that I, necessarily, also renege on any attempt to define what is meant by *know*.) It is clear that there is no possible single answer here that would satisfy both the empiricist- and rationalist-oriented epistemologists among us. In fact, it is likely that there is no single answer to the question of how we know. It seems more likely that we come to know about the world in which we are embedded by a number of different strategies. A thoughtful discussion of the several possible ways in which we must be able to acquire knowledge and to "know" is to be found in J. Royce's (1974) essay on cognition and knowledge subtitled "Psychological Epistemology." Figure 1.3 depicts the three basic paths to knowledge that Royce believes func-

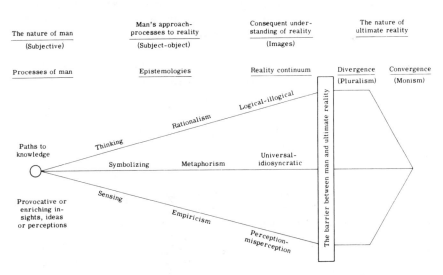

FIG. 1.3. The three different means of acquiring knowledge (from Royce, 1974).

tion as communication links between the internal mind and the external world. In addition to the classic rationalist–empiricist dichotomy of logical thought (thinking) and experience (sensing), Royce also adds the route of symbolization (metaphorizing) as another alternative. It is through this pathway in particular, he asserts, that one mind gets to know another mind. This pathway, he believes, as I do, is necessitated by the intrinsic intrapersonal privacy of each mind.

I do not believe that even the most hard-nosed, contemporary empiricist would now argue that raw sense data are absorbed by an observer into his base of knowledge without the mediation of some sort of symbolization and/or rational thought process. The classic days of a naive acceptance of the *tabula rasa* by empiricists seem long gone. Rather, it seems that the very existence of the three epistemologies to which Royce alludes is itself evidence, not of antagonistic theories, but rather of the fundamental truth that all three strategies must be in use, each to at least some degree. Of course, nothing can possibly be learned without some sense data, but, equally well, nothing is possible without some kind of thought or information processing dependent upon the existing knowledge, state, or set of the organism. To suggest otherwise is to carry human mentation to a level of automaticity that is far beyond what I believe to be argued by even the most radical contemporary empiricist.

Similarly, just as I have had to turn again and again to metaphors and analogies (i.e., to syntactically nonidentical, but semantically related symbols) to ascribe meaning to the vocabulary items dealt with in this chapter, the human being must constantly turn to metaphor to learn new ideas or, more importantly, to appreciate what another being is feeling or sensing. Systems of these metaphors have been called by many names by psychologists (e.g., *schema*, *frames*, or *scripts*), but they all share a common function—to provide linkages between new sense data and old experiences that give meaning and significance to what otherwise would be an overwhelming barrage of meaningless and insignificant sensory inputs.[4]

In this book, I am concerned mainly with the one of Royce's three strategies that he called "perceiving." I have to relegate analysis of his other two pathways to knowledge—thinking and symbolizing—to others. My present goal, furthermore, is to attempt to answer this epistemological question only in part—only in terms of our experiences and responses to the spatio-temporal geometry perceived stimuli.

---

[4] As I write these sentences, I must continually acknowledge the circularity of the vocabulary that I am forced to use. Such words as thought, knowledge, mentation, and experience are also subject to the same definitional difficulty as the others I have explicitly tried to define and are themselves, therefore, inadequate and incomplete. It is at this point that philosophers and scientists alike have to wink and say, "You know what I mean," thus behaving like purveyors of illicit drugs or dirty postcards who try to avoid the commitment to specifics that could get them into serious trouble. But, what is really being evidenced is the ubiquity and necessity of metaphorical thinking.

2. The Mind-Brain Issues

The preceding three questions are the historically universal and conceptually grand philosophical issues from which all the others flow. They define the overall goals that have guided the development of psychology, as well as all of the other sciences and, indeed, much of organized human thought, for over 6,500 years since the dawn of civilization and the freeing of intellect that occurred with what was clearly one of the great social inventions of all time—the specialization of labor. The next class of questions to be treated in this section concerns the nature of the relationships that may exist among the real physical and the real mental elements of this universe, in particular between the neural and psychological measures of brain activity. This is the modern manifestation of the classic mind-body (only recently termed, as I have already noted, the mind-brain) problem. The traditional problem has currently been concretized by raising related issues or, at least, rephrasing the issue in modern terms. These days students of mind-brain relationships are now asking such questions as:

a. What Is the Proper Level of Analysis of the Brain if Our Goal Is to Explain Mind and/or Perception? Contemporary students of this problem, certainly stimulated by developments in neurophysiology and computer technology, respond to this question by asserting that the aspect of the nervous system essential to mental processing is, in fact, the pattern of interconnections among the components of the neuronal network. (See Uttal, 1978, pp. 11–14, for a discussion of this topic.) Many of the other extensively studied aspects of the brain are not, in fact, germane to this question, even though they are important in their own right in a metabolic or supportive context (e.g., Which are the ionic forces and molecular structures involved in maintenance of membrane potentials?) or at a far more macroscopic level of analysis than the details of neuronal networks (e.g., Which nuclei of the brain seem to be associated with which psychological functions?). Thus, the critical aspects of brain that appear to distinguish it from the liver (for example) as a potential organ of mind and interesting object to study are the details of the rich and both varied and valuable network of interactions among the individual neurons. It is this property of brain—the network of information-processing interconnections—that is in my judgment most closely associated with mind. Having asserted this fundamental premise as a putative answer to this question, the next questions follow directly.

b. What Is the Relationship Between the Discrete Neuronal Actions and Their Interactions and Molar Psychological Activity? This is the specific form into which the mind-body problem has evolved under the influence of modern neuroscientific research. Although much more precisely specified than the classic version, this form of the question turns out to be (with the exception of a few special cases of simple invertebrate networks) equally refractory as the classic one. Indeed, it (or other corollaries of the query into the relationship between the microscopic and macroscopic) may be the most perplexing empirical and theoretical problem currently to be found in all of science. It remains the great chasm that our philosophy, mathematics, and empirical science have not yet bridged, nor have we even begun to conceptualize the kind of bridge that might be built despite the hopes of some theoreticians in the field. Whatever the answer to this question, it most certainly involves spatial and temporal interactions at several levels of complexity.

The reason, however, for this chasm is quite different than that classically invoked to explain the absence of a conceptual bridge. Previously, the difficulty most often invoked was either that the two were not closely enough related—separate levels of reality—or that the method was inappropriate—speculation as opposed to experimentation. The modern network form of the mind-brain problem is, on the other hand, now believed to be *computationally*, rather than conceptually or methodologically, refractory; analysis at the neural network level of organizational complexity involves computations that are now appreciated to be extremely difficult to carry out for the simplest of practical reasons. Combinatorial problems involving multiple interactions and complex feedbacks may require unrealizably large computers operating for inordinate lengths of time for their solutions. Although in some formal sense theoretically finite, problems of this genre are, for all practical purposes, unsolvable because of the very large number of computations involved. The exasperating fact is that it seems likely, and in fact it may be formally proven (see chapter 6), that there is no possibility of ever answering this question for specific neural network-percept relationships within the complex vertebrate nervous systems.

Nevertheless, there has been a host of neurophysiological laboratory studies that purport to show the role of single neurons in the encoding of mental processes. These vary from studies of sensory communication, (e.g., the extremely influential work of Hubel and Wiesel, 1962, 1965), to motor output (e.g., the work of Ranck, 1973, and Mountcastle et al., 1975), and even to spatial maps (e.g., the work of Olton , Branch, & Best, 1978) among many others. In general, I believe that these responses are descriptive only of the action of individual neurons and do not properly speak to the main issue—how the interaction among neurons comes to represent molar mental processes.

Some modest progress has been made, however, in understanding some of the general classes of interactions that may occur between discrete elements and molar behavior. In particular I refer here to the work of W. Hoffman (1966, 1980, 1985) using the Lie algebra in his study of topologically constant (dimensionally isomorphic) visual phenomena. His theoretical approach is considered in detail in the next chapter. In preview, I must state my intuition that Hoffman is probably closer to some fundamental kind of truth regarding this matter than are most other theoreticians, even if he is not correct in all of the details of his theory. Hoffman's work, quite appropriately, is intended to be very limited in scope, but it is at least a step toward a model of how holistic processes may emerge from the action of discrete components.

Nevertheless, I am convinced that it is unlikely that the general problem of the relationship between the neural and perceptual processes will be solved in the context of the psychoneural equivalences that exist between these two domains in the central nervous system. However, the following sub-section presents a closely related question regarding the peripheral nervous system on which considerable progress has been made.

c. How Do the Neural Responses (Codes) of the Peripheral Nervous System Represent Stimulus Information So That It May Be Effectively Communicated from the Transducing Receptors to the Brain? The relative simplicity of the peripheral communication mechanism and the predominantly monodirectional flow of information have made the problem of peripheral sensory communication a much more assailable one than those of central integration and the identity of percepts and neural network state. Much is known about peripheral communication codes even though relatively little is known about psychoneural equivalences deeper in the nervous system. (The subject of peripheral codes was the topic of my earlier work; Uttal, 1973b.) Indeed, we are very sure of some answers to this question. For example, we now appreciate that any variable dimension of neural activity can, in principle, encode any stimulus dimension (dimensional isomorphism is not required in the peripheral nervous system any more than it is in the central nervous system), and that there are common principles operating in all of the sensory modalities. We even know, in a much more particular way, which codes are used in which cases. Clearly much progress has been made toward a general answer to this peripheral communication coding question.

3. The General Perceptual Issues

The questions in the previous section collectively characterize the mind-body (brain) question as it has evolved up to the present, but, as important as they are in setting the stage, they are not the specific issues that are the targets of this volume. At this point we move on to the third level of questions dealing with perceptual processes of such complexity that, I believe, they can be discussed only in mathematical or verbal terms far removed from the language of the neural nets in which the answers to the preceding questions are usually framed. Here I list what I believe are the major issues dominating the study of perception in general.

a. What Is the Nature of the Internal Representation of Visual Thoughts, Percepts, and Memories? This conundrum is both increasingly evident and increasingly important in contemporary discussions of psychological processes in general and perception in particular. Shepard (1981) for one, believes it to be primary; he states that the problem of internal representation looms as the central problem of perception'' (p. 283). Needless to say, the problem of internal representation is an issue that has generated considerable heat and controversy among theorists of various persuasions. However, given what I have already said about the representation of peripheral *sensory* codes, it is also important to note that this issue is quite different from the sensory coding issue and one on which much less progress has been made. In the present context the question of representation is aimed mainly at resolving whether or not *symbolic, linguistic,* or *analog* representations are used to encode ideas or percepts in the central nervous system. This is not the same as the matter of neural responses in peripheral pathways; it is something quite different. The codes alluded to in this case of central representation are themselves molar rather than cellular and microscopic.

Pavio (1978) reviews three possible kinds of representation possibilities. Two of the representation types he lists are: *linguistic or verbal*—in which words are used as codes—and *nonverbal*—in which the representations are analog or pictorial, more like the objects themselves than the abstractions represented by words. Even though there is some conceptual overlap of the verbal and nonverbal representation schemes, as well as some uncertainty about what each definition incorporates, I believe that the kind of nonverbal coding to which Pavio alludes is intended to be more like the *semi-pictographic* coding scheme of written Chinese than like the "toy in the head" isomorphic representation that less sophisticated theorists (particularly those discussing three-dimensional perception) have proposed.

The third, and final, category listed by Pavio (1978) is neither pictorial nor verbal, but is classified by him as *abstract and amodal*. It is similar in concept to (but certainly not the same as) the mathematical or numerical encoding scheme found within a computer. That is, a series of abstract symbols (in the computer, these would be the 1 and 0) that are neither verbal nor pictorial are used to represent ideas. As Turing (1936) has proven, such an abstract coding scheme can, in principle, represent any idea, no matter how complex it may be. Given Turing's formal proof, as well as what we know about neurons and computers, it is hard to understand why there is any resistance to the abstract and amodal category as a representational schema or why it has not come to dominate theory in this domain. Whether ideas are amodally represented in a similar way at the level at which cognitive psychologists are working is, however, a slightly different question. To understand this better, let us briefly consider some examples of representational theories at this more molar level.

The linguistic representation approach is epitomized, according to Pavio, by Whorf's (1956) suggestion that all sensory inputs are immediately reencoded as verbal strings. The pictographic, or nonverbal, approach is typified by the work of Rosch (1975) who argues against the linguistic representation (or, in the even stronger sense championed by Whorf, among others, of linguistic determination of our percepts). Incidentally, though it is not scientific evidence of the kind likely to convince my empirical colleagues, I find the biographical and historical review of mental imagery among scientists written by Shepard (1978) to be a personally compelling argument for a nonverbal basis to many kinds of thought. Shepard's article is also, it should be noted, a "jolly good read" and would be enjoyed by anyone interested in the topic.

The third, amodal, approach to representation is championed by both Osgood (1957) and Chomsky (1981), who support an abstract coding scheme within the brain. Their work has been especially influential in recent years but is still not universally accepted.

Pavio's (1978) review surveys the various kinds of evidence that have been marshaled to support each of the three views, and I shall not repeat his arguments here. But it is interesting to note that, as so often happens, data mean different things to different observers, and that is certainly the outcome in this case. Pavio and I come to different conclusions with regard to the answer to this query. He argues for a combined verbal and nonverbal (i.e., pictorial) system of representations, whereas I believe that the idea of an abstract code underlying our internal representations, comparable to the one operating at the neurophysiological level, is even more likely. But the issue is complex; there remains considerable debate not only concerning the alternatives (and it must be remembered, the alternatives may not be mutually exclusive; each may in part be correct), but also with regard to the actual resolvability of the matter. This brings us to the next question.

b.   Can the Issue of Internal Representation Be Resolved by Behavioral Techniques?   This is a kind of metaquestion that probably should have been considered, if not resolved, before we attempted to answer the preceding one; nevertheless, for pedagogic reasons it would have been difficult to do so. Indeed, this question—the resolvability of the preceding question—itself is a matter of considerable theoretical controversy. Among those on the one side is Anderson (1978), who believes that the matter of internal representation is not resolvable with behavioral methods. (I reiterate another previously discussed obstacle to progress in the study of internal representation; because of the number of neurons involved, it is unlikely to be resolved neurophysiologically either.) Anderson's main antagonist in this debate of resolvability is Pylyshyn (1979). He asserts that the issue is capable of adjudication; this is an assertion with which I, for one, am not comfortable, and in the absence of an answer to the question of resolvability, I believe we only turn to our-all too-biased prejudgments, opinions, and indirect arguments when we consider the matter of which internal representation is likely to be used in any particular mental process. Because of its special importance we return to consider this issue several times later in this book.

A particular situation in which this debate has become embodied is in the lively discussions between Ratcliff and Hacker (1981, 1982) on the one hand and Proctor and Rao (1981) on the other. The issue in this case was whether reaction time differences between positive and negative responses are satisfactory criteria for distinguishing between alternative models of matching tasks. The specific question is whether reaction times reflect processing times accurately—an association that if well founded, it is argued by some, would allow a reductionistic model of the underlying processes to be developed.

Ratcliff and Hacker point out that the reaction measures are indeterminate with regard to the duration of the underlying processes and that a model more like Ratcliff's (1981) descriptive statistics that does not employ precise deterministic description of the properties of the underlying mechanisms is more suitable. I believe that Ratcliff and his colleagues are arguing a specific case in the context of a particular experimental exemplar of the more general hypothesis of psychophysical indeterminacy that I have presented here.

The strongest and most general argument against the resolvability of internal representation, however, is probably to be found in the aforementioned work of Moore (1956). Moore is a mathematician who has worked in the field of finite automaton theory. A *finite automaton* is a device that is deterministic (as opposed to probabilistic or random) and has a finite number of internal states, a finite number of possible input "symbols," and a finite number of output "symbols."

One of Moore's theorems (Theorem 2) is directly related to this argument: "Theorem 2: Given any machine S and any multiple experiment performed on S, there exist other machines experimentally distinguishable from S for which the original experiment would have had the same outcome" (p. 140).

Moore continues: "This result means that it will never be possible to perform experiments on a completely unknown machine which will suffice to identify it from among a class of all sequential machines" (p. 140). And, finally, Moore qualifies this conclusion:

> If, however, we restrict the class to be a smaller one, it may be possible. In particular, much of the rest of this paper will be concerned with the case where the class consists of all machines with n states or fewer, m input symbols or fewer, and p output symbols or fewer. Such a machine will be called an (n,m,p) machine. (p. 140)

It is certainly arguable whether or not Moore's (1956) theorem is applicable to the representation problem in human perceptual science. But it appears to some of us, at least, that it is, that the mind-brain is a finite automaton (even if very large numbers of states and neurons are involved, the number is finite); and, further, that this theorem, because of its broad applicability to the class of systems to which we humans seem to belong, will necessarily place severe constraints on some of the work currently carried out by theoretical and experimental psychologists. This is particularly true for cognitive psychologists who seek to understand, measure, and define the detailed nature of internal mechanisms, representational and otherwise, by behavioral means alone. But it was also relevant to the long-lasting controversy between trichromatic and opponent mechanisms in a simpler kind of psychophysics.

Moore's theoretical answer to the question of the identifiability of automata makes the arguments over internal representational schemes in memory and perception curious dialogues, indeed. If Moore is correct and if his theorem is generalizable to human mentation, then many of psychology's goals may be patently absurd. If, on the other hand, his theorem is inapplicable and Pylyshyn and others are correct, then the next steps in the logical sequence are implacable. Full consideration of the matter of representation demands that we must also ask the following two corollary questions concerning transformations between different levels of representation.

c.   How Are the Information Patterns Defined in the External World by the Stimulus Scene Converted into Whatever Representation Scheme It Is That Is Used Internally   and

d.   How Is Our Perception of the External World Then Reconstructed from the Internal Representation System, However Abstract, Verbal, or Pictorial It May Be, Inside the Head?   Answers to these two questions are the domain of a kind of psychological research other than the one with which I am concerned here. Therefore, I do not dwell on them, other than to state that whether they are answerable in detail or not, it is clear that the nature of human perception and cognition and the known facts of the neuronal system constitute two legs to an existence proof that such processes as encoding, representation, and decoding can and do successfully occur regardless of whether or not we will ever be able to understand them fully. Somehow we do manage to both encode stimuli in central neural representations that are the equivalents of mental acts and then to decode these representations into a model of the external world that is, at least, behaviorally adaptive: We do manage to respond to the dangers and opportunities of our environment in a way that indicates that whatever the mental map is like internally, it is usually appropriate. For the moment I do not have anything further to say about these two issues. They are usually studied in the context of memory paradigms (for example, the perceptual matching of current and recalled stimuli) that are beyond the scope of this volume.

e.   The Problem of Stimulus Equivalence.   Another classic issue that has confronted students of visual perception for decades (and philosophers for millennia in the related context of ''universals'') is the ability of the perceiver to treat widely distorted retinal maps as being equivalent in terms of their conceptual and categorical nature. That is, we are able to perceptually designate two stimuli as representing the same physical object (or to be a member of the same category) although one may have been transformed from the other by magnification, translation, rotation, inversion, or even some more drastic distortion. A dinner plate is perceived as a circular object that is the same as another plate although it may be viewed from an oblique angle or from a distance other than the one at which it was first encountered: Simple transformations, translations, and rotation make the retinal projection a highly distorted "model" of the real object, and yet, the "model" may be perceived easily to be the same as the object. The visual-constancy literature is replete with data suggesting that the transformed stimulus object is not just "recognized" as belonging in the same class of objects as the untransformed object but is actually "seen" as being equivalent to the untransformed object to a degree that perceptually goes far beyond simple categorization.

The existence of such a powerful and ubiquitous perceptual process as constancy is an a priori indication that any simplistic model of recognition based upon a set of stored isomorphic templates is unlikely to be adequate as a description of human visual-recognition behavior. Not only would a very large number of templates have to be stored, but one would be hard pressed to explain the matching of a stimulus scene with a template of a scene that had not, in fact, been previously experienced. Furthermore, size constancies can be affected by independent estimates of the distance to the stimulus or even knowledge of what size the object "should" be. None of this speaks to the existence of a template-matching process in perception.

The obvious alternative to a template hypothesis is that it is not the comparison of the specific geometry of the stimulus with a template that is of significance, but rather the nature of the *relative* relationships among (i.e., the arrangement of) the geometrical parts of a scene that is the key to visual form perception. This is quite a different mechanism than those underlying any conceivable hardwired feature recognizers or Fourier spatial-frequency analyzers of the kind that have so frequently been proposed to account for one or another aspect of form perception in recent years.

Theoretical solutions to what at first glance should seem to be the enormously difficult problem of stimulus equivalence are surprisingly prevalent. Lashley (1942) was probably the first to propose the idea of repetitive representations interacting via interferencelike patterns as one possible solution. This idea has been clothed in the terminology of the more modern technology of holography by Pribram, Nuwer, and Baron (1974), but the ideas are essentially the same. An image placed anywhere in the retina will produce multiple representations throughout the relevant portions of the brain. This concept is also closely related to the Fourier analysis ideas that are currently popular. Recently, computer engineers have joined the ranks of practitioners of this point of view. Abu-Mastafa and Psaltis (1987) argue that optical computers, using large memories to store vast numbers of templates, model human form-recognition mechanisms as they match stimuli against stored images. Although this may work as a useful engineering gimmick it is almost certain that they are wrong in believing that this is the way recognition occurs in the human visual system.

An alternative approach to solving the stimulus-equivalence riddle is the discrete neuronal nerve-net model that was originally proposed by Pitts and McCullouch (1947). Their model is based on a different kind of neuronal computation but seeks to achieve the same goal of explaining stimulus equivalence, or, as they so eloquently put it, "How we know universals" (p. 127).

f. Are Some Dimensions of the Stimulus Primary and Some Derived?   This is the classic perplexity most clearly enunciated (and resolved to his satisfaction and almost no one else's) by Bishop George Berkeley in his classic *Essay Towards a New Theory of Vision* (Berkeley, 1709/1954). Berkeley distinguished between mediate visual stimuli (such as those influencing the perception of depth) that he believed had to be processed by the nervous system in a very indirect manner to be perceived, on the one hand, and stimuli that could be processed in an immediate manner by the organism, on the other. An argument can be made, and I have made it elsewhere (Uttal, 1983) in both empirical and theoretical contexts, that this dichotomy is a fallacious one. This counter argument (to Berkeley's dichotomy) asserts that all perceptual experiences are so indirectly related to the stimulus dimensions that all stimuli must be considered to be mediate rather than immediate. This stance is analogous to Helmholtz's (1968) philosophy of unconscious inference as well as to the constructivist theories of modern cognitive psychologists.

This question has been formulated in other places and at other times in forms that seem to mean exactly the same thing. We may ask: Which aspects of percept are driven by the stimuli and which are constructed by the observer? or, alternatively, Is vision active or passive? Though the words differ, these queries convey virtually the same meaning as the one heading this section. My personal opinion is that with few exceptions (those I classified as Level 0, 1, or 2 in my 1981 volume) the perceptual system is remarkably active and mediate in the way it handles stimuli. As we see in chapter 2, this issue is the fundamental core of some of the major disagreements in form-perception theory.

g. Is Visual Perception Innate or Learned?   This question is obviously closely related to the preceding one. The suggestion that there exist stimuli that may or must be meditated necessarily implies that there be some process or mechanism, either innate or learned, responsible for the mediation. According to one point of view, that of the empiricists, the mediating mechanisms must be acquired by experience; we must learn to perceive the mediated dimensions of the stimulus. This logic is what led Berkeley (1954) to assert that we must learn to see the mediated stimulus dimensions (such as depth) by linking them with the immediate dimensions (like height, width) sometimes appreciated through the medium of other modalities such as proprioception or touch. The opposing point of view, associated with classic rationalism, supported the existence of innate ideas or mediating mechanisms that did not have to be learned but were either a part of the organism's organization from birth or emerged as a result of growth rather than experience.

The controversy is, of course, not simple, and there is probably not a single instance in which a perceptual task has been universally accepted by theoreticians as being unequivocally either innate or learned. The statistical and methodological difficulties involved in studying learning effects at the same time that an organism is going through its maturation cycle are profound. It is probably not too farfetched to suggest that the entire field of developmental psychology has grown up solely in an effort to unravel this tangled knot. Nevertheless, the debate rages on. An eclectic position with regard to this issue seems to be a prudent choice, and I place myself among the prudent in this regard. From my point of view, perception, in large part, is the outcome of some measure of experience operating on some innate mechanisms. I suspect, however, that the two influences—experience and growth—may not be easily separated in the near future to everyone's satisfaction.

h. Is Visual Perception Holistic or Elementalistic? There is no question that there is a strong elementalistic tendency on the part of much modern thinking about perception that has been stimulated by the extraordinary intellectual accomplishments occurring in neurophysiology and computer science. Nevertheless, there is a strong undercurrent in contemporary psychological thinking reflecting a rejuvenation of the commitment to the holistic point of view originally championed by the Gestalt psychologists. This yet barely revealed and minority undercurrent seems to me actually to be closer to the "correct" answer to this question than that proposed by mainstream elementalists. Substantial amounts of psychophysical data and many straightforward demonstrations argue that people see more in terms of the arrangement of parts than in terms of the nature of the parts. I place myself among what I hope is a growing minority of holists, but acknowledge that the pendulum has swung back and forth many times not only in my own thinking but also in the history of this profession. This question is examined in detail in this book.

i. What Is the Natural Geometry of Visual Space? The phenomenal space in which psychophysical processes occur is not identical or even congruent with the physical space of the external world. Many studies have shown that systematic distortions are introduced by the transformations that occur in the perceptual system. What is the nature of these distortions? And Are there specific shapes that are best perceived because of their similarity to this distorted perceptual space? The work of Luneberg (1950) and Blank (1959) speaks directly to this issue. Joseph Lappin of Vanderbilt University has also been studying the nature of the metric of visual space. This is another form of the same question. Many other research projects, particularly concerning stereoscopic depth, implicitly illustrate that Euclidean geometry is inadequate to describe visual space phenomena. Again the issue is complex: Some investigators (e.g., Wagner, 1985) assert that phenomenal spatial geometry depends on many observer and task variables and thus may vary from situation to situation and from observer to observer.

These, then, are the major scientific issues generally guiding perceptual research. It is important, in concluding this list, to note that there are some other questions, not included in the tabulation, that seem at first glance to be of great import but, in fact, are nearly totally unassailable because their constituent terms are so poorly defined. For example, there has been great interest over the years concerning the possible "voluntary" nature of perception. Can we consciously filter our percepts? I believe this to be essentially a nonquestion in the sense that its premises are so poorly spelled out. The concept of "voluntary" (i.e., "free will" in an older jargon) is itself so poorly construed and defined that we are hard pressed to know how to even approach this issue in the laboratory. The empirical (as opposed to the patently philosophical) fundamentals of whatever it is that is meant by words like "voluntarism" and "free will," and even "responsibility," are not yet within the reach of experimental psychology in spite of the fact that ambiguous material can often be organized in alternative ways "at will." What this means is as mysterious as the phenomenon is solid. With this disclaimer in print, I can now turn to the fourth class of issues that are more specifically related to the perception of form and are suitable for empirical investigation.

4. The Form-Perception Issues

Questions pertaining to form perception are subsidiary to those of the previous section on the General Perceptual Issues just as those were subsidiary to the even more general issues of the section on the Mind-Brain Issues. We are now at a level of specificity in this tabulation of issues motivating research to concern ourselves with visual form perception in particular rather than perception in general. It is here that the specific parameters of geometry enter the discussion in a way that can be manipulated in the laboratory.

a. The Specific Attribute Question.   I have repeatedly (Uttal, 1975, 1983, 1985, 1987) called attention to the fact that although there has been a very large amount of research on matters tangentially related to form perception, there have, in fact, been relatively few investigations directly targeted at what may be the most important and fundamental issue in form perception—the *specific attribute issue*. A few others, including Sutherland (1967) and Zusne (1970) have preceded me in also raising the hue and cry concerning this oversight. Nevertheless, our cry is largely unheard, it seems, and the main psychological community still seems to prefer to consider things such as the temporal integration of forms or how we remember and recall forms rather than to examine the central issue. That central issue, the specific attribute question, can be spelled out succinctly in the following ways: *What are the attributes or characteristics of a form that regulate its detectability, discriminability. or recognizability?* It is important to appreciate that I use the word *attribute* here to emphasize that I am concerned both with the *global* properties of the form and the *local* features. I intend there to be a greater inclusivity of the term *attribute* than there is of the word *feature*. It is, as I have noted, the difference between some aspect of the overall *arrangement* of, as opposed to the *nature* of, the component parts of a form that seems to dominate form perception.

Attribute to me is a word that includes both the relationships defining the overall arrangement (organization) and the nature of the component features. This approach is in close agreement with the use of the terms *attributes, dimensions,* and *features* by W.R. Garner (1978). He makes the following distinctions and defines the terms in a particularly complete way that is extremely useful:

> Component properties (attributes) consist of either dimensions or features. Dimensions are variables for which mutually exclusive levels exist, and quantitative dimensions are distinguished from qualitative dimensions on the basis of the role of zero: Zero is a positive value for quantitative dimensions but simply indicates absence of dimension for qualitative dimensions. Features are variables that exist or do not exist, so that zero is confounded as a level on a variable and as absence of the feature. Holistic properties can be simple wholes, templates, or configurations, with simple wholes (and possibly templates) not being more than the sum of the parts; configural properties are emergent properties, thus other than the sum of the parts. Component and holistic properties are different aspects of the same stimulus, because they coexist and are not independent. (p. 99)

There are three practical reasons for the long neglect of the specific attribute question. First, as I noted earlier, there is as yet no adequate means of quantifying what we mean by the word *form*, thus it is difficult to precisely specify the attributes of a form. Although some authors have suggested statistical families of forms that are alike in some general way, there is no single dimension along which form may be continuously varied comparable to electromagnetic frequency in color research or acoustic frequency in pitch research.

Perhaps the fundamental reason for this difficulty lies in the fact that the spatial and temporal attributes of forms are intrinsically multidimensional, and in present-day psychology we still tend to think mainly in unidimensional terms. Forms, in the absence of a unique descriptive dimension, are often generated in a more or less arbitrary manner and are equally often defined as experimental stimuli on the basis of some vaguely articulated ad hoc rule. The stimulus forms (dotted arrays) I most often use in my personal research effort are also more or less arbitrary, although in some cases a continuous variable (e.g., variance or the order and coefficients of a polynomial expression) does satisfy the immediate needs of a particular experiment.

The second reason that the specific attribute problem was ignored for so long is that heretofore there has been no practical way to manipulate even arbitrarily defined forms in stimulus displays. As I also noted earlier, Gestalt psychology was damaged perhaps even more by this practical difficulty than by the empirical falsification of its fragile neuroelectrical field theories. Those enlightened, but unfruitful, pioneers simply did not have the technical capabilities to carry out the obvious experiments. One must wonder what the state of contemporary perceptual psychology would have been if those holistic perceptual scientists had possessed the information-manipulation tools now available to modern perceptual researchers. The advent of the laboratory computer, in particular, has ameliorated this practical difficulty. Forms of great variety and complexity in two, three, and even four dimensions (i.e., x,y,z,t) are today easily generated in any laboratory interested in doing so.

The third reason the specific attribute problem has been neglected is that the manipulation of the form of continuous figures usually leads to a confounded outcome. That is, changing one attribute of the global arrangement of the parts of a form also often covaries some other local attribute. For example, varying the area of a geometrical form also varies the perimeter of that form, and we do not yet know much about the psychophysical interaction of such dimensions. Such a confounding often makes the actual causal relationship between any particular attribute of the form and any measure of the perceptual response uncertain. All that is certain is that the specific attribute question remains a formidable task for both empirical testing and theoretical analysis.

b. How Do the Attributes of a Stimulus Form Interact?
The troublesome question posed here is the one to which I alluded only in passing in the previous paragraphs. It concerns the effect of the relationship among the attributes of a stimulus when we perceptually process them. A number of contemporary researchers (including Garner, 1974; Garner & Felfoldy, 1970; Krumhansl, 1984; Lockhead, 1970, 1972; Shepard, 1964) have attacked this problem from the point of view of the interactions or integrality of the geometric dimensions of a stimulus form. (The issue is also, of course, closely related to the whole-vs.-element controversy previously mentioned but in a much more general way than that posed here.)

Another guise in which this same issue arises is in terms of the independence of our ability to localize a form in space and to identify that form. The now well-demonstrated existence of two separate pathways from the retina to the cerebral cortex (the retino-geniculate pathway—supposedly mediating form perception—and the collicular pathway—supposedly mediating localization and orientation) suggests the physiological independence of these two processes, but the psychophysical details of their putative lack of interaction have not been worked out.

However, the issue transcends geometrical attributes such as shape and location per se. Other attributes of stimulus forms, including aspects of their meaning or significance, are also known to affect the perception of a form. Aiba and Granger (1983), for example, has studied the interaction between color and position in another attack on this problem. This issue is even further complicated by the fact that meaning can be conveyed by the merest abstraction or caricature of an object in a way that makes the detailed geometry virtually irrelevant. These nongeometrical but semantic information-loaded aspects must also be taken into account in answering the question of the influence of the attributes of a stimulus form on perception.

A related, but not the only other, way in which the matter surfaces again is with regard to masking. Masking, as I went to some lengths to clarify in the previous volume in this series (Uttal, 1981) and update in this volume (see chapter 3), is not a single process but, rather, may be any one of a half-dozen or more separate processes. The kind of masking with which I am most concerned here is letter-recognition masking in which the presence of additional non target "noise" letters in a display may inhibit (mask) or in some cases even enhance, letter recognition tasks. This phenomenon has been studied by Estes (1972), Bjork and Murray (1977), and Santee and Egeth (1982), among others. A vigorous controversy has been engendered between theorists who believe that characters are processed independently (e.g., Eriksen & Lappin, 1967, and Gardner, 1973) and those who believe that the characters interact (e.g., Estes, 1972, 1974). The object- and word-superiority effects, in which a letter or a line can be seen better in a meaningful context than when isolated, are also phenomena that speak to this fundamental issue of interacting stimulus elements. I have much more to say about these topics later in this book.

c. Are the Attributes of a Stimulus Form Processed in a Serial or Parallel Manner? This issue is one of internal mechanism, and therefore like the general matter of internal' representation to which I alluded earlier, *may* be intractable to the tools of both behavioral (because of the black-box problem) and neurophysiological (because of sheer complexity) research. However, a great many psychologists are currently concerned with this question, and it would be incomplete to not at least mention it here, despite the possibility that it might be an unanswerable one. The concern in this context is with the way in which our brain's (or mind's) logical mechanisms process stimulus forms. I specifically avoid the use of the word *analyze* here. *Analyze*, of course, is a prejudicial term that is the outgrowth of the elementalistic zeitgeist. Its use actually begs the question posed; it is at least conceivable that there is no analysis in the sense that forms are dissected or broken apart into their constituent parts. Rather, it seems very likely that they may be dealt with holistically; "any" analysis may be tantamount to losing the integrity of their form and, thus, their significance.

Nevertheless, it has often been suggested that one way the perceptual system may work is to break the stimulus up into parts of some sort and then deal with the individual attributes in sequence just as we would handle several problems serially at a molar level. Hebb's seminal theory (Hebb, 1949) was of this genre. One extreme alternative to this hypothetical serial processing is some form of simultaneous or parallel processing in which all attributes of a stimulus are jointly processed by a distributed mechanism capable of executing large numbers of processing steps at the same time. From the neurophysiological point of view, it is self-evident that parallel processing could easily occur. Billions of neural events are associated with each psychological event, but the question is usually framed by cognitive psychologists in a more molar context.

A familiar problem at this more molar level is that a fast serial processor can behave very much like a slower parallel processor, and the input–output and timing relationships may be indiscriminable to psychophysical probes in either case. Indeed, for each serial process there must exist, in principle at least, an equivalent parallel processor capable of carrying out the same process. The distinction between the two possible mechanisms, therefore, usually depends upon *relative* time measurements of processes for which we have relatively poor information concerning their absolute temporal properties. Furthermore, the absolute timing characteristics of these systems may strongly interact with the task or experimental design in ways that confuse the issue in a fundamental way. (This is the same point made by Ratcliff & Hacker, 1982, with regard to reaction time to which I alluded earlier).

This is not a promising situation if one is seeking a definitive answer to the serial-parallel question for a particular instance of perceptual information processing. Therefore, this controversy may be another one of those frustrating issues that reduces to a tautology at one level (almost certainly processing is parallel at the neurophysiological level) and yet is intractable at another (thought may or may not be serial at the molar psychological level). On the other hand, the interested reader may consult Snodgrass and Townsend (1980) for an expression of a situation (reaction times) in which it is believed that serial and parallel models may be distinguished. Bergen and Julesz (1983) also point to another situation (texture discrimination) that they believe illustrates distinctive differences between parallel and serial processing. The serial processes in this case are not computational in the same sense as Snodgrass and Townsend's processing, but should be denoted as a molar kind of attentive scanning.

d. The Great Mystery of Perceptual Construction. Next, we encounter the great perplexity of how it is that we go about carrying out the complex computations, constructions, and invariance extractions in those cases in which we go from stimulus forms that are incomplete, ambiguous, or downright misleading, or in which the key information is hidden, encoded, or cryptic, to more or less veridical and complete perceptual experiences. There are many different examples of figural organizations and completions of the kind to which I here allude. The *subjective contours* made famous by Gaefano Kanizsa (1974, 1976); the strong tendency, highlighted by the Gestalt demonstrations, to fill in gaps; and our ability to literally move interferences in the stimulus space to less informationally significant places in the perceptual response space (Snyder, 1972; Warren, 1970) are but a few of the many examples of the powerful ability our perceptual system possesses to construct complete percepts from the simplest and most abstract or incomplete and degraded hints. The plainest fact of all is that these constructed percepts may have influences on our experience as powerful as the responses to real stimuli[5]; this fact alone attests to the extraordinary constructive capabilities of the human perceptual system and mitigates the impact of any theory based upon a rigid stimulus-response or passive determination.

The important message carried by these sometimes trivial-seeming, but in fact extremely challenging, demonstrations is the power of the constructionist abilities of the nervous system. To the extent that we can understand these abilities in these contexts, we may also be able to understand perception in general. Sadly, little progress has been made in this regard, and, indeed, the suspicion remains that this problem, too, may be intractable in terms of the microscopic level in which it would be desirable to frame an explanation.

e.   Is Visual Form Perception Microgenic? Can It Be Analyzed into Sub-processes?   This question is generally answered, at least implicitly, in the affirmative by contemporary psychologists. And, frankly, such a taxonomic dissection of "perception" into subprocesses is probably necessary in order to provide the necessary conceptual framework for the rest of this book and, much more important, to permit progress in the science. I raise this question here, however, in order to at least acknowledge that some doubt exists with regard to the separate biological reality of many of the processes that are discussed and studied in what is so often assumed to be psychophysical isolation from each other. It is entirely possible that the putative hierarchy of visual processing stages that is a cornerstone of so much of our thinking (see, for example, Bachmann, 1980; Uttal, 1981; Werner & Wapner, 1952) in perceptual science is, in fact, purely an artifact of a profound human drive towards taxonomic classification (a highly evolved version of a much more primitive curiosity) or, even worse, of the limited methodological paradigms that we are forced to use to examine what may be intrinsically much more holistic processes. The existence of these doubts, however, does not prevent me from asking the following related question:

f.   Given That They May Only Be Pragmatic Conveniences, What Are the Subprocesses We Find Convenient to Study in Our Search for Understanding of Form Perception?   In other words, what is the best way to dissect the global process we call *form perception* into subprocesses that will allow us to meaningfully apply the Cartesian and Millsian method of detail? To conduct experiments on problems of sufficiently low levels of complexity so that they are amenable to control and manipulation is, of course, the practical, if not the theoretically fundamental, reason that we continue this attempt to define perceptual subprocesses; it is a search for a level of manipulable simplicity carried on

---

[5] It is often possible to show by careful experimentation that a constructed percept does not behave in exactly the same way as the response to real stimulus, but the emphasis here is on the nature of the raw percept itself.

even though the underlying biology of the situation may not justify this kind of analysis. Given what we have learned about form perception in the laboratory and what we may plausibly speculate, we ask here: What are the manipulable and simple subprocesses that could possibly unite to make up the whole perceptual process?

Having asked this question, I now note that I have already answered it, in part, in my minilexicon presented earlier in this chapter. Many of the terms that I attempted to define there were just those subprocesses I now seek.

The question of the existence of form perception subprocesses has two very important corollaries. First, given that these subprocesses exist in biological fact and are not just conceptual conveniences, what are the mechanisms of each? Second, what theories can be invoked to describe and explain each subprocess? A main goal of a considerable body of psychological theory development, as well as of this book, is to answer these two corollary questions.

g. What Are the Phenomena of Form Perception and What Are Their Properties?

Finally, we ask about the phenomena—the perceptual experiences (or measures of them) themselves. This is *not* the same question as the one just asked about the processes. The processes *produce* the experiential phenomena but they *are not* the phenomena. The phenomena of form perception, as I use the term, include both the data obtained in experiments that are indicative of the experiences and the subjective experiences of the perceiver themselves. The awareness of (or responsiveness to) grouping or texture, the perception of depth, or the discrimination of one form or another are all the phenomenal outcomes of perceptual processes. These outcomes or responses must be identified, categorized, and defined in terms that are different from those used to categorize the processes that give rise to them. The processes are, in a very real way, much more abstract than the phenomena in that they must be inferred from the phenomena; they are not directly observable either by the perceiver or by the experimenter.

It would be impossible for me to attempt to list all perceptual phenomena here. A list of just those examined in contemporary psychological laboratories would be much more varied and longer than a comparable list of processes. And, indeed, the purpose of much of the rest of this book is to emphasize the theories that "explain" perceptual experiences and to attempt to categorize, describe, and, to the extent possible, explain them in terms of a smaller number of more general categories—the processes—that underly the phenomena.

Nevertheless, there are many corollaries to the question of the nature of the phenomena that also must be answered. Two of them are:

h. What Are the Functional Relationships Between the Dimensions of the Stimulus and the Dimensions of the Psychological Experience?

This is the descriptive question asked by psychophysicists. In other words, what are the laws governing the transformations between stimuli and percepts?

i. What Is the Best Explanation (as Opposed to Description) of Each Phenomena? This is the question asked by theoretical psychologists. In other words, how do we see?

The purpose of this introductory chapter is to orient my readers to my own theoretical biases. My goal here has also been to make a broad general point. The plain and simple fact is that perceptual scientists are actually motivated to do things in the laboratory (even though it may not be explicit in their thinking) because they (or the community of which they are a part) are trying to answer broader issues than the specific empirical questions being asked and the manipulations being made in experiments. This is all too often overlooked—these questions may not be explicitly stated, but they are ubiquitous nevertheless. The degree to which one is doing quality science that transcends the mundane collection of empirical measurements is closely associated with the degree to which one understands this fact.

E. PLAN OF THIS BOOK

This book has a somewhat different flavor than the three that preceded it in this tetralogy. My goal in this book is to emphasize theories and concepts rather than data. Of course, data cannot be ignored entirely, but the field is so broad that, in my judgment, the chances of producing a successful synthesis will be enhanced by concentrating on the unifying principles and theories of the processes rather than trying to exhaustively enumerate the entire data base of visual research. This book is divided into an introductory chapter and five others. Chapter 2 is intended to provide a broad survey of the history of perceptual theories, with a special effort made to define the logical clusters into which theories fall. Chapter 3 concentrates on the ideas inherent in theories of detection. Chapters 4 and 5 are aimed mainly at theories of discrimination and recognition, respectively. In each of these three chapters, I also spell out some of the concepts, terms, and ideas that have been both the targets and the motivating forces behind theory development in these three respective fields of visual research. In chapter 6, I summarize and criticize what I see as the current state of form-perception theory.

It should be obvious that chapters 3, 4, and 5 represent the hard content core of the book, whereas chapters 1, 2, and 6 represent commentary on those major themes. It should also be obvious that chapters 3, 4, and 5 represent an implicit taxonomy of these higher order visual processes that has within it a very explicit theoretical commitment of its own. To organize a book is to express such a taxonomy, and my acceptance of these categories is tantamount to accepting an affirmative answer to the question of microgenesis—perception is, according to my current view, made up of a series of perceptual molecules. It is for the future to decide whether these categories are the correct ones or, for that matter, if this microgenetic orientation is correct.

2

THEORIES OF FORM PERCEPTION

A. INTRODUCTION

The ultimate purpose of form-perception research is to *explain* the means by which organisms process and perceive stimulus-forms. In spite of the fact that most of our energy and time is spent in the laboratory, the true mission of our science is only secondarily to *describe* and *measure* form-perception phenomena. Most of the perceptual phenomena we study are, in fact, of only minimal intrinsic interest; they are used in the laboratory merely as exemplars to suggest the underlying transformations so that a general understanding of more universally important perceptual processes can be achieved.

The assertions of the previous paragraph (which summarize some of the thoughts of the previous chapter) are, of course, a reflection of a highly personal perceptual credo. I must acknowledge that it is possible, in fact likely, that this point of view is a minority perspective in the crisp cold light of the vast amount of purely descriptive data collection that goes on and the relatively small amount of solid explanatory theory that appears in print in this field. What the preceding paragraph is intended to express is my belief that there is an exaggerated emphasis on data *collection*, as opposed to data *integration* and *explanation*, in our science. A strong need exists, therefore, to at least partially offset this misemphasis by presenting a discussion of both the historically significant and some of the more general theories of form vision that are currently popular early in this book. This is the purpose of this chapter. It is here that I consider the various interpretations that are the essence and the purpose of form-perception research. More specific theoretical approaches are dealt with later. It is here that a particular conceptual context from among many possible ones is established for this book.

Before I begin to discuss the many general theories, prototheories, metatheories, and points of view that have been put forward by students of form perception over a history that spans millenia, there are some general theoretical and conceptual points that must be made. One important caveat, best expressed at the outset of this discussion, is the simple warning that, although it may sometimes appear otherwise, it is unlikely that the two major opposing schools of thought (rationalism and empiricism, to be explicitly defined later) in this field are really exclusive antagonists of each other. There is, in fact, a highly complementary relationship between theories stressing the immediate role of the stimulus in determining percepts and those stressing the mediated role of the organism in determining its perceptions. One would be hard pressed to find a proponent of either point of view of such extreme and radical rigidity as to reject *all* of the premises of the opposing point of view. Rather it seems that the major difference between the two groups is the emphasis that each places on the salience of certain classes of phenomena.

Such a complementary merging of what may superficially seem to be diverse and even antagonistic theories will be seen to be entirely appropriate in the light of the undeniable fact that some perceptual experiences are best explained in terms of peripheral processes that are *more* dependent on the nature of the stimulus and the receptors and afferent mechanisms, whereas others are best understood in terms of more central mechanisms that are *more* powerfully influenced by less automatic and more symbolic action by the organism. It is this kind of relativistic approach to theory—one of complementarity and emphasis rather than of exclusion—that should mitigate any extremism in most theoretical controversies. Many strident controversies, therefore, are actually empty passages in the dark rather than vigorous conflicts of great substance over important issues that illuminate understanding. All too often it seems that the proponents of the two schools of thought speak past each other rather than to each other. Often they do not even seem to be considering the same phenomena. The heart of this science is to be found in specific controversies over particular issues based on jointly shared data bases, not the vacuous debates between metatheories evolving from overlapping findings that actually never come into conflict on any specific issue.

A wonderful way to graphically depict these differences in emphasis and the ubiquitous lack of focal points of conflict between different metatheories was presented almost 50 years ago by Brunswik (1939) and is still relevant. He devised a schematic diagram (reproduced in Fig. 2.1) analyzing the various levels at which psychological processes and events occur. Brunswik pointed out that different fields of psychology are concerned with different relationships among the various components of the system. Psychophysics, for example, is interested in the relationship between the distal stimuli and the molecular behavioral components. In his model, Brunswik lumped together virtually all of the topics about which I have written in the tetralogy of which this book is a part under the single category "intraorganismic events and dispositions." All of the theories discussed in this

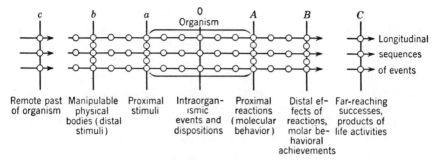

c *b* *a* 0 Organism *A* *B* *C*

Longitudinal
sequences
of events

Remote past / of organism | Manipulable / physical / bodies (distal / stimuli) | Proximal / stimuli | Intraorgan- / ismic / events and / dispositions | Proximal / reactions / (molecular / behavior) | Distal ef- / fects of / reactions, / molar be- / havioral / achievements | Far-reaching / successes, / products of / life activities

FIG. 2.1.   A multilevel analysis of the ways in which psychology can study the behaving organism, but at a coarse level (from Marx & Hillix, 1973, after Brunswik, 1939).

book and in its predecessors speak to various subdivisions and levels of this category. If Brunswik's 0 level is expanded, as shown in Fig. 2.2, which is an elaboration on my part of his diagram, we can see how the various metatheories may only rarely even come into contact and thus may never conflict. Global theories often attack a particular level, a particular aspect, or a particular mechanism of form perception without intruding into the intellectual territory of what might have initially seemed to be a potentially antagonistic theory.

A closely related matter concerns the goals of any particular theory. What a particular theory is trying to do is often unappreciated because it is often not expressed or, at least, is underexpressed by its author. For example, one of the most popular trends in contemporary perceptual theory is the application of what we have discovered about the trigger-feature sensitivity of individual neurons in the peripheral nervous system to the psychological processes of form detection. The distinguished work of David Hubel and Thorsten Weisel, as well as an army of other contemporary neurophysiologists who have added to their pioneering and revolutionary neurophysiological discoveries, has established beyond doubt

Intraorganismic Events and Dispositions

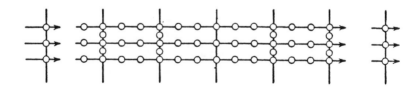

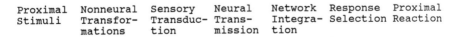

Proximal / Stimuli | Nonneural / Transfor- / mations | Sensory / Transduc- / tion | Neural / Trans- / mission | Network / Integra- / tion | Response / Selection | Proximal / Reaction

FIG. 2.2.   A finer multilevel analysis of the ways in which psychology can study the behaving organism concentrating on what Brunswik (1939) referred to as the "intraorganismic events and dispositions."

that individual neurons *are* specifically sensitive to particular spatio-temporal attributes of the visual scene. Of the validity of this *neurophysiological datum* there is no question! However, neurons sensitive to particular spatio-temporal forms (even if they were to be found in our own nervous systems) are not necessarily the same thing as the psychological data describing our molar perception of those forms, much less the psychoneural equivalent of the phenomena themselves.

Indeed, a little reflection suggests they are not even plausibly the same thing. Hubel (1978), in particular, as one outstanding counterexample, explicitly stated his view that *findings from his laboratory are not germane to the problems of cognitive psychology*. All of the neurophysiological data of this genre are, in fact, helping us to understand something else, he reminds us; that is, he and his colleagues have taught us about the attributes of the components of the *communication pathway* conveying information from the peripheral receptors to the central nervous system. None of these data adequately speaks to the problem of the more central psychoneural equivalents of the cognitive mechanisms underlying form-perception processes and phenomena in either Hubel's or my opinion.

There certainly is, however, an abundance of both neuroreductive and non-neuroreductive *theories* of various kinds that are intended to speak directly to the form-perception process. As one surveys these theories, both in their historic and contemporary versions, it quickly becomes evident what are the essential characteristics of the two main schools of thought. All theories of form perception can be ordered along a single dimension that ranges from one extreme—a radical empiricism—to another—a radical rationalism—with various intermediate positions along that axis corresponding to the relative conceptual proximity to either extreme. This main dimension along which form-perception theories, in particular, vary is but one of the three main dimensions that collectively characterize theories of visual perception more generally. I have already presented (Uttal, 1981, chapter 2) a schematic drawing that depicts this tridimensional theory space. That drawing is reproduced here in Fig. 2.3. In the present context I ask

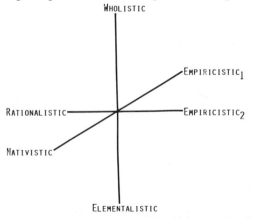

FIG. 2.3. The three-dimensional space within which perception theories can be classified (from Uttal, 1981).

the reader to direct attention specifically to the axis labeled Rationalist–Empiricist$_2$.[1]

The terms *rationalist* and *empiricist* have been appropriated from philosophy and refer respectively to two generic classes of perceptual theories. One— rationalism—has traditionally emphasized the impact on the response of active conceptual central processing by the perceiver; the other—empiricism—has stressed the determination of the response by the stimulus and by automatic peripheral processing mechanisms. Traditionally, rationalist philosophers have supposed that information had to be processed by already existing "cognitive mechanisms" before it could have meaning attached to it— that is, before it could be perceived. Thus, rationalist theories have usually emphasized the existence of some preexisting system of "ideas" and the active manipulation of the incoming information by those ideas. Typically, classic rationalists suggested that these ideas are innate, but this premise is not essential to their position, as I suggest in Footnote 1; a theory could also assert that ideas might be learned and still be within the rationalist fold. According to adherents to the rationalist approach, the perceptual experience is the more or less indirect result of the application of deductive principles to the stream of sensory stimulation by an entity that actively interprets the incoming signals. The preponderance of perceptual processing in this case is often said to be *subjective*.

The empiricist tradition, on the other hand, has stressed a much more direct processing of incoming sensory signals by the perceptual system. To the empiricist, we perceive because of the direct impact of the incoming messages on what is essentially a passive or, at least, an automatonlike perceptual nervous system. The transmitted properties of the stimulus object, to a significant extent, determine the response—a response that is a much more direct outcome of the stimulus than that postulated by the rationalists. Complex ideas are built up by a process more akin to induction than to the deductive logic proposed by the rationalists and without the mediation of complex interpretative or inferential processes. Processing is much more automatic, deterministic, and algorithmic. In this case the preponderance of perceptual processing is, therefore, often described as *objective*.

These two radical and extreme points of view present a dichotomy that can be characterized in other ways. The rationalist, or indirect, theories typically invoke some kind of a top-down processing in which the existing central mechanisms in some way interpret, infer, construct, or otherwise modify the significance of

---

[1] The subscript 2 was used in that volume (Uttal, 1981) to distinguish this dimension of direct-indirect or empiricist-rationalist processes from another use of the word *empiricist* (subscripted *1*) more closely associated with the context of the innate-versus-learned nature of perception controversy. Though empiricist$_1$ and empiricist$_2$ dimensions are often uncritically linked together, in fact, they represent quite distinct aspects of the problem and should be kept separated. In this volume, we are concerned only with the direct-indirect dimension (and not with the learned-versus-innate dimension) and, therefore, can drop the subscripts. It is to be understood, from this point on, that the use of the word *empiricist* is restricted to the subscript 2 meaning.

the afferent flow of information. In this sense these theories are organism driven—the dominant influence (although hardly the only one to even the most radical proponent of this philosophy) is the interpretative processing executed by a higher, more central, or more complex process on a lower one. Perception is *indirect*, in the sense that the stimuli do not determine the response. Effortful attention is often invoked by this class of theoretician. Processing is *active*, in the sense that manipulations are made on the sensory information by a "rational," "constructivist," "knowledgeable," "understanding," or in Shaw and Bransford's (1977) terms, "adumbrative" interpreter. The intent of the latter psychologists is to have the term *adumbrative* connote some sense of the creation of an ensemble cognitive structure (i.e., concept) from the suggestions of the incomplete, disorganized, and particulate sensory information.

The empiricist theories, on the other hand, emphasize the impact of the stimulus and the automatic, lower, preattentive processing levels on perception. Empiricists typically consider the perceptual experience to be the result of a much more direct influence of the stimulus on a rigid algorithm-evaluating nervous system than is usually allowed by the rationalist. Thus the perceptual nervous system is considered to be a more passive system in that it responds directly to the *geometry* of the stimulus form rather than to any subtle *implications of the geometry* of the stimulus. To the empiricist, the medium is relatively more important than the message. The influence of the organism is exerted mainly through the execution of more or less inflexible algorithms rather than through the construction, addition, or "knowledgeable" interpretation of semantic information. The stimulus–response school of thought that dominated mid-20th century behaviorism is an example of a strongly empiricist interpretation of how perceptual processes might work. In general, theories that are categorized more towards this end of the rationalist–empiricist dimension tend to be bottom-up approaches in which the stimulus and peripheral neural mechanisms determine the perceptual experience more than do the central mechanisms of the perceiver. Such theories postulate automatic and direct modes of processing by automatonlike mechanisms. The processing is passive in either of two ways. Either the response is totally dominated by the stimulus, or the stimulus is processed by relatively simple mechanisms that do not themselves exhibit any processing capabilities that are sensitive to the logical or semantic attributes of the stimulus or of the perceiver. The raw physical properties of the stimulus (geometry, luminance, etc.) are of the greatest significance from this point of view.

It should be noted that there is a subtle difference in the way that the terms *rationalism* and *empiricism* are or have been used in psychology and in philosophy. Before Kant, philosophers traditionally designated the terms as being mutually exclusive methods of discovering the "truth" about the world. On the one hand, rationalism asserted that we attain knowledge by interpreting and understanding the *meaning* of sensory information. Empiricists, on the other, asserted that the pyramiding of experience by the accrual of raw sense data is the only reliable source of knowledge. The development of epistemology from Bacon through Kant is essentially a series of elaborations on the tension between the two views. Neither view, from a purely philosophical standpoint, necessarily depends for its validity on the existence of a "physical world" as we generally understand it.

As used in psychology, however, both terms presuppose the existence of a physical environment; the distinction being made with the terms in this venue is not methodological but, rather, descriptive. Whereas philosophers are concerned with rationalism and empiricism on at least two levels—first, to generally validate (or invalidate) particular philosophical approaches to answering questions, and second, as descriptive terms in the (supposed) resolution of particular epistemological questions—experimental psychologists proceed on the assumption that an empirical approach is necessary if anything concrete is to be determined. Only the descriptive function remains for the terms, and the debate turns to whether, or to what degree, perceptual information is processed automatically or is mediated by a "mind." (Here, *empiricism* is used in the sense of "empiricism$_2$," as given in Footnote 1). Hence the terms as used in psychology need not conflict so violently as they do in philosophy; they can be viewed as the extremes of a continuum (which is not easily done in many, particularly rationalist, philosophical systems), and they lose the overtones of sophistry and constant contradiction that they have acquired through their use in philosophy. Readers who are familiar with the terms primarily in philosophical contexts may feel some slight confusion with the way they are used in the taxonomy of psychological theories, but I hope this comment clarifies my use of the term.

The two radical and extreme versions of form-perception theories that I have presented in the preceding paragraphs are, of course, caricatures. Most contemporary theories are not so radical (although as we shall see, extreme radicalism is not totally absent even in this esoteric arena). It is more often the case that the different theories of form perception *tend* toward the top-down or bottom-up approaches while, in fact, usually containing aspects of both approaches. We have a rich body of neurophysiological data that makes it no longer a matter of speculation or debate whether or not the nervous system of the perceiver does a substantial amount of preliminary peripheral processing of the afferent signal. That is axiomatic nowadays and must be accepted. On the other hand, perceptual and cognitive psychology laboratories have made it equally certain that the perceptual experience is not generally just a passive reflection of the stimulus. This is also the message conveyed by the evidence we have concerning illusions (see for example, the wonderful collection of books authored by Coren & Girgus, 1978; Luckiesh, 1965; J. Robinson, 1972; and Tolansky, 1964—a group of authors who obviously get great delight from their work).

Another introductory conceptual point must be made here. By no means should it be thought that to be a rationalist one must assert the proposition that there is anything mysterious about the cognitive mechanisms that process the incoming stimuli to any greater extent than do empiricists. Many *neo*rationalists, among whom I now (somewhat to my own amazement) include myself, are thorough-going monistic reductionists *in principle*. Each and every cognitive or rational process is, a neorationalist of this genre agrees, the outcome of the action of myriad individual neurons. It is solely the action and interaction of neurons that permits simple precognitive elements to produce cognitive processes when concatenated into sufficiently large ensembles. There is, according to this psychobiological monism, no metaphysical mystery to the emergence of global behavior from the microcosm of the neurons, only a practical, computational difficulty. This philosophy asserts that the ability to execute complex information processing is an intrinsic attribute of neurons (or any other logical element) that becomes manifest when they are gathered together in sufficiently large numbers, In other words, one can be a rationalist without necessarily asserting the old saw "The whole is greater than the sum of the parts"—an incantation left over from pre-information science days. It is not clear why it is so difficult for so many to ac-cept the simple idea that we cannot fully explain the entire nature of the parts until the totality of their individual nature is fully expressed. The simple fact is that a part is only fully described when we know how it interacts with other parts within larger systems.

As I noted in chapter 1, the relationship between microscopic, prerational, neural elements and macroscopic rationality is one of the most important and perplexing intellectual challenges of all time. Our continual concern with this perplexity is based upon the fact that the bridge joining the two domains has not yet been built even though scientists have been attacking it from two main directions—that of the synthetic simulator who practices the art of artificial in-telligence (AI) computer programming and that of the analytical neurophysiologist. Neither field has yet cracked the problem of how neurons become minds or has even made much progress, but this current lack of success should not be used as an argument against a radical psychobiological monism.

The reasons for the failure of AI researchers to provide us so far with good theories of human perception are twofold. First, there is a serious conceptual problem rampant throughout the field—many workers appear not to appreciate the limits of an analog as a putative theoretical explanation. No matter how close the apparent similarity in performance exhibited by examples of human and machine perceivers, we cannot assume that we have explained anything about the way in which human perception actually works by allusions to the computer-simulation programs. It is all too often believed that the *analogous behavior* of program and man implies *homologous mechanism*.

For example, propinquity of addresses in programmed list structures (i.e., lists of items stored in a computer memory) can closely simulate behavior that seems to reflect similar semantic associations between ideas. Birds, airplanes, and dragonflies are exemplars of a single concept that may be connected by being listed together. However, it is not necessarily the case that all of these flying machines utilize homologous (i.e., evolutionarily and embryologically identical) mechanisms to achieve their flights. Alternatively, the act of flying may be connected by logical relations that can be processed by algorithms sensitive to common meaning without these exemplars ever being present in a common list, just as "flying" can be achieved by completely different mechanisms.

The important idea in this example is that both mechanisms—list structures and semantic analyses—can accomplish the same thing (i.e., associate similar ideas) while using totally different mechanisms. It seems to me that it is highly unlikely that list structures like those used in some of the computer languages simulating associative thinking or form recognition actually exist in the brain—only *performance analogs* of them. By performance analogs, I allude to two mechanisms that perform the same task, but by means of internal mechanisms and processes that are quite different in each case. The lack of homology between associative thought and the list-processing computer program is the point being made. The relationship of the two is an analogy just like the more easily understood case of the different mechanisms used by the flying organisms.

In short, the pseudosemantic links established by list structures or other computer programs and the conceptual similarities elicited by human mentation are most likely to be performance analogs rather than process homologs of each other. It seems unlikely that they are based on the same internal logical processes or mechanisms. For our present purposes, I believe this means that we cannot in the foreseeable future count on a computer-simulation theory to be definitive by itself in its specification of the rules, representations, or internal mechanisms of *human* form perception, no matter how good the imitation. In fact, in terms of internal mechanisms it may be that, in principle, such a model can never be anything more than a remote metaphor that is not even biologically suggestive in any plausible manner. All that a computer program can do is to help delineate some of the transformations that must be executed. It is my conviction, and it is certainly an arguable one, that even though computer programs simulating perception and intelligence superficially seem to be saying something about the microscopic substrate because they are based on elemental logical units—instructions or logic gates—just as thought is based on neurons, in fact all they are actually doing is *describing* behavior in the same manner that molar psychology has traditionally done. That the language of the computer is more precise than the words used earlier does not ameliorate this constraint.

I think this point is also the one being made in an equivalent sense, if a different context, by Bennett, Hoffman, and Prakesh (1988) in their extraordinary new book entitled *Observer Mechanics*. The full significance of this book, merging quantum mechanics and perceptual theory at an extremely abstract level, will not be appreciated for some time. It is possibly one of the most important works of modern time in perception but also sufficient subtle and complex that its impact will most likely be on the next generation of perceptual researchers. In any event, these authors raise the point that only some of their "observers" are compatible with the Turing model, and thus computers, in principle, can not model the observer in general.

This limit on the power of analogs to *explain* is but one problem faced by AI research. It is an annoying, but equally compelling, practical fact that few, if any, AI research programs have even come close to a successful imitation of perception. It could be fairly claimed, in spite of some highly dramatized demonstrations, that they have succeeded in doing nothing beyond performing very limited image-processing operations in highly circumscribed microenvironments. Among the best work so far is in the field of letter-by-letter recognition. Among the least developed is in the field of natural language processing.

Furthermore, it is not always appreciated that the expectation and the hope that progress is being made is based upon what is an implicit, though questionable, rejection of the law of diminishing returns. Having invested a million dollars and 5 years to solve 50% of an AI problem is not tantamount to a proof that an additional million dollars and another 5 years will solve the remaining 50% of the problem. The usual effect of doubling investments in the AI field is to solve only 10% (in some figurative sense) more of the problem. The next million dollars and five years may be even less productive. Indeed, additional investments of time and money may serve only to expose the unsolved deeper levels of the problem and thus to drag the solution backward in terms of the proportion of the problem that can properly be considered to have been solved. As we run up against more and more intricacies, we often come to realize that the original 50% percent was not really 50% percent at all.

Dreyfus (1979), in his book *What Computers Can't Do*, has been among the most outspoken critics of the AI field in terms of its limited accomplishment. His critique has emphasized the utter lack of success exhibited by even the best modern simulation programs in generalizing their peculiar kind of perceptual skills from whatever microworld in which they may have originally been programmed to operate, to other, even closely, related microworlds. No program, according to both Dreyfus and my own experience, has yet successfully generalized its function in a way that suggests the presence of ''understanding'' comparable to that of humans as opposed to a merely mechanical evaluation of specialized algorithms. According to Dreyfus, in each and every instance in which AI conceptual generalization has been claimed, it was actually accomplished by the addition of the necessary algorithmic primitives to extend the microworld within which the program could function. There was, therefore, simply an *accretion* of program steps rather than a *generalization* of understanding or a broadening of the utility of the previous program segments. Dreyfus has thus called attention to the fact that there has, in fact, been little pyramiding of the algorithmic foundations of one program into the conceptual superstructure of other more intelligent ones. In Dreyfus' words, current AI programs deal only with ''constructing and manipulation of symbolic descriptions''. He goes on to say that ''the notion that human perception can be explained in terms of formal representation does not seem at all obvious in the face of the actual research on perception and everyday concept formation''. In my words, AI programs operate by empiricist rather than the rationalist rules that seem to be better descriptors of human perception.

This is exactly the same criticism made by Fodor (1978) who points out that programs like those that manipulate the block-filled microworlds work only because they have been specifically designed to have precise properties; properties that both allow the algorithm to work and permit these algorithms to be "verified" as plausible theories. But, Fodor also points out that the microworld and the program that manipulates it cannot be generalized to any other world.

Dreyfus (1979) specifically calls attention to another implicit premise of this field, which he calls the *metaphysical assumption*, that he believes to both ubiquitous in the AI field and fallacious. This assumption asserts that the background environment of meaning and relationships, within which objects of a stimulus microworld fit, can itself be programmed as a set of well-defined relationships. Dreyfus believes that this is not, in general, correct, and that in fact the web of real-world interrelationships in which any object is bedded is not well modeled by formal algorithms in the sense we understand them currently. For this reason, he believes there is a fundamental limit on how far computer-simulation research can go in actually simulating the logical roots of organic intelligence.

Watanabe (1985) is also critical of the intellectual accomplishments of this field. According to him, the following shortcomings of AI researchers are that they:

1. Do not clearly realize the basic distinction between induction and deduction, therefore, do not know what part of their programs represents inductive and deductive processes.
2. Are usually trained strongly in logic and very poorly in natural sciences. Therefore, they emphasize the logical aspect, and suppress the inductive aspect of human reasoning.
3. Usually smuggle man-made heuristic rules or principles into the program, without saying so, then pretend that everything man can do can be performed by a computer.
4. Are little concerned about a general theory and, with a few exceptions, their papers or books describe individual particular problem-solving algorithms. (pp.127–128)

Another psychologist who has misgivings about the relationship between AI and psychological theory is Braunstein of the University of California at Irvine. Braunstein (1983) asks rhetorically: Should technology recapitulate phylogeny? and suggests that the answer should be no. His argument is that the process of evolution has imposed some severe constraints on and created special properties of human vision that make it considerably different from computer vision. Braunstein's conclusion is that because of these special constraints and properties "the effectiveness or lack of effectiveness of a perceptual process in a computation system is not evidence for its presence or absence in human vision" (p. 85). (This criticism is essentially the same as the fallacy of analogs of which I spoke earlier, [p. 56 and Uttal, 1973b] and to which I refer again in chapter 6.)

The three special constraints to which Braunstein alludes are:

1. *The primacy of depth perception*: Human (and for that matter, all animal) visual perception is deeply concerned with the appreciation of depth both as a means of avoiding predators and of gathering food. Without depth perception it is unlikely that man could have evolved or would have survived as a species. Computers, on the other hand, need not deal with depth directly and reduce many of the problems of depth to two-dimensional problems that virtually ignore the actual three-dimensionality of the world in which they operate.

2. *Human perception and contradictory knowledge*: Braunstein's second constraint is that human perception sometimes operates in seeming contradiction to what the observer may come to know through other sources of information. An illusion may persist in spite of the fact that the observer knows full well that the observation is only illusory. A computer, to be most efficient, would want to reduce these conflicts early in its analysis of a scene; yet somehow the human functions perfectly well in spite of them.

3. *Heuristic processes in perception*: Braunstein then goes on to note that there are many processes in human vision in which there is no direct, automatic, algorithmically processible link between the stimulus and response. Rather, the human generates approximate solutions to the geometry of the stimulus on the basis of soft rules of approximate inference. The important point is that these rules may not, in Braunstein's words, be "decomposable into simpler arithmetic computations" (p. 91).

Although all three of the points raised by Braunstein (1983) are arguable, it is his overall perspective that I believe is very important in the present context. His aim is to point out that human and computer vision systems are likely to operate under different criteria and constraints. He also says:

> Just as it is unreasonable to conclude that there are no similarities between the processes found in human and machine vision, it is also unreasonable to conclude that there are no substantial differences. The processes used by the human visual system are not necessarily the processes most suitable for image-analysis programs, and those most suitable for image analysis are not necessarily found in human vision. (p. 86)

I hope it is clear now that this is a point of view with which, I strongly agree. The fact that a several of us share such sentiments does not necessarily make our view correct, but it is comforting to have company when you play the role of a cynical gadfly or a critic.

It is also interesting to have observed the evolution of AI systems and approaches over the years for within that evolution is an implicit self-criticism. Originally, formal models and either deductive or analytical algorithms were invoked to do things like play checkers or to solve "general problems." Recently, however, a new approach has come to the fore—the "expert system" in which large "data or knowledge bases" are inserted into the system. The distinction between the two approaches is instructive: In the former, rules of very specific kinds are utilized from which intelligent behavior was expected to emerge. In the latter, information relations are expressed as "knowledge"—that is, preexisting knowledge that, to be sure, might have been logically manipulated but in fact is usually dealt with as a long look-up table of listed relationships. Rules of process have given way (to exaggerate a bit) to dictionaries of relationships.

It is not too much a stretch of the situation to point out that this suggests that the evolutionary change occurred when formal rules of deduction and induction and of mathematics were found to be inadequate to simulate intelligent behavior. Current models, therefore, seem to be expedients enlisted to do what formal rules and symbolic relationships could not be made to do. Nowadays we seem to be more willing than previously to turn to prestored bases of knowledge than to *generate* it in a dynamic way.

A real question, therefore, has arisen: Did the AI field actually take a step backward when it turned from formal algorithms to the exhaustive catalogs of the so-called expert systems? Are "expert" systems the swan song of a dying field of inquiry reflecting the surrender of our hope that we can actually develop artificial intelligence? This pointed and contentious question will have to be answered in the future by others, but I, for one, am convinced that "expert systems" do not represent any kind of a model of mental processes.

Neuroscience's theoretical assault on the mechanisms of perception faces similar and perhaps equally fundamental difficulties, not the least of which is a very practical obstacle. From one point of view, the difficulty may be thought of as arising out of the most substantial advantage the neuroscientist possesses over other approaches to the study of mind. The AI researcher cannot be sure that the elements out of which he or she is building his or her perceptual systems are the correct ones (in the sense of being the same as those used by the human nervous system); there are a very large number of nearly equivalent logical subsystems or instructions that could have been used. On the other hand, the neuroscientist knows at least one thing for certain; that is that the neurons out of which the brain is composed *are* the building blocks of this particular system. The difficulty itself comes from the fact that there are so many of them, they are so complexly interconnected, and there are so few analytical tools that can be applied to examine the nature of this complex web of interactions among the individual neurons. Unfortunately, the fact that neurons are known to be the elements means that the neuroscientist is constrained to live with this complexity if his or her theories are to possess any biological validity.

This brings me to another very important matter that bears reiteration in the present context. If one is to ask: What is the critical level of neural analysis of perceiving systems? my answer, as we saw in the previous chapter, is that it is that very complex pattern of interactions of which we certainly know virtually nothing in mammals and only a little about in a few primitive invertebrates that fortuitously have both anatomically stable and simple nervous systems. The fact that so much has been learned about the biochemistry of neurons or of the molecular dynamics of ion flow across membranes, therefore, is not germane to the problem of how mind, in general, or perception, in particular, emerges from neurons. The very mass and the exciting successes of neurochemistry serve only to perpetuate the illusion that we are learning a lot about the perceiving mind-neuron relationship by understanding the metabolism of neurons. However, this is not likely to be true. These metabolic aspects of neurophysiology are all but irrelevant to the emergence of intelligence from interacting aggregations of microscopic cellular elements.

The point being made is that it is the spatial and temporal pattern of organization of neurons and not the nature of neurons that is important in understanding how mental states emerge from neural aggregates. The unimportance of the particular kind of logical elements (except with regard to timing considerations) used in a computational engine has been repeatedly demonstrated in the evolution of computer technology over the last four decades. We have gone from the relays and vacuum tubes, to discrete transistors, to small-scale integration, to today's large-scale integration in computer architecture. However, the fundamental logic, the way in which these varying parts have been combined remains virtually constant. The elegant new 450,000 or 1 million logic gate, or whatever it is by the time this book is published, large-scale integrated computer chip announced by some frontier manufacturer is virtually identical in logical principle to the Burks, Goldstine, and von Neumann (1947) *stored* program, digital computer invented 40 years.[2] Only recently have new forms of more parallel logics begun to be considered seriously. Progress in this field is rapid and several processors of varying degrees of parallellicity have been announced just in the last year.

I appreciate that I am using a computer metaphor here to make a psychobiological point (that the nature of the individual element is not important), but in this case I believe the metaphor is apt. In the brain, of course, there are many different types of neurons, but it may be that the diversity of their anatomy is

---

[2] The *stored* program digital computer is generally attributed to Burks, Goldstine, and von Neumann (1947). However, many computer historians now believe it to be a derivative of the first special purpose (it could only solve linear equations) electronic digital computer—a device that was developed by John Vincent Atanasoff, then of Iowa State University, in the period 1937–1942. The controversy surrounding the history of the "invention" of the digital computer is spelled out in a paper by Arthur and Alice Burks (1981) and in a multiauthored set of articles starting on page 245 of the July 1982 issue of the *Annals of the History of Computing*. Arthur Burks (1974) also presents an interesting discussion of the problem. Burks sees three distinct stages in this "invention": (a) the Atanasoff special-purpose electronic digital computer; (b) the Eckert and Mauchly general-purpose, electronic digital computer; and (c) the Von Neumann–Burks–Goldstein stored-program general-purpose digital computer.

merely a more or less irrelevant correlate of their need for diversity of interconnectability. Thus, structure emerges from function in an almost irrelevant way.

Even though there has been a large amount of activity in both AI and neuroscience research, much of it is thus irrelevant to developing a real understanding of the foundations and underpinnings of human perceptual skills. Two specific conclusions to which I personally have come are:

1. AI research, though it has proven to be useful in practical applications and defining some fundamental constraints of what is theoretically possible has, in the main, been sterile in providing deep insights into the substrate logical mechanisms of human perception. The analogies offered by workers in this field are at best remote heuristics and, in general, cannot be validated as true models of perception or mind, and

2. The neurosciences have also been totally unsuccessful so far in answering that most important question of modern science: How do global mental skills (like form perception) arise out of the interaction of discrete elements?

The fearful worry is that this twofold lack of success is not simply a reflection of the primitive state of these two arts but actually indicates a fundamental limitation on how far we can go in our quest to link the microscopic with the macroscopic.

Finally, in this introduction to some of the points of view and perspectives that have guided my thinking as I have considered the problems of form perception, I would like to make another general point about the nature of the problem with which we are to be concerned. In a certain sense I have to admit that I may have circumscribed the specific problem dealt with in this volume so tightly that it may have biased my outlook. Specifically I am referring to the fact that I have chosen to deal with form perception rather than cognition in general. *Form* means something very specific to me and to others of my colleagues who are interested in this research area. W.C. Hoffman (1985) has made the issue very clear in describing why many of the mathematical techniques that may be lumped together under the rubric of algebraic topology are so important when one is studying form. But the naturalness of the fit between a kind of formal geometrical mathematics and the kind of perception that we will be considering here may almost be too good. It may have prejudged the issue in a way that must not be overlooked if anyone should attempt a critical analysis of the points that I make. A hopeful sign is that Hoffman also sees the same kind of topological thinking becoming relevant and of interest in the context of higher level cognitive processes. The point is that my doubts may be ill taken and this emphasis on form perception may not be as misleading as it may at first have seemed when other levels of cognitive processing are brought under the theoretical microscope.

In the remainder of the chapter, I briefly review some of the more significant general theories relevant to the form-perception problem. The material is organized in two ways. First, I separate the theories according to the rationalist-empiricist dimension (broadly defined). Within each of these sections, I treat the individual theories in what is roughly a historical progression. The more specific and micro-scopically oriented theories are dealt with as appropriate in chapters 3, 4, and 5.

B. THE EMPIRICIST OR DIRECT APPROACH TO FORM-PERCEPTION THEORY

From a certain point of view the direct, unmediated, empiricist theories of form perception are the more primitive and the most naive. Indeed, in historical fact, the earliest theories of vision were more than less empirical with highly direct relationships postulated between the stimulus and the percept. Mediated or ra-tionalistic perception was a relatively late-coming idea, appearing only after psychologists and their predecessors became aware of the many inconsistencies between physical stimuli and the resulting percepts—particularly with the discrep-ant phenomena called *illusions*. Modern rationalism (neorationalism) can best be dated only as recently as Kantian times (the 18th century), even though some of its historical antecedents date back to classical Greece. The rationalist, mediated approach is detailed in the next section of this chapter. In this section I deal with those theories that stress the direct impact of the stimulus on perceptual experience. Such theories have appeared in many guises throughout the history of thinking about form perception with various degrees of correspondence to the known physiology, physics, and anatomy of the visual process.

I. Aristotle—An Early Empiricist

It is all too easy to read into ancient writings more meaning than was actually intended or appreciated by their authors, but with just a little bit of license it seems fair to include Aristotle (384–322 B.C.) among the early empiricists, if not to identify him as the first to be explicitly so characterized. If Aristotle was not an empiricist in the modern sense of the word, he certainly was a proto-empiricist.

Aristotle rejected the Platonic idea of universal forms—a set of concepts that were considered by Plato's school to be innate and immutable and to be the basis of our appreciation of particular cases of real-world objects. In so doing Aris-totle substituted (for the Platonic forms) an associationism that can hardly be distinguished in terms of its most fundamental axioms from that of the British Empiricists nearly two thousand years later. He was among the first to explicitly teach that sensory experiences were the direct result of stimuli acting on the *soul*—a term seemingly used in much the same sense as we use the word *mind* nowadays. Indeed, one can interpret his philosophy to be identical to that elsewhere called "the toy in the head" theory. For Aristotle, sensory stimuli acted on a more or less plastic and passive internal mind to create an actual neurophysiological (in modern terms) replica that was dimensionally isomorphic to the external object. Aristotle's attitude toward the mind was that it *had* to be passive for perception to occur. Unlike the proto-rationalistic master Plato (who stressed the necessity of the activity of the mind for perception and thought), the proto-empiricist student Aristotle stressed that mental activity would only serve to interrupt the perceptual process.

2. William of Ockham and His Razor

Among the first to actively consider the criteria that were to become the critical distinctions between the rationalist and empiricist point of view was William of Ockham (1280?–1349). William was interested specifically in the problem of whether any mediation between the stimulus and perception was required. His arguments asserting that no such intervention was necessary were logical and based on the principle of parsimony (henceforth, of course, to be known as "Ockham's Razor"). Ockham advocated the idea that there was no reason or need to assume that such an intermediary interpretative process as that invoked by the proto-rationalists and rationalists was actually required to intervene between the external world and our awareness of it. He assumed, purely on the basis of criteria of simplicity, that the action of the stimulus object could just as well be immediate and direct in producing the perceptual experience as not, and that the stimulus was the sufficient cause of the percept without any intervention by any additional and unsensed mechanism such as a rational mind. The invocation of rationalist mechanisms, according to William, simply cluttered up and unnecessarily complicated a process that could be explained with far fewer premises.

In so asserting the direct impact of the stimulus on perception, William of Ockham was reflecting the major trend of visual theory that has held constant since Aristotlian times. His great contribution was to introduce criteria of simplicity and elegance into the debate. And, indeed, even today his "razor" reminds us to keep clear the idea that the most complex mentalistic rationalistic process is probably not different in kind from the simplest neural response; any observed difference being due only to quantity and not quality.

3. Descartes—The Rationalist Empiricist

Between Aristotle and René Descartes (1596–1650) there are few theoreticians other than the Arabic scholars who explicitly dealt with the matter of perception. However, the Arabs' interests were more like those of today's ocular anatomists and optical physicists than like those of contemporary perceptual psychologists, and they do not play a major role in the history of perceptual theory. Descartes' position on the direct-mediated issue was anomalous given the rationalist tone of much of the rest of his philosophy. Although he totally accepted the concept of innate ideas that served to guide mental life, Descartes, like Aristotle, fit very well into the tradition of what was later to be called *psychobiology*. The perceptual or epistemological problem with which he was most concerned was to establish how the material world communicated with the separate mental world that was the other fundamental realm of his dualistic metaphysics. Descartes' supremely psychobiological solution to the epistemological quandary was to invoke the pineal gland as the mediator between the physical and mental worlds. Though this particular anatomical idea is completely rejected now, and the idea of a mediator between separate mental and physical realities is rejected by most contemporary psychobiologists,[3] it is clear that Descartes thought of the perceptual process in much the same terms as later empiricists, rather than in the mode of Kant or Leibniz, his rationalist compatriots. To him, as to Aristotle, the percept was a very direct result of the stimulus acting on a passive, algorithmic mediator. Indeed, Descartes hypothesized a pictographiclike relationship between the internal and external realities. He believed, as did Aristotle, that the nervous system acted (in mysterious ways he admitted he did not totally understand) to produce some kind of a replica of the object in the mind. The relationship between the object and, at least, the immediate percept was considered to be uninfluenced by innate ideas or the other concepts that Descartes shared with his rationalistic successors.

The oft-told story about Descartes and the bull's eye is probably correct in identifying and characterizing the intellectual roots of his radical empiricist theory. Having seen the image of the outside world as it was focused onto the inside of an excised bull's eye, Descartes used this optical projection as the metaphorical basis of his theory of perception. A similar "image," he wrote, was somehow projected back along the optic nerve to the pineal gland. Thus, the technological model that he used as a heuristic (as so many others before and since have used other technologies) for his perceptual theory was nothing other than the optical properties of a bull's eye.

4. The Empiricists (British and Otherwise)[4]

The historic idea of a direct impact of stimuli on perception flowered in the seventeenth and eighteenth centuries into a full-blown philosophy called *empiricism*. Thomas Hobbes (1588–1679) laid the foundation stone of perceptual empiricism in his classic work *Leviathan* (Hobbes, 1651/1962), in which he articulated a mechanistic philosophy in which mental acts were depicted as direct physical reactions (even as motions) to the "pressures" exerted by physical stimuli.

Hobbes' physicialistic empiricism was radical and extreme, as evidenced in his own words from another of his seminal works *De Corpore* (1665). When a physical stimulus "presses" on the organ of sense, that ". . . pressure, by the mediation of the nerves, and other strings and membranes of the body, continues inwards to the brain and heart, causeth there a resistance or counter pressure,

---

[3] For an exception see the work of Eccles (1979) and Popper and Eccles (1977).

[4] Some of this material has been borrowed from an earlier work (Uttal, 1981) and has been revised and edited for inclusion here.

or endeavor of the heart to deliver itself, which endeavor, because outward, seemeth to be some matter without'' (from *Encyclopedia of Philosophy*, 1967; Vol. 4, p. 37).

The emergence of such materialistic, mechanistic, and, some would argue, positivistic points of view as Hobbes' concerning mind in general, and to an amazing degree, sensations in particular, led to the specific development of British empiricism. The evolution of the several sequential intellectual stages of this school are well known. British empiricism is usually dated specifically from John Locke (1632–1704) who set the stage for the development of empiricistic epistemology by spelling out a number of fundamental principles that have had an enduring effect in the intellectual life of our civilization.

Locke's theory of perception (best summed up in 1690 in his work *An Essay Concerning Human Understanding* (1690/1975), was highly mechanistic, elementalistic, and empiricistic. However, as we see frequently, he was not exclusively committed to direct stimulus determinism. Locke also explicitly advocated the concept that percepts more complex than simple sensations were created by aggregating or associating the basic sensory experiences through a process of "reflection." Locke's "reflection," an antecedent of Helmholtz's unconscious inference (as well as contemporary cognitive constructionism) was a quasi-rationalistic concept that contrasts somewhat with the more automatic associationistic premises of the later empiricists. The empiricist Locke's quasi-rationalism should also be contrasted with the rationalist Descartes' quasi-empiricism to emphasize the potential overlap of the two approaches.

The next major figure in the development of British empiricism, Bishop George Berkeley (1685–1753), was in general agreement with Locke's associationism. Berkeley's major point of contention with Locke dealt with the latter's concept of primary and secondary qualities. Locke had asserted that each physical object had two different sets of properties. One set, consisting of the primary qualities (e.g., length), was a basic characteristic of the object itself, whereas the other set, made up of the secondary qualities (e.g., color), was meaningful only when expressed in terms of and referenced to the observer's mental processes. In other words, Locke had said that secondary qualities were inferred by the observer. (This is an interesting and intuitive precursor of distinctions we now know exist in the sensory coding schemes used by the nervous system.) Berkeley, however, believed that only secondary qualities existed and that *all* properties of a perceived object were meaningful only when defined in terms of the observer. Berkeley thus holds a particularly interesting position in the empiricist school because he was not a *materialistic* monist but, rather, one of the few examples of that rarity, an *immaterialistic* or *idealistic* monist. The assertion that all qualities are secondary is equivalent to a kind of radical idealism. Berkeley's most important work on perceptual theory was his book, *An Essay Towards a New Theory of Vision*, first published in 1709 (Berkeley, 1709/1954). A modern discussion of this work can be found in Armstrong (1960).

David Hume (1711–1776) attempted to remove Berkeley's theological and idealistic metaphysics from the otherwise mechanistic philosophy of empiricism. Hume made an especially important contribution in his far-sighted suggestion that the mind was better considered as a *process* (by which the various sensations, ideas, and memories circulated from one point to another) than as a *thing*. Hume's most important books, *A Treatise of Human Nature* (1739/1941) and *Enquiry Concerning Human Understanding* (1748/1966), are critically analyzed with regard to his perceptual theory in Price (1940). Hume was particularly concerned with the causal connections between the stimuli and mental percepts. He carried Locke's associationistic philosophy forward to a new high of mechanism by proposing that the laws of association were of exactly the same nature as the laws of interaction between physical objects. This same idea emerges anew in Bennett, Hoffman, and Prakesh's (1988) important book.

Both Hume and David Hartley (1705–1757), the next important figures in the development of British empiricism, concerned themselves with the problem of how the associations between the elemental sensory impressions developed. Both at one time or another in their writings expressed the idea that simple contiguity in time and similarity in meaning or significance of stimuli were sufficient to establish associative bonds between the elements of mental event. This same kind of simple associationism was championed by James Mill (1773–1836), who added the idea that the association of sequential sensations established a temporal order that was preserved when more complex ideas were regenerated. In this regard he was partially anticipating Hebb's (1949) theory of phase sequences (discussed later in this chapter).

Mill's simplistic and direct associationism may be thought of as the epitome of the mechanistic point of view among the British empiricists. Simple contiguity was all that was required for a "mental chemistry" to convert simple sensations into complex percepts. Meaning and conceptual similarity were concepts that were ejected from his philosophy.

British empiricism mainly evolved into a strict sensory associationism. Interestingly, at about the same time in France, Étienne de Condillac (1715–1780) proposed a much more extreme empiricism that did not involve the concept of associationism. Condillac championed the hyperempiricist idea that sensations alone were all that were required for mental processing and awareness. Condillac's philosophy was thus an extreme empiricistic elementalism that did not involve the concatenation or association of primitive sensory experiences into more complex perceptions or ideas. It is similar to some of the contemporary direct realisms, as we see later.

In the present context, another important lasting contribution of British empiricism was its role in perpetuating those mechanistic foundations of modern psychobiology that were originally suggested by Hobbes and Descartes. According to the empiricist tradition and its intellectual descendants (structuralism, behaviorism, and neurophysiological reductionism) perceptual responses to stimuli are more or less direct and automatic. The perceiver is, to a very great extent, a passive transducer operating by means of simple mechanical and deterministic processes.

5. Ernst Mach—The "Critical Empiricist"

Ernst Mach (1838–1916) was another one of those remarkable polymaths (like Aristotle, Leonardo da Vinci, Helmholtz, and William James) whose span of interests includes the perceptual processes among a vast array of other topics. He was originally trained in physics and came to study auditory and visual sensory processes because of his interest in philosophy—in particular, epistemology. Indeed, Mach is now also well known for his work as a physical and biological scientist as well for his pioneering work in the contemporary field of the philosophy of science. His contributions to science were profound and manifold. Albert Einstein describes Mach as one of the main influences leading to his (Einstein's) creation of the theory of relativity. It was Mach who was among the first to appreciate that physical measurement of time and space had to be made relative to each other, an idea that greatly diverged from the widely held Newtonian absolutism of his time.

Although his interests were wide-ranging, it is fair to say that Mach was, first of all, an epistemologist, both in theoretical and applied contexts. Much of his specific experimental work on the senses was aimed at learning about the general problem of the acquisition of knowledge. He had read Kant as a young man and was knowledgeable about his contemporary Helmholtz's idea of unconscious inference. Nevertheless his response was to reject both of these rationalistic approaches and deal with sensory experience as if it were produced in a very automatic and direct manner, consistent with the view of the British empiricists, and, in particular, David Hume.

Mach's philosophy must also be considered to be one of the major precursors of Gestalt psychology. He considered forms to be attributes of a stimulus in the same way as are size and intensity. Many of the demonstrations described in Mach's magnum opus *The Analysis of Sensations* (1959) were later to be used by the Gestaltists in their concentrated attack on the perceptual problems raised by the phenomena of form perception. Mach's attitude toward psychology was that it should be, to the fullest possible extent, physiological and reductionistic. Nevertheless, he was also a reasonable eclectic and did not totally reject other approaches of a more cognitive or "intellectual" kind. Indeed, in *The Analysis of Sensations* he, too, oscillated between empiricism and rationalism. For example, Mach (1959) asserts that there is more to vision than just the physiological responses to stimuli: ". . . it is clear that recognition is not the result of geometrical considerations . . . but of intellect" (p. 106). Clearly Mach, despite his formidable reputation as an empiricist, also appreciated that there were psychological processes influencing perception that transcended the direct and unmediated theory of perception with which he was mainly concerned.

Perhaps Mach's greatest contribution to the psychobiology of perception was his invention of nerve-net theory. His contribution was phrased in a terminology that seems totally modern today both in the verbal and the mathematical languages in which he spoke. He had earlier discovered the Mach Band phenomenon, the illusory (in the sense that the perceptual response does not agree with independent measures of the physical stimulus) dark and light bands on either side of a gradient of stimulus intensities. The full story of this discovery and the neural theory that Mach suggested is eloquently and elegantly presented in Ratliff (1965) and does not need repetition here.

The important point in the present context is that Mach hypothesized that these illusory bands were produced by interactions (of an inhibitory kind) among adjacent regions of the retina. It is a remarkable fact that the papers he wrote between 1865 and 1868 on this topic are still considered to be the prototypical example of a still acceptable, in fact, outstanding neuroreductionistic theory in sensory psychobiology. Indeed, the neural mechanisms about which Mach could only have speculated have just recently actually been observed with our modern technology.

In large part Mach's contribution of the idea of a passive neural-net processing of stimulus information was a critical response to the Kantian and Helmholtzian notions of rational or inferential processing by an "active" mind. He believed that these arguments were not satisfactory explanations in a reductive sense, and thus he was stimulated to seek explanations in the physical and physiological language with which he was more comfortable. It is striking that in spite of the absence of the necessary neurophysiological data he was able to draw out of psychophysical findings such precise insights into what the underlying neurophysiology must be.

Mach is thus an empiricist of a more than less radical kind; he accepted psychophysical responses as direct and unmediated when it came to the analysis of the sensory experiences with which he was most concerned. Nevertheless, as we have seen, he did not reject completely the idea of other processes that might be less direct or more interpretative as an outcome of the complexity of neural networks of which we still know very little.

A comment should be made here about the difference between the terms *direct* and *indirect* on the one hand and *empiricist and rationalist* on the other. Both of these pairs of terms reflect the extremes of the same quantitative dimension but, in fact, these extremes may not differ in kind in some deep sense. That is, what appears to be indirect may be only more complex and thus more inscrutable than that which appears to be direct and easily understood. Again and again we will see the theoretical orientation being determined by the nature of the phenomena of interest. Mach's interests were directed toward the "simple" sensory phenomena. He did not, however, reject rationalism in its proper place, that place being among the more complex phenomena; neither, for that matter, did the rationalists totally reject "empiricist," direct, unmediated processing by the peripheral nervous system.

6. William James

William James (1842–1910) was one of modern psychology's most important scholars and the author of one of the most significant literary milestones in its history—the monumental *Principles of Psychology* (James, 1950/1890). This treatise is considered by some to be the first truly scientific book about psychology. Although well known also as a physician, physiologist, anatomist, and philosopher, James's special contribution to psychology was teaching his contemporaries to deal with it as an independent science in an analytical and descriptive manner.

James's attitude toward perception and sensation was of this same genre. Though only a part of a much more expansive system of psychology, his analysis of the perception of space, in particular the third dimension of depth, is particularly germane to the topic of this book. The issue in this case was the one previously wrestled with by Berkeley—whether the perceived third dimension differs from the horizontal and vertical first and second dimensions because it does not have an immediate retinal correlate. James was among those who chose to make no distinction between the three perceived dimensions, unlike Locke and others of the empiricist school of thought who believed that depth was different from length and width. James asserted that the experience of depth was, in actual fact, as immediate as the experience of the other two dimensions. His argument ran counter to the idea that length and width were more "direct" because they were more immediately related to the retinal mapping whereas depth was only encoded by invariances in disparity. James ignored this peripheral coding distinction to assert his belief that "the third dimension forms an original element of all our space sensations" (p. 269 in Vol. 2 of the Dover Edition), and thus placed himself among the empiricist school of thought in at least this context and others as well.

To James there was no such thing as a rationalistic or indirect construction of percepts from stimulus cues, but, rather, he argued that depth, like height and width, acted directly on the nervous system to produce an unmediated sensory experience. Indeed, there was not even any need for the intervention of another sense, such as the often-invoked somatosensory tutor for visual depth, to provide the basis for the perceptual appreciation of space or, for that matter, form. Of course, James's famous expression describing the mind of the neonate as a "blooming, buzzing confusion" suggested that he felt that some experience was necessary to guide the development of perceptual skills, but these were simple, computationlike, and not rationalistic, processes that had to be learned.

James wrote that there were two processes involved in this educational experience: (a) "reducing the various sense-feelings to a common measure"; and (b) "adding them together into the single all-including space of the real world" (pp. 268–269, Vol. 2 of the Dover Edition). To "measure" space, the observer had to sense objects under various conditions and to thus assign "values" to their dimensions, some of which were immediate attributes of their real shapes and some of which were only signs of that shape. In this manner, according to James, we come to appreciate the nature of particular forms or the nature of space in general and eventually to respond automatically on the basis of those past experiences whenever the stimulus is presented again. There is, in this radical perceptual empiricism, nothing like Helmholtz's construction by inference, but only "the recall of previous space sensations with which the present one has been associated and which may be judged more real than it" (p. 269, Vol. 2 of the Dover Edition).

James, the father of the "stream of consciousness" and the philosopher-psychologist who could discuss will and decision making in such a modern context (see chapter 26 in his *Principles*), was thus somewhat surprisingly a thoroughgoing empiricist in the sense I have used it in this book when he turned to the discussion of perceptual topics.

7. Wilhelm Wundt and E.B. Titchener: The Structuralists[5]

The first laboratory exclusively dedicated to the experimental study of psychological processes, including perception, was set up by Wilhelm Wundt (1832–1920) in 1879 at the University of Leipzig. Wundt's longest lasting contribution to perception lay in the specific statement of the premises of a truly scientific and fully psychological theory of mind, the theory that was later to be called *structuralism* by his most famous student, E.B. Titchener (1867–1927). Wundt emphatically stated that the proper subject matters of this new laboratory-based psychology were the mental processes and perceptual phenomena themselves, and that the method to study such mental processes was specifically *subjective introspection*. Although this is not too unsettling today, both at his time as well as during the heyday of modern behaviorism, such a perspective was both revolutionary and extremely irritating to many more positivistically oriented scholars.

Heavily influenced by his training in Wundt's laboratory, Titchener spent his career at Cornell University championing the structuralist approach to psychology. Titchener was also, like Wundt, a thoroughgoing elementalist in the associationist tradition, believing that all percepts, images, and affective states were composed of aggregations of elementary psychological units. For percepts, the topic of the present discussion, the elements were primitive sensations produced as a direct result of the stimulating environment. Titchener's structuralist elementalism went to extremes in championing this notion of sensory elements. In one of his books, *An Outline of Psychology* (Titchener, 1896), it is reported that he calculated that there were 44,000 distinct sensory elements from which percepts were formed! The physiological elements of Titchener's theory were also influenced by Johannes Müller's (1801–1858) doctrine of the specific energies of nerves. Whatever the elements, psychological or physiological, the concept of the analyzability of complex events into elements was the keystone of Wundt's and Titchener's structuralism and clearly an empiricism of the kind we are considering here.

---

[5] Some of the material in this section has been adapted from my earlier work (Uttal, 1981).

8. The Gestaltists

The specific position of members of the Gestalt school of thought (including Max Wertheimer, 1880–1943; Kurt Koffka, 1886–1941; and Wolfgang Köhler, 1887–1967) on the rationalist–empiricist dimension has always been somewhat ambiguous. However, after some reflection, I have now come to believe that they are better classified in the empiricist than in the rationalist tradition. In general, the Gestaltists asserted that the interactive forces (of a form that forced it to be grouped or that acted to establish its "goodness" are exerted within the neural representations of the nervous system. Although this places the forces determining the nature of the percept within the organism, the interactions that they postulated were relatively simple algorithmic ones more akin to the neuroreductionistic theories I shall discuss shortly. For this reason, and their general lack of concern with the cognitive aspects of mental life, it seems quite appropriate to consider the Gestaltists as being exemplars of the empiricist classification.

9. The Direct Realists[6]

In recent years a new tradition that has came to be called *direct realism* and that is also clearly a radical empiricism has acquired a number of followers. Before describing their particular interpretations of form perception, let us consider the general nature of both direct and indirect versions of realism. (The concept of realism, of course, does not denote a perceptual theory per se, but is a philosophy dealing with the nature of physical reality. A realistic world is, as we have seen earlier in chapter 1, one that exists independently of the presence or absence of an observer.) Shaw and Bransford (1977) spell out the specific nature of direct and indirect realism in the language of perceptual theory. A direct realism is one in which the physical world itself is perceived by the organism. An indirect realism, in Shaw and Bransford's lexicon, is one in which some surrogate of the real world (such as retinal contours or the retinal mosaic) is the intermediary between external reality and perception. The indirect realist would assert that we reconstruct a mental model of what the world must be like from those secondary, surrogate "representations" of the real world.

There is a great deal of subtlety in this dichotomy because the nature of the stimulus, so casually invoked in the preceding sentence, in fact, is a matter of some disagreement. Is the stimulus the proximal physical event on the retina? Or is it the neural responses of the receptors? Or quite to the contrary, is it the distal physical object itself? Shaw and Bransford would presumably consider most of the empiricisms that I have described in this section to be indirect realisms, because they all assume that, however direct the analysis, the processing of stimulus information is carried out on a representation, an encoding, or a transfor-

---

[6] Some of the material in this section has been adapted from my earlier work (Uttal, 1981).

mation of the original stimulus. According to them, the very concept of "information" or of "neural codes" implies an indirect processing that is quite different from the direct interaction between the objects and attributes of the external environment by the perceptual system.

Shaw and Bransford also go on to draw another dichotomy. They note that either a direct or indirect realism may be either *naive* or *critical*. The naive realist (direct or indirect) philosophy blends smoothly into a kind of idealism: The world to the naive realist is exactly as it is perceived and thus external reality becomes a resultant of the perceiver's action upon the external world. However, Shaw and Bransford also note that either the direct or indirect realist can accept the fact that there may be illusions, perceptual distortions, reversible figures or any other kind of perceptual nonveridicality under certain conditions and thus either approach may be classified as a critical realist. A critical realist (either direct or indirect), who accepts these imperfections, assumes that our senses are not completely accurate keys to knowledge, that we cannot fully know the nature of external reality, and thus our awareness is incomplete and possibly erroneous. In the best known critical and direct realism, that of the late James J. Gibson, any discussion of the attributes of the proximal stimulus, of the transduction, or of sensory coding is eschewed. The only relationship that is considered to be important is the direct interaction between the observer and the observed physical object or environment.

Gibson's (1950, 1966, 1979) version of direct realism has come to be known as ecological optics. Ecological optics is a radical direct realism, by which I mean that it emphasizes the direct casual effect of the stimulus in generating the percept almost to the exclusion of the properties of the observer. The observer, in Gibson's description, attends to the information in the "optic array," but does not create the meaning or significance that is attendant to the percepts; that is largely predetermined by the environmental stimulus scene itself. Meaning is thus inherent in the role played by the stimulus in the external environment (i.e., its ecological function).

Gibson's theory can be interpreted to be a reaction against both an empiricistic associationism that suggested that perceptions are created by the aggregation and concatenation of simpler sensations and a rationalism that suggested that some organizational, rational, or logical processes within the observer are required to construct perceptions from incomplete or ambiguous stimulus information.

Gibson's theory of perception has had a significant impact on current theoretical thinking. Neisser's (1976) book attempts to incorporate many of Gibson's ideas into the framework of contemporary cognitive psychology. But the work of Shaw, Bransford, and Turvey seems to me the most important step forward from Gibson's original position. These important theoretical psychologists have begun to develop a new radical direct realism in a series of articles (Shaw & Bransford, 1977; Shaw & Turvey, 1981; Turvey, 1977; Turvey & Shaw, 1979; Turvey, Shaw, & Mace, 1978). They have presented a deeply thoughtful argument that perception is not the result of distant relationship between the external physical environment and the perceiving observer mediated by nonisomorphically encoded signals, but rather that it is a much more intimate transactional relationship between the perceiver and the environment. In Shaw and Turvey's words elsewhere, "the objects of perceptual knowing are functionally ascribed directly to objects in the knower's environment." Direct realism of this sort asserts that the experience is not of the brain state triggered by the stimulus, but of the "functionally specified environment" itself. Shaw and Turvey's theory postulates that this interaction is in the form of a "coalition" between the observer and the environment. Their approach, therefore, ties together the observer and the observed into a unified entity; perception is not understandable, according to them, without consideration of both observer and observed and the interactions between them.

The work of another direct realist, Hans Wallach, was particularly concerned with the relations and retinally projected stimuli. In particular, Wallach (1939, 1948) directed theoretical attention at the invariance relationships that existed in the retinal image that he believed were the direct and unmediated cause of visual perception. Ratios of illuminance, of velocity, and of shapes, rather than the absolute local values of the stimulus, were the antecedents of perception in much the same way that optic arrays led to perception in Gibson's thinking.

In the next two sections of this chapter I consider two major clusters of form perception theory. They are in turn: analytic models of visual perception; and neural models invoking highly specific biological processes. These two categories are, of course, not mutually exclusive, but the emphasis of each approach does tend to be directed, as indicated, toward a particular aspect of the problem. The one thing that both of these classes of theory share is that they are all empiricist at their most fundamental axiomatic roots. Not all are as direct as the theory the direct realists would choose to assert, but each reflects the action of a more or less automatic processing system, perceptually responding in accord with well-defined rules or algorithms that do not insert meaning beyond that already conveyed by the stimulus array.

10. Analytic Models of Visual Perception

One synoptic guide to the nonprobabilistic approach to mathematical theories of vision can be found in Caelli's (1981b) concise review of the nature and application of what is generally referred to in mathematics as *analysis*. Analysis includes algebra, calculus, differential and integral equations, vector and tensor analysis, and a number of other kinds of mathematics that involve functional relationship among the dimensions of a deterministic, as opposed to a statistical or probabilistic, nature.

Caelli surveys both the methods and the applications of analytic mathematics in vision. Specifically, he describes Fourier analysis, convolutional mathematics, network analysis, and vector representation of geometrical forms (including cross-

and autocorrelations). He considers the application of these methods to such diverse topics as contrast and intensity, texture, discrimination, illusion, movement, and stereopsis. Certainly, my own use of the autocorrelation function (Uttal, 1975, 1983, 1985, 1987) as a predictor of form detection falls into this same category. Caelli's own work is among the best exemplars of this approach (e. g., Caelli, 1980, 1981a, 1982, 1985; Caelli & Dodwell, 1980).

In general, Caelli's strategy, as are those of other, theoreticians who use analysis, is to find a descriptive model that reproduces the transformation between the stimulus and the observer's response. Caelli offers us a list of the following goals for a science of form recognition. His list differs in fundamental goals and purposes only slightly from the one I have expressed in this chapter. The aim of Caelli's science is "to develop computational procedures for how man and machines may best recognize shapes and objects of arbitrary type and specified invariances" (Caelli, 1987). He then goes on to note that there are three fundamental means of representing images. A two-dimensional image for which $F(x)$ is a function of intensity alone; a two-and-one-half-dimensional image in which $F(x)$ also carries surface information; and a three-dimensional representation that, in addition, carries object information. For each of these three representations Caelli suggests that there are certain fundamental problems that must be solved. Table 2.1 lists his version of these "basic issues" or problems.

Caelli next breaks each of these issues down into specific algorithms or fundamental procedures that can be used to solve each of the constituent visual problems. Without going into the details of each of these methods, I would like to note that each of the proposed methods of solution is a specific computational or mathematical operation. I believe, therefore, that Caelli has proposed what is essentially a perspective on or a theory of form perception that is mainly constrained and driven by the available mathematical tools and not primarily by the psychobiology or phenomenology of the perceptual experiences he studies. I have no doubt that many of the techniques that he proposes will be powerful and useful, but to let the methodology dominate the specification of the fundamental issues

TABLE 2.1
Caelli's Tabulation of the Fundamental Problems of Pattern Recognition
(redrawn from Caelli, 1977)

Fundamental Problems		
2D	2½D	3D
• Decomposition/ feature extraction processes	• Extracting/ shape from intensity maps	• Object representation
		• Matching procedures
	• Surface rep.	• Topology
• Matching/classi- fication algorithms		
	• "Glueing" surfaces → 3D	
• Invariance coding		

places one in a position that is terribly prone to ignore some of the psychological phenomena that should be of primary interest. It also suggests a kind of prejudgment that this kind of analytical mathematics is the most appropriate one with which to study human form perception, and that conclusion is by no means certain.

Caelli's perspective as expressed in his tabulation of the problems of form perception in man and machine is, in fact, a very specific theory, but one in which such processes as decomposition and feature extraction are taken as premises rather than only as hypothetical answers to the problem of how we see forms. Feature extraction, as well as features themselves, are the implements of only one theoretical approach to form perception; one against which substantial criticisms can be made. Caelli's formulation of the field of form perception ignore many global, holistic, and synthetic aspects of how we see.

I have much more to say about such an analytic or feature-oriented view of form perception in later chapters. For the moment, I present Caelli's work as an important alternative view of what the issues are, one which I believe is based upon a particular view of what methods are available rather than the perceptual aspects of the problem. However great the theoretical differences between his view and my own, such an explicit attempt to organize the problems faced in form perception is rarely encountered; it must be noted with admiration. At the very least, he has made enormous contributions to computer image processing.

II. Neuroreductionistic Models of Form Perception

In the previous section I discussed a number of different mathematical approaches to explaining visual processes. Noticeably absent from this list of theories was any allusion to the neurophysiological mechanisms that could underlie the processes that were being described by the equations and formulas of those models. Although it is not generally appreciated, all of the mathematical models are indeterminate with regard to the underlying neural mechanisms. Another generic approach to a theory of form perception has come much more directly out of the neurophysiological laboratory. Whatever neurophysiological data base that is currently in vogue has a habit of becoming the heuristic for generating the premises and axioms of a neuroreductionistic theory of visual form perception. Typically, such theories are devoid of mathematical formalities; their originators are much more likely to invoke the observed attributes of the individual neurons or aggregates of neurons as models for what, at first glance, seem to be related perceptual processes. A list of neuroreductionistic theories (Uttal, 1981) displays the following five main categories:

- The lateral inhibitory interaction model
- The single-cell feature detection model
- The spatial-frequency detection model
- The neuronal-network model
- The continuous field model

Each of these theoretical approaches emphasizes one or another aspect of the properties or arrangement of the neural mechanisms that are known to make up the nervous system. This is often done in ways that are only weakly linked to the psychophysical phenomena they purport to model and may have no formal mathematical representation. I have critically reviewed these models in that earlier book (Uttal, 1981) and need not repeat that critique here. It is helpful, however, to briefly abstract that discussion to identify what I believe are the specific premises of each of these neuroreductionistic models and indicate some important contemporary examples of each.

a.   The Lateral Inhibitory Interaction Model.   The fundamental premises of the lateral inhibitory interaction model are:

1. There exist horizontal connections between neural units within the same anatomical level. In addition, many different levels contain these lateral interconnections.

2. These interconnections are primarily inhibitory. However, over short distances most current expressions of the theory allow that the interactions may be excitatory, thus producing receptive fields with concentric excitatory and inhibitory regions.

3. The degree of interaction is dependent upon the distance between the mutually inhibiting units.

4. The lateral inhibitory interactions in the neural space are the direct and immediate precursors (the critical processes) of similarly organized phenomena in subjective experience.

5. All lateral interaction theories assume that the subjective magnitude of the percept is monotonically related (i.e., is topologically isomorphic) to the amplitude of a neural response; for example, reduction in perceived amplitude is an immediate outcome of a reduction in neural activity.

6. According to these theories some afferent information is irretrievably lost as a result of the lateral inhibitory interactions.

The lateral inhibitory interaction model has been used in efforts to explain such diverse perceptual phenomena as metacontrast (Breitmeyer & Ganz, 1976; Bridgeman, 1971; Weisstein, 1972), aftereffects (Ganz, 1966; Wade, 1978), and binocular rivalry (Abadi, 1976; Thomas, 1978).

b.   The Single-Cell Feature Detection Model.   This model, rather than emphasizing the inhibitory interactions among neurons, concentrates on the specific sensitivities of individual neurons. Single-cell models assert that there is a direct relationship between their behavior and the organism's perceptions. Barlow (1972, 1982) has been the most outspoken champion of this approach and indeed was the one to formalize the specific premises of this approach to neuroreductionism. His statement of the premises underlying the single-cell approach can be paraphrased as follows:

1. To understand nervous function one needs to look at interactions at a cellular level, rather than either a more macroscopic or microscopic level, because behavior depends on the organized pattern of these intercellular interactions.

2. The sensory system is organized to achieve as complete a representation of the sensory stimulus as possible with the minimum number of active neurons.

3. Trigger features of sensory neurons are matched to redundant patterns of stimulation by experience as well as by developmental processes.

4. Perception corresponds to the activity of a small selection from the very numerous high-level neurons, each of which corresponds to a pattern of external events of the order of complexity of the events symbolized by a word.

5. High-impulse frequency in such neurons corresponds to high certainty that the trigger feature is present.

The applications of single-cell theory in the 1970s were virtually beyond listing. It became almost a *sine qua non* that no one could even consider visual perception without invoking the elegant neurophysiological data of Hubel and Weisel (e.g., 1959, 1962, 1965) as putative explanatory theories of virtually all kinds of form perception. The incontestable selectivity of feature-sensitive neurons at all levels of the nervous system has contributed greatly to the explosion of the neuroreductionistic zeitgeist in recent decades.

The theory has been taken to its most extreme form in the work of Konorski (1967), who proposed that all concepts and ideas, no matter how complex, were in fact encoded by single cells or single-cell types. Evidence to support Konorski's radical theory is scanty, but continued publication of such papers as that of Perrett, Rolls, and Caan (1982) and Kendrick and Baldwin (1987) who report single cells in the monkey or sheep cortex specifically sensitive to faces continue to fuel this approach. There are, however, many arguments against the interpretations of these data, notwithstanding the undoubted validity of the measurements.

c. ***The Fourier Channel Approach.*** Vying with, and to a degree supplanting, the single-cell-geometrical-feature-sensitive-cell ideology described in the preceding sections is a newer approach asserting that there exist anatomically discrete channels in the visual nervous system that are selectively sensitive to the spatial-frequency components of a visual stimulus. The concept of a two-dimensional Fourier spatial-frequency analysis as a code for vision was initially proposed by Campbell and Robson (1968) and has received enormous attention in recent years. Papers at major scientific meetings of visual societies now sometimes seem to be totally dominated by the spatial-frequency approach. Specifically, adherents of this view assert the following premises:

1. There exist anatomically discrete channels in the nervous system that selectively respond to the two-dimensional component spatial frequencies of the stimulus. The whole visual stimulus is thus analyzed by a Fourier-type process implemented by these channels acting as spatial frequency filters.

2. The channels are relatively narrowly tuned. They respond only to a narrow bandwidth of spatial frequencies.

3. These channels are relatively independent of each other.

4. Perceptual information is represented by the relative amount of activity (a multidimensional vector) in the channels.

5. Different stimulus patterns produce different vectors, and different vectors are equivalent to different perceptual experiences.

6. The channels are each individually sensitive to spatial frequencies across broad areas of the visual field.

It is very important to appreciate that a Fourier channel, neuroreductionistic theory does not necessarily involve the analytic mathematics of a formal Fourier description and, vice versa, a good Fourier mathematical analysis does not necessarily imply the existence of spatial-frequency channels. Such a formal model may, therefore, be developed without allusion to neurophysiological channels. There have been many examples of a combined mathematical and neuroreductionistic analysis, but the approaches are, in fact, independent and each can exist without the other.

Once again, because of the wide popularity of this approach and the way in which it is so often embedded in experimental research, I do not attempt to review the many applications of this model in recent years. The interested reader might look at a book by Harris (1980) for a good discussion of the Fourier approach. I deal directly with the relevance of the Fourier model to detection in chapter 3.

d. The Neural Network Approach. Whereas the preceding two theory types, invoking the specialized single feature-detecting neuron and the spatial-frequency-detecting channel respectively, concentrate on the properties of spatially tuned subunits of the brain, an alternative approach concentrating on the pattern of interactions among relatively unspecialized neurons has been lurking just behind the scenes—the neural-net model. As mentioned earlier, there is an immense difficulty associated with this model, however. That difficulty revolves around our inability to analyze a complex system of this kind. Nevertheless, it seems to many theoreticians that the network idea may, in fact, be the closest to some kind of neuroreductionistic truth than any of the other models. Neural-network theory asserts the following:

1. Perceptual information is represented by patterns of activity in distributed networks of neurons.

2. The state of the network at any moment encodes the current state of the perceptual process. That is, the pattern of activity is the psychoneural equivalent of the perceptual process.

3. The "state" of the network is constrained by statistical considerations. No particular neuron or set of neurons is critical; what matters is the central tendency of the overall system. Any neuron can be replaced by many others in any given process.

4. Even the simplest perceptual process involves many millions (billions?) of neurons.

5. Most neurons are physiologically unspecialized in logical function and depend on the nature of their interconnections as to what their role will be in the network.

6. Any individual neuron may participate in several different network functions, perhaps even simultaneously.

(The reader interested in a critique of both Barlow's single-cell theory and my version of a neural network theory might be interested in reading W.A. van de Grind's very interesting paper on Decomposition and Neuroreduction of Vision in a book entitled *Limits in Perceptron* that was edited by A.J. Van Doorn, W. Van de Grind, and J.J. Koenderink and published by VNU Science Press in Utrecht in 1984.)

The question is: Can we go beyond these imprecise verbal statements to a precise statement of the implications and significance of a neuronal-net model? In this context, it is interesting to note that the detailed specification of the network interactions occurring within a man-made digital computer, a device of orders of magnitude less complexity, is never done (other than in the engineering diagrams) even in the act of writing a program. Boolean algebra may be used to represent limited-size switching circuits, but the overall design (and thus analysis) of a computer is still very much an artistic rather than a precise scientific process. Nowhere is this art form better illustrated than in the tales woven about the design of new microcomputer systems (see, for example, *Byte* magazine, January 1984, for a fascinating discussion of the evolution of the Apple Macintosh Computer, or the book *The Soul of a New Machine* [Kidder, 1981]).

The suggestion arising from this metaphor is that it is unlikely that, however correct in principle, the neuronal network will ever be a precision model in the sense that it will be possible to formally represent mental processes either by means of quantitative expressions or by means of simulated or artificial neural networks. Neural-net models have been around, and promise to remain around, for many years, however. I have already noted Mach's invention of the idea. McCulloch and Pitts' (1943) important paper was another milestone in this history, as was

Hebb's (1949) cell-assembly theory. Dodwell (1970) has also presented a very specific neural-network theory of form perception. What promises to be an especially exciting approach by a neuroscientist who seems to have especially good judgment in his concept of what a neural-network theory should be like is the work of Schwartz (1977, 1980). His synthesis of the neural geometry of the primate visual cortex and visual perception is compelling and lucid. Especially significant, however, is Schwartz's appreciation of the limits of this approach. This topic is considered at length elsewhere in this book.

e.   The Continuous Field Model.   Finally we come to the continuous field theories. Field theories, it must be acknowledged at the outset, are essentially dormant today, representing a theoretical approach that has a very modest, if any, contemporary following. Even the holographic theory proposed by Pribram, Nuwer, and Baron (1974), which uses the field-like terminology of the interference hologram as a metaphor for brain activity (an idea that is directly derived from Lashley's (1942) concept of cortical-interference patterns) is actually based upon a set of assumptions that are very difficult to distinguish from the other neuronal-network theories I have already described. Any theory of brain function that is based upon either local ephaptic (soma to soma or axon to axon transmission) or broad electrotonic interactions as major means of communication between different regions is inconsistent with the most basic postulates "of modern neurobiology—the neuron synaptic theories. All electrotonic field theories involving passive current spread (as opposed to those reducible to neuronal-network concepts) were effectively laid to rest by the definitive studies of Sperry, Miner, and Myers (1955) and Lashley, Chow, and Semmes (1951), which showed that the insertion of short-circuiting metallic foils, pins, and wires into the cortex did not disrupt visual discriminations to any significant degree.

Fields, therefore, are descriptions that are at best holistic metaphors of, or molar analogs of, what is actually going on in the nervous system, in much the same way as is the mentalistic vocabulary of psychology. In spite of this analogy between molar fields and molar minds, there is little interest in this approach these days. I exclude the work on evoked brain potentials and electroencephalographs from this statement, particularly the work of Freeman (1981, 1983); they constitute a somewhat different conceptualization of the problem. Nevertheless, these macropotentials are also best understood as cumulative, quasi-statistical processes reflecting the overall behavior of networks consisting of millions and millions of discrete neurons. Be that as it may, the theory that electrotonic fields serve as a means of processing sensory information and representing perceptual processes is, for all practical purposes, extinct in the 1980s. All of us have been irretrievably influenced by the microelectrode and the electron micrograph in spite of the lack of correspondence in scale and time between the mechanisms these devices probe and molar psychological processes.

In conclusion, all of these neurophysiologically oriented models are concerned

mainly with specifying various kinds of neural mechanisms that might be involved in the processes of form perception, but all are as devoid of precision as any
purely behavioral model. They provide only an illusion of true reductionistic explanation. Neuroreductionistic models are only infrequently tested against the
psychophysical data in the same demanding way as were the descriptive mathematical models described in the previous sections. Rather, they (with the specific
exception of the Fourier models) tend to be presented as loose metaphors that
are shown to be "not inconsistent" with perceptual findings. In retrospect, we
can see that there is often a very loose logical and conceptual linkage between
the processes observed at the microscopic neuronal level and those observed at
the macroscopic psychological level. Whether it is a single cell or a neural network, the neural processes are presented as basic logical elements rather than
as synthesized systems that must in the aggregate encode or represent perceptual
processes. It is only in the rarest cases that computational tests are carried out
on these neural models in which the imprecise metaphors are tested in a quantitative way. This has been done with the Fourier models and the lateral interaction models to a far greater extent than with the neural network or single-cell
models, however. Yet, even in those cases, it is really the mathematical formularizations rather than the neural premises themselves that are being tested.
As I have noted, it is very likely that the two are separable. Even then, these
models usually work only when the stimuli are from a narrowly defined universe—
such as gratings—and fail when other stimulus sets are used.

An important point is that there is no intrinsic antagonism between any of the
neuroreductionistic approaches and any of the macroscopic or mathematical formularizations. The various theories are usually directed at different aspects of
the total problem and must be considered to be complementary to each other rather
than as alternatives. However, one thing they all do have in common is that all
of the theories mentioned so far are clearly empiricisms describing the nervous
system as an entity that operates by passive, algorithmic rather than active,
cognitive rules.

In conclusion, although contemporary neural models carry an aura of "scientific modernity," in fact the real importance of the matter of neuroreductionism
seems to lie at a deeper philosophical and logical level than that methodological
or technological one. Few of us, however, pay much attention to such issues nowadays. Exceptions can be found in the distinguished work of Teller (1984), whose
study of "linking hypotheses" is among the most thoughtful and useful exposi-
tions of the logical foundations of this topic in recent years. In a less detailed
manner, I dealt with many of the same issues in my 1973b and 1978 works, *The
Psychobiology of Sensory Coding* and *The Psychobiology of Mind*.

12. Computational Models of Form Perception

In recent years, with the advent of the information-processing digital computer—
the tool par excellence for psychologists and other theoreticians concerned with
information processing mechanisms—a new trend has been developing in form-

perception theory. This new attack on the problem emphasizes the detailed nature of the local functional processes that possibly are being executed within the perceptual system. It does so by simulating putative visual processes with simple algorithms that are often relatively uncomplicated computationally but grow in behavioral complexity as they are concatenated. Indeed, in the aggregate the total array of computational processes is so complex that it is often difficult or even impossible to formularize these processes with specific analytical equations. Rather, computational algorithms, more comparable to the patterns of interaction observed in physical electrical networks or in the activity of the microscopic neural elements themselves, are programmed into a set of discrete computer instructions—that is, a program. Both the probabilistic or analytic mathematics used in the formal models and the detailed neurophysiological attributes of the nervous system's components are sometimes ignored because the functions performed are simulated by what are often nonnumerical statements describing the local interactions among the constituent components of an idealized system. It is only when the outcome of these local processes are displayed in ensemble that the molar behavior of the system becomes evident.

Thus, the computational approach that I now describe falls somewhere between the totally molar mathematical or psychological models and the totally microscopic neural approaches described in the earlier sections. Thus, the computational theories (and theorists) tend to view the visual image as an array of a large number of quasi-independent elements and the visual mechanism as a parallel processing system made up of an ensemble of interacting neurons encoding these stimulus elements.

It is interesting, in fact, amusing, to note that the hypothesized parallel nature of the visual system is exactly the opposite of the way in which the conventional Von Neumann computer actually functions; the computer, in its traditional form, is almost always a serial processor that sequentially calculates events and outcomes at one local point in time or space, then goes on to another point to carry out the same local computations. It is only by repetitive or iterative reprocessing that a stable solution to the process under study can be developed. This serial point-by-point processing, although formally interchangeable with a parallel processor, is quite different from the kind of parallel processing that actually must be going on in the brain or that is implied by the models of the computational theorists. In spite of this discrepancy, it is certainly true that most of the basic concepts underlying computational theories of human form perception evolved from techniques emerging from the field of computer image processing. A good general introduction to this latter field can be found in Cannon and Hunt (1981). More technical discussion can be found in Rosenfeld (1969), Andrews (1970), Andrews and Hunt (1977), Pratt (1978), and Rosenfeld and Kak (1982).

Another very important attribute of computational theories, in the sense I use the term here, is that they do not, in principle, require the use of a digital computer. Computers are convenient and often are used in practice to perform the calculations, but this is not the essence of the computational approach. Rather the term is used here to indicate theories involving the evaluation of a set of equations or interactions that simulate or imitate the kind of simple and local logical or informational processes that are thought to be carried out by the components of the nervous system itself or by some mechanical system that functions in an analogous way. Thus, in principle, computational algorithms might be evaluated by a system of simultaneous linear algebraic equations or a system of differential equations. Mathematics of these kinds can often be evaluated on an analog computer as well as digitally.

The difference between discrete (algebraic) and continuous (differential) equations to which I allude is thus the one between an analytic solution of a system of equations representing some global attribute of a whole form on the one hand, and one in which each local interaction is independently and discretely evaluated on the other. To be sure, both means of evaluating systems—discrete digital computation and continuous analysis—may be perfectly good analogs of each other, but the discrete computational evaluation has one overriding advantage that is denied to the analytic method. Functional processes can be represented and evaluated that, because of their (the processes') enormous complexity, can neither be formulated nor solved using analytic mathematics. Iterative, discrete processing allows highly nonlinear systems, or systems with repeated discontinuities, for example, to be analyzed with virtually the same ease with which an actual physical model of the device could be constructed. The influence of irregular or analytically nonrepresentable stimulus patterns (such as those obtained from a discrete digitalization of a scene) can be evaluated with the discrete computational approach with as much ease as a simple continuous function.

Because the same algorithm would work in either an analytic or a discrete version, the digital computer is not generally used by computational vision theorists to numerically solve global, continuous differential equations of the genre considered here, but rather is chosen to solve a very large number of very simple algebraic interactions among discrete regions of the simulated physical space. It goes without saying, however, that the two procedures must necessarily fade into each other, and some numerical evaluations of analytic functions must, in fact, be identical in terms of the specific programming steps to the discrete, local computational transformation of a stimulus pattern.

These, then, are some of the practical concerns that guide this increasingly important branch of form-perception theory. No one, perhaps, has been more explicit in describing the tenets of this new approach or applying it to practice than the late David Marr, an exceptionally productive young scientist who was one of the leaders of the MIT school that has been so significant in pioneering this new school of thought. Marr, in the last few years of his life, had the energy, courage, and opportunity to write what many agree is a quite remarkable book (Marr, 1982), in which he put forth the essential aspects of his personal view of a computational theory of vision, in general, and form perception, in particular. I return to discuss his work in detail in chapter 5.

To gain just a brief idea of the breadth of other mathematical and computational techniques that have been applied to just one part of the form-vision problem—that of recognition—over the last several decades, consider the following list developed almost 20 years ago by Brick (1969). Two general categories of mathematical treatment of images are distinguished in his list: those processes that are useful to transform the irregular information array of a scene into a more canonical or quantitative form and those processes that act as decision rules to carry out the categorization or recognition itself.

1. Transformations
   - Clustering (for compacting classes or for maximally separating patterns)
   - Clumping (for developing class centers)
   - Intuitive transformations or features
   - Functionals and operators (such as lineal discriminants, or quadratic functionals, etc.)
   - Dimensional reduction (via, e.g., coordinate transformations followed by rejection of least important dimensions or straightforward rejection)
   - Templates (prototypes or the most characteristic shapes)
   - Perceptronlike or neural (brainlike) techniques
   - Eigenfunction generators
   - Decision-theory techniques
   - Mode seeking
   - Correlation-type techniques
   - Factor analysis
   - Matched or inverse filtering
   - Entropy techniques
   - Stochastic-process techniques
   - Hill-climbing algorithms
   - Other techniques for picking the most important features (with relevance to the objective function of the recognition problem)
2. Classification and Recognition Techniques
   I. Probabilistic techniques—Partitioning
      - Bayes' rule techniques (probability distribution known)
      - Approximate Bayes' rule techniques
         - Partitioning surface approximated by simple surface (e.g., linear, piecewise-linear, quadratic, etc.)
         - Probability distribution estimated
         - Functional of exact or estimated probability
         - Distribution used
         - Estimation-of-decision rule
      - Deferred or sequential Bayes techniques
      - Techniques using metric or similarity relationships
      - Stochastic techniques
   II. Nonprobabilistic Techniques
      - Use metrics or similarity relationships directly
      - Partition based on metric or similarity

- Relationship
- Partition intuitively
- Partition by interactive means
- Partition by frequency of co-occurrences
- Neural or perceptionlike partitioning
- List-processing techniques (pp. 90–91).

A rich lode of potential perceptual theories is implied here that may be extremely stimulating to psychological theory, even though exploring human perception is certainly not the main goal of the AI field.

There are many other more recent methods, of course, but this list is sufficient to make the point. There is a rich variety of different mathematical and computational algorithms by means of which various kinds of human form-perception processes can be imitated. Computer scientists interested in machine perception have drawn upon this rich technology, of course, to develop their computer vision machines. In the final analysis, however, it must not be forgotten that the goals and purposes of the two schools of endeavor—computer vision and perceptual theory—are quite different.

13. Other Important Contemporary Empiricist Theories of Form Perception

The general approaches that have been described so far do not begin to do justice to the rich variety of empiricist-type theories that have been proposed in recent years. Indeed, with the exception of the cognitivist school (which I argue is fundamentally rationalist) the empiricist approach has dominated thinking particularly among biologically and mathematically oriented perceptual theoreticians. No reasonably sized list can be complete because of this plethora of empiricist theories. It is inevitable, therefore, that in attempting to list exemplary theories in this and subsequent chapters, I shall offend some whose favorite (or personal) approach is not listed. I hope those readers will appreciate, therefore, that the following list is just a reflection of the theories with which I am familiar and that I believe represent something especially important in contemporary thinking. Many others have noted the enormous variety of formal models that have been specifically applied to model visual form perception processes. Recently, for example, Grossberg (1983) listed the following additional kinds of mathematical models that he was aware had been applied as theories of visual form perception:

- Fourier analysis
- Projective geometry
- Riemannian geometry
- Special relativity
- Vector analysis

- Analytic function theory
- Potential theory
- Cooperative and competing networks

These are just some of the formal, mathematical ones. Grossberg also discusses the question: Is a unified theory possible? and then answers his question in the affirmative by suggesting what he believes is a step toward such a theory. He raises a profound issue, of course, perhaps as important as (if not identical to, although in another guise) the issue of how we go from neurons to minds. The reader should pay attention to this very important perplexity as the following list is surveyed. In both their strengths and weaknesses, all of these theories speak to this issue at least partially. In the following subsections I briefly introduce these theories. In later chapters I return to consider some of them again in the context in which they are particularly relevant.

a. The Perceptron Tradition.   One persistent and popular approach to the form-recognition problem, and among the earliest to be applied with any success in the AI field, is based upon the pioneering work of Rosenblatt (1962). Rosenblatt proposed that a randomly organized, triple layered network of receptors, integrators, and classifiers (or responders) could be suitably trained (by simply repetitively presenting exemplars of stimulus forms) to recognize stimulus forms. This was accomplished by selectively reinforcing "synaptic" interconnections on the basis of the degree to which they were actived by the stimulus. It is now known (Minsky & Papert, 1969) that such systems, called *perceptrons* by Rosenblatt, include many different kinds of devices with different properties, only some of which could possibly perform the "recognition" processes suggested by Rosenblatt. Recent research has reinvigorated perceptron ideas from what had thought to be the lethal critique by Minsky and Papert.

Thus, the idea of a self-organizing, multilayered network of simulated neurons continues to be a popular approach to understanding pattern recognition. Some modern theories are very similar to Rosenblatt's original model with only minor modifications. For example, one modification of Rosenblatt's system would be to modify only those "synaptic" contacts emerging from *the* single cell that is responding maximally.

Kunihiko Fukushima of the NHK laboratories in Japan has been a modern leader in pursuit of this approach (Fukushima, 1975; Fukushima & Miyake, 1982) and has developed an advanced, multilayered perceptronlike device he has called the *cognitron*. Later, a version that was not sensitive to most orientation, size, or localization differences as was the original algorithm was developed and called the *neocognitron*. To the degree that perceptronlike devices work (in Japan, some of the alphabetic and Kanji characteristics recognizers based upon such logic work very well, indeed, according to my own personal observation) and to the extent they reflect human perceptual idiosyncrasies (as does Fukushima's neocognitron) such devices may be considered to be quasi-theoretical models of human form-recognition processes.

b. The Nerve-Net Model Approach.

Another main theme of contemporary form-perception theory can be discerned in the work of some other scholars who use formal mathematical treatments of neural networks. Simplified networks are used as surrogates for the very complex plexi actually found in the nervous system. Preeminent among those who practice this brand of theory in which mini-networks model more extensive systems is Stephen Grossberg of Boston University. Grossberg has contributed a large number of papers over the last 20 years in which he has striven to develop a general theory of perception as well as of learning and other psychological processes. Throughout this extensive series of contributions (which are summarized in Grossberg, 1983), he has primarily used differential and algebraic equations to describe the behavior of relatively small networks (a few neurons) as prototypes of the much larger networks that certainly must actually constitute the psychoneural equivalents of the perceptual processes themselves.

In general, however, all models of this genre use a kind of mathematics whose utility depends on a certain degree of regularity in the nervous system. A qestion remains concerning their suitability to model the quite irregular systems that actually underlie realistically complex mental processes. Furthermore, there is little evidence that the logical processes that exist in the brain follow the rules of either calculus or of the interactions of small networks of neurons.

A difficulty with this kind of work is that there has been inadequate validation of the specifics of his model with psychophysical data specifically elicited to distinguish it from other equally plausible models. A criticism that can be made of many mathematicians who enter the field of perception is that well-established and quantified psychophysical data is often irrelevant to the specific predictions of their models, or the associations between data and theory are too qualitative to provide compelling arguments that the one is a good model of the other. As is so often the case, the real proof of a theory is not its general fit with ''classic'' demonstrations, but rather its precise fit with data collected specifically to test the prediction in particular situations at which the model is precisely aimed.

Notwithstanding these limitations, Grossberg's approach is a formidable intellectual superstructure and a significant contribution toward our understanding some of the putative mechanisms that may exist in the visual system. There is much yet to be verified concerning his approach, however. The interested reader may also wish to read the commentaries included in the Grossberg (1983) article for a wide sampling of opinions concerning his work.

There have been many other examples of similar, though less extensive and comprehensive, models published in many different journals in many different disciplines—far too many to be exhaustively listed here. But one other related and notably interesting approach has been reported by Nagano and Fujiwara

(1979). They use a similar method—a network of a few neurons represented by algebraic equations—to simulate the behavior of directionally sensitive neurons that have so frequently been described in recent years by neurophysiologists. Nagano and Fujiwara's model works well because it is a basic unit of a repetitive and regular supersystem of neurons—the retina. In cases like this, the action of any unit is characteristic of the action of any other. Furthermore, the rules of concatenation are relatively straightforward so there is little that is unexpected emerging as the network enlarges. This kind of organizational regularity is not a property of most regions of the vertebrate brain, of course, but rather of those relatively well-ordered peripheral structures of the sensory and motor nervous systems. The application of this kind of modeling to less well-ordered neural networks remains a highly controversial procedure.

Models of movement detection in neuronal nets have been one of the hottest areas of perceptual modeling in recent years. Adelson and Bergen (1984) and Watson and Ahumada (1985) have all proposed increasingly more complex networks of hypothetical neurons that can extract moving objects from stable backgrounds using linear motion-selective filters. This work builds on the classic studies of Barlow and Levick (1965) of the rabbit retina.

c. Julesz's Texton Theory.   Bela Julesz (1981, 1984) has suggested a theory of texture perception that is based upon fundamental units of preattentive visual form perception that he calls *textons*. Textons are attributes of the stimulus to which the visual system is selectively sensitive. His suggestion that processing occurs and, further, that it is carried out by specialized neural elements is based upon the unique roles these particular attributes play in allowing us to discriminate between different regions of textured surfaces. Julesz has noted that, in general, human observers are not able to distinguish between textures that have the same second-order but differing third-order statistical properties. (I define these statistical properties more precisely later and expand upon these ideas in chapter 4, in which I discuss discrimination.) However, there are some exceptions to this generality. Certain attributes of the texture elements do permit discrimination between regions that do have the same second-order statistics. These special attributes are the textons of Julesz' theory and are the manifestations, according to him, of the action of the simple, complex, and hypercomplex cells originally described by Hubel and Weisel (1965) in the mammalian visual cortex. In particular, Julesz lists the following elements as the fundamental textons of preattentive texture perception.

- Elongated blobs (line segments)
- Line endings
- Line crossings
- Binocular disparity
- Movement disparity

- Temporal flicker
- Color

Each of these, he asserts, is associated with some fundamental neurophysiological property of the single cells in the visual system, presumably produced by a parallel processing mechanism that is insensitive to some attributes of the individual textons such as orientation and, indeed, size.

Julesz's theory of textons is an informal, descriptive one in most regards in that it is not framed in a particular mathematical formulation. It does represent an interesting linkage between the molar behavior of the visual system and the microscopic functioning of the individual neurons of the brain in a much more mature way than was characteristic of the earlier single-cell theoretical approaches to form recognition. In this regard, it is similar to the Hoffman's Lie algebra theory that is now briefly described.

d. Hoffman's Lie Algebra Theory. The work of mathematician William Hoffman is a particularly important model of perceptual phenomena and, in my opinion, one of the potentially most fertile. Hoffman (1966) originally proposed the use of an existing mathematical system (the Lie algebra of transformational groups) on which work independent of vision had been done for many years (Auslander & Mackenzie, 1963; Cohn, 1957; Mostow, 1950) as a model of visual perception. Hoffman noted the many similarities between the transformations that were describable by the abstract mathematics of the Lie algebra and those that occurred in visual perception. These are summarized in Fig. 2.4. He suggested,

Transformation groups on $\mathbf{R}^2 \times \mathbf{T}$

Perceptual invariance	Lie transformation group	Orbits
Shape Constancy	*Unimodular Group* SL($\mathbf{R}$, 3)	
Location in the field of view	Horizontal translations Vertical translations	
(Form memory)	Time translations	
Orientation	Rotations, SO$_2$	
Afferent binocular vision	Pseudo-Euclidean Rotations	
(Efferent binocular function)	Pseudo-Euclidean Rotations in plane-time: $\mathbf{R}^2 \times \mathbf{T}$ (Invariant: xyt)	
Size constancy	*Dilation group (Homotheties)*	
Motion-invariant perception	*Lorentz group of order 2*	
Cyclopean, egocentered perception	Group of rotations, SO$_3$, in Plane-time: $\mathbf{R}^2 \times \mathbf{T}$	

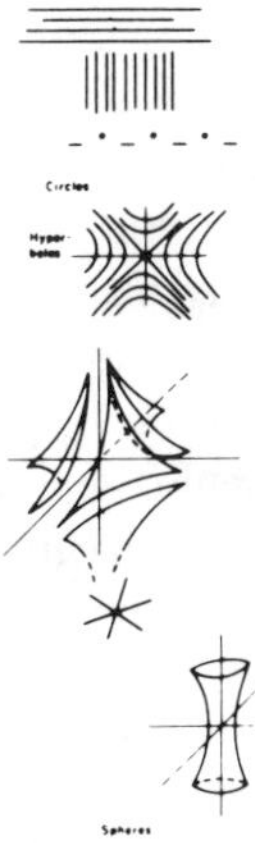

FIG. 2.4. Relationships between certain visual illusions and the Lie transformation algebra (from Hoffman, 1978).

in light of these analogies, that the Lie algebra would prove to be a powerful means of describing and analyzing visual processes. W.C. Hoffman (1967, 1970, 1971, 1978, 1980) has pursued this line of inquiry extensively in recent years, applying the model to movement perception, constancies, and perceptual development.

Recently in this work he has extended his model by invoking possible neural explanations of perceptual transformations that are largely dependent on the discovery by Hubel and Weisel of the orientation-sensitive detectors. Although the use of the Lie algebra as a descriptive model of vision seems appropriate, I believe there is less support for the neural hypotheses Hoffman proposes. And though it is possible that the neural-network-mediated transformations invoked by Hoffman are the basis of the perceptual transformations he describes, it is also possible that such percepts are the result of higher level processing and do not, in fact, depend on the orientation sensitivities of Hubel and Weisel's cells.

The mathematical model and approach used by Hoffman cannot resolve the issue of the neuronal substrates; it can only test the plausibility of his premise that the cumulative effects of a manifold of orientation detectors may be responsible for such processes as constancy. It is neither a test of necessity nor sufficiency, however, and other quite distinct, though analogous, assumptions (e.g., that the transformations occur as the result of constructionistic interpretations mediated by exceedingly complicated and very high-level neural nets) also remain viable.

e. ***Watson's Feature Vector Model.***   Watson (1983) has improved substantially upon what now must be considered to be the conventional Fourier model of visual form perception by substituting for the scene-wide set of orthogonal sinusoidal components a set of orthogonal functions that are the multiplicative products of those extended spatial sinusoids and localized Gaussian functions. This resulting set of alternative localized orthogonal primitives known as Gabor functions or, as he calls them, spatial features, can be convolved with a stimulus in the same way that one would carry out a Fourier analysis. The result of this convolution of the stimulus with the set of primitive spatial features is a "vector" with as many components as there were different spatial features. The features are conceptually unlimited in variety but Watson thoughtfully uses only a small set that varies in spatial frequency, height, width, orientation, and phase. Thus, each stimulus will produce a multicomponent characteristic number (compared to the spatial frequency power spectrum obtained in the Fourier model) that can be manipulated to either detect or recognize a form.

The Watson model is conceptually of the same genre as the Fourier model—a set of primitives are convolved with the stimulus—but the advantage in this newer model is that the localized primitives Watson uses are more physiologically reasonable than were the spatially diffuse set of sinusoids. One of the great difficulties of the original Fourier model had been the implication that the component sinusoids must exert their influence over very broad regions of the retina.

No physiological or anatomical evidence of such enormous receptive fields existed to support this hypothesis, however. Watson's Gaussian-limited spatial features are a step forward in that they ameliorate this physiological difficulty. Nevertheless, there still remains the theoretical difficulty that this model would work even if there were no physiological equivalents. It is, in a very general sense like the Fourier analysis, all too powerful. A set of mathematical abstractions is called on to mathematically analyze the stimulus and, in principle, can do so even if the underlying mechanism is different in kind.

A more serious misconception concerning this approach is that it is really not a form-perception model, but a form-transformation one. That is, after the convolution of the stimulus with the family of spatial Gabor functions, one is left with as formidable a discrimination or recognition task as one confronted at the outset. The subsequent evaluation of the transformed vector is a process that takes Watson (along with many others interested in this aspect of form perception) into a domain of statistical modeling that is not dealt with in the type of convolution model presented in the 1983 paper.

f. Connectionism: Psychology Discovers Neural Nets. In the past few years there has been a "discovery" by theoretical psychologists of an intellectual movement that has been quite popular among other sciences for perhaps two decades. This is the theoretical approach that incorporates neuronlike units into relatively large parallel-processing networks to simulate mental and behavioral processes. The enthusiasm for this movement has been enormous, as described in an excellent critical review by Schneider (1987) and I do not need to repeat his discussion of the seemingly exponential increase in work of this genre here.

Schneider does perform one particular service that fits well within the scope of this book, and I summarize his codification of the premises of the "connectionist" school. The defining features of a connectionist theory, as paraphrased from Schneider (1987, p. 74) are:

1. Processing occurs in a population of simple elements.
2. Information is stored in terms of the weights of the connections between these simple elements.
3. The interactions between elements are all simple combinations (e.g., addition or multiplication) or nonlinear transformations (e.g., saturation).
4. Learning occurs because of simple changes in the weighting between elements.

This neural-network philosophy is consistent with the general trend toward ideas of brain function based on parallel processes among large numbers of neurons. It is, therefore, a step forward from the naive single-cell hypotheses. It is, however, from another point of view not as novel a development as suggested by many of its afficianados because many computational theorists, perceptual psychologists, and neurophysiologists have been following this line of thought for over two decades. As applied to learning machines it is almost certain that some of the problems with the early perceptron approach will be overcome and that the connectionist models will successfully simulate some forms of human cognitive function. Unfortunately, as I discuss later, no matter how successful the simulation is, there can be no convincing evidence presented that the particular network constructed in any connectionist exercise is any more valid as a explanation of how the brain does the comparable task than any other mathematical or computer model. The connectionist approach must, therefore, be considered to be an evolutionary development of parallel-processing ideas that have come to be increasingly common in the AI community with specific application to psychological theory rather than a revolution in psychological theory. Any criticism of AI models, furthermore, also holds for the connectionist models.

Connectionist models, nevertheless, do represent another bit of progress in psychology. With their parallel, multiple (but simple) neural-element-interaction approach, they are a step in the right direction. From my perspective, they are more biologically valid as a general theory than other theories stressing local action or single-cell representations of complex psychological processes. Complete discussions of what obviously is going to be an important movement in the cognitive psychology of perception and learning can be found in Hinton and Anderson (1981), Rumelhart, McClelland, and the PDP research group (1986), and McClelland, Rumelhart, and the PDP research group (1986).

These are but a few of the more notable empiricist-type theories that have been proposed by psychologists and mathematicians to describe one or another aspect of visual form perception. There are many others that have not been mentioned, that probably should have been, but sheer number makes any exhaustive review impossible. I have at least illustrated the type of thinking that permeates this field, and others are mentioned as appropriate in later chapters.

The essential and important general point is that all of the empiricist-type theories that have been considered so far in this section propose some kind of an automatic, algorithmic, passive processing by neural networks either explicitly or in terms of some computational analog. We now turn to the other half of the great theoretical dichotomy and consider the theories of form perception that have grown up in the rationalist tradition.

C. THE RATIONALIST OR INDIRECT APPROACH TO FORM-PERCEPTION THEORY

The modern version of the idea that the incoming stimulus information does not directly produce a phenomenological response, but rather had to be mediated by the "mind," central nervous system, or some internal state of the organism in a way that involved *meaning* more than *geometry*, is relatively new. Correct or not, some thoughtful scholars feel that this is a more sophisticated idea than the passive, automatic, and stimulus-determined approaches propounded by the modern empiricists and their predecessors. Before the Middle Ages, and indeed well into that period, most scientific attention concerning vision had been directed at the optics and anatomy of the visual system rather than at its psychological functions. Only the epistemological philosophers had been concerned with the higher mental events that today we call "perception." Even Plato, who had concerned himself with universal "forms," had been mainly concerned with the nature of the optical, rather than the perceptual, aspects of vision. It was he who suggested that some force was actually emitted from the eye to make contact with the object. This *extramission* theory was immediately challenged by Aristotle, who suggested that some force came from the object to the eye—the *intromission* hypothesis. It is surprising to discover that there was still some debate between the Platonic extramission and Aristotlian intromission theories of light well into Medieval times. This was so in spite of the fact that Arabic scholars like Alhazen (965–1039?) had, for all practical purposes, demonstrated the inadequacy of the extramission model much earlier. The psychological influences on the perceptual process came to theoretical attention only much later. This seems a natural progression; before one need worry about the subtle central influences of attention, learning, perceptual filling, or distortion, the more peripheral and immediate problems concerning how light gets into the eye have to be resolved.

As we have seen, the early work in vision simply finessed the problem of central or mental influences on perception and typically assumed some sort of an isomorphic, one-to-one relationship between the percept and the stimulus object or retinal image. This may be considered to be a proto-empiricism! Important contributions were made by Alhazen and later by Johannes Kepler (1571–1630) in suggesting what we now appreciate was the seed of the concept of point-for-point encoding as well as the idea that the visual image in the eye was not necessarily the psychoneural equivalent of perception. From the latter intellectual breakthroughs arose the idea of *symbolic representation*, a process that was just beginning to be appreciated as one that occurred much deeper in the nervous system. Herein lies the germ of the emerging rationalist philosophy.

It is possible to easily read into Alhazen's approach a primitive kind of constructivist or interpretive rationalism. According to this interpretation, he was beginning to assert that the brain, through the medium of the *"ultimum sentiens"*—the ultimate sentient power—"perceives" the events communicated by the optic pathway. Alhazen's idea of a central processor of incoming information— an "ultimum sentiens" that is a physiological, as opposed to a philosophical, construct—can thus be read as a prototype of the rationalist, indirect approach. If one accepts this analogy, then obviously rationalism has roots that existed much earlier than is often appreciated. Nevertheless, this prototypical rationalist organ— the brain-mind—was not Alhazen's main interest; most of his studies were directed at explaining how something that would later come to be called "information" passed from the external world to the brain. He was only incidentally interested in what happened after it got there. The full story of this remarkable man can be found in Lindberg (1976), my main source for this part of the discussion.

The development of perspective art in the Late Middle Ages was another factor that emphasized the differences between the stimulus and the perceptual experience. Therefore, this development also began to focus attention on the active role played by the more central portions of the visual nervous system in determining the nature of the perceptual experience[7] thus contributing to the emergence of the modern rationalisms.

a.   Kant—The First Perceptual Rationalist.   The first major, explicitly perceptual rationalism, emphasizing the primacy of the observer rather than of the stimulus in determining the perceptual experience, was that put forth by Immanuel Kant (1724–1804). Kant had been significantly influenced[8] by Gottfried Wilhelm Leibniz (1646–1716), who dealt with perception as if it were a "confused state of thinking" but whose concept of aggregates of monads ("singular and ultimate units of being") was surprisingly associationistic—and thus empiricistic—in its fundamental quality. Unfortunately, Leibniz's philosophy was so thoroughly mixed with his theology that it is hard to call it science, and the first truly scientific elaboration of rationalism for perception is usually attributed to Kant.

Kant's perceptual theory assumed that all sensory signals were classified according to a system of 12 fundamental and innate categories. The categories are specified in his monumental *Critique of Pure Reason* (Kant, 1781), *reason* being defined as being pure when it is innate and uncontaminated by sensory experience. Kant's categories were the three quantitative ones (universal, particular, and singular); the three qualitative ones (affirmative, negative, and infinite); the three relational ones (categorical, hypothetical, and disjunctive); and the three modal (problematic, assertoric, and apodictic). Each of these categories or dimensions of "pure" innate reason acted on sensory inputs to the point that the percept was as much, if not more, a result of the perceiver's "pure reason"' than of the stimulus. This is, of course, the essence of the rationalist approach explicitly stated

---

[7] There is a curious inconsistency of events here, for it was also about this time that philosophers such as Bacon (1561–1626), Descartes (1596–1650), and Hobbes (1588–1679) also began to look upon the human organism as more of a mechanism than had been acceptable to their predecessors (with the extraordinary exception of the anachronistic genius Robert Grosseteste, 1168–1253). With this came an increase in the palatability of the ideas of treating man both as an object of science and as an automaton. Yet at virtually the same time there emerged an appreciation of the active role played by the human "mind" in determining what we see. To a certain degree, these ideas still seem inconsistent with each other, a controversy that became increasingly apparent in later years.

[8] Surprisingly, Kant's perceptual philosophy deviated greatly from that of Descartes and some of the other great traditional pioneers of rationalism. Descartes believed, as we have seen, in the direct impact of the sensory signals on the mind via the pineal gland and was actually an empiricist in this domain.

and painstakingly ornamented with concepts that today are thought to have no empirical reality or conceptual utility. It is interesting to note that Aristotle also had 12 categories, some of which had the same names as Kant's, but they were even less comprehensible than the Kantian conceptualizations.

To Kant, space and time themselves were not "objective and real," but "subjective and ideal." This was a form of an idealist (as opposed to rationalist) line of thought that ran counter to many of the realistic philosophies that were dominant even in his own time. To him the perceived "reality of space" was introduced by the mind, prepared for the task by the existence of concepts that had been instilled into the nervous system by many generations of historical evolution. Kant, thus, is also championing the concept of "innate ideas," an idea that is central to the classic rationalist tradition.

However, alternative interpretations abound of his complex philosophy. Kant may also be construed as having viewed both space and time as being "fundamental axioms" that "represent the form of experience rather than its matter"—the point being that these attributes of existence are prerequisite to the possibility of sensation. To say merely that he thought of them as "subjective and ideal" is therefore incomplete. Although space and time are constructed in Kant's system, his view seems to be that they are logically previous to the categories of pure reason. Furthermore, they are constructed automatically—they are "wired in," and hence implcit in perception—an idea which has about it at least a taint of an empiricist flavor.

The primary dichotomy in Kant's metaphysics, prior to the space and time categories, and the processing agents or categories, is that between *phenomena*—the world as we know and experience it—and *noumena*, or the postulated world "out there" which cannot be directly known. In Kant's system the question of whether the world "really is" the way we experience it, actually becomes meaningless, because nothing can be experienced or known, even in theory, except as phenomena mediated by the categorical system.

In discussing Kant, it is important to remember that his predominantly rationalist philosophy (in that he deemphasized the external world and the passive processing of stimuli) was not motivated by the desire to answer questions pertaining to perception per se, but rather by his interest in the nature of both physical and mental realities in a metaphysical sense. The bridge between the two realities, according to him, was perception itself. This is *the* motivation behind Kant's attention to perception and, thus, the reason behind his influential role in perceptual theory.

Kant's attitude toward perception, in summary, was prototypically rationalist; he asserted that perception is a flawed bridge between those external physical and internal mental realities and that it could never be expected to provide more than a partial truth about the world to the perceiver: In other words, he believed we can never fully know the world through our senses. The main reason for this failure of sensory-based knowledge was the essence of the rationalist thesis—that

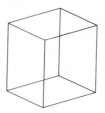

FIG. 2.5. The classic, often trivialized, but compelling (both theoretically
and perceptually) alternating illusion—the Neckar Cube.

the stimuli do not determine the phenomena. Quite to the contrary, according
to Kant, the mind's rational powers interpret and modify stimulus-borne information and thus may distort the image of the external world. Kant was, in short,
arguing that the empiricist point of view, in which the stimulus directly determined the percept, could not be correct, and the kind of processes we now classify
as cognitive or interpretive must affect even the rawest forms of perception. Nevertheless, just as the empiricist did not totally reject rationalist ideas, he did not
reject the need for sensory input. To Kant, as to the empiricists, such inputs were
necessary, but not sufficient to explain perception. Kant, to sum it all up, may
be considered to be the first constructionist and a harbinger of modern cognitive
psychology.

b. Necker and Reversible Figures.   It is not often appreciated that the amusing parlor demonstrations that are virtually always presented in elementary
psychology courses (sometimes it seems for the same reason that the bearded
lady or the dog-faced boy were *always* to be found in the circus midway) originally
were at the core of esoteric theoretical and philosophical disputes between rationalists and empiricists (Necker, 1832) had originally used the reversible cube
that now memorializes his name as prima facie evidence that the nervous system
can create a specific form in situations in which the stimulus is inadequate or
ambiguous: Thus, he argued that perception *must* be rationalist in nature. The
reversible cube, which can be seen in two alternative spatial orientations, is shown
in Fig. 2.5. This object is perceived according to some attribute or factor that
varies with the internal state of the organism, not in accord with the stimulus.[9]
This, to Necker, was a compelling argument for the addition of meaning or phenomenological form to the stimulus by the mind in a manner that transcends
stimulus determinacy. The dynamic nature of the inferred form was, therefore,
considered to be a powerful argument for some kind of rationalistic processing,
and Necker's demonstrations, though still unexplained, were originally presented
in exactly that theoretical context.

---

[9] One perceiver-controlled function that does seem to regulate the perceived orientation of the
Necker cube is that involving which corner is foveated (see Kawabata, Yamagami, & Noaki, 1978).
Another is the degree of preadaptation to a nonambigous form (see Emerson, 1979).

c.   Helmholtz and Unconscious Conclusions.   The process of transformation of perceptual theory from a primarily philosophical to a primarily scientific enterprise received a major acceleration with the publication of Herman W. von Helmholtz's (1968) masterpiece *Treatise on Physiological Optics* in 1866. Helmholtz was the scientific generalist and polymath par excellence. He worked in applied medicine, physiology, physics, and psychology as well as producing speculative books on a variety of philosophical topics. He was an opto-mechanical inventor as well, and was responsible for the first practical ophthalmoscope. He studied the sense of hearing as well as vision, and his contributions are considered to be monumental in both sensory fields. In addition to his optical treatise, he also published the epochal *Die Lehre von dem Tonempfindung (On the Sensations of Tone as a Physiological Basis for the Theory of Music)* (Helmholtz 1863/1948.)

Our interest with Helmholtz here, however,is with a very specific aspect of his manifold contributions—the conclusions that he drew from his studies concerning the nature of visual perception. Clearly Helmholtz was an empiricist in one sense of the word; he believed, unlike Kant, that we do, in fact, learn about the external world mainly through the medium of sensory experience. He concluded that there are no innate ideas as such and in this regard must be considered to be an empiricist. Equally clearly, however, Helmholtz was not an empiricist in the sense of how the word is used in the present context. Like Kant, he argued strongly that the central nervous activities that are subsumed under the word *mind* actually are necessary to construct the perceptual experience from the raw stimulus information. It is true that he did not like mentalistic psychological constructs such as "mind" and rational construction, but he found it impossible to avoid their use. Although much more precise and constrained in his language than Kant—it must not be overlooked that the domain in which Helmholtz operated was science and not philosophy—it is clear that Helmholtz is thinking in exactly the same vein as Kant with regard to the nature of perception when he makes the following assertions:

> The general rule determining the ideas of vision that are formed whenever an impression is made on the eye, with or without the aid of optical instruments, is that such objects are always *imagined* as being present in the field of vision as would have to be there in order to produce the same impression on the nervous mechanism, the eyes being used under ordinary normal conditions. (p. 172)

> The psychic activities that lead us to *infer* that there in front of us at a certain place there is a certain object of a certain character, are generally not conscious activities, but *unconscious* ones. In their result they are equivalent to a *conclusion*, to the extent that the observed action on our senses enables us to form an idea as to the possible cause of this action; although, as a matter of fact, it is invariably simply the nervous stimulations that are perceived directly, that is, the actions, but never the external objects themselves. (p. 174)

These *inductive conclusions* leading to the formation of our sense-perceptions certainly do lack the purifying and scrutinizing work of conscious thinking. Nevertheless, in my opinion, by their peculiar nature they may be classed as *conclusions*, inductive conclusions unconsciously formed. (p. 195)

In my earlier works I named the *conceptual connections* occurring in this process *unconscious conclusions*. Unconscious, in respect to the major premise based upon a sequence of experiences, each of which had long since disappeared from memory and entered consciousness only in the form of sensory impressions, not necessarily as sentences framed in words. New sensory impressions occurring in ongoing perception form the minor premise to which we apply the rule stamped in our mind by previous observations. Later I avoided that term, "unconscious conclusions," in order to escape from the entirely confused and unjustified concept—at any rate so it seemed to me—which Schopenhauer and his disciples designate by this name. *We are obviously concerned here with a basic process which underlies all that truly can be called thinking, although it lacks the critical sifting and completion of individual steps found in the scientific formulation of concepts and ideas.* (p. 220)

(All of these quotations are from Warren and Warren, 1968, from Southall's translation of Helmholtz, 1925, and from the Warren translation of Helmholtz, 1879. Italics have been added in all cases.)

The important point to be gleaned from these quotations is that Helmholtz was thoroughly convinced that the stream of raw sensory impressions had to be interpreted by the inductive and inferential processes of which he spoke to be made semantically useful. In spite of his deep commitment to a sensation-dominated empiricism ("All knowledge must ultimately come through the senses"), Helmholtz was thus a rationalist in the sense presented in this chapter; the significance or attribution of meaning to the sensory signals was accomplished by means of mechanisms that he described in terms that were classically rationalistic. Sometimes in his writing it seems that this very empirical scientist was dismayed by this need to turn to mentalistic concepts. Nevertheless, it seems clear that Helmholtz felt this eclectic empiricist–rationalist theoretical approach was as obviously necessary in his times as it is in ours.

d. The Transactional and Probabilistic Functionalists.   Although there were other intervening theorists between Helmholtz's time and the theorists of the 1920s and 1930s who invoked central, cognitivelike processes for processes other than perception, one later distinctly perceptual school of thought that was obviously and directly influenced by the rationalist trend was that of the American functionalists. The functionalists stressed the adaptive aspects of mind and the utility of the perceptual or behavioral response to the organism. Utility-driven psychological importance rather than geometrical form guided the response of the perceptual system to the stimulus. Their emphasis was, therefore, on the interaction between the human cognitive processes and the external environment.

Two different functionalist points of view, that of the transactional functionalists and that of the probabilistic functionalists, have been distinguished. The transactional functionalists, including John Dewey, Adelbert Ames, and William H. Ittleson (see especially Ittleson, 1952), believed specifically that there was no direct causal relationship between the stimulus and the percept; rather a "transactional relationship" existed between the external world and the observer's past experiences, attitudes, and needs. In emphasizing this aspect of perception, they stressed the inner mental state of the observer as an overriding determinant of the perceptual response in much the same way as both previous and future rationalistic theorists.

The other school, the probabilistic functionalists, most clearly exemplified by Egon Brunswik's work (see especially Brunswik, 1955) was in accord with the idea, to which I have already alluded several times, that the set of stimulus cues is but a fuzzy shadow of the real world—that any physical stimuli are at best incomplete and inadequate clues to the nature of external reality. The task of the perceiver, according to Brunswik, is to rationally interpret these partial cues and hints in order to form a conclusion about the most probable nature of the external world that fits these incomplete signals. The particular perceived world that is conjured up by the cognitive mind is thus only one of the many possible worlds but it is the most perceptually probable one. Thus was the qualifying adjective—*probabilistic*—attached to Brunswik's form of rationalist functionalism.

*e. **The Neorationalist Psychologists.*** The idea that some central mental state of the observer, rather than the stimulus, is dominant in determining perceptual phenomena is thus an idea with a moderately long history. In modern times this idea persists in the theoretical expressions of a very large number, if not the majority, of those who explicitly would categorize themselves as "perceptual" psychologists, as well as a large number of contemporary cognitive constructionists interested in other psychological functions. In the following paragraphs I briefly describe a number of the more visible members of this group of my colleagues who share with me the idea that the internal state of the organism and some kind of mental interpretation of the proximal stimulus information are important, if not dominant, in the specification of the perceptual experience.

1. Irvin Rock's Cognitive Decision Theory.

Irvin Rock's (1975, 1983) recent writing about form perception is very much of the same genre as were Helmholtz's ideas. Rock suggests that the attributes of stimulus form are largely disorganized when they arrive at the critical central portions of the nervous system in which discrimination, recognition, or grouping occur. It is at this point that he invokes cognitive processes that are strongly in the rationalist tradition. In fact, Rock asserts that the visual system carries out virtually the same processes as were suggested by Helmholtz. Indeed, the perceptual system's role, according to Rock, is one of inquiry—it asks the same questions that Helmholtz believed it asked; both see perception as a form of problem solving. In Rock's (1975) words, "the stimulus information is cognitively evaluated, albeit unconsciously and nonverbally, on the basis of the question 'What entity or entities in the objective world are most likely producing this stimulus distribution?' "

Rock, as was Necker, is especially interested in ambiguous figures, and points out that they are particularly salient as clues to the nature of perception. He notes that they demonstrate the variation in perception that occurs even in those situations in which the stimulus remains absolutely constant. The solution to these perceptual puzzles posed by the stimulus is carried out in much the same way as any other kind of problem-solving behavior, according to Rock. He agrees that the rational problem-solving process is, as suggested by Helmholtz, nonconscious. Rock also believes that the impact of the Gestalt laws of grouping is mediated by this central, nonconscious processing. The resulting grouped percepts are reasonable approximations to a hypothetical real-world stimulus form that is capable of plausibly producing such retinal stimulus patterns. Though nonconscious (or preconscious), an explicitly cognitive decision has been made by the perceiver as to what he will see, according to the fundamental assumptions of Rock's theory. Once again the observer, rather than the stimulus, becomes the focus of this theoretician's interest in perception, and Rock, by so asserting, places himself squarely among the neorationalists.

2. Neisser New and Neisser Old

Ulrich Neisser has been one of the most influential cognitive psychologists of the last two decades. Originally he was very much a proponent of the idea that visual perception occurred by means of a process that was analogous to the "reconstruction of a dinosaur skeleton from a few bone fragments" (Neisser, 1967). The synthesis of a percept from stimuli was considered by him to be identical to the process of visual imagination. One process produced phenomena that were closely associated with immediate cues, whereas the other led to percepts that depended on cues that had less recently entered the perceptual system and were, therefore, more a part of the memory base than of the current sensory input.

More recently, however, Neisser, acknowledgedly influenced by his late but very distinguished colleague at Cornell University, J.J. Gibson has altered his theoretical position (Neisser, 1976). Neisser has now drawn away from the idea that it is the perceptual experience that is constructed or synthesized by cognitive process to the idea that it is the expectations, or, as he calls them, "anticipatory schemata" that are constructed. These schemata "prepare the perceiver to accept certain kinds of information rather than others and thus control the activity of looking" (p. 20). By assuming this stance, Neisser was attempting to accommodate into his theory many of Gibson's ideas which, as we have already seen, are remarkably empiricist in tone. In doing so, however, Neisser does not reject the constructivist concept, but rather changes its focus. No longer does he assume that other percepts are themselves rationally constructed, but rather the new suggestion is that the observer constructs the schemata that filter stimuli to allow only certain parts of the rich flood of information into the optic array to be directly processed in the empiricist manner championed by Gibson. Clearly, this is a compromise between a radical empiricism and a radical rationalism, with the perceptual aspects reflecting a surprising (in terms of Neisser's previous views) empiricism.

Neisser, however, is not doctrinaire in his attitude. He also adopts an eclectic attitude toward theories in visual perception, asserting that in his opinion (as in my own) there are no gross inconsistencies among the different theories, only differences in the target phenomena emphasized by each. Nevertheless, a major portion of his thinking, even after this transformation, involves active mental processes operating to construct schema that select incoming stimuli. The essence of the rationalistic process is still present, but heavily modulated by his new empiricist perspective.

3. Information-Processing Theories

The earlier version of Neisser's constructionistic approach is also the essence of at least one version of the information-processing theoretical zeitgeist that has attracted considerable attention in recent years. We can also see how there is a strong overtone of stimulus determinism in at least some of the information-processing theories: Algorithmic evaluations are often purported to be carried out prior to the perceptual "construction" process. The differences among the various schools of thought within the various information-processing theories revolve around the amount of any kind of central rationalistic processing that is performed in addition to this peripheral, empiricistic, algorithmic processing. If the processing is limited to a hierarchical kind of concatenation of geometrical features, the minitaxonomy of theories utilized here would place such a version of the information-processing approach among the empiricist theories discussed in the previous section. If, on the other hand, the mental processing is purported to deal more with semantic relationships and the act of perceptual construction, then the thrust of that particular information-processing theory would place it in this section among the neorational ones.

A particular, and explicitly eclectic, version of a rationalist information-processing theory has been developed by Rumelhart (1977). It involves peripheral empiricist components, but also a pattern "synthesizer" (i.e., a constructive component) that embodies the safe kind of interpretive determination of perception that is characteristic of the rationalist approach. Figure 2.6 is a reproduction of his model.

The main element of all of the various versions of the information-processing theories of form perception seems to be that there are identifiable functional pro-

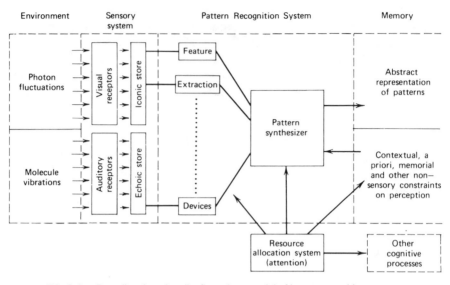

FIG. 2.6. Rumelhart's rationalist flow chart model of human cognitive processes including perception (from Rumelhart, 1977).

cesses represented as separate blocks in a graphic flow chart model of the psychological processes. "Information" flows from, to, and among the various boxes within which various subprocesses occur. The specific element of those versions of the theory that suggests that they should be classified as neorationalism is the existence of some component in which the information is processed in a mediate manner; that is, which actively constructs a plausible and meaningful percept instead of simply passively reproducing an isomorphic representation or transformation of the incoming array of stimulus information. This classification of cognitive-information processing theories as rationalist, of course, is severely clouded by their merger in recent years with more empiricist-type computational models. In the final taxonomy, each of the many different theories will have to be inspected individually to determine to which school of thought it actually belongs. Indeed, given some of the other limits to understanding internal structure I consider in this book, an extremely complex set of even passive transformations may be in principle indistinguishable from active, cognitive construction. If any neural theory of mind is correct, this becomes a truism.

4. Jean Piaget

The great Swiss developmental psychologist Jean Piaget wrote extensively on perceptual theories and in doing so has expressed another form of a neorationalism. Piaget was a remarkably energetic man. I heard him speak in Paris in the 80th year of his life. His paper concerned his scientific plans for the next 10 years! Although Piaget was not able to fulfill that plan, he did leave us with a rich legacy, including his deep insight into the development of the perceptual process in children. Among his many writings, the one most relevant to us in his book on *The Mechanisms of Perception* (Piaget, 1969).

Piaget distinguishes between primary and secondary illusions—those that are relatively simple (but not necessarily genetically innate) and those that are more complex, interdimensional, and characterized by activities that increase with age. The secondary effects may, Piaget asserts, eventually swamp out the primary ones. But, more germane to our present discussion is Piaget's unwillingness to separate perception and cognition into two mutually exclusive categories. Rather, as he asserts elsewhere "Action as a whole is both the point of departure for reason (cognition) and a continuous source of organization and reorganization for perception."

Piaget (1969) goes on to specifically reject empiricism (in the sense that we can gain knowledge only through our senses) by turning to Kantian notions of a kind I have discussed earlier. He concretizes this issue by asking: "To what extent is perception a 'copy,' or at least a faithful translation, of the object, and to what extent does it make additions. . .to structures which derive from the activity of the subject?" (p.362). This is a wonderfully succinct way of expressing the focus of the tension that exists between the rationalist and empiricist (in the sense I use the words here) school of thought. Piaget's (1969) answer to this question is clear and phrased in a language with which my readers should be familiar by now:

> In the end, the relative adequacy of any perception to any object depends on a constructive process and not on an immediate contact. During this constructive process the subject tries to make use of whatever information he has, incomplete, deformed or false as it may be, and to build it into a system which corresponds as nearly as possible to the properties of the object. He can only do this by a method which is both cumulative and corrective. (p.365)

This is a statement of a confirmed rationalist, without doubt, and an answer that is as clear as the question that was asked.

5. Other Rationalists

The list of other psychologists who espouse the rationalist view is long. It includes Lloyd Kaufman, who in his excellent text *Sight and Mind* (1974) asserts:

> The position taken here is that there is no such thing as immediate experience either of objects and events or of the observer's own inner states. All the events that might be termed instances of immediate experience are themselves constructions occurring over time and after the fact. Hence any program designed to account for immediate experience is doomed to failure. (p.16)

And there are many others. Indeed any theory that suggests that the "mind" plays an active role in interpreting stimuli or constructing percepts is in the terms of the present taxonomy a neorationalism. Included in this category, therefore, are the hypothesis theory of Gregory (1970, 1974); the schema-type theories of Arbib (1975) , Miller, Galanter, and Pribram (1960), and Abelson, (1973); Bruner and Postman's (1947, 1949) directive state theory; Braunstein's (1976) "heuristic" theory of motion perception; and the ideas of a host of other psychologists who have in one way or another noted the nonveridicality of the human perception of physical objects.

D. RAPPROCHEMENT—A CONTEMPORARY VIEW

The discussion presented so far is an all-too-brief review of the major approaches to a theory of form perception. In the few pages that I have been able to dedicate to this topic, I have discussed the two main themes—empiricism and rationalism—that I believe characterize theory in this field. It should be obvious that I necessarily have had to omit or gloss over the work of some important scholars in this field and perhaps have placed an unnecessary emphasis on some historical figures that are no longer of general interest. Nevertheless, I believe that it is especially important for contemporary students to appreciate that the roots of what are often quite spirited modern debates are to be found well back to antiquity. It is important to realize that the two opposing themes have persisted, not because one or the other was incapable of administering the coup de grâce to the other, but rather because each had something positive and correct to say about the visual process. This is the main message of the historical survey I have presented.

My purpose here is to stress that form perception is the result of a mixed bag of strongly interacting processes. Certain processes carried out by the visual system are more or less passive, automatic, algorithmic, and direct (empiricist in my lexicon), whereas others (which at some level of logical primitives are based on exactly the same neural principles) are so complex (because so many logical primitives have been concatenated) that they *seem* to characterize a system that is operating on the basis of rules and laws that are active, indirect, logical, or semantic. I profess that both kinds of processes must be present. A surprising fact is that the complexity of the phenomena under consideration is not a good clue to which of the two kinds of processing is actually occurring. Simple geometrical illusions are as likely candidates to be handled by highly complex and rationalist processes as are some recognition tasks involving stimuli loaded with meaning of a more subtle kind.

Having asserted my belief in the need for an eclectic approach to form perception here at the end of this discussion, I must also emphasize that I am not alone in this point of view. The reader may have noticed that throughout this discussion I have repeatedly had to hedge on the categorization of many of the theories to which I have alluded; many of the theoreticians stress their empiricistic or rationalistic premises only to recant in a footnote or in brief secondary paragraphs indicate acceptance of the partial validity of the opposing view. Many explicitly accept the idea that some aspects of form perception are certainly direct and immediate while others must be indirect and mediate. The particular stance taken by each theoretician is mainly associated with his choice of the particular phenomena with which he is concerned.

In summary, any rigid doctrinaire attitude toward explaining form perception seems unjustified. Many different explanations working at many different levels of the perceptual system are necessary to fully comprehend the incredible versatility and power of this particular aspect of our mental life. In the chapters that follow, I examine the various theories that are used to explain form perception and attempt to draw forth a contemporary view of the nature of and multiple explanations of this wonderful property of the human mind.

3

THE DETECTION
OF VISUAL FORMS

A. INTRODUCTION

In this chapter I consider those psychological processes, phenomena, and models that are specifically concerned with the detection of particular stimuli in a surround. *Detection* is, as we have seen, a curiously misused and abused word in the lexicon of psychology. Some uses often encroach upon the definition of other well-defined visual processes. In other cases the intended meaning of the word is so inclusive as to make it virtually meaningless as a scientific designator. One appropriate use of the word, but one with which I am not concerned in this chapter, is *energy detection*; that is, the constellation of phenomena and processes associated with the absolute threshold for luminosity—in other words, the process by which an observer determines if there is any photic stimulus there at all. Though there are certainly some cognitive overtones to even this kind of absolute threshold (usually associated with the *criterion levels* used by an observer in accepting or rejecting a near-threshold event) in fact, our knowledge of the mechanics of the absolute luminosity-detection threshold convinces most contemporary visual scientists that it is an ensemble of properties of the photochemical-receptive processes in rods and cones (as well as the statistics of individual quanta) that regulates this kind of detection behavior. Indeed, the absolute threshold of luminosity detection has been known for many years (Helson & Fehrer, 1932) to be virtually unaffected by the shape or form of a stimulus as long as it is within the integration area defined by Ricco's law. Helson and Fehrer also note (a conclusion for which I have found no subsequent refutation) that it takes "25 times as much light to perceive forms correctly . . . as compared with just noticeable light. . . ." (p. 101).[1]

The energy-detection problem is also well known to be almost a nonproblem because the human visual system (and that of many other animals) is virtually as sensitive as it can theoretically be. Under ideal conditions of observation (30 min dark adaptation; 10 msec exposure time; 10 min of visual angle spot; 20 deg in the periphery of the retina; 510 nm light) detection thresholds are of the order of five to seven photons, according to Hecht, Shlaer, and Pirenne (1942) or one photon, according to Sakitt (1972). In either case the individual rod is certainly capable of responding to a single photon, the smallest amount of light possible. The entire concept of an absolute luminosity threshold thus becomes meaningful only in other than the ideal conditions of this experiment and as a differential measure, for example, at different wavelengths.

The word *detection* is also used in another context (other than measurement of the limits of luminosity thresholds) by students of alphabetic-letter perception. The task of finding one particular letter among many is sometimes said to be illuminating an aspect of form "detection." However, a close inspection of this kind of paradigm suggests that what is actually being studied in this case is a kind of successive-recognition behavior. This is not what I am interested in, either, in this chapter. Letter "detection" experiments of this recognition genre are, therefore, considered in chapter 5.

The kind of detection with which I deal in this chapter is of a higher and more complex level than the mere detection of luminance and of a lower and less complex level than the classification and recognition of forms in a search experiment. Presumably, detection of the kind discussed here is associated with neural computational processes located more centrally than the simple, peripheral networks of the retina, lateral geniculate body, or even the lower levels of cortical representation. It is at these higher levels (and not at those mediating the detection of luminance per se, as Helson and Fehrer,1932, correctly showed) that the effects of form become measurable. On the other hand, the processes relevant to form detection are not so central[2] as to involve effortful cognition: Most detection processes of the genre dealt with in this chapter seem to occur effortlessly, and automatically at some level intermediate between what we call *receptor* and *cognitive* processes.

---

[1] Helson and Fehrer go on to note that in recognition-type experiments, however, form does play an important role, but in curiously inconsistent ways. Interestingly, they find that rectangles can be seen more often and with fewer confusions at lower luminosity than any other form. This result is consistent with "the rule of linear periodicity" emerging in my own work (see the discussion later in this chapter). This similarity in outcome suggests that the results from dotted-stimulus experiments may be generalized to continuous forms, at least in this regard.

[2] The anatomical phrases "more central" or "more peripheral" used in these paragraphs, of course, are only metaphors. In fact, we have no idea where detection or recognition is localized in the brain. Indeed, neither may be localized at all, but each is more likely to be the outcome of widely distributed mechanisms throughout the brain.

The processes of detection with which we deal in this chapter are mainly concerned with the segregation of a stimulus-form from the other parts of a scene in which it may be embedded; that is, with the organization of the stimulus scene into figure and ground or with the extraction of a salient figure from a complex or visually noisy irrelevant environment. Such detection processes are of the kind I classified as Level 3 in my earlier work (Uttal, 1981). This chapter, therefore, in part reiterates and expands some of that material in the light of new data and insights that have emerged recently. It also deals with some other aspects of the detection process I did not consider there.

A main characteristic of this level of processing is the preattentive, almost automatic, way in which the salient aspects of the stimulus are separated from the irrelevant. This aspect of my taxonomy and the initial plan to dedicate this book totally to what had at first seemed to me to be a completely attentive (Level 5) kind of processing of visual form thus stand modified.

It would, however, be dissembling not to acknowledge that any such taxonomic decision is arbitrary. Thus, the essential issue now arising is: Is the segregation of the three types of visual processing (detection, discrimination, and recognition) into distinct categories a proper and plausible foundation on which to build a taxonomic analysis of visual form perception? The question must be asked because it is evident that this is not always done by contemporary theoreticians; many of my colleagues have chosen to develop models of visual perception that essentially deal with all three of these stages of perception in a unified manner.

My predilection to do otherwise is based upon a number of considerations. One is the unarguable truth that the total visual perceptual process is so complex that to not use John Stuart Mill's "method of detail" or Descartes' *methode* would quickly submerge the investigator in a sea of confounded experiments and conflicting and overlapping theories. Results that appear contradictory, on the one hand, and antagonistic theories, on the other, arise in the literature exactly because the component perceptual processes are intrinsically ambiguous, uncertain, and interactive from one stage of processing to another. And yet many of our research paradigms uncritically examine vision as if it were a unified entity.

Another argument for a separatist view of perception that transcends this issue of complexity is much more practical. It appears to be the case that the three perceptual processes with which I am concerned in this volume can, in empirical fact, be separated by appropriate experimental procedures. In my own laboratory I have found strong evidence that form detection can occur at more severe levels of masking or degradation than can discrimination or recognition. The disassociation of these processes by means of the dot-masking paradigm is useful just because the experimental paradigm is unusual and unconfounded to a degree that is not possible in letter-recognition experiments, for example. The experiment to which I refer (more fully described in Uttal, 1987) was carried out by elastically (i.e., mathematically) stretching a prototypical planar array of dots into seven of the standard forms of solid geometry as shown in diagram in Fig. 3.1. These forms were displayed stereoscopically and thus appear to be three-dimensional. We then

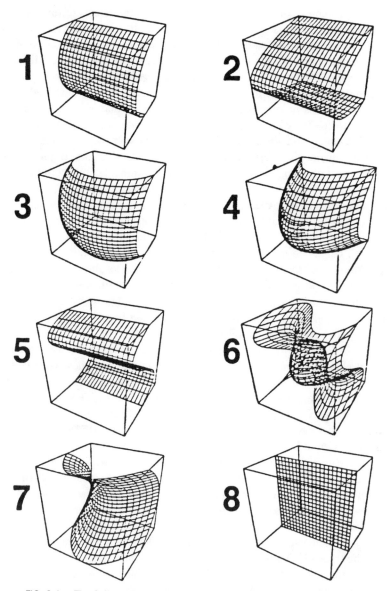

FIG. 3.1.   The 8 three-dimensional surfaces used in the dot perception studies (from Uttal, 1987).

compared the detectability, discriminability, and recognizability of these eight (seven stretched shapes and a plane) in a dot-masking paradigm in which the dotted forms were embedded in an array of random dots distributed throughout the viewing space. Briefly, let us consider what happened to support the separability of process idea.

In order to achieve the dual goals of determining the effects of form and task and to make the comparison as precise as possible, it is necessary to reduce one particular source of variance—the individual differences that previously confounded many experiments of this type—to a minimum. That was accomplished by the logistically difficult task of keeping the same group of observers throughout the entire time period that the experiment was being carried out. Under most previous conditions holding a single group for more than a single experiment had proven to be nearly impossible, but a system of bonuses, alternate observers, and gentle cajolery did succeed for the first three experiments. The three parts of this experiment, therefore, used the same stimuli, the same observers, and nearly identical psychophysical procedures to determine the impact of the task—detection, discrimination, and recognition—on performance.

In the first part of the experiment, the observer's task in this case was to report in which of two sequential one-second presentations a dotted stimulus form had been presented by depressing one of two handheld push buttons. One of these two stimuli contained the stimulus-form and a number of randomly positioned masking dots. The other contained the same masking dots plus a number of additional randomly positioned "dummy dots" equal to the number of dots in the stimulus form. After each response a plus or minus sign was displayed on the oscilloscope to indicate if the observer's choice had been correct or incorrect. The next trial was then automatically initiated.

The second part of the experiment was carried out using the same group of observers who participated in the first part, but in this case they were asked to discriminate (rather than detect) between pairs of stimulus-forms selected from the same set of stimulus-forms. The observers were successively presented with the two of the geometrical forms and asked to specify if they were the same or different. In this case, both presentations contained organized stimulus-forms. The pairs chosen to be discriminated in each trial were constrained so that only equal dot densities were compared with each other. This was done to assure that the task depended upon shape alone and not upon a not-so-subtle density cue.

The discrimination experiment involved one other parameter; it was possible to specify in what proportion of the trials the two stimuli should be identical. For this experiment, it was decided to use 33% as the value of this factor. That is, the two stimuli were constrained to be identical on a randomly chosen one third of the trials. This is an important variable because it does interact with the number of alternatives to determine the level at which the observer would perform if he or she saw nothing and was merely guessing.

The third part of the experiment required the observer to name which one of the eight geometric forms had been presented by orally uttering a code name ("cylinder," "arch," "hemisphere," "paraboloid," "cubic," "double," "saddle," and "surface") into a microphone. These code words were used to signify the (a) circular cylinder, (b) the parabolic arch, (c) the hemisphere, (d) the paraboloid of rotation, (e) the y- or one-dimensional cubic, (f) the x-y or two-dimensional cubic, (g) the hyperbolic paraboloid, and (h) the square planar surface. These words were chosen to both maximize the ease of learning for the observers and the discriminability of the sounds to a speech-recognition system.

To correctly compare these three curves, the data are plotted in Fig. 3.2 in a normalized form. The transformed scores from the three tasks look very much alike. However, there remains, and this is the key point, a residual ordering of performance as a function of the task even when normalized. The effect of masking dot density is still clearly differential; performance drops off more rapidly for recognition, discrimination, and detection, in that order.

It is clear that the differential effect of masking dot density over the ranges of the three tasks is greatly reduced if considered in this normalized context. The sequence in which the outcomes of the three parts of the experiment are ordered is also consistent with the idea that additional information is needed to progress from one of these perceptual tasks to the next, and, therefore, a hierarchy of separable perceptual processes seemingly does exist. It is also possible, of course, that different qualities or kinds of information are required for each task and that the hierarchy is due to differences in acquiring or processing this information.

The premise that therefore permeates the organization of this book is that the three stages of visual processing are actually separate from very fundamental biological, as well as methodological, points of view. The main argument for this assertion is based upon the empirical fact that by use of an appropriate ex-

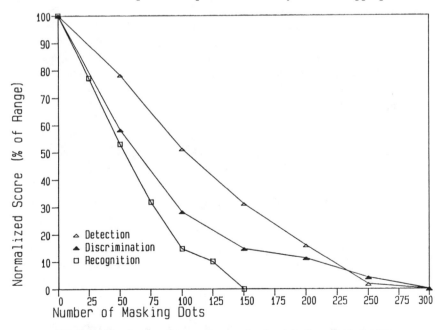

FIG. 3.2. The three performance curves for the detection, discrimination, and recognition of dotted forms in dotted noise (from Uttal, 1987).

perimental paradigm, as exemplified in the experiment reported in the previous paragraphs, the three processes can be dissociated, examined, and studied separately, and that in such situations detection, discrimination, and recognition often exhibit quite different properties. Detection of a target form must logically occur prior to or, at the very least, no later than identification or classification of that form. It is hard to imagine how something could be recognized without being detected, although it is easy to conceive of an unrecognized form being detected. Yet, all too often the two processes are fused experimentally into a single measure. Sometimes the fusion is intentional and researchers in the field may consciously take the tack of studying such unified processes as a universal form of information acquisition or perceptual processing, two terms that are far less precise than the operational definition for detection, discrimination, and recognition given elsewhere in this book.

The choice of experimental paradigm is thus critical in determining what observations are appropriate for inclusion in this chapter. As I noted earlier, letter recognition or, as I believe they are mistakenly called, "detection" experiments rarely deal with the process that I would consider to fall within the rubric of form detection as it is used here. Rather, the very act of *searching* for an *particular character* among many in an extensive stimulus set identifies this approach as a recognition-type experiment. All of the characters are obviously detectable, and each must be examined and recognized in order to be classified. As a contrary example, camouflage-type or signal-in-noise–type paradigms actually obscure or degrade the form of the individual stimulus; that form must actually be extracted from the clutter or *detected* before it can subsequently be classified or *recognized*.

I must note, and this is clearly a view that may be highly colored by my personal preoccupation with a relatively pure dot-masking detection-type study for over a decade, how few other perceptual psychologists these days seem to be interested in the kind of detection behavior discussed in this chapter. Somewhere between the absolute detection of a dim light and the ability to discriminate between two forms as being different from each other lies another constellation of phenomena and processes. This constellation is characterized by luminance levels well above threshold, yet requiring some perceptual (although generally preattentive) organization or analysis before the stimulus-forms become perceptually evident; in other words, before they are *detected*. That all visual scenes must be perceptually organized so that the forms can be detected seems self-evident, but somehow this problem area has not attracted the attention it should have. Perhaps this is due to the fact that detection falls between the interests of the receptor-process-emphasizing, physiologically oriented psychologists on the one hand and the recognition-emphasizing, cognitively oriented psychologists on the other.

Whatever the reason for this lack of attention, the essential aspect of the psychological-research paradigms studying the intermediate level of processing we observe in detection performance is that they all involve degradation of one kind or another. That is, in order to explore detection processes it is necessary to make the task more difficult than it would normally be. The perceptual system's ability to detect forms (as well as to discriminate and recognize) is astonishingly powerful, and in most ordinary situations it does so effortlessly and virtually flawlessly as long as the threshold for luminosity detection is exceeded. To study this elusive (elusive just because of its powerful ability to do its job) process it is necessary to make the task more difficult and to challenge the perceptual system with extraordinary viewing situations. This is accomplished in a number of ways, which are elaborated upon later. For the moment, a few sample means of degrading stimuli should be mentioned: These include contrast reduction, the addition of visual "noise," and fracturing the continuity of either the characteristic features and contours or the entire global form of the stimulus.

Thus, the topic considered in this chapter (as well as the study of detection in general) relies heavily on some kind of degraded form as its prototypical stimulus. The form is hidden by visual noise, is obscured by low contrast, is incomplete or the exposure is short, and the observational skills are thus challenged to detect the stimulus object. It is an empirical question, only partly answered in some special experimental situations, as to what degree detection in each of these situations is accompanied by an equally immediate form-recognition experience. In accord with the premises of the organization of this book and the results of experiments similar to the one described earlier in this section, however, I consider the detection aspects independently of the others.

To make the goal of this chapter more concrete, I now tabulate the empirical and theoretical approaches that are considered here:

- Detection of gratings varying in contrast
- Dotted-form detection
- The detection of symmetry
- Masking

As we cover these topics, the reader should be alert to the fact that we are attempting to answer some specific questions concerning form detection. In particular:

- What is the effect of form on detection?
- What is the effect of stimulus uncertainty on detection?
- Does spatial-frequency-channel hypothesis reflect the underlying anatomy?
- What is the effect of signal-to-noise ratio on detection?
- How is detection affected by masking or camouflage?

B. THE DETECTION OF CONTRAST GRATINGS

As my readers must be fully aware by now, I believe that the hypothesis of anatomically distinct, physiologically separable, spatial-frequency channels in the visual nervous system is yet unproven. In spite of this view, I am a strong advocate of the value of the two-dimensional Fourier frequency-analysis method both as a means of specifying stimuli and as a procedure for analyzing the results of psychophysical experiments utilizing gratinglike stimuli. My argument with the Fourier theory is that the undeniable utility of this precise and elegant means of quantifying inputs to and outputs from the human "black box" in no way justifies the totally distinguishable and independent concept of anatomical spatial-frequency analyzers in the nervous system. It is a fact (and this was the most important meaning of Fourier's original theorem) that any function, no matter what are its inner mechanisms or origins or how convoluted the complexity of its shape, can be formally analyzed by this mathematical procedure as long as it has a finite number of both discontinuities and maxima and minima[3] and the law of linear superimposition holds (i.e., the amplitudes of the constituent sub-functions add linearly). Fourier's theorem is known to hold in one and two, and presumed also to hold in three dimensions, although three-dimensional calculations of this kind often exceed the power of even our most powerful computers. It is only in special circumstances that three-dimensional Fourier analysis can be carried out. One of these is in the context of the dotted (discretely sampled) stimuli that I have used in my laboratory work. Such sparsely sampled stimuli allow intermediate-size computers to evaluate the triple integrals required for the analysis of three-dimensional forms. The resulting transformations are four-dimensional graphs, (i.e., the coordinates on the three spatial frequency axes and the value of the integral at each point in that frequency space must be encoded) thus requiring false color coding or some other artifice to be displayed.

Fourier analysis can utilize any set of component orthogonal wave-forms (usually, but not necessarily sinusoidal functions—a rich variety of other orthogonal sets can be found in Pratt's excellent book, 1978) that can be superimpositioned to reproduce any arbitrary function. This analysis, Fourier himself must have appreciated, would work even if their were no generators of sine waves, square waves, or any other orthogonal functions actually present in or underlying the function being so analyzed. The anatomical analog to this mathematical theorem is that the Fourier mathematics can be extremely useful even if the putative "channels" of selectively sensitive spatial-frequency neurons do not exist. This is a point with which even John Robson, one of the most important figures in the spatial frequency channel scene, agrees. He says (Robson, 1983):

I am therefore going to describe some of those neurophysiological findings which

---

[3] It is interesting to note that a wave-form does not even have to be continuous to be represented by a Fourier analysis, only to have a "finite number of discontinuities."

seem to me to be most relevant to an understanding of the image-processing role of the visual system particularly as revealed by studies mainly conceived, executed or interpreted in spatial frequency terms. *It is worth emphasizing that while some of these studies have certainly been undertaken by people who have believed that the visual system is indeed performing some sort of spatial frequency analysis. it is certainly not necessary for this to be correct for their experimental approach to be useful or the results significant.* (p. 75; italics added)

The important idea is that Fourier analysis is a means of *mathematically analyzing* a system; the system does not need to be actually *structurally implemented* in the form of a system of orthogonal functions in terms of its underlying mechanisms for the mathematics to work. Thus, the proven *Fourier mathematical methodology* must be distinguished from the *anatomical hypothesis of spatial-frequency channels*. The spatial-frequency-channel hypothesis makes a specific statement about the mechanisms and implementations within the nervous system that the Fourier mathematics does not imply and, indeed, as a matter of principle cannot. For the Fourier mathematics, the internal anatomical mechanics are merely excess conceptual baggage.

Of course, there can be and is a quite distinct body of neurophysiological evidence that is purported to support the idea of anatomical spatial-frequency-analyzing channels or cells. Much of this work has come from the laboratory of Russel DeValois (see, for example, DeValois, Albrecht, & Thorell, 1982) but the possibility of alternative interpretation of their indisputable neurophysiological findings remain. The data they observe may reflect other deeper levels of sensitivity, just as these findings have tended to replace the simpler interpretation of Hubel and Wiesel (e.g., 1965) concerning the trigger sensitivities of "simple" and "complex" cells.

Even the most modern reconceptualization of the channel problem in the form of the so-called Gabor or Mexican Hat function (resulting from the cross-multiplication of sinusoidal and Gaussian functions—a product that is shown in Fig. 3.3) is subject to this same difficulty. This set of orthogonal features was introduced to overcome the blatant but often overlooked discrepancy between the need for broad Fourier spatial-frequency components specified in the mathematics

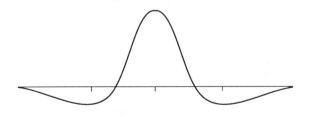

FIG. 3.3.   Cross section of the mexican hat transfer function: A sinusoid multiplied by a gaussian distribution.

and the absence of comparable wide-ranging physiological interactions across the visual fields.

Interestingly, Gabor functions are very similar, if not formally identical, to the "sinc" function that is known to be among the most efficient means of reconstructing sampled images (Pratt, 1978), and, thus, their relationship to the center-surround receptive field may just be fortuitous. (Of course, the nervous system could have evolved toward this optimum shape for the usual adaptive reasons, but that is another matter.) In short, an orthogonal set of Gabor or sinc functions is a mathematical construct of great power that, like the sinusoidal set used in Fourier analysis, would work even if there were no neural-receptive fields possessing the same Mexican Hat shape present in the visual nervous system. And, indeed, this construct does also seem to work to describe visual perception—it has been applied very successfully as a formal model of shape coding by Watson (1983).

Another important point is that a Fourier analysis is only a transformation of the stimulus-form from one representation into another. The output of any convolutional transform of this kind is but another, sometimes more complex, form. The problem of detecting, discriminating, or recognizing forms remains unresolved—the transformed images must still be processed by some other decision-making mechanism to account for experimental and simulated outcomes. In principle, the transformation from the spatial domain to the frequency domain does not solve any of the perceptual problems even though it may simplify them.

Having made these distinctions and having expressed these caveats, I also feel compelled to note that it must not be underestimated just how fruitful and influential Campbell and Robson's ideas of a Fourier visual system containing spatial-frequency channels have been. Their ingenious approach has stimulated a wide variety of novel experimental paradigms of which we literally could not have conceived previous to the introduction of this important concept into experimental studies of vision.

The initial suggestion that spatial-frequency-analysis techniques might be applied to study of visual phenomena can be attributed to Selwyn (1948) and to Schade (1956), who used the spatial frequency idea in a way that implicitly assumed that the visual pathway is a single-channel system that simply operates differently at different spatial frequencies. They measured the threshold contrast of spatial-sinusoidal targets. Lowry and De Palma (1961) were, shortly after, the first to use the spatial frequency idea to study contour enhancement. Without question, however, the major milestone in the more recent development of the spatial-frequency approach was the now classic paper by Campbell and Robson (1968), who seem to have been the first to suggest that different spatial frequencies are handled separately by anatomically different portions of the visual system. This revolutionary idea was based upon two important observations: First, that prolonged adaptation by particular spatial frequencies led to a diminished ability to detect that frequency—an idea expanded upon later by Blakemore and Campbell (1969); and second, that different "channels" seemed to be separately sensitive to the different component harmonics of a square wave—an idea subsequently expanded upon by Graham and Nachmias (1971).

Campbell and Robson's seminal, and (at the risk of offending many of my distinguished colleagues) so-far unsubstantiated, physiological-anatomical idea was that there are actual multiple, anatomical, spatial-frequency-filtering channels in the visual system that operate more or less independently to represent not the local geometrical features or the global shape of the stimulus scene, but the Fourier spatial-frequency components of the pattern.

Exactly what it is that is meant by the key idea has been much argued. To go straight to the source, however, let Robson (1983) himself interpret what he and Campbell meant:

> Although these findings [i.e., Campbell and Robson's] are obviously of some intrinsic interest, their main attraction has derived from their use as a basis for the suggestion that the visual system performs some kind of spatial-frequency analysis of the visual input as a primary step in its image-processing function.
>
> Much of this argument has centered around the bandwidth of the spatial-frequency-selective visual mechanisms since it is maintained by some that a degree of spatial frequency selectively would be shown by many mechanisms which could be much better understood in other terms. Higher degrees of selectivity would be more truly indicative of a frequency-analyzing mechanism. (p. 74)

In this quotation, Robson seems to deemphasize the mathematical aspects of the Fourier theorem in favor of the physiological one. In doing so, I believe he is deviating from the simplest and cleanest possible explanation of the utility of the Fourier model—its value purely as a mathematical, as opposed to a physiological, theory. However, Robson clearly sees the difference between Fourier analysis as a descriptive methodology and the anatomical-physiological mechanism actually analyzing stimuli into quasi-orthogonal channels sensitive to the various component spatial frequencies.

The full range of research that has been generated by the Campbell–Robson contribution in recent years is staggering and patently unreviewable in this book or any other with any aspirations to generality. One cannot go to a contemporary meeting of visionaries (as some visual scientists, not immodestly, are beginning to call themselves) without being overwhelmed by the impact of Campbell and Robson's original concept of visual spatial-frequency analyzers. In this section, I consider the application of their hypothesis to but one aspect of the problem, the results that deal specifically with the detection of gratings.

The detection problem of particular and most fundamental interest in the current context is the determination of the conditions of spatial frequency and contrast at which a gratinglike stimulus can be detected, as opposed to being perceived as an equiluminous area. The spatial frequency, of course, is relatively simply defined by the number of cycles of a repetitive, usually sinusoidal or square wave, stimulus that is present per degree of visual angle.

Contrast, however, is defined in a more complicated way. Consider for a moment the cross-section of a spatial pattern f (x, y) that varies in luminance in accord with the following sinusoidal rule:

$$L_x = A \sin wx + C \tag{3.1}$$

where L_x is the luminance at any horizontal locus x; A is the maximum luminance; and w is the spatial frequency in cycles per unit of x. In this expression, c is a constant ''pedestal'' of uniform luminance upon which the sinusoidal oscillations are superimposed. Such a spatial sinusoid is shown in both plan view and in cross-section Fig. 3.4. The dimensions of the cross-section, it should be noted, are x (the distance along the horizontal axis)—all cross-sections taken along any vertical line being the same in this situation — and the luminance L_x at any x as defined by the equation just given. (Because there is no actual functional variation in y, in fact, it must be appreciated that this is actually a one-dimensional stimulus in a formal sense, I return to consider this matter in more detail later.)

The amplitude of the sinusoidal-luminance variation has two critical values of special importance to this discussion—luminance of the trough (L_t) and the luminance of the peak (L_p), the lowest and highest values respectively of the fluctuations in stimulus intensity. Contrast or, more precisely, contrast ratio (CR) is defined by the following expression.

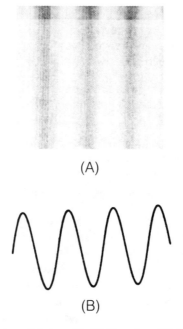

(A)

(B)

FIG. 3.4.   A spatial sinusoid: (A) Plan view; (B) Cross section.

$$CR = \frac{L_p - L_t}{L_p + L_t}$$
                                                          (3.2)

Such an expression takes into account not only the difference between Lp and Lt, but also the magnitude of the 4 pedestal (as reflected in the term $L_p + L_t$).[4]

With these definitions in hand, we can now turn to the original problem: How do the spatial frequency and contrast of a grating jointly determine the ability of the visual system to detect such a spatially fluctuating luminance distribution? In all cases contrast will be degraded by adjusting the CR upwards from zero, a value representing a uniformly illuminated area, to 1.0, a value representing a grating with perfectly black and white lines.

To answer this general question, there are several issues that must be considered separately. First, what is the pattern of detectability when a single spatial sinusoidal grating varies in frequency and contrast? Second, what are the parameters of detectability of compound gratings constructed from two or more single frequency sinusoids? The first issue has been answered in great detail, and the relevant response curve is well understood; in fact, it is almost a classic. The second issue is less well understood and lies at the heart of much of the current controversy in this field. I present the relevant psychophysical data independently of the neural hypotheses in which they are usually entangled.

Let us first consider the detectability of pure, single-frequency, spatial sinusoids. Qualitatively, the nature of the response is best illustrated by the diagram in Fig. 3.5. This figure displays a sinusoidal stimulus-field that varies in spatial frequency (across the horizontal dimension) and in contrast (across the vertical dimension). This figure was originally prepared by Campbell and Robson (1968), but has been published so many times in so many different places that it has now virtually taken on the role of a cult object. Notwithstanding this near deification of what is otherwise an interesting demonstration, the point of this figure is that the detectability of gratings depends both upon their contrast and upon their spatial frequency. In general, the lower the contrast, the lower their detectability. This can be seen by attendiing solely to any narrow vertical region on Fig. 3.5. Gratings always disappear at the lower portions of the vertical segment as the contrast is diminished.

Detection sensitivity as a function of spatial frequency, however, varies in a more complex manner that is also displayed in this figure. The least detectable contrast (i.e., the lowest point on the vertical axis at which a grating of a particular spatial frequency is visible) varies from frequency to frequency and is optimal at an intermediate spatial frequency. Depending upon how far away this book is from your eyes (and the vagaries of print reproduction), this intermediate point may vary. However, at a normal reading distance it should be near the region

---

[4] A clearly written "primer" of Fourier analysis can be found in Naomi Weisstein's totally enjoyable tutorial entitled "The Joy of Fourier Analysis" (Weisstein, 1980).

FIG. 3.5.   The modulation transfer function graphically demonstrated (from Barlow & Mollon, 1982).

"5 cycles per degree of visual angle." In fact, if the spatial frequency is controlled very precisely by holding the viewing distance constant, and if the contrast is regulated better than can be done with the reproduction process available to book publishers, then the peak spatial frequency sensitivity actually is closer to 10 cycles/deg. This optimum spatial frequency is measured by determining the threshold contrast (i.e., the lowest contrast at which the grating can be seen as a fluctuating spatial pattern, as opposed to an equally luminous surface) over a suitably wide range of spatial frequencies. This function is now known as the *Contrast Sensitivity Function* (CSF) in opposition to the purely optical transform known as the *modulation transfer function* (MTF) (see Fig. 3.6).

It is very important for the reader to realize that the "tuned" or "resonant" peak occurring at 8–10 cycles/deg in the CSF relating spatial frequency and contrast detection is neurophysiological-psychophysical property of the entire visual system. The MTF of the optics of the eye, on the other hand, must be measured in a different way, by measuring the dispersion of light around what should be a sharp image of a scare wave grating on the retina. In this case, the MTF curve does not show a "resonant" peak at 10 cycles/deg, but is monotonic, decreasing progressively with increasing spatial frequency. The reduction in contrast in this case is primarily because of the "leaking" or "blurring" of light sideways from the otherwise well-focused grating lines because of purely optical aberrations in the light path within the eye. Both a typical monotonic optical MTF of the optics of the eye and a typical tuned or "resonant" psychophysical CSF are shown in Fig. 3.6.

As I noted, the results obtained in a compound grating-detection experiment are much less clearly understood and more controversial than when only a single spatial frequency is involved. One reason, of course, is that the stimulus situation is much more complex than when a single spatial frequency is utilized. When one spatial sinusoid is involved, there are only two salient degrees of freedom—contrast and spatial frequency. When two spatial sinusoids are mixed, however, both the contrast and the spatial frequency of each as well as the phase angle between the two can vary independently, and thus there are at least five degrees of freedom that have to be specified to fully define the stimulus situation. As the number of constituent sinusoids in a compound wave increases, the number of degrees of freedom increases even further. Furthermore, new, more complex

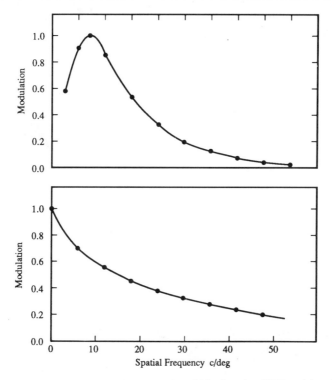

FIG. 3.6.   The subjective (A) contrast sensitivity function (CSF) and the objective (B) modulation transfer function (MTF) (redrawn from Ohzu & Enoch, 1972).

waveforms (other than simple sinusoids) are formed from the destructive and constructive interference of the two spatial sinusoids.

To begin our discussion of the detection of compound gratings, let us first consider a relatively simple case—a mixture of two spatial sinusoids of different frequencies, as shown in Fig. 3.7 a & b. When these two components are added together, there is a summation and subtraction of their respective luminance peaks and troughs such that the combination luminance pattern shown in Fig. 3.7c obtains. The interesting psychophysical question to be asked of such a stimulus is:

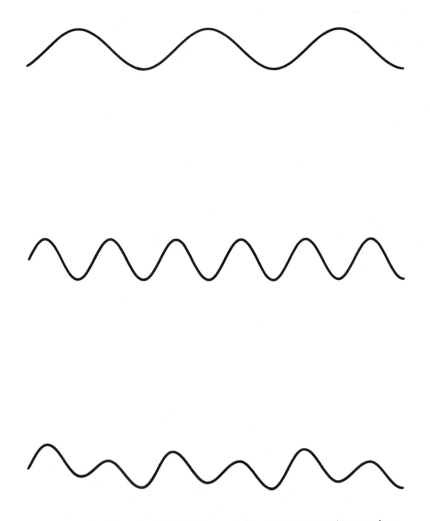

FIG. 3.7. Two sinusoids (A & B) summate to produce a complex wave form (c).

What is the relation between the just detectable contrast of the combination stimulus and the just detectable contrasts of the two individual components? The answer to this question, obtained in many independent studies (but, perhaps, best exemplified by the pioneering work of Graham & Nachmias, 1971) is that the combined stimulus, even though it has a substantially larger contrast ratio than either of its two components, exhibits only a slightly enhanced detectability. That is, the detectability of the high-contrast combination of two low-contrast spatial sinusoids is just slightly better than the detectability of the more detectable of the two components themselves.

This surprising result is considered by many (including Graham, 1980, and Julesz & Schumer, 1981) to be strong evidence that a multiple-channel Fourier analyzing system (as opposed to a single-channel system) underlies many aspects of spatial vision. The key idea is that the putative channels are independent in terms of their detectability and that the contrast threshold of the most sensitive channel alone determines the threshold of the combination stimulus. Because there is actually no energy at the spatial-frequencies defined by the irregular-appearing peaks and troughs of the combination stimuli (a fact analogous to the absence of energy at the combination frequencies of auditory tones), and the putative spatial-frequency channels are thought to respond only to the components where energy is actually located, the suggestion of independent channels is supported. In other words, the threshold to the combination stimulus seems to be determined by the most sensitive threshold to the individual frequency component where physical energy is present and is not affected by the combination waveform that possesses no real energy. In this case it is the combination waveform that is the mathematical fiction, just as in Fourier analysis it is the derived sinusoidal components.

This does not explain, however, why the actual thresholds measured in this prototypical experiment in which two spatial frequencies are superpositioned are, in fact, slightly lower (i.e., compound gratings can be detected at somewhat lower contrasts than that of the individual components) than those measured when the same components are presented singly. The answer proposed (originally by Sachs, Nachmias, & Robson, 1971) was that a kind of *probability summation* occurs in this situation. Specifically, near threshold, they suggested that each individual channel has a certain stochastically varying probability of detecting its particular spatial frequency. Therefore, the joint probability of either of two channels actually ''seeing'' a grating is likely to be somewhat better than of one alone for purely statistical reasons that are totally unrelated to the shape of the compound stimulus. This observed slight advantage of two independent detectors over a single one occurs even if the two detectors are not interacting in any way other than simply contributing their individual probabilities of detection to a joint output.

Probability summation of this kind is modest in amplitude compared to the increased sensitivity that would have been displayed to the enhanced peaks and troughs of the resultant contrast of summating spatial frequencies if the channels were not independent but, rather, were interacting. It is just the kind of subtle influence that could account for the slight increase in detectability of a compound stimulus in spite of the fact that the visual system exhibits no sizeable increase in sensitivity to the greatly enhanced contrast of the combination stimulus.

For more complex composites of three or more sinusoidal spatial frequencies, the possible increase in amplitude of the combined wave, and thus the contrast, is even larger, but the results are comparable. There is typically only a slightly reduced contrast threshold to the combination beyond that of the most sensitive-spatial frequency component.

There is some uncertainty concerning the influence on the CSF of the phase relationships between the component spatial frequencies of a compound wave.[5] In some task situations, phase seems to matter very little, whereas in others it is of great consequence in determining the contrast threshold. For example, when the spatial sinusoidal stimuli are both very close to their own threshold contrast, phase is not an important variable in vision. However, when one of two spatial sinusoids is very luminous relative to the other, then distinct differences in the CSF occur as the phase relationship between the two components is varied. A key study of this problem was reported by Nachmias and Webster (1975). They measured an effect of phase but discovered that it occurred only when the two component spatial frequencies were relatively close to each other. Specifically, the high-frequency grating had to be no more than three times the frequency of the low-frequency grating for the phase relationship between the two to affect the CSF. Indeed, it seems to be generally true that phase relations matter only within this 3-to-1 range and then only if at least one of the signals is much above its contrast threshold. This conclusion has recently been confirmed and elaborated by Lawden (1983). Sagi and Hochstein (1983) also show strong phase effects for two suprathreshold gratings in a discriminability task, but only within the limit of these constraints.

When compounds of several sinusoids are used as masks, however, the results are not so clear-cut in a detection task. Nachmias and Rogowitz (1983) have shown that the detectability of a 2.2 cycles/deg sinusoid is strongly affected by the phase of a masking mixture of 8.8, 11, and 13.2 cycles/deg sinusoids. Here all three components exceed the 3-to-1 frequency difference limit expressed previously, but presumably the combination frequency, despite its zero energy, can in some way play the role of a lower frequency mask.

There are, however, situations beyond simple contrast detection in which phase can be shown to play an important role. For example, the phase relation between a complex mask consisting of several superimposed sinusoidal frequencies and a target consisting of a single pure sinusoidal spatial frequency has been studied

---

[5] Simply put, the phase relation (or phase) indicates the relative time or position at which each wave-form exhibits equivalent values. For example, if two wave-forms both peak at points 3 deg apart, that 3 deg would be their "phase difference."

by Lawton (1984). She found that the observer's ability to detect such a sinusoid when it was masked by a mixture of other sinusoids varied as a function of the phase angle between the single-masked and the combined-masking sinusoids. Curiously, the effect of phase angle did not vary continuously but only between zero deg and 90 deg. More extreme phase shifts (between 90 and 180 deg) showed no such functional effect.

Lawton's experiments demonstrate an important point—that in some contexts phase can matter, even though in others that may seem to be very closely related it exerts only a minimal influence. It is essential, however, to appreciate that her experiment was not a pure threshold contrast-detection experiment. Rather, it was a signal-in-noise detection task that had more in commom with the dot-masking experiments to be discussed later in this chapter than with the contrast-detection paradigm just discussed. This is but another example of a situation in which a modest change in psychophysical procedure can drastically change the obtained results.

The general significance of this work on phase lies in its contribution to our knowledge of the nature of the underlying processes that may account for the Fourierlike behavior of the nervous system. It is a mathematical fact that any system that does not maintain phase when it analyzes a waveform into compo- nent orthogonal functions will not provide the information necessary for the reconstruction of the original wave form. Any measured phase sensitivity reflects such an ability to preserve that information and thus adds a certain amount of plausibility to the Fourier models. It is, in a sense, unfortunate that the results concerning phase are so ambiguous. A firm result in either direction would help enormously to resolve the controversy over this particular theoretical model.

In the preceding discussion I concentrated on the effects of spatial frequency and phase, but there are, of course, other aspects of spatial frequency that might also differentially affect the action of the putative spatial-frequency channels or some other analogous mechanism. One of the major alternative dimensions that has been glossed over is that of stimulus uncertainty. That is: What effect does prior knowledge of what and where the stimulus will be have on detectability of a grating? Davis, Kramer, and Graham (1983) have explored this aspect of the spatial frequency problem and have determined that uncertainty on the part of the observer with regard to the position and the spatial frequency of a low- contrast grating does affect its detectability. However, if the contrast is the dimen- sion that is uncertain (in terms of what it will be in any given stimulus trial), then this uncertainty on the part of the stimulus has no effect on detectability. They also interpret this result to support the spatial-frequency channel idea.

The effect of uncertainty on grating detectability is not the same as with other stimuli. When alphabetic letters are used (Posner, Snyder, & Davidson, 1980), then there is a much smaller effect of uncertainty. Indeed, when alphabetic characters are used, the whole edifice of the spatial-frequency hypothesis is threatened. The predictions of the model just do not fit the data. For example, when alphabetic characters are used in a recognition type experiment (Coffin, 1978) the spatial-frequency components of the characters did not provide a good explanation of the confusion errors among various characters; the frequency components of various characters simply did not correlate in the same way as the confusion errors. It should be noted that in other situations, however, simply varying the number of stimulus alternatives (this is, of course, one way to manipulate the degree of uncertainty) as evidenced in the work of Staller and Lappin (1981) as well as Lappin and Uttal (1976) can and does produce strong effects on the measured detection scores. As another example, Swenson and Judy (1981) have also shown strong effects of stimulus positional uncertainty in a detection task involving noisy pixel-type stimuli that simulated CAT-scan displays. Davis (1981), Cormak and Blake (1980), and Graham, Robson, and Nachmias (1978) have all also demonstrated that uncertainty concerning the spatial frequency of a to-be-detected grating reduces its detectability. Indeed, in most cases in the now classic signal-detection literature, we see uncertainty reducing detectability.

In terms of the limits of the Fourier model it is important to also appreciate that the work that has been done in the past in this field of the Fourier analysis of visual processes has largely been one dimensional. "Two-dimensional" gratings, of course, are actually one-dimensional functions because they do not vary as a function of one of the orthogonal axes—the vertical or y axis. A true analog of the spatial-frequency filtering properties of the eye is more likely to be found, it has been suggested, in a true two-dimensional approximation to a Fourier stimulus such as the one shown in Fig. 3.8. A number of investigators have begun to appreciate the limited approximation to a real-world stimulus that

Space domain

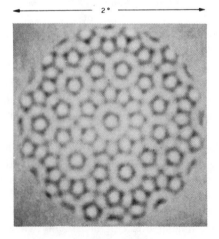

FIG. 3.8. The two-dimensional Fourier spectrum of a stimulus defined in both planar dimensions (from Daugman, 1984).

a grating represents and the importance of this two-dimensional representation to our testing of the plausibility of real spatial-frequency channels in the eye. As mentioned earlier, Watson (1982) has proposed that there are units in the visual system that are better approximated by the two-dimensional grating patches in which a sinusoid was modulated by a Gaussian as shown in Fig. 3.3.

Perhaps the most intriguing analysis of the two-dimensional problem has been carried out by Daugman (1984). Daugman not only discussed the nature of the more appropriate stimulus and thus clarified the true two-dimensional nature of any putative Fourier "channels," but also carried out psychophysical masking experiments using stimuli like those shown in Fig. 3.8 in order to define the characteristic "shapes" of the receptive fields of those channels. His data were analyzed in terms of the threshold elevation (for detection) of a two-dimensional stimulus of variable spatial frequency when it was masked by a similar (but constant) grating stimulus (with a 9 cycle/deg spatial frequency) oriented vertically and with a constant 32% contrast ratio. Daugman plots his data in the form of a two-dimensional graph with the height of the peaks all normalized to about 2,000% of the unmasked contrast of the stimulus to show the masking effect. This allows him to describe the true two-dimensional attributes of the putative Fourier channels. His results suggest a different channel shape than is usually assumed, one that, although elliptical, is much more like the classic receptive field profiles than most visual scientists had previously assumed. An even symmetric and an odd symmetric version of the field shape are shown in Fig. 3.9.

The experiments concerning contrast detection in both masked and unmasked contexts that are discussed so briefly here merely tap the surface of a very much more extensive set of experimental data that has accumulated in recent years concerning spatial-frequency detection. The elucidation of the putative nature of the Fourier channels (which may or may not exist in the nervous system, a matter yet to be resolved) has been accompanied by a number of specific mathematical theories describing how such multiple-channel mechanisms might account for the phenomena associated with the detection of compound gratings. Julesz and Schumer (1981) review many up to that date and, in addition to the ones already mentioned, note should particularly be made of the work of Norma Graham (in particular Graham, 1977), and MacLeod and Rosenfeld (1972a, and 1972b). Many other attempts to describe the data of grating detection in purely formal terms also exist, and new ones emerge constantly.

Again, a caveat must be expressed—No matter how well any of those formal models fit the data, their physiological assumptions are separable, and a good methematical fit does not necessarily establish anatomical truth. One hopes this important aspect of Fourier's original message will not be lost in our enthusiasm for this otherwise exciting development in perceptual theory.

It should also be mentioned in passing that the visual detection of temporally varying stimuli—for example, flicker or gaps in a train of flashes—is also a vigorously researched topic that should be of interest to students of this field for

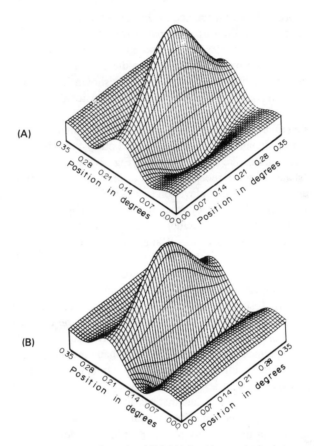

(A)

(B)

FIG. 3.9.   The two-dimensional filter obtained from a single observer assuming (A) even and (B) odd symmetry respectively (from Daugman, 1984).

many reasons, not the least of which are the temporal-spatial relations that are uniquitous in this domain. The main interest in this book, however, is with the spatial attributes of vision, and that temporal work is, therefore, not immediately germane. To leave this topic without at least noting that some of the spatial attributes of vision interact strongly with some of the temporal ones, however, would be negligent. The reader is directed to articles by D. H. Kelly (1972) and R. M. Boynton (1972) in Vol. 7/4 of the *Handbook of Sensory Physiology* (Jameson & Hurvich, 1972) for comprehensive reviews of this topic.

C. THE DETECTION OF DOTTED FORMS IN DOTTED NOISE

In the preceding section I considered a detection task in which the degradation of the stimulus-form was achieved by reducing the contrast. The threshold contrast thus became the dependent measure of the observer's ability to detect the nonuniform luminance pattern that has been quantified in the form of a spatial-frequency pattern. In this section I consider a somewhat different experimental paradigm—one, the reader should be forewarned, in which there are many formal similarities to the grating experiments just described hidden among what are really only superficial methodological differences. Specifically, I expand upon my discussion of the detection of dotted forms in dotted noise, an experimental approach that has dominated my own laboratory research for most of the last decade and was briefly introduced in another context at the beginning of this chapter. As with the spatial sinusoidal gratings, the stimuli in this case (dotted stimulus-forms displaying some kind of order, are well enough above threshold luminance that energy-dependent detection is not an issue. In the undegraded form in which it is shown here, such a stimulus can be detected, indeed even recognized, with great ease even when presented in very brief exposures. If presented in this unattenuated and undegraded form, performance on most visual tasks would be virtually perfect.

Therefore, to use this stimulus-form as a probe into the mysteries of human form perception, it must be degraded. Degradation of dotted stimulus-forms is accomplished by superimposing upon each stimulus-form a constellation of other identical, but randomly positioned, dots. Thus, this experiment becomes a prototypical example of a signal-in-noise detection task comparable to the electrical communication or auditory signal-in-noise paradigms, but in two (or three) dimensions rather than in one. An example of a stereoscopic dotted stimulus is shown in Fig. 3.10.

This type of detection task is particularly suitable for explorations concerning the influence of pure spatial organization or arrangement on visual form perception. Overall or global form effects are emphasized just because local features do not, in fact, exist. Dots are components that possess no features of their own

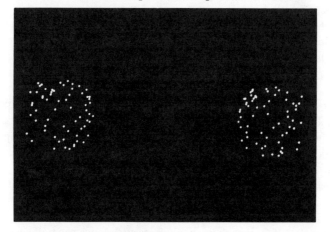

FIG. 3.10.   A random dot stereogram of a paraboloid of rotation convex toward the observer.

other than locus and, inconsequentially, brightness. It is only because of the global organization of a constellation of dots that an organized form may be perceived.

The dotted stimuli in dotted-noise-masking procedure is a paradigm that can be used to study the detection of forms in two, three (using stereoscopic disparity as a cue), and even in four dimensions if temporal variables are introduced in the experimental design. The technique is particularly easily implemented with the kind of modern computer-controlled, point-plotting displays that are now becoming ubiquitous in psychological research laboratories.

Another important aspect of this technique is that it can be applied to the study of geometric forms that are somewhat closer to real visual forms than are the already transformed abstractions represented by square or sinusoidal gratings. Although this judgment is admittedly controversial, and one must not lose sight of the incontestable fact that there are many similarities in the two techniques, a dotted form is arquably more realistic (i.e., more like real stimulus-forms) than is a grating in terms of the spatial Gestalt. This is so even though in principle all of the attributes of one can be simulated with the other. It is just a practical consideration that a somewhat different mathematical algorithm may be more conveniently applied in one situation than in another. In the case of dotted stimuli, a discrete autocorrelation or cross-correlational transform is more natural than the spatial Fourier analysis that is appropriate for continuous grating like figures. Furthermore, there are formal similarities between the Fourier and autocorrelational analyses by means of which they may be interconverted. Therefore, at a theoretical level they must, by definition, be equivalent to each other and neither can say more or less than the other about how we see.

In summary, the dotted-signal-in-dotted-visual-noise paradigm does emphasize some aspects of visual information processing that are not so evident when one uses the Fourier approach, simply because it is operating in a space (x,y,z) that is more familiar than the Fourier frequency domain (u,v,w).

The dot-masking paradigm has proven over the years to be a rich source of data and ideas related to problems of form perception. I have reported over a decade of laboratory research in a series of papers and in four major monographs (Uttal, 1975, 1983, 1985, 1987). The purity of the stimulus-forms used in this study (i.e., their freedom from both energy-driven receptor influences and context-dependent semantic and cognitive influences) allowed my colleagues and I to examine some subtle information-processing attributes of visual detection processes that are often hidden or overwhelmed by other energy-sensitive, peripheral, or meaning-dominated central effects when nondotted, natural, or realistic stimulus-forms are used.

The history of dot masking as a formal experimental procedure (it probably existed in an analogous form as practical visual tasks in real-life, camouflage-type situations long before this date) goes back to a largely overlooked paper by R.S. French (1954). French implicitly foresaw the advantages of a methodology in which the signal-to-noise ratio (somewhat arbitrarily measured by the number of dots in the stimulus-form and in the mask, respectively) could be used to vary the visibility of a visual form. The idea of using dots is important just because it minimizes the role of the *nature* of the components and emphasizes the role of their *arrangement*. Given the ubiquity of data suggesting that this is, in fact, the way human beings see, this was not a trivial advantage. Another early publication in which many of the same ideas were developed was written by Goldmeier (1965). He had been working with rather noisy radiographs of cancerous tissue and noted the analogy between those poor-quality and naturally degraded X-ray pictures and the dotted-forms-in-dotted-noise paradigm. Some of his pictures could well have been used as stimuli in my own experiments.

One of the early major discoveries ccncerning form perception that was made using this method was the very straightforward and undeniable fact that some constellations of dots are more detectable than others, even when dot numerosity, spacing, and indeed all other variables other than arrangement itself are tightly controlled. That is, the global geometry, per se, of a constellation of dots (and presumably other kinds of stimulus-forms) influences detectability above and beyond the specific details of the constituent local features. This is the essence of the controversy between holistic and elementalistic theories of form perception. I return in chapter 4 to consider this issue in detail, but for the moment it should be noted that a holistic point of view permeates much of the rest of my discussion. It should not be overlooked in the interim, however, that it is also possible that the issue is really confused by a matter of scale. That is, it is possible that the parts or whole aspects of the physical stimulus may be less important than their relative size in the perceptual representation of the observer.

When dotted stimulus-forms are used as stimuli the local features have been reduced to nil and it is only their global arrangement that seems to matter. In most of our experiments the results seem not to be greatly affected by the clarity or focus of the individual dots. Indeed, for those stimuli whose exposure duration is very brief it is moot whether they are in good focus in even the best refracted eye, the sharpening effects of lateral inhibition not being evoked to overcome the normal amounts of image blur due to retractive errors in even the best eyes until long durations (> 100 msec) are used.

For the detection of two-dimensional forms and, possibly, three-dimensional forms as well, although the results in that case are somewhat equivocal, many of our results can be summarized as reflecting the operation of a general law— "The Rule of Linear Periodicity." This rule emphasizes the prepotency of straight, periodically spaced dotted lines in human dotted-form detection. It is important to appreciate that despite the human sensitivity to straight-lines and the traditional role that straight lines have played in neurophysiology under the influence of Hubel and Wiesel's many distinguished neurophysiological studies, other sensitivities are both conceivable and physiologically plausible. For example, Fukushima (1970) has proposed a curvilinearity detector in the form of a computer model that is also based upon known physiological principles.

Nevertheless, the facts obtained in our form-detection experiments also indicate that lines are the prepotent stimulus for human dotted-form perception in two-dimensional viewing. Additional support for the prepotency of dotted straight lines has come from the work of Foster (1979) who, using a discriminability task, observed a degradation in performance when the dotted stimuli that had to be compared by observers deviated from linearity. My own study (Uttal, 1973a) also speaks to this same fact as do the results of a longer monograph (Uttal, 1975).

The reasons for special visual sensitivity to straight lines are suggested, but the underlying physiological mechanisms are not illuminated or explained, by a specific mathematical transformation—the autocorrelation that was developed in the monograph (Uttal, 1975). This transformation is embodied in a formal model that has been developed to describe the data obtained in a series of experiments using the dotted-form-in-dotted-noise. The autocorrelation model is a means of processing simulations of the dotted stimulus-forms in a manner that produces results that have been shown in many cases to be analogous to the way in which the same stimuli are processed by the human visual system. To the degree that the autocorrelational transformation and psychophysical phenomena agree, it can be asserted that the model is sensitive to many of the same attributes of the stimulus as is the perceptual skill. Beyond this statement of analogy, however, interpretations concerning the exact details of the underlying physiological mechanisms become highly speculative.[6]

It is, therefore, extremely instructive to apply the autocorrelation model, which does a surprisingly competent job of actually predicting the psychophysical detectability of two-dimensional dotted stimuli, to the psychophysical data. This is so even though the model does work well in a three-dimensional stimulus environment.

The autocorrelation transformation is a special case of a convolution integral based on the following formula:

$$A_c = \iint f(x, y) \cdot f(x + \Delta x, y + \Delta y) \, dy \, dx \qquad (3.3)$$

where Δx and Δy are shifts in the positions of the points of a stimulus-form $f(x,y)$ required to produce a shifted replica: $f(x + \Delta x, y + \Delta y)$.

Although this formula is presented here in terms of the integral calculus and in the terminology of infinitesimals, in the actual computer model that was developed, the transformation is implemented in the form of a discrete approximation to this equation. Indeed, some of my mathematical colleagues, more precise than I in their terminology, may prefer to call it an "autocorrelationlike"

---

[6] I must reiterate a point made earlier. There is nothing unique about the autocorrelation. If it works, so too then must a Fourier-type analysis, since the Fourier transform of the autocorrelation must be the same as the power spectrum density and vice versa. However, there is a different emphasis and a different point of view that makes the autocorrelation approach especially useful. Furthermore, different mechanisms must be implemented to produce the power spectrum and the autocorrelation respectively, so there are real differences in implementation between the two theories.

transformation, a nomenclatural purification I would happily accept. A complete description of the discrete computational algorithm actually used to compute the autocorrelation has been presented in Uttal (1975). A family of A_c values must be computed for all possible Δx and Δy combinations to fill the autocorrelation space.

The autocorrelational space for a two-dimensional surface is made up of a number of peaks distributed in the Δx, Δy space. By applying the following empirical expression:

$$F_m = \frac{\sum\limits_{n=1}^{N} \sum\limits_{i=1}^{N} (A_n \cdot A_i)/d_{ni}}{N} \tag{3.4}$$

a single numerical "Figure of Merit" (F_m) can be generated for each autocorrelated stimulus pattern. In this expression, A_i and A_n are the amplitudes of peaks taken pairwise, D is the Pythagorean distance in the Δx, Δy space between the two peaks, and N is the number of peaks. The purely arbitrary and ad hoc expression produces families of F_m's that are closely associated with the relative psychophysical detectability of sets of stimulus-forms.[7]

In one of the earlier monographs (Uttal, 1975), I reported how the effects of variation of a number of different attributes of two-dimensional stimulus-forms were evaluated in a series of psychophysical experiments using only two-dimensional visual stimuli and masks. Specifically, I considered the effects of each of the following attributes and found the results indicated for each of the following dimensions:

1. Dot numerosity—more dots, more detectable.
2. Line orientation—no effect.
3. Deformation of straight-lines into curves and angles—more deformation, less detectable.
4. Collinear dot-spacing irregularity—more irregular, less detectable.
5. Transverse dot-spacing irregularity—more irregular, less detectable.
6. Missing parts in triangles—sides more important than corners.
7. Polygonal orientation—no effect.
8. Distortions of squares into parallelograms—more distortion, less detectable.

---

[7] It is interesting to note that however arbitrary and ad hoc the figure of merit actually was originally, it is the one part of this theoretical system that actually may have a *physiological correlate*. Professor Ken Goryo of Chiba University in Japan and I have recently observed an evoked brain potential that is highly, but inversely, correlated with the figure of merit. The potential is evoked by stimuli for which the figure of merit is known; its amplitude is small for ordered forms and large for poorly ordered forms. This interesting lead suggests a kind of physiological reality for the figure-of-merit expression that had not been anticipated.

9. Organized straight-line patterns versus—"pick-up-sticks" patterns composed of the same lines—more organized, more detectable.

10. Distortions of squares and triangles by misplacing one or more corners—more distortion, lees detectable.

11. Figural goodness as defined in Garner and Clement (1963)—no effect.

In the next series of experiments, reported in Uttal (1983), I turned from two-dimensional stimuli hidden in two-dimensional masks to stimuli that, while still two-dimensional themselves (single dots, lines, and planes), were embedded among random visual masking-dots that were arrayed in three-dimensional space. This work also achieved a number of interesting results:

1. Just as in the first series of experiments, as an unmitigated generality, increasing the number of masking-dots monotonically reduced the detectability of a dotted stimulus-form when all other variables are held constant. In other words, the raw signal (stimulus-dot numerosity)-to-noise (masking-dot numerosity) ratio was a powerful determinant of dotted-form detection. Although not surprising, this outcome was an important cross-referencing parameter between different experiments and is of interest in its own right. This outcome confirmed and extended the findings concerning signal-to-noise ratios from the earlier study with two-dimensional stimuli.

2. The position of a repetitive flashing dot within the apparent cubical space exerted only a minor effect on its detectability. A dot placed far off the rear, lower, right-hand corner was seen slightly less well than dots at other positions, and one centered in space was seen slightly better. Although I presented no equivalent data concerning the translations of lines or planes, within similar limits and on the basis of my two-dimensional results, I believe this result also holds for such multidimensional stimuli.

3. Repetitively flashed dots with interdot intervals of 100 msec were seen better than those with shorter or longer intervals when the number of flashed dots was held constant. The function relating single-dot detectability to interdot interval was thus nonmonotonic and suggests the existence of an optimum interval of about this duration.

4. In dotted-form discrimination, there was a substantial advantage gained by using a dichoptic viewing condition that allowed the perceptual construction of depth compared to either binocular or monocular viewing conditions in which no disparity cue to depth was present. Somewhat surprisingly, binocular viewing produced higher detection scores than did monocular viewing, in spite of the fact that there was no information difference between the stimuli in the two nondisparity viewing conditions.

5. Increasing the interdot interval between sequential dots in a plotted straight-line of dots led to a monotonic and nearly linear reduction in the detectability

of the line. It is unclear whether this was a result of the increase in the interval per se or due to the increased number of masking-dots encompassed by the duration of the dot train. What is certain is that apparent movement did not substitute in any way for simultaneity.

6. Very surprisingly, irregularity of the temporal intervals between the plotting of successive dots did not appreciably diminish dotted-line detection. A high degree of interdot-interval irregularity could be tolerated without reduction in detection scores.

7. Spatial irregularity of the dots along a straight line affected detectability at short interdot-intervals ($\leq$ 30 msec). However, at longer dot intervals these same spatial irregularities exerted little influence on detectability. In some manner, visual mechanisms seemed to be able to compensate for these spatial distortions if sufficient time elapses between the plotting of sequential dots.

8. An increase in the disorder of the sequence in which a series of regularly spaced (in time and position) lines of dots was plotted produced only a modest, though monotonic, decrease in the detectability of the form. This form of irregularity, so extreme that it violated the spatiotemporal topology of the stimulus-form, could still be partially overcome, presumably by the same mechanisms that were capable of "smoothing" temporal and spatial irregularity.

9. Dotted-line orientation in space was ineffective in influencing detectability scores. Visual space was isotropic for diagonal lines.

10. When two planes were to be discriminated from each other with regard to their respective depths:

   a. The greater the dichoptic disparity between the two planes, the more easily one was discriminated from the other.

   b. The effect of the number of dots in the two planes was relatively small. Indeed, discrimination of a highly reduced stimulus consisting of only two dots was easily accomplished.

   c. A reduction in viewing time led to a progressive though modest reduction in the discrimination of the two planes.

   d. When a burst of masking-dots followed the presentation of a dichoptic stimulus, stereoscopic performance was especially degraded at intervals less than 50 msec.

11. The form of a planar stimulus composed of even a relatively large number of randomly arrayed dots had a surprisingly small effect on its detectability, given what we had previously learned in the earlier two-dimensional studies with dotted-outline forms. Even when the viewing time was reduced, the effect of form remained small. Furthermore, the effect of even as drastic a manipulation as changing the stimulus-form from a square to an elongated rectangle was slight. However, this conclusion did not hold for forms defined by dotted-outlines. Dotted-outline forms showed a strong increase in detectability as they became more oblong.

12. There was virtually no effect on detectability when a static-viewed planar stimulus-form defined by a random array of dots was rotated to different positions around the y axis. When the form was rotated in more complex ways around two or three axes the experimental outcome was equally unaffected. Space also appeared to be isotropic for planes of this kind.

13. The gradient of form detectability was very steep between 88 and 90 degs of rotation, but virtually flat over the entire range from 0 to 88 degs.

14. When a frontoparallel-oriented plane was placed in different positions within a cubical space filled with masking dots, it was most easily detected at the center of the cube. Detectability diminished, therefore, where disparity was greatest in either the crossed or uncrossed direction.

These, then, are the major findings that were obtained in the study of the influence of stimulus-form on the detectability of two-dimensional dotted forms masked by a three-dimensionally dispersed array of masking dots.

The autocorrelation transformation also successfully modeled these psychophysical data. Because of the essentially two-dimensional nature of the stimulus-forms it was easy to represent many of the stimuli that were utilized in these experiments with the autocorrelation mathematics and to calculate the Figure of Merit. Some striking findings emerged when this was done; most notably, evidence was obtained to support the prediction of both qualitative and quantitative differences between planes composed of random arrays of dots and those composed of dotted outlines.

In the next study (Uttal, 1985) using this paradigm, my laboratory concentrated on the detection of truly three-dimensional forms, nonplanar surfaces that were created by elastically stretching planar prototypes into quadric and cubic surfaces. A number of interesting results also came from this work:

1. Different nonplanar stimulus types were detected with varying degrees of ease in the dotted-surface-in-dotted-mask-type of task. A parabolic arch was detected slightly better than the average, and a double cubic and hyperbolic paraboloid were detected slightly less well than the average. However, these effects were all surprisingly small.

2. Distributing the dots of the mask throughout the perceived space by means of disparity-controlled stereopsis has the effect of dedensifying the mask and increasing performance when the stimulus-forms were generated from random-dot arrays but not when they were generated from regular grids.

3. The degree of deformation of simple types of polynomial-generated, nonplanar surfaces, however, had little effect on detectability. Simple types are those in which the surfaces possessed less than two maxima or minima. This null result obtained in spite of the fact that the apparent surface of an elastically stretched stimulus may have a greatly enlarged area compared to its planar prototype and thus lower apparent stimulus-form dot density.

4. The degree of deformation from a plane to a nonplanar stimulus surface, however, did exert a measurable, though modest, influence on detectability when more than a single maximum or minimum was present on the nonplanar surface.

5. As the number of maxima and minima increased—for example, as regulated by the spatial frequency of a sinusoidal surface undulating in depth—detectability decreased further. However, close examination of such stimulus-forms indicated that a major portion of the effect of this parameter of form could be attributed to inadequate information being available to define the shape. At lower stimulus-form dot densities, the sampling density was insufficient for even an ideal observer to reconstruct the form. The human observer did only slightly less well than the limits imposed by the sampling theorem—a remarkable outcome in itself.

6. The signal-to-noise ratio was a strong determinant of the detectability of a form. Either increasing the stimulus-form dot density or decreasing the masking-dot density increases the detectability of the form. In sample experiments in which the effect of form was negligible, over 90% of the variance in performance scores was accounted for by the signal-to-noise ratio alone. There are several paradoxical or puzzling results implicit in this list that should be especially noted:

   a. *Dedensifying* the dots of a random-dot array *stimulus-form* by stretching it into three-dimensional space did not reduce the form's detectability. However, the stereoscopic procedure did strongly reduce the effect of a given number of masking-dots compared to monocular viewing. Therefore, *dedensifying* the *masking-dots* did reduce detectability of a stimulus form.

   b. The size and mix of the stimulus set often influenced the detectability of individual members of the set.

   c. Grid stimulus-forms did not exhibit even a slight sensitivity to nonplanar shape compared to that exhibited by forms generated from random-dot arrays.

The absence of a strong form-effect in three dimensions comparable to that observed in two dimensions can be interpreted in terms of limits on our ability to process the spatial information contained in the constructed three-dimensional information. Some computer theorists have suggested that true three-dimensional form recognition is not possible (even though we can construct three dimensions from two and can recognize three-dimensional objects by processing their two-dimensional projections). If this is true, the inability of the visual system to differentially detect different three-dimensional forms is at least consistent with the mathematical limitations observed in artificial intelligence work.

The data reported in Uttal (1985) suggest a new rule or law of dotted-nonplanar-form detection that can be added to the "Rule of Linear Periodicity" that worked so well for planar and linear structures: "The Rule of Three-Dimensional Non-computability"—nonplanar surfaces (and presumably also solid objects) cannot be processed in the same way as two-dimensional objects. Geometrical sensitivity existing in two dimensions does not exist in three dimensions because the nervous system (and possibly many other computers) does not have the power to directly process three-dimensional geometry.

It turns out, however, that the situation is very much more complicated as we add other kinds of visual tasks to the detection task that was the main object of interest in the discussion so far. This was the goal of the fourth study (Uttal, 1987) in this series. We also considered what would happen if the observer was asked not only to detect, but rather also to discriminate or recognize the three-dimensional dotted forms used as stimuli. Although these results should properly be considered in a later chapter, their close relationship to the present discussion makes it useful to at least mention them now. The results are:

1. Detection, discrimination, and recognition appear to be generally organized into a hierarchy in which successively higher amounts of information are required to overcome the degrading effects of masking random-noise dots.

2. In a few exceptional conditions, typically at high masking-dot densities, discrimination sometimes occurs at lower signal-to-noise ratios than does detection.

3. Detection and discrimination performance both appear to be relatively uninfluenced by the shape of the surface in terms of their raw scores. Recognition scores are idiosyncratically influenced by stimulus shape varying with observer groups and stimulus set. Both discrimination and recognition, however, do show a very reliable sensitivity to form in the error matrices for the various combinations that must be discriminated or the confusion errors in the recognition task.

4. The errors of discrimination and of recognition indicated in the error matrices are strongly diagonally symmetrical, indicating that no significant response bias occurs and that the responses are largely stimulus driven.

5. Detection, discrimination, and recognition data both show a prepotency of the regularly sampled forms over the randomly sampled one.

6. In the discrimination experiment with random stimuli, certain confusions (i.e., poor discriminations) occurred. The strongest ones were:

   a. The cylinder was difficult to discriminate from the arch and the saddle.

   b. The hemisphere and the paraboloid of rotation could not easily be discriminated from each other, but were quite discriminable from all others.

   c. The two-dimensional cubic was difficult to discriminate from the one-dimensional cubic and the plane, but the one-dimensional cubic was easily discriminated from the plane.

7. In the recognition experiment, using random stimuli, the pattern of results was virtually identical to the strongest confusions in the discrimination experiment, but the differences between the first and second tier of error scores were greater in recognition than in discrimination.

   a. The cylinder, arch, and saddle were confused with each other.

   b. The hemisphere and paraboloid were confused with each other.

   c. The one-dimensional cubic and the two-dimensional cubic were frequently confused and the two-dimensional cubic (but not the one-dimensional cubic) was confused with the plane.

   8. When an elastic plane is rotated to different positions in a rectangular space, it does not vary in detectability in spite of the fact that there is a greater than two-to-one variation in its apparent dot density. This result negates any possibility that local-region effects can account for the null effect of stimulus-form in the raw correct percentage graphs.

   At this point, I deal with one perplexing and continuing problem of this kind of research. Throughout this entire group of studies, it has repeatedly been the case that experiments in which mixed groups of different stimulus-forms (i.e., different geometrical shapes, not different degrees of distortion) have been used, we have obtained inconsistent results when the findings are plotted as a function of the stimulus-form. Experiments that are nearly the same reflect different shape or form functions. Furthermore, observers behave quite idiosyncratically (i.e., they exhibit stronger individual differences) when faced with, for example, the eight different standard forms (utilized throughout the present work) rather than a single form varying in density or degree of deformation. In other words, when mixed sets of stimulus-forms are used and the response patterns of individual observers are compared, they typically do not show the same pattern of sensitivities to shape.

   Recent personal discussions with Brian Rogers of Oxford University suggest that stereoscopic vision experiments, in particular, are subject to a great deal of variability from task to task, from observer to observer, and from condition to condition. It may be that this reflects either some higher level intervention or the increased difficulty of the task. No general answer to this problem is known at the present time.

   The problem seems to lie in the individual differences of the observer's responses to the specific stimulus-forms used in the experiment. Several explanations are possible for this aggravating situation. One explanation is that in spite of what are considered to be adequate controls, different observers may in some subtle way be noting some aspect of the local geometry of the stimulus patterns and cueing in on this aspect of the stimulus rather than the global shape cue we wish them to use. Such local cueing would be very much more difficult to do in a set of stimuli based upon the same stimulus-form than in a set of different forms.

   A second possible explanation is more psychologically subtle. It may be that the explanation is, in the words of Peterson (1986) some "nonstimulus contributions to the perceptual organization" of the stimulus-form utilized here. That is, perhaps the processes being assayed in this study are not as totally preattentive as we think. Perhaps different observers "perceptually organize" the stimuli in different ways and this organization breaks through to influence their visual response. Others (e.g., Haber, 1966; Hochberg & Peterson, 1985; Kahneman & Triesman, 1984) have also suggested this possibility for what otherwise appears to be very low-level perceptual processes.

Disconcertingly, both of these speculative answers, as well as most others that could be invoked to explain the present data, are framed in terms of the observer's cognition and of higher level mechanisms than I have tended to invoke in my theories of dotted form perception. Is the difficulty to which I have alluded a matter of individual differences or idiosyncratic cognitive mechanisms rather than the automatic stimulus-driven preattentive processes I believe to be most influential here? I cannot answer this question; I can only report that in every instance in which I have invented some strategy to seek closure or completion in this work, it has turned out that the situation is far more complicated than it had seemed.

Thus, there were variations of several different kinds in the obtained results from the several parts of the experiment. These variations illustrate, once again, the fact that general or universal rules seem to be absent in this type of perceptual research and that slight changes in procedure can often have dramatic effects on the outcome of what seem at first glance to be very closely related experiments. I return to consider this matter in chapter 6.

In summary, of the questions motivating dotted-form-perception research that have been of greatest concern to me in the past, the one dealing with the effect of form on the visibility of dotted stimuli in this signal-from-noise extraction task is probably the most intriguing. It is surprising how little attention has been paid to this specific attribute question. The reasons for this neglect are manifold, but include:

1. Technical difficulties in the manipulation of forms (a difficulty that has largely been ameliorated by the further development of real-time control computers and novel display devices).

2. The absence of a general notational system for geometric form (the analytic geometry used in my work and the arbitrary forms used in others' are, at best, band-aids over great conceptual wounds).

3. The complexity of geometrical forms themselves. Researchers often have generated an ideal *gedanken* experiment only to discover that it was impossible to implement because of some intrinsic confounding arising out of the inherent linkage of two or more attributes of the stimulus (e.g., perimeter and area). This kind of deep-seated, structural obstacle is not easily surmounted by any kind of ingenious experimental design. Rather, it is a difficulty that is built into the essential nature of geometric forms.

It is a simple fact that there are some experiments that "should" be done but that cannot without altering the experimental paradigm in such a way that dimensions other than those with which we are mainly concerned would be concurrently manipulated. For example, some might say that any stimulus-form could, in principle, by presented in a random-dot stereogram possessing no monocular cues. In fact, the process of converting something like a dotted straight-line into a random stereogram changes the essence of the line so thoroughly that it would no longer be the stimulus of interest. Rather, each line element would be replaced by a relatively broad array of dots that would destroy the very geometrical feature (the linear order of a series of single dots) that is emphasized by the rule of linear periodicity.

Such reasons partially explain the paucity of studies in which the specific geometric attributes of a visual stimulus have been examined to determine their effect on a visual performance task. It is also for these reasons that researchers have, in general, tended to turn to studies of other aspects of geometric stimuli that are, in fact, only secondarily associated with the specific-attribute question. The heroic bibliographies compiled by Zusne (1970, 1975, 1981) not only demonstrate the enormous and varied interest in the general problem of how people see forms, but also the relative paucity of studies of the influence on visual performance of the specific geometrical attributes of those forms. Instead, efforts are aimed at almost every other dimension or aspect of the problem, from perceptual development to perceptual persistence to perceptual aesthetics. Only a few items in Zusne's three bibliographies deal directly with what he refers to as stimulus variables—the specific attributes.

A popular alternative has been to examine temporal effects rather than geometrical ones. For example, my laboratory, along with others that are thoroughly reviewed in Breitmeyer's (1984) splendid book, carried out a number of studies on the temporal dynamics of the dot-masking process (Uttal, 1969a, 1969b, 1970a, 1970b, 1970c; Uttal & Hieronymous, 1970; Uttal, Bunnell, & Corwin, 1970). Research of this kind, I now believe, is probably best considered to exemplify what the ethologists would call ''displacement activity''—actions that are not germane to the task at hand but which keep the organism busy until it can decide what to do with the real problem it faces. The real problem in form perception, in my opinion, has always been the specific-attribute question—an issue of spatial, not temporal, influences.

I have, however, considered the specific-attribute question in studies that are directly concerned with geometric form. Form investigations include those reported in Uttal (1973a, 1976, 1977) and, of course, the four monographs previously cited (Uttal, 1975, 1983, 1985, 1987). Some others have considered the spatial geometry of stimulus-forms from the same perspective. Most notable are the works of Hughes (1982), the large body of highly relevant knowledge from T. Caelli's laboratory (e.g., Caelli, 1982; Caelli & Yuzyk, 1985); the work of Julesz on textures (see especially Julesz, 1981), the studies on density discrimination carried out by Horace Barlow and his colleagues (e.g., Barlow, 1978; Burgess & Barlow, 1983) and their work specifically on form (Barlow &

Reeves, 1979; van Meeteren & Barlow, 1981), and most germane, the work from Joseph Lappin's laboratory (see especially Falzett & Lappin, 1983). This, I believe, is the context within which our work falls. Ginsburg's (1983) work is also of this same genre.

The texture works of Julesz, Barlow, and others are considered in the next chapter because I believe the emphasis in their studies is directed more toward discrimination than detection. But a brief comment about an important outcome from Barlow's laboratory is appropriate here. The workers found that the human observer operated at about a 50% efficiency level compared to an ideal observer. In fact, this is a highly efficient performance level and it is remarkable how well observers do in two-dimensional tasks of this type. The failure to be affected by three-dimensional form uncovered in my experiments thus may be a very precise estimate of the limits on the computational power of preattentive spatial vision.

D. THE DETECTION OF SYMMETRY

Other kinds of dotted-form-detection processes are of course at work in the human visual system than those I have studied. One of these is thought to be exquisitely sensitive to the detection of global symmetry in otherwise random dot arrays. The phenomenon of interest in this case was first reported by Julesz (1971): When a random dot texture is reflected over a vertical axis (which then becomes its central axis of symmetry) so as to produce a symmetrical figure, the symmetry is immediately obvious to the observer in a preattentive and automatic manner; that is, it is immediately detected. This phenomenon from at least one point of view is an extraordinary result, simply because the two halves of the symmetrical stimulus may individually display no order at all. Nevertheless, when this structureless form is reflected about an axis of symmetry, the new organization and structure so generated stands out in a striking and obvious manner. It is of interest to consider what this has to say about the size of the field over which these interactions occur and what it says about the nature of form perception in general.

In recent years this phenomenon has been studied most extensively by Jenkins (1982, 1983a, 1983b, 1983c). Jenkins manipulated several parameters of the symmetrical stimulus pairs including the linearity of the centers of the pairs of symmetrical dots (i.e., the linearity of the axis of symmetry) plotted on an oscilloscope. In one example of his work, each symmetrical (or, rather, quasi-symmetrical) pair of dots defined a center point that either was distributed along the center line or distributed over a wider region. The width of this "axis of symmetry" was the main independent variable in his experiments. The observer had to detect the symmetrical or quasi-symmetrical stimulus when two patterns were presented; the nontarget one possessing no symmetrical structure at all, and the target one possessing a variable degree of symmetry as controlled by the vertical collinearity of the center points of the various symmetrical pairs of dots on either side of the midline.

The main result of Jenkins' experiment was that the wider the region over which the midpoints of the point pairs were distributed, the poorer the symmetry-detection performance. Although this is not an unexpected outcome, a rather surprising result was that his observers were always able to detect symmetry to at least some degree even when the range over which their midpoints were perturbed varied by as much as 4.41 deg—a value almost as wide as the total stimulus (5.0 deg). Thus, global symmetry detection seems to be a process that is built into the visual system as a powerful and efficient preattentive tool for processing dotted (and presumably other) forms.

Jenkins rejects the notion that there has to be some kind of a single symmetrical neural structure in the nervous system to account for this powerful ability to detect symmetry. Rather, he proposes a set of three cooperating processes that could explain this phenomenon. He suggests, first, that there is some sort of algorithm built into the nervous system for detecting the uniformity of orientation of the pairs of dots and that this mechanism works independently of the distance between pairs of points. Second, he proposes that there is another mechanism that is able to combine the most important pairs into what he calls pseudo-features (this is reminiscent of Julesz's (1983) textons and Triesman and Patterson's (1984) special features). Third, and finally, he suggests that another mechanism exists that is capable of making the actual evaluation as to whether or not the figure is symmetric. These three mechanisms, Jenkins asserts, can be thought of in terms of networks of neurons, perhaps capable of accomplishing other spatial analyses simultaneously. The important thing he believes, is that human visual systems are symmetry information-processing systems without being intrinsically symmetrical themselves in terms of their internal mechanisms.

It is unfortunate that the formal properties of these three mechanisms were not pursued further by Jenkins in his interesting studies. The properties exhibited by the visual system when it detects symmetry seem to have close analogies to the kind of functional processes that are well modeled by the kind of transforms used by Marr or myself in processing global form in other contexts. It seems likely that some kind of correlational mechanism might do a very good job of simulating exactly the action of the triplet of mechanisms invoked by Jenkins in his verbal model.

Explanation of the data in experiments of the genre considered in this section has been attempted from many other points of view that are distinctly different from the autocorrelation model I have proposed or Marr's functional algorithms. The detection of signals in noise (other than dotted forms) is a classic area of perceptual research and other theoreticians have emphasized such factors as the Gestalt organizational principles (e.g., Banks & Prinzmetal, 1976), the features of the stimulus (e.g., Estes, 1972), perturbations of the stimulus (e.g., Wolford, 1975), and even, in some cases, Fourier-type models (Graham, 1980). The problem of the equivalence of their models to the autocorrelation transform or to Jenkins' three processes remains to be resolved.

In summarizing the work on symmetry, I call attention to what I believe is the most significant conclusion to be drawn from this work. That conclusion is that human visual perception is powerfully driven by the global organization of a form. There is no simple way to understand Jenkins' work in terms of local interactions or features. Rather, it becomes meaningful and understandable only in terms of sensitivity to the overall structure or to parts that are very distant from each other. Such distant loci can not interact in terms of local processes, but only in terms of wide-ranging ones. It is this outcome that makes this work so especially important.

E. MASKING—A LABORATORY MODEL OF CAMOUFLAGE

Camouflage may be defined as any kind of disguise or concealment that makes an object less conspicuous. In the present context, camouflage is defined to be any geometric property of the stimulus or its surround that makes the stimulus less detectable. It is important to appreciate that there are many such natural protective mechanisms that have evolved for defense against predation that are not camouflage in the sense I use the term here. Some evolutionary outcomes, for example, may make an organism even more conspicuous than earlier generations had been. In some cases this can produce a mistaken identity in which the organism mimics something other than itself that is, in fact, much more dangerous. We shall not concern ourselves with such nonconcealing, but misdirecting, devices that make an object look more ominous than it really is or those that mimic a poisonous creature. In the natural world, concealment (i.e., a reduction in detectability) may be accomplished by appropriate changes in coloration or design that break up distinctive features of an animal or plant so that it blends into its background. The main purpose of this section of this chapter is to consider a number of experiments from the much more artificial world of the laboratory that deal with the influence of context or surround on the detectability of a stimulus-form. This influence is epitomized by what is referred to as a "masking" experiment.

Camouflage comes in many guises: An example is a visual scene in which a natural object is hidden by a complex surround such that its geometrical structure blends into that of the environment. This occurs mainly because some of the most salient cues for detection are broken up or made discontinuous by the respective coloration or design of the object and the surround.

Another kind of camouflage occurs when the object is embedded in the form of the surround. In this case the object is not obscured by the degradation of its coloration or design, but rather by the fact that it is a very useful and functional part of the surrounding scene in which it is embedded. This may be a kind of geometrical embedding or an example of what has classically been called "functional fixedness''—invisibility due to the object's role in the normal *function* of the scene. This latter example is obviously not a detection problem related to the geometry of the scene and preattentive processing, but of what is certainly a result of a higher, cognitive level of processing.

The laboratory analog of many of the kinds of camouflage that have just been discussed has been referred to as ''masking by pattern'' by Breitmeyer (1984), among others. As so often happens in this context, however, there is disagreement about the types of detection tasks that should be pooled under this rubric. Whereas Breitmeyer lumps metacontrast, masking by random noise, and masking by structured elements together, I feel that the distinctions among these categories are significant enough that so that they should be dealt with as separate entities. Even though the experimental paradigms of each of these three categories of masking are very similar, it seems (to this student of perception, at least) highly unlikely that the mechanisms that account for nonoverlapping metacontrast could possibly be the same as those accounting for masking by overlapping patterned forms.

It is now appreciated that visual stimuli are reduced in detectability when a spatial mask is superimposed on the stimulus within some now well-understood limits of temporal propinquity. The criterion characteristic of this kind of masking is the same as that observed in the examples of natural camouflage discussed in the previous paragraphs. Namely, that the component features of the mask and the target are very similar, such that the former tends to break up the distinctive features of the latter. The superimposition of a patterned mask on the stimuli thus tends to reduce the distinctive features and organizational properties of the stimulus that allowed it to be detected and/or recognized.

An important corollary of this process of masking by pattern, although not one that is essential to understanding its basic nature, is that the mask and the stimulus-form need not be presented simultaneously. The normal persistence of the visual response is sufficient to allow both to interact and thus for the reduction in detectability to become manifest. It must be appreciated that the measure of visual persistence produced by variations in the interval between the stimulus-form and the mask is not an answer to the issue of the nature of the masking process itself. These temporal attributes of the stimulus-form-mask interaction provide a convenient means of manipulating detectability in a way that allows us to measure the temporal attributes of the interaction, but it does not assay the effects of geometry and form of particular interest to us here. As I indicated earlier, the reasons that the temporal interval played such a large part in the masking literature and why temporal interaction effects were so often studied were practical, not theoretical. Previously, there was no easy way to vary such attributes of the experimental situation as the density of the pattern mask. On the other hand, it was very easy to manipulate the temporal interval between the stimulus-form and the mask. Indeed, the standard instrument of masking research, until recently, has been the fluorescent-tube-illuminated tachistoscope in which there was little control possible over the luminosity characteristics of the light sources and in which it was a difficult and cumbersome procedure to change the stimuli from one trial to another.[8]

The digital computer used on a laboratory control device has changed this situation drastically. Both raster-scan (TV-type) and point-plotting cathode ray tubes can be driven by computer programs to paint a new stimulus form and/or a new mask in fractions of a second with exquisite precision and great flexibility. Thus, only in recent years has it begun to be possible to manipulate the attributes of the mask itself rather than only the interval between the mask and the stimulus form.

This technical inability to manipulate the attributes of the mask is not a trivial difficulty that can be overlooked. In some of the most important experiments in this field, only single masks had been used throughout entire studies, and serious questions remain as to whether or not observers become so familiarized with that single mask that they were able to read through them in the same way that one can easily discern the pattern is a fractured figure once one has become familiarized with it. What seems to have been a minor technical problem might indeed have seriously biased major experimental programs.

With that caveat in mind, let us consider some of the major studies of masking by patterns and search out the generalities that describe this kind of visual process.

One main point I think should be made, however: Masking phenomena are the result of many different kinds of underlying processes. The fact that they are so multiply determined has been the source of considerable theoretical confusion. The similarity of protocol among the various kinds of experiments has clouded the fact that there are at least six different kinds of phenomena and, therefore, theoretical explanations. Specifically, masking may be caused by:

- Temporal summation of two spots
- Figural superimposition
- Neural interaction
- Indiscriminable surface properties
- Gestalt grouping
- Metacontrast

The first two items in this list (two-spot and figural superimposition masking) are probably strongly dependent upon the most peripheral luminosity-dependent mechanisms of the eye. The third (neural interaction) is intended to categorize

---

[8] Of course, it is not impossible to manually introduce neutral density filters into the optical path of a tachistoscope or to *manually* change masks as well as stimulus-forms in random order in that device. However possible, the history of the situation is that it is improbable that these manipulations would actually be carried out with sufficient persistence and discipline to avoid experimental confounding. Even experimental psychologists have limits on their tenacity.

those that are the result of more central, but still relatively peripheral, processes, whereas the next one (indiscriminable surface properties) usually turns out to be a problem of discrimination rather than detection and will be discussed in the next chapter. The latter two (Gestalt grouping and metacontrast) are clearly the result of central interpretive mechanisms that hide, mask, or reduce our capability to detect by virtue of what we should refer to as cognitive processes. In the following section I have elaborated, edited, and updated discussion of the several types of masking phenomena that clearly influence detectability from my earlier work (Uttal, 1981).

a. *Two-Pulse Interaction: Masking of the First Kind.* If two stimuli are presented to the same eye in rapid succession and the second is both more intense and larger in extent than the first, then the first stimulus may be obscured or masked to a degree that is a function of the interval between the two.

The classic observation of this "bright flash" type of masking was made by B. H. Crawford (1947). Crawford used a long-duration (.5 sec) masking flash and a brief, dimmer test flash, both of which were circular and concentric. In the context of our present discussion, the most interesting result of his experiment was that the bright flash could suppress detection of the dimmer flash even when it did not begin until 50 msec after the test flash was presented. In this case the differential latencies of the two different amplitude signals probably artifactually altered the period of interaction. Even if the two had equal latencies, the persistence of the response to the first stimulus would have allowed the two to interact and thus set up a situation in which the more intense flash could inhibit the less intense one by simply reducing the contrast between the target and the background. Masking of this sort is now appreciated to be effective when the two stimuli are presented to the same eye but not when the stimuli are presented dichoptically. Thus this kind of masking is most likely peripherally mediated and quite distinct from several other kinds of masking with which it shares many operational similarities. I refer here to bright-flash masking as masking of the first kind.

b. *Figural Summation: Masking of the Second Kind.* The two-pulse interaction technique just described is a procedure for measuring temporal integration that depends mainly on relatively simple luminosity-detection measurements. However, sequential visual stimuli also interact in ways that may lead to either a diminishment or enhancement in performance on certain more complex tasks. Although the basic process underlying both the simple and complex tasks may be exactly the same, the nature of the more complex task has sometimes obscured the essential identity of the responsible processes.

The essential point in this discussion is that because the temporal acuity of the visual system is relatively poor, two stimuli that are not physically simultaneous may appear to be so. Thus as a result of this apparent simultaneity, figures that may be incomplete in two or more partial presentations may appear to be complete if the parts are presented in rapid-enough succession. Furthermore, figures that were individually recognizable may be masked or hidden by the merging that results from the mixture of a "target" and a "mask." Whether the interaction is summative and enhances perception, or inhibitory and degrades perception, is not so much a matter of the underlying process as it is one of the nature of the stimuli and the task that the observer is required to perform.

My dot-masking experiments, as described earlier in this chapter, are examples of the inhibitory kind of masking. Kinsbourne and Warrington's (1962) work with checkerboard masks, or Sperling's (1963) and Schiller and Smith's (1966) work with random fragments are also of this same genre. Many other more recent relevant studies are described in Breitmeyer's (1984) book. Whether the mask and the target are presented in the same eye or in different eyes, the phenomena are comparable (with the possible exception of forward dichoptic masking); the target is hidden in the confusion of the superimposed image. The critical factor in producing the superimposition, it seems, is the prolongation of the response long past the duration of the stimulus.

Excellent reviews of the very extensive pattern-masking literature up to 1968 can be found in Kahneman (1968). However the most significant paper in the field of masking has clearly been Turvey's (1973) experimental and theoretical analysis of this kind of masking. Turvey carried out a series of 19 experiments that led him to conclude that there were two levels of processing involed, even when identical stimuli and tasks were used. His experimental design was a simple one. He used either random noise or a field of letter fragments as a mask, alphabetic characters as targets, and determined both the forward or backward masking effects.

Turvey concluded from this extensive study that both peripheral and central phenomena were involved in this kind of masking, but that these processes were not sequential in time; that is, he suggested that they were essentially simultaneous and operated in parallel, although the central process depended, of course, on whatever transformations had been made by the peripheral one.

For the moment, let us consider only Turvey's conclusions about the peripheral-masking processes. Peripheral masking, according to Turvey, is very similar to "masking of the second kind" described in this section. According to Turvey, peripheral masking is characterized by a multiplicative law; that is, the energy of the target, multiplied by the minimum interstimulus interval between the target and the mask that allowed the masking effects to be completely overcome is a constant for peripheral masking. Central masking, according to Turvey's model, is better described by an additive law in which the target duration plus the minimum interstimulus interval eguals a constant.

More specifically, Turvey's (1973, p. 48) conclusions for the central and peripheral masking processes were (in excerpt) as follows:

1. Although energy variables significantly affected the degree and direction of peripheral masking, they were relatively immaterial to masking arising centrally.

2. Forward masking of peripheral origin was more pronounced than backward masking of peripheral origin; moreover, the severity of peripheral forward masking increased with increases in mask intensity, whereas the severity of peripheral backward masking did not.

3. When two stimuli, target and mask, were presented monoptically in a backward-masking arrangement, the upper limit on masking was set by either peripheral or central processes depending on the energy of the target and the relation between the target and mask patterns.

4. A nonmonotonic U-shaped function was obtained monoptically with overlapping target and mask when the target energy was greater than mask energy. It was hypothesized that this function reflected the transition from peripheral to central masking with increasing delay between the two stimuli.

5. Individual differences were more obvious in central than in peripheral masking.

There are, of course, experimental paradigms other than masking that also reflect the same mechanisms of visual persistence and summation underlying these visual noise-masking results. Hogben's (1972) dissertation utilizes an ingenious task in which missing dots must be detected in a rectangular dot matrix that is distributed over time. The temporal distribution is achieved by interjecting a constant interval between the sequential plotting of the dots of the matrix. The general result in Hogben's studies was that the longer the interval between the dots, the less likely the observer was to detect a missing dot. The implication of this finding is exactly the same as the others I have just described—if the temporally distributed presentation of the stimulus dots takes place quickly enough, the entire matrix is simultaneously visible because of the persistence of the visual response. Observers are thus able to use global organization cues to locate the missing dot in a way that is not available to them when the stimulus dots are spread over so great a time that the pattern cannot be seen as a whole.

In summary, there is a broad class of different experiments that seem to be well explained by simple superimposition or fusion of two stimuli presented in quick succession occurring as a result of response persistence. Depending upon the nature of the stimulus material and the task, there may either be an inhibition (masking) or an increase in the detectability or recognizability of the form resulting from this fusion. It should be noted, however, that there is some limited evidence that contradicts the simple temporal persistence and summation explanation of the phenomena that I have analyzed here. McFarland (1965) , for example, designed an experiment in which he asked observers to judge the apparent simultaneity of triangles in which the corners and the sides were presented in sequential order rather than physically simultaneous. He found that there was a difference in judgments of simultaneity when the corners, as opposed to the sides, were presented. Similarly, in another study using the sides of squares rather than triangles, McFarland and Prete (1969) went on to show that the presence of other lines in the field surrounding the square could alter the judgment of simultaneity when the sides of the square were presented in sequential order. The fact that simultaneity judgments were affected by both the form and the nature of the surround supports Turvey's suggestion that some components of the masking processes may be due to central levels of processing.

Another aberrant result further mitigates the simple peripheral-integration-period explanation of these summative phenomena. For some unexplained reason, dichoptic forward situations (target to one eye and noise mask to the other eye) do not produce a substantial masking effect comparable to either a dichoptic backward mask or a forward or backward monocular mask. This result has been replicated too many times for there to be any doubt of its validity. The absence of forward dichoptic masking has been shown by Smith and Schiller (1966), Greenspon and Eriksen (1968), and Turvey (1973).

Thus the theoretical situation is still somewhat equivocal, and the explanation of what leads to these effects of fusion somewhat uncertain. In general, however, there does seem to be a consensus in the theoretical literature suggesting that they are mainly due to persistent responses in peripheral portions of the visual system.

c. Lateral Inhibitory Interaction: Masking of the Third Kind.   In this section I briefly consider some masking phenomena that appear to be directly based upon inhibitory interactions among neurons in relatively peripheral portions of the visual system.

A widely accepted current model asserts that simple lateral inhibitory interactions exist in the vertebrate nervous system that are comparable to those found in the compound eye of arachnids. Although the initial neurophysiological data confirming this model came mainly from invertebrates, in fact, most of the basic concepts had been suggested many years earlier by Ernst Mach (see Ratliff, 1965, for a good history of this problem) on the basis of human psychophysical findings. At present there is some neurophysiological evidence that inhibitory neural mechanisms capable of mediating contour enhancement exist in the vertebrate retina. Enroth–Cugel and Robson (1966), for example, have demonstrated a peaking of response rate in a ganglion cell of the cat retina when a step illumination was moved across it, comparable to an effect observed in the invertebrate compound eye by Ratliff and Hartline (1959). The whole problem has become exceedingly interwoven with the problem of receptive field structure, however, and much of the evidence for inhibitory interaction in the retina is couched in those terms. For our present purposes, it is sufficient to note only that there is virtually universal acceptance of the idea that such inhibitory interactions exist in the most peripheral portions of the vertebrate visual system as well as the invertebrate.

There is also considerable psychophysical evidence that the processes that lead to the Mach bands and related phenomena, in fact, are quite peripheral. This evidence is usually obtained by comparing the results of dichoptic and monocular stimulus presentations. The repeatedly demonstrated absence of this kind of interaction between dichoptically presented stimuli is one of the most compelling arguments that the peripheral interactive processes are, at least, sufficient, if not necessary, to account for many of the phenomena I consider in this section.

However these findings should not be interpreted to mean that inhibitory interactions are exclusively peripheral and occur only in the inner and outer plexiform layers of the retina. Some evidence also exists indicating that central lateral inhibitory mechanisms are operative in some instances. One study seeking inhibitory neural interactions that might be associated with certain comparable psychophysical phenomena (Gardner & Spencer's 1972a, 1972b studies of "funneling") actually found those neural interactions to be present only in the central nervous system and not in the peripheral nervous system. Although the analogy between this study and the visual system is somewhat farfetched (their study was done on the somatosensory system in which there are no synaptic interconnections that would allow lateral interactions to occur in the periphery), Gardner and Spencer's work does serve as an existence proof that lateral inhibitory interactions can occur centrally as well as peripherally.

d. Surface Cues: Masking of the Fourth Kind.   The physical properties of an extended stimulus are, of course, limited to the same set of dimensions that must characterize any other physical stimulus. The stimulus characteristics of a surface are limited by the wavelength spectrum, luminosity, spatial extent, and patterned variations of these properties within the region being examined. The phenomenal response to a surface, however, may have many more degrees of freedom. *Surface color* is the term that has been traditionally used to describe the wide variety of experiences attributable to an extended region. Jacob Beck, in a virtually unique analysis of surface colors (Beck, 1972), has listed a very large number of dimensions along which surface appearances many vary. The main contemporary area of interest in surface cues, however, deals with texture, and for the most part, this stimulus attribute has been examined with discrimination tasks rather than detection ones. For this reason this type of masking is discussed in the next chapter.

e. The Gestalt Rules of Grouping: Masking of the Fifth Kind.   The rules of grouping the figural components of a complex scene have been a matter of concern to the Gestalt psychologists since the inception of their school of psychological theory. Study of the Gestalt "rules of grouping" was the keystone around which most of the rest of their holistic theory was itself organized. The word *Gestalt* itself is virtually synonymous with the terms *pattern, form,* or *group.* An explicit search for the rules of grouping was, therefore, an important part of Gestalt psychology's research program and has been one of its most lasting contributions. Eleven main rules, first explicitly enunciated by Max Werthheimer (1923), governing the perceptual grouping of the elements of a multielement display, are usually tabulated. Of these, 10 refer to influential properties of the stimulus pattern, and the eleventh to an internal state of the observer. The first 10 are:

1. The rule of spatial proximity: All other things being equal, elements of a pattern that are close together in space tend to be grouped together.

2. The rule of temporal proximity: All other things being equal, elements of pattern that occur close together in time tend to be grouped together.

3. The rule of similarity: All other things being equal, elements of a pattern that are geometrically similar tend to be grouped together.

4. The rule of continuity: All other things being equal, elements of a pattern that represent a continuation of a pattern defined by the organization of other elements of the pattern tend to be grouped with those other elements.

5. The rule of closure: All other things being egual, elements that form a closed pattern (i.e., a pattern without discontinuous boundaries) tend to be grouped together.

6. The rule of uniform density: All other things being equal, elements of a pattern that are distributed with egual spacing tend to be grouped together better than irregularly spaced elements.

7. The rule of common fate: All other things being equal, elements of a dynamic pattern that are moving in the same direction and at the same velocity tend to be grouped together.

8. The rule of symmetry: All other things being equal, elements that are arranged in a symmetrical form will be grouped together.

9. The rule of common orientation: All other things being equal, elements sharing a common orientation (i.e., vertical, horizontal, oblique) tend to be grouped together.

10. The rule of Prägnanz: All other things being equal, the elements of a pattern that produce the "best" figure (the figure with the highest degree of "goodness" or minimum amount of "structural stress") tend to be grouped together.

(*Prägnanz* is, as so many others have noted, a terribly difficult term to translate from the original language—German—and, perhaps more important, from the original linguistic philosophy in which it was originally formulated by Koffka, 1935. In an attempt to catch the flavor of this word, we can only say that the Gestalt psychologists believed that each stimulus figure has inherent in it one best form that was the easiest for the observer to organize. Thus, an equilateral arrangement of three dots displays the highest degree of "Prägnanz" for a triangle, even though it could be forced or perceptually stressed to represent three points on a circle or other curve. *Prägnanz* has also been defined as the minimally complex figure into which a pattern can be organized. In that context, it has close denotative relations with such terms as *entropy* and *information*. However, to this date, no one has yet been able to propose a quantitative metric for Prägnanz; the use of this word is still highly qualitative and somewhat arbitrary. The important thing about this concept is that the Gestaltists assumed that it was a property of the stimulus, whereas modern thought is more likely to attribute it either to the properties and characteristics of the observer or to an "interaction" between the stimulus and the observer.)

The eleventh rule is:

11. The rule of Einstellung: All other things being equal, elements of a pattern will be grouped in accord with the "objective" set (Einstellung) of the observer. If the observer has been preconditioned to expect a triangle, when three dots are presented, he or she is indeed more likely to see a triangle; and if that observer has been preconditioned to see a bear in astral constellation, the bear is more likely to be apparent than any other form. (This, of course, was the Gestaltist's only bow to the experiential and attentional factors that now dominate thinking about perceptual grouping.)

In recent years, the emphasis in the study of these rules of perceptual organization has changed dramatically. The current stress is on how to use them as independent variables rather than to measure them as dependent variables. The goal in the most modern research is usually to determine the effect of grouping on a task such as target detection or memory rather than to study the factors that influence grouping. A general outcome of this emphasis has been to highlight further the fact that simple feature-detection models are not, in general, adequate models of target-detection behavior and to show that the fluence of configurational or organizational factors on memory and detection is even more powerful than the influence of local features.

The theory tested in many such studies has been the specific feature-detection model proposed by such workers as Estes (1972, 1974) and Bjork and Murray (1977). The general philosophy expressed by these psychologists is that there are independent channels (conveying feature-specific information) that interact to account for the masking effects of letterlike stimuli on each other. I refer to this type of masking paradigm as masking of the fifth kind—that is, a reduction in visibility produced by the entanglement of an element of a target pattern in a Gestalt or grouped pattern in a way that reduces the probability of its being detected or recognized as an independent element.

The major counterargument to the Estes, Bjork, and Murray feature-sensitive channel theory, which clearly is a genre similar to those that I criticized in the previous chapter, has been the demonstration that the Gestalt configurational effects, which are not well accounted for in such theories, are in fact dominant in modulating the detection of letters in this kind of experiment. Such an argument has been presented by Banks, Bodinger, and Illige (1974); Banks and Prinzmetal (1976); and Prinzmetal and Banks (1977). In the first of these papers, Banks, Bodinger, and Illige (1974) reported that increasing the separation between a target T letter and a set of masking F letters increased the detectability of the target by perceptually extracting it from a group in which it had been embedded. This experiment was well controlled for lateral interaction effects; the authors thus felt confident in attributing the release-from-masking effect purely to the reduction of a Gestaltlike proximity factor than to a reduced spatial interaction between any putative feature channels.

In the second of these studies, Banks and Prinzmetal (1976) showed that the grouping of the elements in the target and the mask strongly affect both the speed and accuracy with which a target letter could be detected and recognized. If the stimulus pattern was organized so that the target letter was a part of a Gestalt or perceived grouping that included the noise characters, then the target letter was detected less well than when it was separated from the group. This reduction in visibility of the target occurred even when the number of masking letters was larger in the well-grouped stimulus than in the poorly grouped condition.

In the third study, Prinzmetal and Banks (1977) discovered that a target character could be hidden by being made a perceptual part of a pattern that exhibited good continuity. The target letter was far less easily detected when it is placed alongside a line of masking characters than when it was colinear with that line. This result is so robust that it holds even when the latter discontinuous positioning would bring the target into closer proximity to a larger number of masking characters than when it was at the end of the line.

The important point made by all three of these experiments is that the global configuration of the stimulus exerts a powerful, if not dominating, effect even on such processes as target detection, which are often considered only in terms of the details of their local geometry. From my perspective, there is no way that such phenomena can be satisfactorily attributed to the function of hypothetical "channels" or "feature-detectors" in the way that the Estes, Bjork, and Murray theories attempt.

Similarity is also very important. A study of the effect of the relative orientation of a single stimulus line (which differed in some property from the masking lines) and multiple masking lines was carried out by Michael Young (1985) in my laboratory. The observer's task in this experiment was to specify in which of two sequential presentations a target line appeared. In both presentations the stimulus was obscured by various numbers of horizontal dotted lines. Furthermore, the stimulus lines could be either horizontal, as were the masking lines, or could be tilted so that they formed an angle of either plus or minus 5, 10, or 15 degrees with the horizontal. The main parameter in the study of interest in the current context is the difference in detectability produced by the relative orientation of the target line and the masking lines, respectively.

Young's study showed that the detectability of the target line was reduced to a minimum when it was oriented at the same angle (horizontal) as the many masking lines. Thus, the detectability varied as a function of the similarity of the context and the target—in this case, that similarity has been operationalized as similarity of orientation.

In a similar study, Oyama and Watanabe (in press) showed that the ability to count the number of lines in a multiple-line stimulus array also declined as the orientation of a set of target lines and a set of masking lines became more similar. In this interesting experiment the task was somewhat more complicated than mere detection—the observer had to "subitize," that is, automatically count the number of lines in the target, but the effect of orientation was also comparable. The more alike the orientation of the target lines and the masking lines, the lower the correlation of the reported numerosity and the actual numerosity of the target-line set. Indeed, the orientation of the target and masking lines was not the only dimension in which similarity could be manipulated to influence the accuracy of subitizing. Oyama and Watanabe also showed that color differences could produce essentially the same effect. If the masking lines were the same color as the target lines, then subitization was much less accurate than when the colors were different. The point is: It is not the linearity of the line per se that is the key to understanding this phenomenon, but rather that any dimension of the stimulus will produce similar effects as the target and mask become more or less similar.

f. Metacontrast—Masking of the Sixth Kind. Another form of temporal interaction that has attracted considerable attention in recent years is known as "metacontrast." Metacontrast is a backward-masking phenomenon in which the first of two nonoverlapping stimuli is reduced in subjective brightness (often to the point of nondetectability) as a result of its interaction with the later coming second stimulus. Any of several stimulus patterns including concentric ring and discs has proven to be effective in eliciting the phenomenon. A "target" or "contrasted" stimulus (the central disc) is presented previous to a "masking" or "contrasting" stimulus (the ring). The effect usually occurs best within some specific range of intervals between the contrasted and contrasting stimulus. Because this is a backward-masking effect in which a retroactive effect of a subsequent stimulus on an earlier stimulus is measured, this phenomenon has been of especially great interest to perceptual scientists; it is not intuitively obvious how one stimulus that has occurred as long as 100 msec after the presentation of another could affect that earlier stimulus. No other explanation being available, metacontrast would have had to have been considered as an example of backward causation—a process disdained by thermodynamicists, philosophers, and psychologists alike.

As we see here, however, other explanations are available. Models involving transient and sustained channels or neurons of differing conduction velocities have been invoked to reduce the need for invoking as unpalatable a concept as backward causation. Constructionistic processes in which percepts are assembled after all stimulus have occurred also provide another alternative solution to this dilemma. Interest in a closely related phenomenon, paracontrast, in which the contrasting stimulus occurs previous to the contrasted one, has been considerably less, simply because of its lesser challenge to our notion of the unidirectionality of time and our knowledge of the persistence of visual responses. In general, the contrasting stimuli are set at the same color and luminance and, therefore, no model invoking variable latent periods in the receptor (with the resultant possibility of one signal catching up with another) is as plausible as it was with the kind of bright-flash masking that I discussed in an earlier section.

Metacontrast is a very distinct kind of masking, even though it is often confused with some of the other kinds I have already mentioned. The characteristics that distinguish this particular kind of masking effect from others are:

1. The contrasting and contrasted stimuli are similar in shape.
2. The contrasting and contrasted stimulus patterns do not spatially overlap.
3. The measured effect is exerted On the apparent brightness or detectability of the preceding stimulus; it is a backward effect.
4. The stimuli are relatively large and widely separated, and the effect is global over the entire area of the masked stimulus.

Metacontrast illusions were first reported and named as such by Stigler (1910), and were subsequently brought to modern attention in the publications of Werner (1935), Pieron (1935), Cheatham (1952), and Alpern (1953). A number of excellent reviews of this active research topic have been published in recent years, attesting to the widespread interest in this temporal interaction illusion. Among the most highly recommended ones are those by Raab (1963), Kahneman (1968), Weisstein (1972), Lefton (1973), and Scheerer (1973).

However, a considerable amount of controversy has revolved around the actual shape of the metacontrast function and its origins. This controversy takes the form of a disagreement between those who feel that the metacontrast phenomenon (its U-shaped function of interval between stimuli in particular) results from high-level judgmental, or "subjective," factors on the one hand, and those who feel it is mediated by a more peripheral process, on the other. The issue has been most explicitly raised by Eriksen and Marshall (1969) and Eriksen, Becker, and Hoffman (1970), who have suggested that the U-shaped curve so often reported was an artifact of the response required of the observer. In other words, they suggest that the observer actually changed the response criterion during the course of the experiment as the experimental conditions varied. This subjective explanation of the U-shaped function, which incidentally has been supported by the work of Hernandez and Lefton (1977), was supposed to occur in those experiments in which observers ranked or rated the apparent brightness of the masked stimulus using magnitude-estimation procedures. Forced-choice procedures were at first proposed to negate the U-shape outcome and produce a monotonic curve.

It must also be acknowledged, nevertheless, that there is a substantial body of information evidencing the robustness of the U-shaped function in a wide variety of experimental paradigms and with a variety of different stimuli. Weisstein, Jurkens, and Ondersin (1970) were the first to challenge Eriksen and Marshall's suggestion in experiments in which magnitude-estimation and forced-choice procedures were directly compared. And others (e.g., Andreassi, Mayzner, Beyda, & Waxman, 1970; Bachmann & Allik, 1976; Bernstein, Proctor, Proctor, & Schurmam, 1973; Cox & Dember, 1972) have all subsequently found the U-shaped function appearing in a wide variety of experimental designs, including those using forced-choice methods.

Our understanding of the issue has been considerably deepened by Weisstein (1972) and Weisstein and Growney (1969), who have shown that either U-shaped or monotonic functions can be obtained with either forced-choice or magnitude-estimation procedures depending on the luminance relations of the stimulus. When the mask is very much brighter than the target, there is a tendency for monotonic functions to occur. On the other hand, if the target stimulus is adjusted to maintain a constant brightness for all values of interstimulus intervals, the function is always U-shaped. Clearly the point is that the metacontrast function, like the results of so many other Level 4 processes, is not solely determined by either interval, luminance, or any other aspect of the stimulus or response alone but is influenced rather by multiple aspects of the stimulus and experimental design. It is my judgment, after considering the data, that the central "subjective" explanations account for more and are more plausible than any of the more peripheral neural-net models.

Many persistent and fundamental controversies concerning metacontrast continue to occupy the attention of researchers in this field. One continuing perplexity revolves around the problem of whether or not information that has been metacontrasted is physically (i.e., in some more or less peripheral isomorphic image representation sense) suppressed (as would be predicted by those championing neural-net reductionistic-type theories). An alternative view is that physical information is not suppressed, but rather only loses its perceptual significance as a result of interpretative processes that have nothing to do with, say, isomorphic lateral inhibitory interactions operating on the neural representation. The recurrent suggestion is that an image that has been metacontrasted can actually be recovered. Repeated demonstrations showing that the information that is "lost" depends on some aspect of its meaning are compelling counterarguments that the metacontrast is not an act of neural signal suppression alone.

Another important piece of information that indicates that metacontrast is not mediated by simple neural mechanisms is that in some situations enhancement rather than degradation can result from very similar stimulus paradigms. For example, Geiger and Lettvin (1986) have shown an enhancement of perception when a letter or word is flashed at the point of fixation and a letter or word is placed somewhere in the periphery of the visual field. Although there are many complications of shape, contrast, and distance, the general effect of the flashed letter is to "demask" a solitary letter or a letter of a word that had been rendered less visible, presumably by the surrounding letters, when it was a part of the word. The demasking did not occur when the constituent letters were not of the same case; thus, in general, the effects of form per se were stronger than the semantic or cognitive content of the symbols.

The complexities of this kind of masking are obviously far more complex than we had been led to believe by earlier work. What seems certain is that the demasking observed by Geiger and Lettvin is not different in kind from the earlier studies of disinhibition reported by Robinson and his colleagues (1966, 1968) some years ago. These are not simple spatial lateral interactions, but processes influenced by the global form of the character. Like other forms of metacontrast (see Uttal, 1973b), the observed demasking effects did not occur when simple vertical lines are used, only when forms of some complexity like letters were involved. Thus, the effects are form sensitive and not simply due to the raw geometry of the situation.

This, then, brings us to the crux of the metacontrast problem. The value and attention that have been attributed to this peculiar little phenomenon arises mainly out of the fact that it is a useful medium with which to study some of the complex problems of perceptual processing. Metacontrast is, therefore, of interest to the degree that it tells us something about the function and structure of the visual process, that is, to the degree that it becomes a vehicle for theoretical development. In this regard, metacontrast has been extremely fruitful and has stimulated the development of a rich variety of theoretical models. I have already considered in detail the neuroreductionistic models, but many other models have also been proposed. Briefly, some of the more interesting theoretical explanations of metacontrast so far proposed have been Kahneman's (1968) attribution of it to the perceptual disallowance of the impossible apparent motion that must occur in several directions simultaneously when the disk and annulus (or three rectangular stimuli) are sequentially flashed; Eriksen and Hoffman's (1963) and Eriksen and Lappin's (1964) suggestion that metacontrast was an artifact of delayed simultaneous contrast between an image and an afterimage (this is generally known as the "integration" hypothesis); and Kolers' (1968) and Haber's (1969) proposal of an "information overload" hypothesis. This last hypothesis asserts that the first stimulus in a metacontrast paradigm was not allowed sufficient time to be fully processed before the contrasting stimulus "caught up with it," and that the latter thus interfered with the recognition of the former (this is usually referred to as the "interruption" hypothesis).

In conclusion, metacontrast represents a prototypical form of temporal interaction characterized by a backward suppression of detectability that, despite a substantial empirical and theoretical effort, remains largely enigmatic in terms of its origins. In particular, it appears that the several currently popular neuroreductionistic models are inadequate. Their popularity persists mainly because of an absence of alternatives that incorporate knowledge of the effects of higher level influences (e.g., the "judged" impossibility of split apparent motion). The metacontrast effect seems clearly not to be a peripheral one but, rather, to be strongly dependent on central information-processing mechanisms that are considerably more complex than the simple networks proposed by the lateral inhibition theorists.

An argument for the more central or cognitive basis for metacontrast is that the masked, undetectable information is not lost. A number of investigators, to the contrary, have shown that even though a masked stimulus may have been driven below conscious awareness, it may have some subsequent effect on perception. That is, it is entirely possible for a stimulus to be masked to the point of invisibility and still have some influence on the perception of a subsequently presented stimulus. The nature of the effect varies from experiment to experiment, but clearly in such studies as that reported by Morotomi (1981) the specific shape of a backward masked stimulus can have an influence on the recognition of another stimulus that is masked in the forward direction by the same mask. In Morotomi's study he compared a situation in which the pre- and postmask stimuli were identical to ones in which there was no premask stimulus. The effect of the presence of the identical premask stimulus was, somewhat counterintuitively, to actually reduce the recognition scores for the stimulus (Japanese Kana characters). In other situations, controlled shifts in criterion level have varied scores enormously (Pollack, 1972; Schiller & Smith, 1966), even when observers reported that the stimulus was for all practical purposes undetectable. The presence of dichoptic metacontrast is also a strong argument for a central locus of this phenomenon, one that does not depend upon the peripheral interaction so often invoked to explain it. In addition to the classic Kolers and Rosner (1960) paper, new reports of dichoptic metacontrast and its interaction with chromatic induction (Olson & Boynton, 1984) argue strongly that both of these phenomena are mediated by central mechanisms. It is on this note that this chapter is concluded.

4

THE DISCRIMINATION
OF VISUAL FORMS

A. INTRODUCTION

In chapter 3, I surveyed some of the empirical results and theories that pertained to the *detection* of visual forms. In that discussion theories were considered that were intended to explain the outcome of experiments in which the observer was asked to answer a question that was typically structured in the prototypical manner: "Is anything there?" Our attention is now directed to another task—another prototypical question—that of the visual discrimination of forms. In this case, observers are presented with what is informationally a much more demanding challenge in that they have to not only detect the two forms that are to be compared but also to perceive a sufficient amount of detail so that whether they are the *same* or *different* can be specified. Furthermore, the answer to this question is often not so simply dichotomous as it may at first be represented. Same or different judgments are extremes of a continuum, of course, and the decision may be graduated in that the observer can be directed to respond to a query asking to what degree two stimuli are *similar*.

Discriminative mechanisms lie at the heart of a substantial body of empirical psychological research, both current and classic, that probes this particular aspect of the mental processes of visual perception. A substantial amount of theory is also based upon what is at first glance a deceptively trivial psychophysical assay procedure. Theories of discriminability and similarity are among the richest in terms of possessing a relevant data base in the field of visual perception and have the additional advantageous property of generalizing to and linking with many other cognitive processes.

The study of discrimination has been approached from many different points of view. Some researchers have sought to simply determine what are the aspects or attributes of the to-be-compared stimuli that specify whether or not they will be discriminated. But there is also substantial interest in using the discrimination data that have been forthcoming from experiments in which the stimulus materials have relatively little intrinsic interest of their own as surrogates for higher level cognitive processes. In that case the discrimination task becomes a vehicle for questions that deal with such esoterica as whether or not the dimensions of the stimulus are "separable or integral" or explorations into the psychological nature of similarity per se. Other approaches concentrate on the psychophysics of same-different judgments or may even represent steps in the development of methodologies that will allow researchers to approach a problem only tangentially related to the discrimination paradigm itself. For example, the nature of the primitives of visual perception or the nature of the hypothetical Fourier channels that are believed by many to explain pattern perception in general have been targets of research using discrimination paradigms. Our main interest in this chapter, however, is the visual discrimination process per se. What for others has been a medium for analysis is the main substantive topic of this chapter.

It is important to remember that discrimination cannot be examined in isolation from other perceptual processes. The question of the isolatability of the mechanisms identified in chapters 3, 4, and 5 thus arises again. At the outset of this discussion, therefore, it is important to reiterate that discrimination-type experiments, although stressing the judgment of similarity, on the one hand, or of identity or nonidentity on the other, actually involve many other psychological processes than these judgments alone. I have already alluded to the fact that discrimination without detection seems logically impossible (the exceptions nowadays being generally thought to represent subtle procedural artifacts). But there are other indications that clearly suggest that no perceptual process such as discrimination actually exists in total isolation in spite of the previously cited evidence for some kind of hierarchical structuring. We also have to consider that the properties of decision making and other attentive aspects of cognition can and do influence this kind of perceptual processing. Such diverse workers (in the sense that their theoretical orientations are quite different) as Triesman and Gelade (1980) and Grossberg and Mingolla (1985) argue that the raw form of the stimulus is not sufficient to define the percept. Both pairs of investigators speak with deep conviction of the influence of the context or, perhaps to be more accurate, of the observer's attention to the context as a definitive factor in the perception of forms.

In this same vein, it must also be appreciated that there is at least an implicit element of attentive sequentiality in many discrimination experiments that guarantees that this process, in particular, will not solely depend on an instantaneous, automatic, algorithmic response. If the two stimuli to be compared are presented one after the other in the same location the sequentiality is, of course, explicit; but, even if these are presented simultaneously in adjacent locations so the time seems to be of no consequence, in psychological fact attention must sequentially be directed from one stimulus to the adjacent one. This implicit shift of attention introduces time into the discrimination process in almost all experiments of this genre. The few exceptions are exemplified by those in which only a single stimulus scene or object is used; for example, in the texture discrimination studies where two regions are both simultaneously within the field of attention of the observer.

Thus, we see that the discrimination task is intrinsically much more complicated than detection, which, at least at first glance, could be executed by a simple passive network; discrimination involves, at the very least, some short-term storage of the visual information, the judgmental act of the comparison process, as well as all of the processes responsible for the detection of the stimuli. Theories of discrimination, therefore, have much more to explain than those that deal with the detection process alone and the more cognitive tone of the theories discussed in this chapter (compared to the previous one) attests to this increased complexity. This basic fact of complexity explains the existence of what many would consider to be a more mentalistic and active variety of theories and approaches than is found in the study of detection. (One possible exception to this generality can again be found in the work on texture discrimination to be described here that is still conceptualized in a more empiricist than rationalist framework by many, if not all, theoreticians.)

As I noted previously, some theoretical approaches to discrimination are very closely concerned with the psychological salience of the attributes of the stimulus. For example, what exactly is the psychological nature of stimulus similarity? What are the attributes of two stimuli that determine whether they are perceived as being the same or different? Are the dimensions or attributes of the stimuli separable, or are they tied together in some way that prevents them from being perceptually dealt with independently? It is quite surprising how each of these questions has often led to its own distinct literature and how often these separate literatures seem not to overlap in the thinking of the scholars who are studying discrimination. It is on the basis of this collection of sometimes-nonoverlapping sets of questions that this chapter is organized.

Another question that we must deal with in passing concerns the relationship of detection, discrimination, and recognition to each other. Implicit in the taxonomy that organizes this book is the concept that at each of the three levels of visual processing successively higher amounts of information must be extracted by the observer for each of these tasks to be accomplished.

Another way to emphasize this same idea is to assert that the performance on each of the precursor visual information-processing tasks must be accomplished before the other tasks can be carried out. One nonintuitive counterargument to such a hypothesis lies in some relatively rare data obtained from well-controlled comparisons of detection, discrimination, and recognition behavior. Furcher, Thomas, and Campbell (1977), for example, found that reported difference between detection and what they refer to as "discrimination thresholds" of spatial-frequency varying, grating-type stimuli are in most cases accounted for if simple probability-summation considerations are taken into account. Their suggestion, therefore, is that there is no processing hierarchy—both thresholds are achieved at the same information levels at least for this particular kind of stimulus. Other workers have reported this same phenomenon in other contexts—a surprisingly small difference between the detection and discrimination thresholds. It is as if an observer can distinguish what is there virtually as soon as he can distinguish that something is there.

Even more interesting and counterintuitive, however, is that in some situations the performance of the observer may run counter to the predictions of the hierarchical model of information acquisition in an even more astonishing manner. Several workers (Diener, 1981; Doehrman, 1974) have reported that under certain circumstances recognition performance can actually be more accurate than detection performance at the same stimulus information levels. At first glance such a result would imply that the observer is able to recognize something that can not be detected, a result that is obviously contrary to the hierarchical information-acquisition theory as well as the experimental results I discussed at the outset of chapter 3. This result raises the possibility of a paradoxical world in which form identification might even exist in the absence of detection.[1]

However, the actual nonmysterious nature of the possibility of equal detection and recognition, or even the superiority of the latter over the former, has been clarified by Green and Birdsall (1978), who evaluated several alternative explanatory theories. At least one—the disjunctive model—predicts that recognition and detection performance levels should be very close. A specific explanation of the apparent superiority of recognition over detection has been presented by Thomas, Gille, and Barker (1982). They point out, in analyzing an experiment in which either one of two alternative gratings could be present in one of two sequential presentations (the 2 x 2 experimental design that is frequently used in this type of investigation) that it might be possible for an observer to use information from both presentations (e.g., "nothing present" in a spatial subregion of either the stimulus or stimulus-plus-noise presentation may be useful information) to correctly identify a stimulus even when detection was not possible. This sort of process could, according to them, be framed in the context of a low-threshold theoretical explanation of the visual process in contrast to a high-threshold explanation that would preclude identification without detection.

---

[1] There are mythical stories still permeating the psychological literature about something called "subliminal perception" that has been used as a bogeyman to frighten the lay public (the fear is that they may be directed to eat popcorn in a theater when they do not wish to do so or to commit some other nefarious act such as buying an unwanted deodorant.) The so-called problem of subliminal perception is beyond the intended scope of this book, but recent reviews of perception without awareness (i.e., recognition without detection) indicate that subliminal perception is not likely to be a major social hazard. Cheesman and Merikle (1984) and Eriksen (1960) both argue that the methodology used in studies that have reported this elusive phenomenon are seriously flawed, and that the technique is probably ineffective—a contention with which I strongly agree.

B. SOME DEFINITIONS

I. Integral and Separable Dimensions

In order to more easily proceed through some of the following subject matter, it is necessary to familiarize ourselves with certain ideas that have been the focal points of theoretical controversies or empirical research in recent years with regard to discrimination. One of the most important and fertile of these concepts has been the dichotomy of integral and separable dimensions that was originally introduced by Shepard (1964) and Garner (1974).

The idea was an attempt on the part of both of these eminent perceptual theoreticians to precisely characterize the nature of the dimensions that are used in discrimination- and similarity-type experiments. Specifically they were concerned with the way the various dimensions of a stimulus are dealt with by the observer rather than the raw physical description of the stimulus as defined by the experimenter. The separable-integral dichotomy is an explicit effort to deal with the different ways in which two or more stimuli may interact. *Separable* (in Garner's vocabulary—*analytic* in Shepard's older nomenclature) dimensions are defined as those that maintain their independence from each other and which can be analyzed separately even though jointly defining the stimulus. *Integral* (in Garner's vocabulary—*unitary* in Shepard's older nomenclature) dimensions, however, lose their distinctiveness and separateness as they jointly define a stimulus and cannot, therefore, be analyzed separately. Integral dimensions produce stimuli, in the words of another theoretician (Lockhead, 1966, 1972), that tend to be perceived more as undifferentiated perceptual "blobs" or composite experiences than as the combination of a set of quasi-independent properties. (This concept is closely related to the holistic–elementalistic controversy described later in this section, but has a conceptual uniqueness that demands that it be dealt with separately.)

Integral stimuli are typified by situations in which one dimension cannot change without affecting another's value. Separable stimuli can be varied independently. That is, one dimension cannot vary without affecting the value of others in integral situations, but can vary in separable ones. In Monahan and Lockhead's (1977) terms, integrality can be defined as follows: "A stimulus is integral if removal of a physical aspect renders the other aspects unspecifiable or if removal of an aspect removes relational aspects of the stimuli" (p. 109).

Separable dimensions are exemplified by the orientation and size of a semicircle or the size and brightness of a square (see, for example, Nosofsky, 1985); integral dimensions can be exemplified by the classic caricature of a face made up of four lines enclosed within a circle. The size and the orientation of the hemisphere can be described both perceptually and analytically independently of each other; the integral features of a face cannot, and the object is perceived as a whole. If one changes the curvature of the mouth on a caricature of a face, for example, the entire visage may change from an overall happy smile to a globally unhappy frown. Another traditional exemplar of a pair of integral dimensions is to be found in the dimensions of chromaticity; hue and saturation are very difficult to deal with separately by a perceiver. We see colors, not independent hues and saturations.

The importance or the separable-integral dichotomy in discrimination research is substantial. One way in which these two different types of responses to stimulus attributes may influence perception is that they may differentially affect the perceived similarity of stimuli. Furthermore, the mathematical models best suited for describing stimuli characterized by either integral or separable dimensions may be substantially different. A vigorous theoretical controversy has raged around this issue. It is, however, a controversy muddied by large individual differences (see, for example, Ward, 1985) in the way in which stimuli are perceived by observers. That is, observers seem to vary in their tendency to integrate or separate certain dimensions. In the search for universal rules of perception, this is a most disappointing development and may seriously confound our understanding of what had previously been considered to be a built-in process common to all observers. Needless to add, the experimental task also drives performance in ways that are not always under complete control.

2. Wholes Versus Parts

The integral–separable dichotomy is, as noted, also closely related to the whole-part controversy in visual perception. The question in this case, however, has a slightly different emphasis: It deals with whether or not stimuli are perceived on the basis of their overall global structural properties or, to the contrary, are recognized because of a detailed initial analysis of the individual features of which they are composed? The tradition emphasizing the role of local features has its roots in the associative elementalism of the 18th century British empiricists, the structuralism of the early 20th century, and even in the behavioristic traditions that dominated experimental psychology in the 1950s and 1960s. Modern feature analytical models, furthermore, have been enormously influenced by the dual conceptual impact of the elegant neurophysiological work on what are patently feature-triggered single-cell sensitivities and of studies in which computers are used to simulate human visual processes. The enormous progress in these fields has led to a heavy theoretical stress on the analysis of stimuli into their component parts. I believe this emphasis to be misplaced and consider this problem in detail in chapter 5.

The global or holistic approach to perception with its roots in the 18th and 19th century attempts to bring properties such as "relationships" into the discussion of perception. This movement was led by such workers as Thomas Reid, William Hamilton, Ernst Mach, and Christian Von Ehrenfels. Holistic thinking, however, reached its historic epitome in the writing of the twentieth century Gestalt school. (See, for example, the work of Wertheimer, 1923; Koffka, 1935; and

Köhler, 1947.) Modern holistic theories stress the emergence of the Lockhead-type perceptual blob at least in the initial stages of form perception. This is referred to as "global precedence."

Nowadays, as is so often the case, there is a compromise in the works, and the real focus of the current controversy between holism and elementalism seems to be more in terms of determining under which conditions the role of the elements predominate or take precedence and under which the global properties predominate or take precedence. This is an important intellectual step forward compared to the archaic goal of determining which is the sole "correct" approach in any absolute sense. Modern researchers take their lead in this regard from the distinguished work of Erich Goldmeier (1936/1972), who manipulated the size and spacing of groups of lines to determine whether the lines would seem an integrated part of the whole or as elements unto themselves.

The theme of Goldmeier's work has been pursued by Klein and Barresi (1985). They found that when the spacing of dot arrays was large and the dots were few, the number of elements determined similarity, but when the spacing was small and the number of dots large, similarity was more influenced by the spacing than by number. This was interpreted by them to mean that when large, components (i.e., features) of objects were dealt with as independent entities (a precedence of features), but that that when they were small, the features were dealt with as the "material" of an overall form in a way that ignored their local properties.

In spite of this noble trend toward eclecticism, it has to be acknowledged that most contemporary theories are analytic and "part"-oriented, and, without doubt, there is a considerable amount of data to support this point of view. On the other hand, a substantial body of research also demonstrates that humans perceive the general holistic structural relationships of the parts rather than the nature of the parts. Let us now briefly consider two bodies of research that argue for these opposing views as a way of clarifying the two alternative theoretical approaches.

First consider the work of Navon (1977) as an example of empirical support for the holistic view of perception. Navon's paper has taken on some of the characteristics of a classic in the few years since it has been published. He used an ingenious method of determining whether observers depend upon the local geometrical features or the global form in our recognition tasks. Navon's experiments employed stimuli like those shown in Fig. 4.1—an alphabetic letter

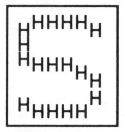

FIG. 4.1.   The stimulus object used by Navon (1977) to study the local versus global controversy.

made up of smaller alphabetic letters, This device was probably first used by Shor (1971) but was also used by Kinchla (1974).

Navon was specifically interested in determining if the larger letters (the global letters) were perceived by piecemeal integration of the small letters (the local features) or whether the entire global form was perceived independently of the detailed structure of those small "features." To anticipate both his results and his conclusions, Navon found that the holistic approach seemed to be the one utilized by the human observer in this type of perceptual situation.

How did Navon arrive at his conclusion? He used a modification of the Stroop name-and-color-interference phenomenon—a modification in which vision and audition could interfere. Stroop (1935) had originally shown that if a word that was *the name of a color* was printed in a color other than that which it named, the observer would have a more difficult time in reading the word than if the word naming the color was composed of letters in the color it named. In his experiment, Navon used visual interference of auditory stimuli as the measure of the impact of the global and local features respectively. The observer was presented with an auditory stimulus consisting of one of two possible spoken names of letters. The task was to identify the letter by depressing an appropriate button. At nearly the same time as this auditory stimulus was presented, the observer was presented with a visual stimulus that could either be the correct response to the auditory stimulus or the incorrect alternative—another alphabetic character. This design was based upon a clear-cut preliminary demonstration that if the visual stimulus conflicted with the auditory one, there would be a profound prolongation of the reaction time in the two alternative, forced-choice, auditory-stimulus-elicited response. This preliminary experiment calibrated the fact that the visual stimulus could interfere with the response to the auditory response.

Navon used the stimuli shown in Fig. 4.1 in exactly this way. That is, the "global" visual letters, constructed from the local letter "features," were used as putative interfering stimuli. The key question was phrased in the following manner: Would the global letter or the local letter interfere more with the auditory naming task? The empirical answer obtained in several experiments was that only the global letter could so interfere, but not the local letters. Therefore, Navon concluded that whatever information was contained in the local structure was not participating in the processes of letter recognition, at least, as he was testing them in this experiment.

Navon went on to consider possible artifacts as letter size and the "speed of conduction" of different letters, and his arguments against artifacts seemed at that time to be convincing in eliminating these potential sources of confounding from consideration. The conclusion to which this work led Navon, along with authors of other relevant studies, along with such practical phenomena as the very great difficulty that copy editors have in proofreading documents, is that visual perception of letters and forms proceeds from the global to the local. In the current jargon, there is a *precedence* of the global form over the local feature in this kind of form perception.

As an aside, it is fascinating to note that, virtually in their entirety, "artificial" intelligence programs work by extracting local features and working up from features to the global form. Similarly, most neuroreductionistic theories of form perception also suggest that it is the local feature that drives the perceptual mechanism. Navon's results and others of the same genre (e.g., Reicher, 1969; Palmer, 1975; Wheeler, 1970; Weisstein & Harris, 1974, 1980) suggest, to the contrary, that no matter how competent the artificial intelligence schemes are, they are not simulating the processes of human intelligence, but rather are operating according to algorithms, rules, and processes that very different from those underlying human perception.

The holistic approach championed by Navon and others has been supported by even others. Gregory Lockhead, who was instrumental in establishing the integral-separable dichotomy, has also placed his own experimental results among those he believes to support a holistic model of visual information processing. Following Lockhead's seminal paper (1972) originally suggesting the holistic "blob" model in which the integral dimensions were processed as an unified whole and specific local features are ignored, Monahan and Lockhead (1977) carried out an extensive series of studies in which observers were asked to identify or judge the similarity of arrays of rectangles or pairs of lines. They interpreted their results to show that it was the vector difference in a multidimensional scaling space (that is, the overall degree of similarity) rather than any putative examination of the local features of the stimuli that determined their observer's performance.

Goldmeier (1982) has presented an interesting review of a number of phenomena that also argues strongly for the precedence of global and contextual attributes of a visual stimulus. In brief, his point is that the perception of a wide variety of stimulus forms is more heavily influenced by the overall visual scene of which they are a part than by the local elements. Some "features" of a scene can disappear entirely (in a perceptual sense) even though they are very much a geometrical part of the stimulus. What we see is what best fits together (as well as what we *remember*). This point of view places Goldmeier's word well within both the classic Gestalt traditions (a tradition that still has much to say to perceptual psychologists even if they do not often listen to the message) and the emerging group of neoholists. Others who have supported the global-precedence hypothesis and who can be categorized within this rubric are Broadbent (1977) and Kinchla and Wolfe (1979).

Reinterpretation and criticisms of the work of Navon and other neoholists, however, was not long in coming. J. Miller (1981) carried out experiments that led him to shift the domain of the Navon phenomenon from the passively perceptual (i.e., preattentive) to the actively attentive. His argument is that the apparent global precedence observed in Navon's study is really due to the twin facts that attention can be directed at the global attributes without attending to the local ones, but that the converse is not true: It is very difficult for an observer to attend to the local feature without attending to the global form. Miller thus suggested that there is no global or local precedence per se—both attributes are simultaneously available in a perceptual sense to the limits of visual acuity. The apparent superiority of one over the other only depends upon which is attended to "post-perceptually."

Thus, Miller rejects a global-precedence phenomenon and asserts a simultaneous availability of both global and local attributes at the preattentive perceptual level. Nevertheless, it must be kept very clear that he does not deny that there is a global advantage of some sort. Attention and decision making, he asserts, do operate primarily in a global-to-local direction. Miller cites an array of studies that he believes supports the concept of global priority or precedence. His main point, however, is that the observed global priority is a result of attention and is not preattentive in the sense invoked by Navon. Indeed, Miller (1981) concludes with a general caveat that might well be reiterated here: "...the present work should be seen as a reminder of the difficulty inherent in attributing effects of experimental variables to perceptual processes, as opposed to decision and to attentional processes" (p.1173).

This statement, of course, is a specialized corollary of the general theorem proposed by Moore (1956) that was discussed in Chapter 1. The general point should not be lost in this clutter of experimental detail. That point is: *Behavioral, stimulus–response, or input–output analysis cannot, in principle, determine the inner structure of a closed system.* Even talk of "convergent operations" cannot obscure the very great possibility that what is being attempted in this kind of theoretical excursion is very possibly not achievable. I believe this to be the crux of what may turn out to be one of the major philosophical crises of late 20th century psychology.

Other criticisms of Navon's work have also been forthcoming. Interestingly, they arise from two diametrically different points of view: One theoretical perspective asserts that the global-precedence effect reported by Navon is actually an artifact resulting from peripheral factors; the other asserts that the effect is not valid because of cognitive processes that were biased in the original experiment.

Peripheral mechanisms able to account for Navon's global-precedence effect have been invoked by Grice, Canham, and Boroughs (1983) . They generalize that the "global-precedence effect" is actually an artifact arising from the fact that the smaller constituent letters or features are more easily degraded by such factors as eye-motion and the location of the stimulus on the retina. When optical and neurological variables such as these were controlled to provide equally clear stimulation for the small and the large letters, these authors report that the reaction-time differences reported by Navon disappeared. Their conclusion is that global precedence is not a primary perceptual principle but rather a derivative of fundamental peripheral, optical, and neurological properties of visual stimulation.

The other point of view attacks Navon's findings by asserting that they are the outcome of high-level cognitive mechanisms. Kinchla, Solis-Macias, and Hoffman (1983) suggest that the whole global-versus-local-precedence argument is ill-posed. That is, they suggest that, to the contrary, either one may dominate depending on the attentional set of the observer. According to Kinchla and his colleagues, the observer has the ability to select alternative visual strategies, sometimes attending to the microscopic or local details and sometimes attending to the macroscopic shape, and that each of these strategies will emphasize the influence of the part or parts of the stimulus to which it is especially tuned. Thus, they reject both the *bottom-up*, peripherally oriented objection of the global-precedence effect supported by Grice, Canham, and Boroughs (1983) and the *top-down* perceptual effect itself originally championed by Navon. Kinchla and his colleagues are suggesting a third alternative—a hypothetical *middle-out* process in which intermediate aspects of the form are first sampled. They assume that the perceptual field of view of the observer can then be expanded or contracted at that person's cognitive discretion to more global or more local aspects. This point of view has also been championed by Hoffman (1980). In fairness, it should be noted that the great individual differences in this kind of work support their contention.

However, even this eclectic and compromising point of view has its challengers. Hughes, Layton, Baird, and Lester (1984) have reported new data that not only supports the idea of global precedence, but also suggests that high level cognitive factors cannot account for the phenomenon itself.

Obviously this is a field in a very fluid theoretical state and one that is currently involved in a very vigorous controversy. The question can be raised: Is this controversy resolvable, or are the authors of the studies attempting to do something that is in contradiction in principle to what automata theory tells us about the impenetrability of the inner mechanisms of a black box?

It would be incomplete, however, if we did not also hear from other champions of the feature hypothesis. The opposing (to the global-precedence hypothesis) feature-oriented point of view is, perhaps, best currently exemplified by the work of Anne Triesman and her colleagues. They (Triesman & Gelade, 1980; Triesman & Patterson, 1984: Triesman & Schmidt, 1982; Triesman & Souther, 1985; Triesman, Sykes, & Gelade, 1977) have presented a strong counterargument that they believe supports the contention that the local elements of a scene are processed prior to the organization of the whole form. Triesman and her colleagues have focused their interpretation of their findings by referring to it as their "feature integration theory." The main axiom of their argument is that local features are processed first by the nervous system and only subsequently are they organized into integrated forms or percepts. Furthermore, and this is a major deviation from most current theories, they hypothesize that *to so integrate the feature requires effortful attention.* (I believe, however, that the nearly automatic recognition processes to be described in the next chapter speak to the contrary on this point. I also expect that there will be a great deal of controversy concerning this point in the future.) The idea proposed by Triesman and her colleagues is not entirely novel. It reflects a kind of feature integration that was a central axiom of an earlier form-perception theory proposed by Hebb (1949). In Hebb's model, the features were first perceived by assemblies of cells and then united by "phase sequences" programmed by eye-movements. Though tachistoscopic exposures have relegated the eye-movement hypothesis to the theoretical rubbish heap, one can substitute shifts of attention for actual orbital motion in Hebb's theory and come up with what is essentially the very same theory proposed by Triesman and her colleagues.

The general outline of the Triesman feature integration theory is shown in Fig. 4.2 in a diagrammatic fashion. The main point of relevance in the present context is that Triesman postulates that many different feature maps are generated during the early, preattentive processing, perhaps (but not necessarily), by the well-known feature-triggered neurophysiological systems that have been the object of so much attention during the last two decades. (These operators, of course, are the analogs of Hebb's cell assemblies.) It is her belief that a substantial amount

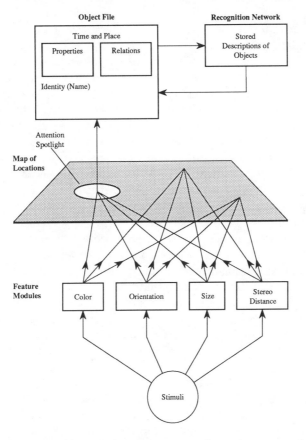

FIG. 4.2.   A model of the human form perception system as conceived by Triesman (redrawn from Triesman, 1986).

of empirical data speaks to the hypothesis of an initial local-feature analysis as opposed to the global models proposed by Navon and others. Specifically, she (Triesman & Patterson, 1984) cites the following classes of evidence to support this approach to visual information processing.

1. The existence of feature specific neurons in the neurophysiological research data base.
2. The fact that selective adaptation occurs to specific features of a stimulus.
3. Additive effects in similarity judgments.
4. The influence of selective attention in feeding and sorting tasks.

Triesman and her colleagues have also reported the results of a number of new experiments that are presented in support of the "features before wholes" precise of her feature-integration theory. These include studies of the conjunction of color, shapes, lines, and angles; visual search for particular geometrical forms; studies of texture segregation; and explorations of illusory merging of elemental features. The latter is a particularly interesting piece of evidence. Triesman's logic is that if an observer occasionally perceives, for example, a red x when presented in a degraded stimulus presentation (for example, by presenting the stimuli in brief exposures) consisting of a green x and a red o (but no red x), this is evidence for an initial analysis into elements. Or, in her own words, "If features can be wrongly recombined, they must have at some level been separately registered as independent entities" (Triesman & Patterson, 1984, p. 14).

That any whole-versus-part-or-feature argument exists has two very important causes. One is essentially psychological—the processes underlying a percept are invisible to the observer and can only indirectly be probed by the experimenter. No one is aware of the codes or transformations that are used in his or her own visual system prior to the emergence of the perceptual experience itself. This lack of even introspective understanding fuels the debate between the local-features and global-aspect theoreticians—a debate that remains very active at the present time with both sides claiming compelling arguments to support their position.

Another way to say this is to point out the difficulty, and perhaps the impossibility, of specifying the internal mechanisms of a closed "black box" by input–output methods alone. The other reason for debate concerning the whole–part controversy is neurophysiological. Even when one does measure cellular responses inside the "black box," the mammalian brain is still so complicated that it is, for all practical purposes, still closed. Beyond these constraints of combinatorics, there are also logical problems.

For example, contrary to popular opinion, no matter how much neurophysiological evidence is accumulated that there is some kind of local-feature analysis of the input-stimulus features, this kind of observation in no way is supportive of a feature-analytical approach to perceptual information processing. Neurophysiological evidence of this kind speaks only to the communication aspects of peripheral sensory coding and not to the interpretative perceptual mechanisms that deal subsequently with that neural information. Cellular responses and mental representations remain completely separate by a vast gulf of ignorance concerning how single cells mediate molar perceptions.

Nevertheless, there is a persistent trend in the perceptual literature to identify specific trigger features as basic perceptual elements. This trend continues the elementalism of the British empiricists and the American structuralists in a modern form. Indeed, the search for the basic elements (fundamental spatial features or "textons," in Julesz's terminology) of perception has become a mainstay of modern perceptual research, almost to the point of begging the more general question of whether the global organization or the local feature takes precedence. Some investigators have based their entire theoretical superstructure on the preassumption that there exists a sensitivity to just these kinds of local features. Clearly, there is no shortage of elementalists among contemporary perceptual psychologists today. But, as I hope I have made clear, the issue is still moot and there is a resurgence of holistic or neo-Gestaltist thinking in contemporary thought. I return to this matter later.

3. Analog Versus Propositional Representations

Another vocabulary issue that must be briefly considered here is the dichotomy established by the antithetical terms *analog* and *propositional*. The context in which this pair of opposing terms is used is that of *representation*—the mechanism by means of which information is stored in the short- and long-term memorial repositories of the brain. The question of specific concern is: In what form is the information that was originally acquired from a visual event as a geometric, physical mapping stored and remembered in later stages of perception? The problem arises because of some very fundamental principles of computation theory, specifically, because of what may be the most important principle in this field. That premier principle is the one proposed and proven by A.M. Turing (1936), in which he establishes that *any idea or concept, no matter how complex, can be represented or encoded by means of a string of binary digits, or any other code, for that matter*. Although the string may become very long and it may even be impractical because of its cumbersomeness to deal with in realistic systems, the point is that there is no way to exclude any particular coded representation of any message on the basis of some criterion of a priori unsuitability.

Turing's principle ("There is no unique code") recurs in one form or another throughout science and technology. Complete computers can be made from a single pair of logical elements (an *and gate* and an *inverter*, for example) that, though inefficient in practice, is perfectly capable, in principle, of carrying out any kind of computation. In the study of the neural coding of sensory messages, one of the universals emerging from many decades of research is identical to Turing's principle: Any neural response can represent any dimension of the message (see my discussion of this vitally important, but usually ignored rule in Uttal, 1973b). There is no dimensional isomorphism required between stimulus and code as long as one knows or can extract the rules of translation. All of the scientific developments in the field of information processing, as well as many of the household joys of our modern telecommunication technology, emerge from the same fundamental source—the innumerable variety of ways in which information can be represented in accord with Turing's theorem.

But these positive developments and joys notwithstanding, many scientific perplexities also emerge from this same flexibility of representation. Because of Turing's proof (in essence saying that any idea can be represented by any code) and Moore's (1956) theorem (in essence saying that the internal mechanisms—including the nature of the codes—of black boxes are unanalyzable by input–output methods) there is a great uncertainty about the ways in which concepts and percepts are represented within the brain. Although it is often obscured by the great successes of single-cell neurophysiology and the general misunderstanding about their relevance to perception (see especially Teller's, 1984, fine article for clarification of this point), it is also certainly true that we have no idea what are the logical processes and codes that are used by neurons of the central nervous system to represent stored information obtained through the sensory receptors. All we know about currently is how they represent *transmitted* messages.

For these reasons, a great deal of controversy exists in the field of memorial, image, or message representation in cognitive studies. Just as with the problem of wholes versus parts, since we cannot establish the answer to this question without equivocation, many different theories of representation have been suggested. Nowhere is this speculative controversy more prevalent than in the perceptual literature.

Theories of perceptual representation fall into two prototypical classes—the *analog* and the *propositional*. At one extreme are the analog theories of representation. The thesis among proponents of this school of thought is that the internal (mental) representation of a stimulus object is in the form of a picture or of a geometric model or some other "analog" that maintains the essential dimensionality and spatial or temporal relationships of the original stimulus geometry. Obviously, this is a kind of representation that is mainly suitable for handling visual information, but one could also imagine an equivalent process for auditory signals in which the melody or tonal pattern was also encoded in a manner that preserved the temporal characteristics of the acoustic signal.

Analog representations of this sort need not be trivial "toy-in-the-head"-type models in which every spatial aspect of the stimulus is geometrically replicated, but may be expressed in the form of elaborate mathematical equivalencies that are in only a formal sense isomorphic to the stimulus. The important thing from the point of view of the analog theorists is that the relationships among the parts are maintained in some kind of a space that is intertransformable with the space of the stimulus.

The opposing (to analog representation) view is generally described as being propositional, symbolic, or verbal. The main theme of this theoretical orientation is that the geometrical or temporal relationships of a visual or acoustic stimulus are not maintained in the same spatial pattern but, rather, that some heavily encoded language is used. For example, a "four-sided equilateral polygon" presented as a visual image could be represented in the brain, not as a spatial replica or dimensional isomorph of the input stimulus with the same geometrical relationships, but by a verbal code—the word *square*. The word has none of the geometrical properties of the original object but it can, and in many cases certainly does, adequately represent that object. Furthermore, many everyday experiences make it clear that such a symbolic representation can lead to the imagined reconstruction of the object virtually as well as the original analog representations of the object cum stimulus.

Much more elaborate propositional codes can be used to carry out the same representational function according to theorists of this genre. For example, a "square" could be described in words as "a figure constructed from four equilength lines organized so that the intersections of each pair form a 90 degree angle in such a way that traversing the figure will bring one back to the point of origin." This is an expression symbolically or propositionally equivalent to both the shape itself and to the word *square*, but expressed as a series of propositions that bear little geometrical resemblance to either.

The same concept—a square—could also be represented by a *production system*—a set of statements that allows one to actively reconstruct the form. For example, a square could be constructed from the following set of instructions:

1. Pick a point (x, y).
2. Draw a line in the +y direction one unit long,
3. Draw a line in the +x direction one unit long.
4. Draw a line in the −y direction one unit long.
5. Draw a line in the −x direction one unit long.
6. Stop.

These production instructions are equivalent to a □, to the word *square*, and to the description in the previous paragraphs. They are probably also equivalent to a type of neural representation in the brain that is the equivalent of none of these and that remains, today, totally mysterious despite some fantasies to the contrary.

Research on this topic of representation is particularly active today and represents an area of intense interest to perceptual psychologists. It should not go unmentioned that this study of inner representations would have been anathema to the behavioristically oriented psychologists of only a few years ago. And it may ultimately be determined to represent a bizarre overestimate of the limits of our science—if the brain is a finite automaton in Moore's sense. Though this gloomy prospect looms over the entire analog-propositional debate (among many others in perceptual psychology), for the moment the outcome of the battle between the two theories is unresolved. If I were forced to make a prediction, I would suggest that neither theory is correct in its present specific form, as currently detailed, possibly because both may be present in some way that would satisfy both schools of thought.

C. THE NATURE OF SIMILARITY— SOME THEORETICAL APPROACHES

Although a substantial portion of psychophysical methodology used in discrimination research utilizes a dichotomous "same–different" methodology, much of the modern theory in this field builds upon the somewhat richer idea that some pairs of stimuli are more similar to each other than are other pairs, and that similarity cab be metricized in a graded and continuous manner. It is this assumed variability in the degree of similarity that is the basis of the influential contemporary quantitative models that are inferred from the confusions and discrimination errors that are observed in both the same–different type of discrimination experiments and those in which similarity is itself judged. Tversky (1977) suggests that graded similarity is, furthermore, central to a wide variety of other psychological concepts and ideas. Specifically, he points out that:

> Similarity plays a fundamental role in theories of knowledge and behavior. It serves as an organizing principle by which individuals classify objects, form concepts, and make generalizations. Indeed, the concept of similarity is ubiquitous in psychological theory. It underlies the accounts of stimulus and response generalization in learning, it is employed to explain errors in memory and pattern recognition, and it is central to the analysis of connotative meaning. (p. 327)

However, the astute reader will notice that the word *similarity* that has been used so freely in the previous few sentences is actually another one of those psychological concepts that are so difficult to precisely define. A substantial body of research and theoretical controversy has emerged in recent years in which strong efforts are being made to produce a much more precise and specific definition of the term *similarity* than has heretofore been available. In the following discussion I look at some of these theoretical points of view and, by using them as vehicles, examine in detail the nature of the concept of similarity as it is used in contemporary form-perception research. The main focus of controversy today is between the metric-dimensional theories on the one hand and the feature-set theories on the other. To understand one, we must also understand the other.

One of the main issues in the search for a definition of similarity lies in the nature of the mathematical models best able to describe the relationship among two or more stimulus objects that are more or less alike. Two major points of view have characterized the dominant antagonistic approaches to this controversy in recent years. One is based upon the idea that stimulus dimensions or attributes may be collectively considered to be groups of components that make up a nondimensional "set" of stimulus attributes. The late Frank Restle (Restle, 1961) was probably the first author to propose the hypothesis of the nonmetric or nonordered set of stimulus features as the key to perceived similarity, but the concept has been most fully developed and the underlying axioms made most explicit by Tversky in what is now considered to be a classic piece of scientific exposition (Tversky, 1977).

The alternative to nondimensional set theory is one based upon ordered and metric geometric dimensions or characteristics of the stimuli. The stimuli, from this point of view, are characterized by attributes that can be added and multiplied and that exhibit distance-related functions in a way that is closely analogous to vector manipulations in geometry. Specifically, it is assumed that similarity is monotonically related to distance in a multidimensional space. This multidimensional space is defined and its dimensions designated from empirical data by techniques referred to as *multidimensional scaling* procedures.

The key words in this context are *dimensions* and *metrics*. Dimensions are defined as the salient continuum along which a single attribute or property of the stimulus is varying. By appropriate calculations from the data, which may include direct, but certainly not simple estimates of similarity, same–different judgments, or probabilities of confusions, multidimensional scaling identifies the dimensions being used by the perceiver. For a space to be metric it must meet certain specific criteria (which is discussed later) but in an intuitive sense, a metric space must be capable of being scaled in such a way that quantitative estimates of distances between the items in that space can be established.

One of the first to champion this metric, dimensional point of view was Attneave (1950), but the ideas inherent in his work have led to the development of the formal multidimensional scaling procedures by Torgerson (1958) and Shepard (1962). Although there have been many recent attempts to challenge the metric, dimensional model of similarity that is inherent in the multidimensional scaling technique, the concept has recently been championed anew by Krumhansl (1978) and others.

The most fundamental axiom of the geometric theories (exemplified by the multidimensional scaling procedure) asserts that the distances between objects in an appropriately transformed space are directly related to the psychological similarity of the objects represented in that space. It is this analogy of geometric distance and similarity that characterizes theories of this kind more than any other single principle.

The distinctions between the two points of view—metric, dimensional theories, on the one hand, and set theories, on the other, can be appreciated by a brief review of the main points of each. Let us start by considering one modern version of set theory as propounded by Tversky (1977). Tversky's main argument is that the geometric relationships that are assumed as premises in the metric, dimensional model are not well fit, supported, or justified by the empirical evidence. That is, the metric, dimensional model is based upon certain formal assumptions about the nature of the spatial relationships between the objects in the dimensionalized space that, according to him, are at variance with the way people actually judge similarity. Let us consider the nature of the discrepancies to which he calls attention.

The three central assumptions[2] of the metric, dimensional psychological theory (which are equivalent to the mathematical criteria that formally define whether a space is metric or not) Tversky calls the *minimality axiom*, the *symmetry axiom*, and the *triangle inequality axiom*. These are essentially the same axioms that also define psychological distance in the choice model of Luce (1963) that we briefly consider in chapter 5. The axioms of this psychological theory, of course, are also restatements of the formal mathematical axioms in the parent mathematics upon which this theoretical point of view is based. The interested reader may wish to look at the article on "metric spaces" in the *Encyclopedic Dictionary of Mathematics for Engineers and Applied Scientists* (Sneddon, 1976) for a very formal, but readable, consideration of these ideas independent of their psychological implications.

The first of these three axioms, that asserting minimality, implies that when an object is compared with itself, by definition the distance between the object and itself in the psychological space defined by this model must be a minimum equal to a zero distance in that space. A strong corollary of this axiom is that this null or zero distance must be the same as the distance that would exist when any other object is compared with itself. Psychologically, objects should be identical with themselves and all objects should be self-identical in the same way in a metric space of this kind.

Next, the symmetry axiom asserts that when an object is compared with another object, the distance should be the same as when the second object is compared with the first. Thus, according to Tversky, the metric, dimensional model predicts that it does not matter in which order the comparison is made and the behavior of the observer is commutative.

The third axiom, that of triangle inequality, asserts that the sum of the distance between objects a and b and between objects b and c must be at least equal to and usually is greater than the distance between a and c. Thus, there are no shortcuts in this metric perceptual universe to be made by means of an intermediate stop just as there is no shorter path between two objects in a Euclidean space

---

[2] It is important to appreciate that the discrepancies that Tversky makes explicit are psychological statements; that is, they describe the way in which human observers deviate from the predictions of the specific axioms of the metric, dimensional models when faced with what he believes are relevant stimulus and task situations. The question is: Do the rules predicted the model adequately describe human perceptual behavior? Tversky's strategy is to show that these axioms are not adequately descriptive of human perception and, therefore, at its most fundamental level, the model fails.

than the direct distance between them. In psychological jargon, if two things are dissimilar, then one can not make them more similar by using some kind of an intermediary. In other words, the metric space that is the basis of the multidimensional scaling model can be topologically distorted (i.e., stretched) but it cannot be disordered.

Distance in the metric model is a non-negative number that geometrically represents the perceived similarity of two objects in the metric space that is defined by applying the multidimensional scaling technique.[3] An analogy, therefore, may be drawn between the representation of *similarity* by *space* in this case and other transformations common in the image processing field. There, *physical geometry* is often transformed into *numeric values*: Here, a subjective, nonphysical dimension is converted into space. In both cases a quantitative analysis becomes possible when the non-numeric dimensions of the initial domain are transformed into the numeric dimensions of the transform space. This is the essential reason for the manipulations in each case—the need to provide a numerical and quantitative means of interpreting what is essentially non numerical, nonquantitative data.

In 1977 Tversky suggested that all three axioms defining the metric of a multidimensionally scaled space are either only weakly supported or are totally violated when one examines the related human psychophysical data. His point is that because the properties of a metric space are rigorously specified and these specifications are not met by the psychological experiences it purports to model, then the model is inappropriate and we must look elsewhere for wisdom and understanding. In fact, he goes on beyond the specific details of the Torgerson and Shepard multidimensional scaling model, in particular, to argue that the basic idea of a metric, dimensional perceptual space as a model for similarity may be incorrect; there are simply too many instances, from Tversky's point of view, in which we do not behave with anything like the geometrylike precision of a scaled space in making decisions and in judging similarity.

With regard to the specific axioms, Tversky asserts that minimality is regularly violated because we do not respond with the same probability that two objects are identical when many different identical pairs of items are compared. In other words, the model predicts that all pairs of identical items should be equally often judged to be the same, but in empirical fact, identity judgments vary in probabilistic terms from one stimulus set to another and from one context to another. The distance between an item and itself depends on its environment—a clear-cut contradiction of the minimality axiom.

Next he asserts that the symmetry axiom is also frequently violated and, therefore, cannot be true in general. One of the clearest examples given by Tversky (1977) of a violation of the perceptual symmetry that he believes would be re-

[3] Because the purpose of this analysis is purely conceptual, I make no attempt to present the algorithms and procedures necessary to take a set of data and to form the multidimensional scaling space. The reader is referred to Torgerson's (1958) or Shepard's (1957) papers for the computational and procedural details.

quired to justify the use of multidimensional scaling is in the context of metaphors. He notes that when we metaphorize, in many cases the metaphor simply does not ring true when done in the reverse direction. His example is that we are often willing to say that "an ellipse is like a circle" but it is rare and almost meaningless for one to say "a circle is like an ellipse" (p.328).

He goes on to show that the triangle similarity axiom is not, in general, transitive and that it is, therefore, violated in a way that raises questions about whether or not the metric, dimensional model of similarity is also seriously flawed in this regard. Indeed, he argues that it flies in the face of psychological fact to say that there is any kind of geometrical additivity about the way in which semantic relationships can be combined. Tversky's (1977) example in this case makes the point quite clearly. He illustrates the failure of additivity by noting that "Jamaica is similar to Cuba (because of geographical proximity); Cuba is similar to Russia (because of political affinity) ; but Jamaica and Russia are not similar at all" (p. 329). Thus, as Tversky notes, "the perceived distance of Jamaica to Russia exceeds the perceived distance from Jamaica to Cuba, plus that of Cuba to Russia" (p. 329). Here is a perceptual datum that is in direct disagreement with the third axiom of metric space—the axiom that asserts that the sum of the two distances between similar items must be greater than the distance between the two extremes.

Tversky's critique of the geometrical, metric, multidimensional approach to similarity led him to resurrect the alternative set theory originally proposed by Restle (1961) that had languished in the shadows cast by the apparent successes of multidimensional scaling. Tversky's new formulation of a set model is framed, like its predecessors, in what are essentially nonmetric and nondimensional terms. Thus, in Tversky's new model, similarity is based upon the overlap of sets of features that may not have any geometric or scalar relationship to each other. In short, it is an example of a counting theory in which similarity is defined more by the number of common features than by some quantified estimate of the distance between the objects in a precisely dimensionalized space.

Like the multidimensional, geometrical models he rejects, Tversky's set model is also based upon specific axiomatic foundations[4] as follows:

1. The Matching Axiom: The similarity of two objects is defined as a function of three variables; the subset of features they share, the subset of features that one has but the other does not, and the subset of features that the other has but the first one does not. In general, the larger the number of common features that two objects share the more they are perceived to be alike.

---

[4] It is a compliment to both theories, of course, that their precision is so great that they can be formulated in such explicit terms. This is science at its very best and the level of detail at which their arguments are carried out is very different from the vague, verbal approximations that characterize many other psychological, particularly perceptual, theories. However, the reader should be careful not to confuse good mathematical *description* with accurate specifications of internal mechanisms.

2. The Monotonicity Axiom: In general, any increase in the number of features common to two objects increases their similarity and any decrease in the features they share decreases it.

3. The Independence Axiom: The relative effect of any two features is independent of a third feature they may also jointly share.

4. The Solvability Axiom: The system of similarities that exists must be sufficiently rich so that the equations of the model can be evaluated.

5. The Invariance Axiom: This axiom asserts that equivalence of intervals is maintained from one feature to another. (See the discussion of interval scales in S.S. Stevens, 1951, for a development of this point.)

The set-counting model is championed by Tversky for several reasons. One reason is based on the fact that he believes that symmetrical similarity—the symmetry axiom of the metric, dimensional model—is not required by the set model and that the absence of symmetry is a basic property of perception. It is, therefore, possible for one object to be related to another in such a way that the degree of similarity can be different depending on which way the comparison is being made.

Another reason invoked by Tversky to support a counting-set theory is that there is a strong influence of context and experimental procedure in determining the nature of the similarity effects between pairs of objects. Thus the metric dimensions that are generated by the multidimensional scaling technique, in particular, are not rooted in psychological reality. (In a few paragraphs, we see how this becomes the set piece of the Krumhansl version of a metric, dimensional theory.)

Tversky also believes that although there is no metric space involved in the set hypothesis, there is a set of interval scales generated that can vary from one situation to another. This interval scale is sufficient for the manipulation and evaluation of the degree of similarity existing between two objects and thus can be used to meet the needs of quantitative analysis of similarity data.

The details of the counting-set model (I should say "models" because Tversky presents several different versions that alternatively concentrate on either the ratios or absolute differences in the number of features as predictors of similarity) are much more complex than the brief review that I have given here can possibly indicate. However, for the purposes of this discussion the key difference between the set hypothesis and the metric, dimensional approach to which attention must be paid is that set theory considers stimuli to be a function of discrete features that vary mainly in their numerosity. It is essentially a counting (of features) explanation of the human perceptual similarity. The degree to which the stimulus objects share or do not share certain discrete or discontinuous features is the key to this model. On the other hand, the geometric models of which the metric, multidimensional scaling process is the prototype, consider the stimulus object to be an aggregation of variable dimensions that may themselves take many different continuously varying values and which define the objects' position in an equally continuous multidimensional similarity space.

The important thing, of course, is that both of these theories are attempting to describe perceptual behavior. Therefore, their success or failure lies in the degree to which they are supported by psychophysical data. And, indeed, Tversky (1977) reviews a substantial body of data that he believes supports his set theory and that challenges multidimensional scaling, a review to which the reader is directed for more detail. Without diminishing his accomplishments it should be noted, however, that his counterexamples are often isolated and very specific, almost anecdotal, in quality. Although they do show the fallibility of the metric, dimensional models, they also illustrate the lack of generality that is often characteristic of *any* modeling of this kind.

Since the 1977 paper, which was seminal and an especially significant contribution, Tversky and his colleagues have continued this line of work considering the details of how similarity may be best modeled. Recently, Tversky and Gati (1982) expanded upon Tversky's (1977) critique of the triangle inequality axiom in particular. They noted additional instances in which this axiom seemed to be poorly representative of psychological estimates of similarity. At this point a new idea was introduced: The metric dimensional analysis exemplified by the Torgerson-Shepard multidimensional scaling technique, they suggested, is an acceptable expedient as an excellent means of reducing data from experiments and displaying that summarized information. They are not, however, actually testable theories of psychological activity, in Tversky and Gati's opinion.

In even more recent work Tversky and Hutchinson (1986) have recanted even further and have reconsidered possible areas in which the geometric-type models may, however, be useful and applicable as theories rather than merely as descriptive tools. In general, Tversky and Hutchinson assert, perceptual data involving the neat, discrete, and relatively sparse physical-stimulus dimensions (e.g., from sensory experiments involving only intensity, quality, etc.) do, in fact, fit fairly well within the metric, geometrical approach. On the other hand, they note that when stimuli involve many dimensions and invoke many different features, as do descriptions of countries or people, then the metric geometric models usually turn out to be inadequate in the ways previously described. The distinction these authors draw is between the perceptual and the semantic, but I think that the difference is hardly qualitative, rather, as they also suggest elsewhere, really a matter of the relative numerosity of the constituent features and dimensions.

An important feature of the Tversky and Hutchinson paper is that they provide formal methods for testing the suitability of applying the various models to particular experimental situations. Specific counts of the numbers of nearest neighbors is diagnostic for the applicability of the metric, dimensional or the set models according to them; too many nearest neighbors, however, is a sign that a two- or three-dimension, metric model is inappropriate and that the number of dimensions and/or features is too complex for this kind of analysis. In those instance, the set theory, doting as it does on the number of common features, would be a better model of similarity, and would be preferred. An especially interesting point, not completely unexpected in the esoteric world of formal theory, is that the various models sometimes tend to merge into each other and become formally indistinguishable in intermediate regions of the number of dimensions.

Now let us consider an alternative view—a modern metric, dimensional theory of similarity—in more detail. Perhaps the most articulate champion of such a analysis in recent years has been Krumhansl (1978). In a carefully thought-out analysis, she provides a revision of the metric, dimensional model that she believes overcomes many of the difficulties pointed to by Tversky (1977). Her main point is that many of the criticisms he makes can be overcome if one adds a local density factor to the model producing the multidimensionally scaled space. By invoking a local density factor she is suggesting that the number of neighbors of an object in the metric space actually affect the computed distances between objects. In other words, the number of objects that are similar to the test object will determine how similar the test object is to a comparison object.

Krumhansl emphasizes that the key idea in a metric, dimensional model is that there must be a monotonic relationship between similarity and the distance in the space. Her suggestion for an improvement, in response to Tversky's critique, is a modification of the way in which *distance* is defined. Rather than simply utilizing the metric distance in the multidimensional space, Krumhansl suggests a new definition of distance that takes into account the number of neighboring objects within a local region. This is essentially a means of introducing context effects into the model in such a way that she believes should allow the theoretician to better represent some of the observed psychological effects while at the same time specifically overcoming the violation of the minimality axiom to which Tversky referred.

This modification of the distance function (by taking into account local density) proposed by Krumhansl also allows other degrees of freedom to be introduced into the analysis. For example, the distance between an object and itself will now depend on the local density of its neighbors. The value of the new distance estimate can then be, and in fact according to Krumhansl will usually be, greater than zero. Furthermore, symmetry need not hold absolutely in this revised model, as clearly indicated to be the perceptual case in the empirical examples given by Tversky. Krumhansl's density hypothesis provides an explanation of how asymmetrical-similarity relationships can exist between objects that have different contexts (as do the aforementioned ellipses and circles) in the multidimensional model's space.

Finally, the revision of the geometric model proposed by Krumhansl allows one to understand how the degree of similarity between two objects can vary depending upon whether one asks the observers to judge how much alike the stimuli are or how different they are. This procedural influence was also noted by Tversky as a violation of the axioms of a metric, dimensional model. Thus, the nature of the task can also influence the results in a discrimination task just as can the properties of the stimulus. But this does not fall outside of the realm of explanation in Krumhansl's modification of the model.

Needless to say, in this ongoing debate, Tversky championing set theory has responded. In Tversky and Gati (1982) he and his colleague point out that the density hypothesis proposed by Krumhansl actually raises two separate issues. First, Does it work empirically? and second, Does it work theoretically? Whereas Tversky and Gati are willing to accept the fact that an increase in the local density—that is, an increase in the number of objects that are similar to each other—does lead to a reduction in the perceived similarity between any two objects in that denser region in the multidimensional scaling space, they are not willing to accept the argument that the density hypothesis is sufficiently powerful to account for all of the theoretical discrepancies to which they have pointed. There are still too many axiomatic principles that have to be accounted for from their point of view for Krumhansl's hypothesis to totally salvage a metric, dimensional model of similarity data from their criticisms, in their opinion.

The residual difference of opinion can be partially understood by appreciating that in Tversky's works and that of other set theorists of similarity, order relations are not of importance. Therefore, it follows that the whole concept of distance is irrelevant. Thus, the question of the specific metric used in that space is meaningless. However, from the point of view of the dimensional model, quite a bit of concern must be paid to the specific metric of the visual space. Several alternatives have been proposed. One of these is the city-block metric: How far do you have to travel to get from point a to point b if you are limited to moving only along the horizontal and vertical axes and in unit distances? Another is the Euclidean metric, which perhaps more properly should be called the pythagorean metric because it follows the pythagorean rule $(x^2 + y^2)^{1/2}$. This "crow's flight" distance can deviate substantially from the distance along the orthogonal x and y axes (i.e., the city-block distance) of the perceptual space.

A wide variety of other metrics are possible, however, and Schönemann, Dorcey, and Kienapple (1985) have suggested several, including an average metric (1/2 of the sum of the city-block x and y distances between the two objects); the average power metric (1/2 of the sum of the square root of the distances between the two objects); and a group of other alternatives called "Metrics for Bounded Response Scales" (MBR). Indeed, one of those esoteric MBR scales, in which the distance between two objects was defined as:

$$d_m = (a^* + b^*)/(1 + \frac{a^*b^*}{K^2})$$

where K is an upper bound for the scale and a^* and b^* are projections of the and y distances on to the original metric, was the best fitting of all the similarity metrics tested in their paper.

It is not inappropriate to once again note that all of these models are attempt-

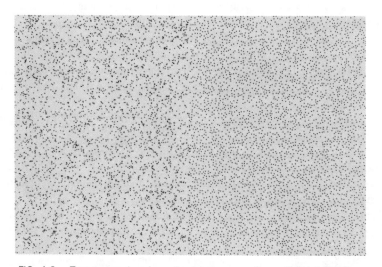

FIG. 4.3.   Two textured surfaces having the same first order statistics but differing in their second order statistics (from Julesz, Gilbert, Shepp, & Frisch, 1973).

ing to describe the vagaries of human behavior, and it is the complexities of the behavior that will determine whether any of these models succeed or fail. They are all trying to simulate, describe and, to the limits of theoretical possibility, explain certain human perceptual processes relating to similarity. If the models seem ad hoc and require too many quasi-formal axioms and hypothesis, this is, of course, a reflection of the complexity of human behavior. The models are all based on a mathematical substrate that was developed to handle much simpler systems and the leap to models of the full complexity of the mind may simply be too great a leap for exact predictions.

D.   THE DISCRIMINATION OF TEXTURES[5]

Most of the material that has been considered so far deals with the similarity and identity (i.e., the discriminability) of single stimulus-forms and objects. We now turn to an aspect of discrimination research that is typically not limited to a single attribute, aspect, or dimension of the visual stimulus but, rather, the interaction of multiple objects. This new topic considers work on the discrimination of *textures*. There is little question that when presented with a stimulus such as that shown in Fig. 4.3 that the elements of the scene are all well above any definition of any kind of detection threshold. Everything is seen, but the perceptual ques-

---

[5] Some of the material in this section has been adapted and updated from my discussions in Uttal (1981).

tion that may be asked is "Are all parts of what is seen perceptually the same?" The observer's task in this case is to discriminate the different regions from each other on the basis of some organized attribute of their local geometry (i.e, of some global property that emerges from the local features), some interactive attribute that changes from one discriminable region to another, some attribute that, admittedly at this point in the development of this science, is still only partially understood.

The perplexity of what feature or qualities of the stimulus-produced distinguishable perceptual regions in textured surface have confounded this field for years. Recently, attention has been redirected at this problem as theoretical and experimental techniques have matured to the point that we can now untangle some of this confounding. Therefore, let us concentrate on the psychophysical and quantitative models developed to analyze this problem.

The renewed interest in the study of texture discrimination has been stimulated by the pioneering studies of Julesz, who for many years has been one of the lights of the A T & T Laboratories. Others have been in the field including Pollack (1973), Barlow (1978), Burgess et al. (1981, 1982), Beck (1966) and recently Triesman and her co-workers (e.g., Triesman & Gelade, 1980). Their respective work is cited as appropriate to flesh out the argument I now present. Nevertheless, the framework upon which we now hang the details of our discussion is mainly based on Julesz's conceptualization of the problem. Julesz's model is, also, one of the most precisely spelled-out theories of form perception, supported both by empirical data and an intuitively satisfying theoretical foundation. Unfortunately, Julesz, as all too many others, has also encumbered his psychophysics and mathematics with neurophysiological corollaries that are not as satisfying. I have criticized neuroreductionism of that kind previously (Uttal, 1973b, 1981) and need not belabor the point here. It should be sufficient for me to note only that many perceptual scientists now feel that the bridge between the perceptual data obtained in psychophysical experiments and electrophysical recordings from single or multiple neurons is yet to be established.

Julesz began his study of texture discrimination some years ago, but recently has developed a theoretical formulation that he calls *texton* theory to explain a curious set of exceptional findings in his work. Texton theory is a quasineuroreductionistic approach to explaining the phenomena he observed. It is based upon certain special sensitivities that the visual nervous system seems to display to particular elements of a textured surface. First, lets us consider some of the observations that Julesz made in his laboratory. Then we look in detail at his theory.

As noted earlier, the key issue in the study of texture is: What are the attributes or properties of the textured visual stimuli that allow different textures to be discriminated from each other? (Texture in this case is defined by the nature of the arrangement or organizational properties of the elements of a repetitive pattern.) To answer this question we have to consider some things about the nature of textured images. Figure 4.3 illustrates a textured surface of this genre.

Textures may vary absolutely—two patterns may differ totally from each other in the density or size of the elements—or relatively, there may be a gradient of change in the density or size of the pattern elements within a single scene. Gradients of texture have been extensively discussed by Gibson (1950) among others as cues to depth. However, his definition was not satisfying and, unlike many other attributes of visual stimuli, until only recently an inadequate and nonnumerical concept of what was meant by texture was all that existed.

A key step in the study of texture occurred when Bela Julesz (Julesz, 1962, 1975, 1978; Julesz, Gilbert, Shepp, & Frisch, 1973) introduced the ideas of orders of statistical complexity as numeric descriptors of the elusive concept of texture. This idea has been very useful and has been a sustained theme of texture-discrimination work for over a decade. It is only in recent years that new ideas such as the existence of features to which the visual system is specially sensitive ("textons" in Julesz's, 1981 vocabulary) and other theories about what happens in the later stages of texture processing (Caelli, 1985) that further progress has been made. I discuss both of these issues later after considering Julesz's statistical model of texture.

Before, I do, however, it may be useful to point out that the distinction between the statistical and texton models is fundamentally similar for the distinction between metric and feature models of similarity. The analogy is straightforward: On the one hand we have models emphasizing the arrangement of the parts, and on the other, the nature of specific parts.

The orders of statistical complexity that Julesz and his colleagues proposed are comparable to the moments (mean and variance, etc.) of descriptive statistics, but, as we will soon see, these two kinds of statistics are not identical. The significance of each of the orders can best be understood if described in terms of dot patterns. The first statistical order of texture defined by Julesz (1975) is closely associated with the mean number of dots in the stimulus, that is, the mean density. Because dot densities are related to the energy being emitted by a surface, whether there are black dots on a white background or vice versa, first-order texture is also linearly related to the luminance of a dotted stimulus pattern. This is a straightforward extrapolation of a simple statistical idea, and it is intuitively obvious just what this first order signifies.

Julesz's second statistical order of texture is not quite so obvious, but it is still possible to achieve a relatively direct appreciation of what it means. The second-order statistic describes an aspect of a dot pattern that is most closely related to the average spacing between dots—a textural property perceived by an observer as the "clumpiness" or "laciness" of the dots. It is analogous to the variance in ordinary descriptive statistics. Thus, two textures might have identical first-order statistics (equal numbers of dots in equal areas) but may differ in their second-order statistics (as reflected in the degree to which the dots are bunched and separated) in a way that makes them appear very different. It is also important to appreciate that the second-order statistic describes much the same information that is described by the autocorrelation function or the spatial-frequency spectrum. The vast literature that relates those kinds of mathematical processes to vision must also necessarily relate the second-order statistic of texture.

Third-order textural statistics are much less easily described in a simple, intuitive way. Julesz described a statistical test in which a sample triangle is "thrown" onto a number of places on two dot patterns. If, on the average, the triangle's corners fall on three dots the same number of times in the two patterns, then the patterns are said to possess the same third-order statistics.

Another way to conceptualize the idea of the the third-order statistics of a pattern more intuitively is to consider it as a common property of the local geometry of the elements that make up the pattern, as opposed to the more global measures—density and clustering—described by the first two orders. For example, Julesz has shown that if a texture is made up of U-shaped objects as shown in Fig. 4.4, a third-order statistical difference is produced between two subregions when the objects are rotated (180 deg.) even though this rotation maintains the same lengths of horizontal and vertical line components in the two parts of the scene. (Such a third-order difference is not discriminable.) However, if the U-shaped elements are rotated 90 degrees, the respective lengths of the horizontal and vertical components in the figure changes. This produces a difference in the second-order statistic. (This difference is immediately obvious to the observer.)

Julesz notes another important general property of textured patterns with regard to their statistical rather than their perceptual role. First, if two patterns have identical statistics at one order, then all lower orders must also be identical. How-

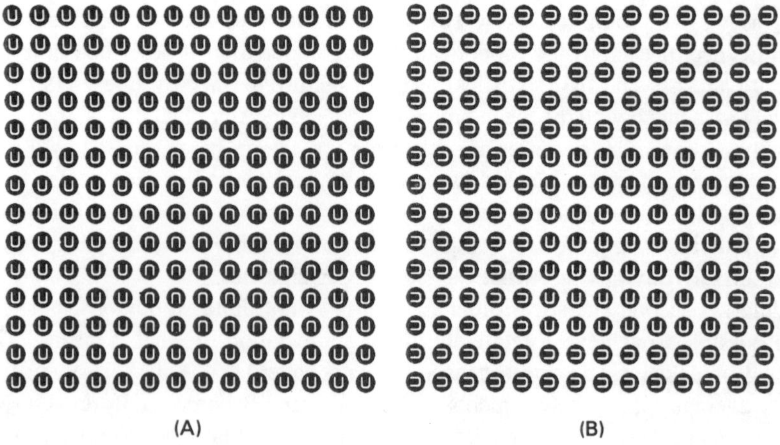

(A)   (B)

FIG. 4.4. Two patterns made up of identical elements. However, in (A) some of the U's have been rotated 180° while in (B) some have been rotated only 90°. Rotation of 90° changes the second order statistics, whereas rotation of the 180° does not. Thus, (B) is immediately discriminable as consisting of two different regions but (A) is not (from Julesz, Gilbert, Shepp, & Frisch, 1973).

ever, as we have seen, the opposite is not true—higher-order statistics are independent of those of lower order. One can straightforwardly produce patterns that are identical in their first order yet differ in their second- and third-order statistics as easily as patterns that are identical in their second-order statistics (and thus necessarily in their first-order statistics), yet differ in their third-order statistics.

So far, I have mainly described the statistical properties of these quasi-random patterns we refer to as texture. More germane to the present discussion is their impact on human perception—in particular, on the ability of an observer to discriminate between different regions that vary in one or another order of statistical regularity. A major study of the discriminability of dotted patterns that differ in their first-order statistics (i.e., in dot density) was reported by Barlow (1978). Barlow was concerned with the ability of observers to detect shaped regions of dots within and beside other dotted patterns that differed only in dot density. Barlow proposed a measure (F) of the statistical efficiency of the human observer based on the ratio of the sample size (i.e., the number of dots) required by an ideal observer and the sample size required by the typical human observer to determine that two patterns were different purely on the basis of the respective dot densities.

The results of Barlow's psychophysical experiment indicated that observers did not quite function as ideal detectors of density differences. Indeed, they rarely performed better than a 50% efficiency. The only condition in which his observers approached ideal discrimination of these first-order statistics occurred in those limiting conditions in which the dot densities were so low and exposures so long that they could actually count the individual dots. At higher dot densities, or shorter durations, their efficiency fell off substantially from the ideal. This result indicated an inability on the part of the observer to carry out this kind of statistical processing at high dot densities at anywhere near ideal levels.

Another important outcome of Barlow's experiment was the lack of any effect of the shape of the stimulus (when it was embedded within the reference region) on d'_{exp} (i.e., the experimentally observed discriminability). This is an important result because it tends to disassociate this kind of overall pattern-information processing from the kind of simplistic feature-detection theory that is all too often misapplied to this kind of finding. The important finding is that global shape did not influence discriminability.

In later work from Barlow's laboratory, Burgess, Wagner, Jennings, and Barlow (1981) have extended this paradigm to include a discrimination task in which their observers were asked to tell in which of two different stimulus fields the denser of two sinusoidally varying density patterns occurred. A major change in this new experiment was that the signals were embedded in random dotted noise so that the observers had to extract the signals from the noise as well as to discriminate the differences between the two sinusoids. By varying the amount of noise in the dotted background, Burgess and his colleagues were able to estimate the statistical efficiency with which humans made this discrimination. In this case it turned out that they did as well as 83% of the theoretical maximum. Obviously the appropriate selection of task and experimental design can elicit human visual discrimination of first-order textural differences at a level that approaches the theoretical maximum. As an aside, it is interesting to note that such slight changes in experimental design can produce such substantial changes in results. This, too, is an issue of major concern in the final chapter of this book.

The data from Barlow, Burgess, and their colleagues are probably definitive in describing the processing of first-order statistics, but I must now turn to other experimental reports to consider the ability of observers to process the higher order statistical properties of those quasi-random dot patterns. There are few good quantitative studies of the ability of observers to process the second-order statistical properties of a stimulus pattern (as opposed to a qualitative demonstration that it is possible). One, however, was reported by Pollack (1971) some time ago. Although he did not use dot patterns in his experiments, but a matrix of printed letters instead, Pollack's work serves as an excellent complement to the present discussion and is one of the few exemplars of an experimental study of second-order textural processing by the visual system. Pollack asked his observers to rank order a set of arrays of x's in terms of their "lumpiness" or "laciness." Because observers could do so in a lawful way, these studies showed that they were able to discriminate between patterns of this kind that varied only in their second-order statistics. As with the work of Barlow and Burgess, Pollack found that his observers did not perform at the level of a theoretically ideal observer. According to Pollack's estimates, his observers could only discriminate among eight different levels of variation in the second-order statistics. His data also indicated that there is an apparent saturation of second-order discriminability that occurs when high dot-density levels are used.

Now let us turn to the problem of stimulus patterns that have identical first- and second-order properties but different third-order statistics. It is here that most of the interesting theoretical activity has been focused. Julesz originally presented a compelling argument supporting the "conjecture" that, in most instances, human beings are not capable of evaluating (i.e., discriminating) third-order statistical differences in texture. In a number of demonstrations (Julesz, 1975, 1978; Julesz, Gilbert, Shepp, & Frisch, 1973) he had shown that, in general, if two textures had identical second- and, therefore, necessarily the same first-order textural statistics, observers were not able to discriminate between them if they differed only in their third-order statistical properties.

A possible explanation of the general ability of the human observer to perceptually process third-order statistical differences in textures is that such high order differences require far more computational power than does the processing of differences in the lower order. That is, although it is easy to measure something like local density or the variance in interdot spacing, the kinds of computations that are required to evaluate third-order differences exceed the brain's ability.

This may also explain why have such a difficult time even intuiting what is the meaning of the third-order differences. Because we can not process these differences, we simply have very little experience in appreciating what such a concept involves and have not developed the linguistic terms necessary to appreciate them.

There is, of course, another way in which this particular datum may be interpreted. If one accepts the idea that the local density (first-order statistic) and the laciness (second-order statistic) are perceivable or defined as global properties of the stimulus, and if the third-order statistic is perceived and reflects only the local attributes of the stimulus, this finding is another argument for a priority of the global over the local in perception. In other words, we can see density and laciness because they are global properties expressed as a simple global aspect of the stimulus, and it, therefore, takes little computational capability to evaluate their significance. However, enormous computational power, beyond even that available from the wondrous parallel processor we call the brain, would be required to evaluate the significance of this ensemble of local indicators. Globality is a short cut, an information-processing, demand-reducing mechanism that helps us to adapt to the environment in a way that is extremely economical in time and processing capability. Julesz's observation that a third-order statistic cannot be so discriminated reflects the limits of this evolutionary development.

The most extensive studies of the third-order statistical properties of dot patterns have been carried out by Caelli and Julesz (1978), and Caelli, Julesz, and Gilbert (1978), who have specifically manipulated the microstructure of the elements of the textured pattern. Figure 4.5, for example, indicates two microelements (among many other possible examples of these two classes) that can be grouped to produce textured regions with identical first- and second-order but different third-order statistics.

However, very few patterns of this type have been shown by Caelli, Julesz, and Gilbert (1978) to violate Julesz's original conjecture of the indiscriminability of patterns differing only in their third order statistics. For example, when arrays of the two kinds of microelements shown in Fig. 4.5 are used to form two regions in a textured stimulus, then the two regions, differing only in their third-order statistics, do become immediately segregated as effectively as if they had differed in their first- or second-order statistics as shown, for example, in Fig. 4.3.

It was this violation of his "conjecture" that was the stimulus for the evolution of Julesz's current texton theory. Early in the development of this work, Julesz identified four pictorial properties that seem to account for the violation of the general conjecture that third-order differences are not discriminable. The properties originally identified included: (a) variations in iso-dipole statistics; (b) quasi-colinearity; (c) corners; and (d) closure.

In the early 1980s a subtle change occurred in Julesz' thinking that was reflected in his publications: Originally, he proposed the conjecture that these four proper-

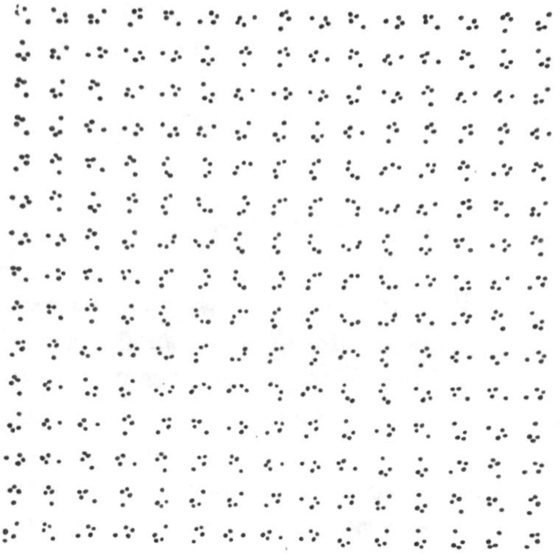

FIG. 4.5.   A textured surface consisting of two parts, each of which has identical first and second order statistics. The two regions should not be discriminable according to Julesz's original "conjecture." Nevertheless, they are, because of "quasi-colinearity" (i.e., a texton-like property; from Caelli, Julesz, & Gilbert, 1978).

ties of the elements of a texture were interesting, but largely irrelevant, exceptions to the rule that differences in third-order statistics could not generally be discriminated. In his more recent work, this line of thought was replaced by the idea that these special visual features were not irrelevant exceptions, but were, in fact, the key actors on this perceptual stage. Julesz now suggests (Julesz, 1981, 1984) that they correspond in some way to the neurophysiological trigger features discovered in the visual pathways by such workers as Hubel and Wiesel. He likens the role played by these special spatial elements (which he now calls *textons*) to that of the primary or fundamental colors in chromatic vision. He considered textons to be "conspicuous" features to which the functional neural units in the visual system are especially tuned so that they operate in an automatic and immediate manner. According to his theory, it is because of these special visual features—the textons—that the human visual nervous system is able to violate the general rule that textures varying only their third-order statistics cannot be discriminated. This is so, he asserts, even though, in general, the computations required for the analysis of third-order statistics are too complex for the visual nervous system to handle; according to Julesz, the textons, because of their relationship to the neural feature filters, provide a short cut that can finesse the limit otherwise imposed by the "combinational explosion" implicit in the computational requirements of third-order statistics.

The next question to ask is: What are the textons of form vision? A second pass at identifying them is by listing properties such as (a) the crossing of line segments; (b) ends of lines (terminators) ; (c) certain shaped blobs such as rec-

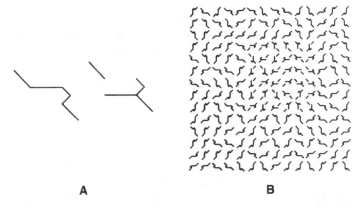

FIG. 4.6.   A textured surface (B) made up of the two kinds of elements shown
in (A). The two components are discriminable even though the component
line segments are the same for the two texture elements. The two elements
do, however, differ in the number of line terminators—in this case the critical
"texton" (from Julesz, 1984).

tangles, ellipses; and (d) single-line segments with appropriate colors, orientations, and lengths. The various textons interact in different ways to produce
discriminable regions. For example, Fig. 4.6 shows a pair of figures that are
nearly similar in having the same number of line segments, but are different in
that there are different numbers of line terminations. These assemblages of textons (note the conceptual and pictorial difference between the idea of a *texton*
and that of interacting *assemblages of textons*) are very discriminable from each
other in spite of the fact that the first- and second-order statistics of the two
microelements are identical.

The determination of what is a texton (i.e., what it is that is fundamental) and
what is not a texton (i.e., what is derivative) is an important goal of Julesz's current theoretical program. As I noted earlier, he originally believe that there were
special properties enjoyed by such stimulus features as line crossings, corners,
closure, and connectivity. However, upon further analysis, in the most current
version of his theory he now asserts that all of these features and the others already
mentioned are derivative, and the conspicuousness of each can be explained by
only three kinds of textons—the line terminator, the line crossing, and the elongated
blob.

In summary, Julesz has modified his original conjecture that texture patterns
that do not differ in their second-order statistics cannot be discriminated. The
empirical evidence showed that there were certain special visual features that did
seem to violate this rule. He still believes that there are limits on the computational ability of the brain to process the third-order differences as he originally
suggested. However, these especially conspicuous features allow what is an apparent violation of that conjecture, but the violation is due to a processing short-

cut and does not necessitate a major revision of what is still felt to be a real limit on the computational ability of the visual system.

Julesz and Bergen (1983) have summed up the current status of their texton theory of texture segregation by asserting the following three "heuristics":

Heuristic 1. Human vision operates in two distinct modes: preattentive and attentive. In the preattentive mode spatial information is processed rapidly, in parallel, as in texture discrimination. In attentive vision the processing is serial and involves attention to small "apertures" of the image.

Heuristic 2. Textons: There are specific spatial properties which are of high sensitivity to the preattentive processes. They include the spatial distribution of "elongated blobs," terminators (end-of-line segments), and line crossings.

Heuristic 3. Preattentive vision is selective only of areas where texton activity is high. (p. 1622)

In accord with the comment just made concerning the global versus local interpretation of Julesz' findings, textons can be thought of in a different way. That is, rather than reflecting the activity of single cells in the communication channels of the nervous system, perhaps these forms are, for some reason as yet not understood, the ones that best allow global structures to be formed. That is, textons are efficient because they shortcut the computational demand by permitting the same sort of *global* perception to be used as in the lower order statistics.

Julesz is not alone, of course, in theorizing about the discrimination of textures. Many other workers have approached this tantalizingly straightforward problem in the hopes of finding out something general about human form perception. Jacob Beck, in work going back over nearly 20 years (Beck, 1966, 1982; Beck, Prazdny, & Rosenfeld, 1983), has invoked what are essentially modern versions of the Gestalt rules of grouping and closure of similar and proximal shapes and good continuity to describe how the elements of a textured surface could be linked together rather than being perceived as independent entities. Grossberg and Mingolla (1985) have built a mathematical theory of the Beck et al. findings based on what they call a boundary-contour model that behaves very much as does the human perceiver in establishing boundaries between textures surfaces. Both of these approaches seem to be consistent with the idea that textons work by generating global structures and thus reducing the computational load on the brain.

Furthermore, as mentioned earlier, some work has been reported by Anne Triesman and her colleagues that deals with the texture problem. Her experiments also suggest to her (Triesman & Patterson, 1984) that something like the primitive visual textons originally proposed by Julesz are at work here. However, the texton of closure that had been eschewed by Julesz appears to Triesman and Patterson to be fundamental, and she includes it in her list of primitive visual features.

Julesz, Beck, Triesman, their coworkers, and I all generally agree on certain aspects of texture perception. First, texture discrimination is seen as being generally a preattentive process that depends upon the interaction of the constituent local features of the textured surface. Second, there seems to be some sort of parallel or global interaction among those elements so that those that are alike are perceptually clustered together. Third, many of the local relationships among the elements (for example, the difference between certain pairs of letters that share common features, but in different arrangements; for example, T and L, C and U, M and W) are invisible or unprocessed at this very primitive level of visual processing. These organizational differences only emerge later when the characters are attentively scrutinized, according to both Julesz and Triesman.

It is obvious that the texton approach, or some variant of it, will continue to be a major theoretical perspective in this field. The search for the form primitives or textons to which the visual system is especially sensitive is likely to continue for some time as individual candidates are tested and either accepted or rejected. It remains for the future to determine if this approach is valid or if textons represent a kind of theoretical subjective surface suggested to the theoretician by metaphor or analogy, visible to the perceiver, but, in fact, representing only an illusory derivative of something much more fundamental.

That the story of texture discrimination is so far incomplete becomes increasingly clear as the days go by. Caelli (1985) has dealt with the issue and has shown that in addition to some kind of special local-feature-extraction algorithm, it is also necessary to hypothesize at least two other mechanisms to complete the process of texture discrimination. The demonstration of the need for textons to go beyond the statistical properties of the stimulus is but one part of his very novel model. Caelli points out that the statistical and texton ideas do not actually say how texture segregation occurs; they only describe the nature of discriminable elements. He sees the actual segregation process as consisting of three subprocesses, each of which must be executed to produce the final segregation. Those three subprocesses are:

1. The detection of the elements of the texture by a nonlinear convolution of the image and the putative ''detector units'' in the visual nervous system.

2. A process of completion by means of a nonlinear enhancement and inhibition of stray and weak signals from the detectors in process 1. This produces a spread of the effect of the detected signals and ultimately perceptual ''filling in.''

3. Finally, a process of grouping similar elements based on a diffuse correlation mechanism. (This is analogous to the hypothesis that global shortcuts can be induced by textons as I just suggested.)

Caelli considers this model to be a precise mathematical formulation of Julesz and Bergen's (1983) statement of the three heuristics of texture perception. He shows the relationship between this model and three heuristics in Fig. 4.7.

In summary, texture discrimination provides both an exciting and interesting area of research itself and also serves as a wonderful fruit fly for a more general

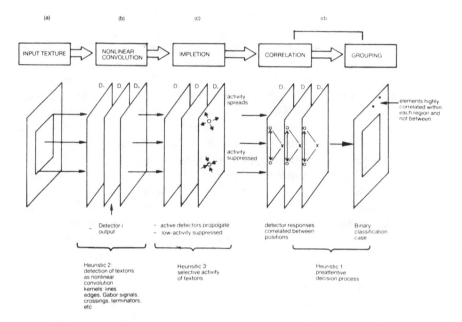

FIG. 4.7.   Caelli's theory of texture segregation (from Caelli, 1985).

analysis of the discrimination process in particular and perception in general. The highly constrained and specific stimulus, our ability to quantify it precisely, and the richness of the phenomena associated with texture perception all have made this a particularly coherent research topic. On the other hand, it is my personal opinion that far too much has been made of some rather superficial analogies between the perceptual units—the textons—and the neurophysiological units—the neurons. I believe, that the "textons" reflect the action of vast networks of interacting neurons (whose collective function is expressed in these special sensitivities) rather than the special sensitivities of individual neurons.

Furthermore, it seems to me that the advantage that is gained by these special units can be mainly attributable to their unusual ability to pull local features together into global structures for which the computational requirements are vastly reduced. Local microstructure that does not contribute to such a global organization are not observed as textons, not because the neurons of the peripheral communication system are less well tuned to them, but rather because the algorithms built into more central portions of the nervous system are not programmed to respond to them. The texton hypothesis, therefore, is closely related to the global–local controversy.

In short, I applaud the technique and the findings of texture research, but I am not comfortable with the neuroreductionistic interpretations made of these findings.

E. THE MATCHING OF VISUAL FORMS

Discrimination as we have defined it and as pursued as a research topic also includes other tasks than the similarity studies of Tversky and Krumhansl, on the one hand, and the preattentive texture discrimination paradigm that has been developed and researched by Beck, Julesz, Triesman, and others, on the other. Another popular research paradigm that approaches the problem of discrimination requires observers equally simply to specify whether two stimuli are the same or different, not in their texture particularly, but more often in their global form. Although this task is, at first glance, simple and direct, it is fascinating to wander through the perceptual literature and read of the many applications of this technique. One distinguished researcher, Michael Posner (1978), has used this simple research paradigm to study a wide variety of perceptual and other cognitive processes. Same–different-type tasks have been applied by him in searches for understanding about preattentive visual processes, the coding of visual forms in short-term memory, and studies of active manipulation of visual images, as well as studies of memory and reading. Obviously there is a strong conviction that this superficially simple research tool embodies a particularly sensitive assay technique that may be applicable in a diverse way as a probe into a very wide range of cognitive processes. Indeed, there is just as strong a belief that a discrimination process of this kind is as central to perception as are the similarity judgments described earlier in this chapter. For example, Nickerson, (1978) says: "The act of comparing one thing with another and determining whether they are instances of the same thing must be a very fundamental type of perceptual activity. Without the ability to make such comparisons there could be no perception as we know it" (p. 77).

The two experimental paradigms—similarity judgments and "same–different" or "matching" discriminations—as I noted earlier, must be considered to be the end points of a methodological continuum. At one extreme is a dichotomous, binary judgment of identity or nonidentity; at the other is a graded evaluation of the degree to which two items are alike. It is very likely that the underlying perceptual mechanisms in each case are very similar, if not identical. Nevertheless, the two approaches have grown up separately and the theoretical and cultural (in a scientific sense) differences between the two traditions are substantial. It is entirely possible to read a paper on same–different judgments that does not refer at all to the work on similarity by Tversky, Krumhansl, or any of the other leaders involved in that aspect of the problem. It is as rare in the similarity literature to find references to Posner or Nickerson's distinguished work using the same–different methodology.

This is another example of the unfortunate compartmentalization of modern scientific psychology, even in fields that are so closely related. It also is an indication of the unfortunate narrowness of most theoretical enterprises in this field.

This segregation of discrimination theories and findings into two separate camps is very likely a serious conceptual error, an overly rigid compartmentalization of the discrimination literature, that has no justification in a biological sense. Some steps have been taken to create a synthesis: I shall discuss Proctor's work, an effort toward unifying some of the matching and similarity data at least, but there may be other opportunities yet forthcoming for some kind of possible intellectual unification that go even further to demonstrate how similarity and matching data are manifestations of the same underlying process,.

Perhaps the main reason for the special attention given to and the broad applicability of the same–different or matching technique is that a number of different perceptual mechanisms have been or can be probed by the same–different process by judicious design of the experiment. At its most primitive level (primitive at least from the joint of view of some theories of perceptual organization), matching involves only a simple templatelike comparison of the perceptual representation of two stimuli or even of their constituent features. At a somewhat more complex level of analysis, and this is where the technique becomes useful to psychologists interested in the representation process or other higher level cognitive mechanisms, the hypothesis that the image is encoded in some way that may not be simply a physical map can be tested. In this context, the invisible symbolic representations of geometrical objects (such as letters, words, or even patterns of activity in neural nets) often become more salient than the simple geometrical properties of the objects themselves. Obviously, there is much more going on here than simply a template match.

At an even higher level of analysis, the active attentional process involved in making same–different judgments can also be explored. A very interesting application in this context is the case in which the comparison requires that some kind of a manipulation or transformation of the visual image or representation is carried out. Experiments have been designed in which the observer is asked to place the two objects to be compared in some kind of canonical spatial configuration, even though the stimuli were not originally presented in that configuration, before the matching process can be undertaken; the objects must be scaled in size or rotated (by what is clearly a very active and effortful attentional process) before the match is made. As we shall see in the discussion of the work of Shepard and Cooper, this approach provides a strategy for studying mental imagery that has been one of the most interesting developments of recent times in cognitive psychology.

Thus the processes of matching or of making what a priori may seem to be a very simple judgment of the identity or nonidentity of a pair of stimulus objects can be a powerful probe of a wide variety of perceptual mechanisms. As with similarity judgments, this experimental procedure has become one of the main tools in the analysis of perceptual mechanisms that may be far more complicated and that go far beyond the most simple notion of discrimination itself.

One way to understand why this simple technique is so broadly applicable is to appreciate that there are usually many different criteria by means of which a pair of forms may be judged to be the same or different. One of the most powerful and influential experiments of the last two decades in this regard was reported by Posner's group. A discussion of his work constitutes one of the central themes of the remainder of this chapter. For the moment, I point out that the work of Posner and his colleagues suggested that observers may utilize at least three different kinds of comparisons, each of which may assay a totally different kind of judgmental process. Their observers could evaluate identity on the basis of a purely physical match, on the basis of a name match, or even on the basis of a match based on a highly abstract rule. For example, in the latter case, the rule guiding the decision might be based on the observer's implicitly asking whether or not two stimulus letters are consonants.

It is a remarkable monument to the ingenuity of Posner and co-workers how deeply this simple same–different paradigm probed the nature of multiple levels of discriminative cognition. However, the very fundamental question must be asked at this point: Is there only one or are there several distinct processes involved in the same–different type of experiment? In other words, does the fact that a single experimental procedure is being used necessarily mean that only one process exists, or are there several different same–different processes potentially at work in this type of experiment?

A completely satisfactory answer to any one of the forms in which this question can be posed is not easy to give. We do know that the simplest changes in an experimental task are capable of drastically altering the behavior and, presumably, which of several possible underlying mechanisms is invoked. One could imagine, for example, that a physical match might require only a preattentive, automatic template comparison, whereas a rule-based (e.g., Are the two letters consonants?) criterion might activate attentive mechanisms executing syntactic-rule evaluating processes that actually have nothing in common with the templatelike comparisons.

As we see, the suggestion that multiple processes are tapped by a single experimental paradigm—same–different judgments—is exactly the solution to the problem that Posner evolved in his search for a conceptual schema for these data obtained in his experiments. In other cases, however, there has been a concerted effort to unify the diverse results and the hierarchy of reaction times. This is the direction that Robert Proctor has taken in his theoretical development, and we also consider this trend in thinking about discrimination.

In this section some of the classic experiments and modern data collection efforts relevant to the same–different paradigm are discussed. I highlight, in particular, the work of Nickerson, Posner, and Shepard. We then look at some of the contemporary theories that deal specifically with the same–different paradigms at all of its many possible levels and return to consider the issue of whether one or many mechanisms are involved when one asks an observer to make as simple a choice as "Are these two objects the same or different?

I. Nickerson on Physical Matches

Since 1965 Raymond S. Nickerson has been studying one of the most curious paradoxes in discrimination research. In a series of papers (Nickerson, 1965, 1968, 1969, 1973, 1975, 1976, 1978) that spans two decades he has concerned himself with the curious fact that an observer in a same–different discrimination task who is confronted with two stimulus objects that are physically the same takes a shorter period of time to assert that they are, in fact, the same than he would have taken to assert that a pair of nonidentical objects are different.

Why is it that this seemingly straightforward datum is so startling and considered by so many scholars in this field to be a major empirical paradox? The answer to this question is, in my opinion, that this finding is inconsistent with the predisposition among contemporary psychological theorists toward a *feature analytical* explanation of the comparison process. In accord with what must certainly be considered to be the "mainstream," if not the most logically correct, of theoretical thinking in recent years, the nearly consensual model of the shape-matching process is founded on the idea that a feature-by-feature comparison must be made in a same–different discrimination task in which the criterion for identity is a physical match. Thus, a theoretician operating from the feature-theoretical point of view would argue that an observer should be willing to assert that any two stimulus objects are different immediately upon establishing that *any single* pair of comparable constituent features are not the same. On the other hand, this feature-centered logic goes on, the fact that two objects are the same can only be asserted after *all* of the pairs of features have been compared and shown to be the same. Thus, it is argued, it should take longer on the average to assert "same" than it should take to assert "different."

Logical as this argument may seem, Raymond Nickerson has repeatedly shown (and many other workers have confirmed) that this is not the way the visual system works. Rather, "same" judgments take significantly less time on the average than do "different" judgments. Herein lies the paradoxical nature of the result and the basis of its special interest to the perceptual research community. Nevertheless, it must be reiterated that this result is paradoxical only in the context of a feature-by-feature theoretical analysis. Indeed, this line of explanation may be an exceptionally clear-cut case of begging the question, in logical parlance. It is entirely possible that there are equally plausible and reasonable alternative solutions, other than the purported feature-by-feature analysis based upon the assumption of a elementalistic solution, to the whole–part controversy. Indeed, this paradoxical result may itself be considered a strong argument that a feature comparison process is not taking place, but rather that our comparison is made on the basis of more global attributes of the stimuli. That this point of view is plausible has been suggested earlier by others, most notably Nickerson (1978) himself who, while speaking of the advantage of "same" over "different" trials in reaction times, noted that: what it seems to suggest is that the *same* judgment in these experiments is not the outcome of an analytic process that compares stimuli in a feature-by-feature fashion and terminates either upon finding a mismatch or after determining that there are no mismatches to be found" (p. 78).

Nickerson then goes on in this same report to discuss some of the support for a nonfeature analytic model of the comparison process. Even more helpful, however, is his discussion of the variety of theories that have been proposed to explain the "paradox" of the advantage exhibited by "same" judgments over "different" responses. He lists the following possible explanations that do not assume a feature-by-feature analysis:

1. An artifact injected by the experimenter in sampling the stimuli such that specific "same" pairs occur too frequently.

2. The priming effect of the first stimulus in the pair to be compared on the second stimulus when the two are identical.

3. The improvement in the memory trace of the second, thus producing a higher "perceptual clarity" of the second when the two are identical compared to the case when the two stimuli differ.

4. Biases on the part of the observer to respond "same."

5. Rechecking in the sense suggested by Krueger (1978) when different stimuli are presented in a pair and the appropriate response is different.

6. Different decision processes for "same" and "different" pairs.

Quite a few theoreticians in this field have not picked up on what is the especially deep insight by Nickerson. If they are wrong, and if Nickerson is correct in his assumption that the decisions in such a comparison may not, in fact, involve a feature-by-feature analysis, the "paradoxical" result is not quite so "surprising" or "paradoxical" as it may have seemed at first glance.

One major alternative theoretical theme, for example, can be based on the premise that the two figures are dealt with holistically rather than elementalistically. If only a single global organizational property of one form need be compared with the same holistic attribute of another form, then quite a different expectation—namely that "different" judgments should be made quicker than "same" ones—would be easily justified.

Egeth and Blecker (1971) have proposed that the "paradoxical" empirical superiority of "same" over "different" judgments can be explained on the basis that the two decisions are the end product of totally different mechanisms. That is, though the task in both cases at first glance seems to be identical, this is but an example of another superficial analogy. They argue that the nature of the stimuli directs the decision process when they are the same to what is essentially a different computational process than when they are different. In other words, the existence of two quite different processes can be invoked to explain the unexpected and pseudoparadoxical result of more rapid "same" judgments. The two mechanisms simply have different properties ("same" judgments are mediated by a process that is just intrinsically faster than a "different" process) and the paradox is resolved simply by altering the premises under which the hypothetical explanation is generated.

The other general theoretical direction in explaining the discrepancy between "same" and "different" judgments is exemplified by Krueger's (1978) "Noisy Operator" theory, a point of view that will be spelled out in more detail in a few pages. To briefly anticipate his model, however, both the identical and nonidentical stimuli are processed by the same mechanism in Krueger's model. But, Krueger (1978) and others propose that the delay in processing different stimuli (compared to the more rapid response to stimuli that actually are the same) is due to the necessity of continuously rechecking the "different" stimuli.

2. Posner on Matches Based on Different Criteria

Another extremely influential line of research on matching has been reported over an extended period by Posner. In a major series of reports that was initiated by a joint publication with R.F. Mitchell (Posner & Mitchell, 1967) and which were followed up with several other important papers including that of Posner (1969) and Posner, Boies, Eichelman, and Taylor (1969), Posner defined an experimental paradigm that has now come to be considered a classic means of studying matching behavior at several different cognitive levels. The key result of this work was the outcome that substantial differences in the way matches were made occurred depending on the nature of the criterion that was used to justify the match. That is, as mentioned earlier, the experimenter may ask the observer to compare two letters on the basis of a purely physical match (e.g., two upper case B's must be reported to be the "same" according to this criterion, but an upper case B and a lower case b must be reported to be different); on the basis of a name match (e.g., an upper case B would be reported to be the "same" as a lower case b according to this criterion); or, finally, on the basis of some more elaborate rule such as whether or not the two letters were both vowels (e.g., an upper case E and a lower case u must be reported to be the "same" if the observer followed this rule).

Other intermediate influences were also examined in the Posner studies. For example, there were differences that depended on the particular letters that were chosen and the type font that was used to produce the stimuli. A more subtle comparison was made between upper and lower case letters that were simply size transformations of each other, (e.g., C and c), on the one hand and letters that were actually different forms in the upper and lower cases (e.g., G and g).

These elegant experiments, simple, direct, and relevant to a broad range of cognitive problems, produced results that were especially clear cut. Posner and his colleagues, using reaction time as their dependent variable throughout this entire series of studies, discovered what appeared to be a hierarchy of processing

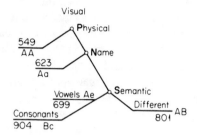

FIG. 4.8. The temporal hierarchy of a series of reaction time experiments (from Posner, 1969).

levels that depended on the specific decision criterion that was imposed on the observer. Identical case letters were reported to be, in fact, identical with the shortest reaction times; letters that were alike in name but were simply different-size transformations of each other were the next fastest; letters that were alike in name but differed in shape were next; and finally, letters that were not alike in name, but were the same only in accord with some semantic or syntactic rule, had the longest reaction times. Figure 4.8 displays some of these results in an unusual form—a reaction-time hierarchy in which the sequential steps of an increasingly difficult (as ordered by their progressively prolonged reaction times) series of decisions is tagged with what are typical reaction times for the particular kind of criterion the observer is instructed to use.

Posner (1978) interprets this empirical chart, which displays the length of time it takes to make a decision for each type of decision criterion, as reflecting the action of a perceptual system that is organized into a hierarchy of relatively independent processing stages. His analysis is based upon reaction times but, in a fundamental way, it is obvious that his scheme is quite different from the classic notion of temporally additive processes suggested by Donders (1868). Posner's "chronometric" method has been used as a source of data to support what is essentially a theory of many parallel channels, some preserving the geometry of a stimulus, some preserving the sound of its name, and some supporting a decision based on some much more subtle semantic aspect of the message it conveys. Posner argues that the different processes may actually go on in parallel rather than in serial order. Posner thus uses reaction-time measurements to support his theoretical conviction that, at the very least, there are separate and distinct encoded representations being constructed and processed in the perceptual system. Both the visual geometry and the verbal names for these alphabetic characters are represented and processed in different cognitively active systems. Furthermore, it is possible for these two systems to communicate in some manner with each other. Thus, name codes and geometrical codes can interact, in ways that are analogous to the Stroop phenomenon (Stroop, 1935; also see my discussion of Navon's work, 1977), quite effectively to interfere with each other.

In other experiments Posner has shown that the semantic or verbal level of processing seems to be totally insensitive to the raw physical characteristics of the stimulus letter (its contrast, luminosity, color, or even its size seem not to affect reaction times when the criterion of choice is the identity of a name or rule match). On the other hand, modifications of these physical parameters can drastically slow up the processing in a matching task in which the observer is asked to use a criterion of physical identity.

A closely related issue that has been investigated by Posner concerns matches between auditory and visual stimuli. He observed that whenever one is asked to make such a cross-modality match (e.g., does the spoken word "Ay" presented to an observer through a set of earphones represent the same thing as the printed letter a?) the reaction times obtained *always* seem to be comparable to those that are typical of verbal matches. The conclusion, therefore, is that cross-modality matches of this sort are mediated by the symbolic names or representations they generate, rather than by any comparison of the primary physical or sensory representations. Data of this sort raise serious questions about some of the dubious subfields of psychological research—specifically, the elusive phenomena called *synesthesia*, wherein, some psychologists assert that auditory stimuli give rise directly to visual experiences.

Marks (1987) provides a useful service in highlighting a possible alternative explanation of synesthesia than direct sensory interactions. He correctly, in my opinion, points out that the conversion of auditory stimuli to visual responses (or vice versa) could be equally as well be understood in terms of semantic or symbolic processes and that the issue is still very much open. Cross-modal transformations such as *synesthesia* have always seemed to me to reflect a peculiar problem for experimental psychology. Perhaps comparison of reaction-time measures of this process with those from Posner's studies will help to resolve their origin.

Another interesting aspect of Posner's experimental design is that it offers an opportunity for studying the process of the transition from visual to symbolic name representations. The work that I have described so far deals mainly with the effects obtained when the two letters to be compared are presented simultaneously. If, on the other hand, one modifies the experiment slightly, as Posner and his colleagues did, and presents the two stimuli sequentially with varying temporal intervals between them, it is possible to study the time at which the visual representation begins to fail and the verbal one takes over. As the interval between two stimuli approaches 2 sec, there is a decreasing difference between the reaction times to two physically identical stimuli and two stimuli that are only alike in having the same name. The obvious explanation of this phenomenon is that the visual representation that is stored is available only for a relatively short time (i.e., less than 2 sec), and that after that brief period has passed the information must be reencoded in a verbal or name form to be retained. Even though this duration is not identical with the measurements made of other forms of visual short-term storage, it is of the same order of magnitude and speaks to the transitoriness of whatever storage mechanism it is that underlies the initial visual representation. The implications for short-term memory studies are, of course, both obvious and profound.

Posner's data and his conceptual model of a system of parallel and nearly independent representations provide far more knowledge about human information processes than just an analysis of the kind of discriminative behavior with which I am interested in this chapter. Indeed, it goes far beyond a description of the initial visual processing of forms that is the main focus of this present work. In extending his analysis to the verbal and semantic codes and processes, Posner takes the discussion into a domain in which not only the form of the stimulus itself but also the modality along which it is presented plays only a secondary role. This is the enormous strength of Posner's analysis, it tends to provide a unifying theme tying together topics that are essentially geometrical and perceptual with topics that are essentially symbolic and cognitive. It is quite clear that the hierarchy of processes that are being assayed by Posner's work ranges from the lowest level preattentive mechanisms (e.g., those mainly affected by the physical properties of the visual stimulus) to high-level processes involving effortful attention (e.g., those requiring the application of semantic rules for their execution.) In this regard, this work plays the same kind of cross-level linking role that Sperling's (1960) invention of the partial report technique did in coordinating our theories of perceptual matters, on the one hand, and memorial topics, on the other. The most rapid skimming of Posner's (1978) book displays the remarkable relevance of the same–different paradigm to a far more diverse set of psychological topics than form perception alone.

Let us concentrate now on the other kinds of theoretical arguments that have been proposed to explain the kinds of matching data that has been obtained in Nickerson's and Posner's studies.

3. Krueger's Noisy Operator Theory

Another theoretical view that has considered the same–different discrimination process has been presented by Krueger (1978). Krueger's main goal was to specifically analyze the basis for the ''paradoxical'' peculiarity in discrimination tasks using same–different judgments that was identified by Nickerson—more rapid ''same'' than ''different'' response times. Krueger confronted this result by developing a theory based upon the supposition that the perceptual responses to the stimuli that are being compared (and, perhaps, also the underlying processing of those stimuli) are intrinsically noisy. That is, stimuli that are being compared cannot be considered to be *perceptually identical* even when they are *physically identical* because of the injection of random fluctuations by the perceptual systems into their representations. Thus the observer should not, if he or she is to optimize performance, immediately decide that stimuli are different on the basis of the mismatch of a single feature or attribute; it might just be a discrepancy due to random fluctuations. Rather, the observer must make a decision on the basis of a process somewhat akin to the decision made in a Theory of Signal Detection (TSD)-type paradigm. Figure 4.9 illustrates the analogy between the enumeration of the number of mismatches that is central to Krueger's noisy operator theory and the strength of the noise and noise-plus-signal distributions, respectively, in the TSD paradigm.

The difficulty faced by the observer, according to Krueger, in the context of a perceived mismatch is that it is far more difficult to exclude a spurious mismatch (due to noise) than it is to accept a true mismatch in his or her comparison. The observer must, therefore, continuously *recheck* the mismatching features, especially when the degree of mismatch is near that which would be generated by the noise introduced into what were originally identical stimuli.

It is at this point that the "paradoxical" efficiency of same judgments begins to be understood, even if one adheres to a feature-oriented conceptualization of the problem. The observer must recheck the mismatching features because truly different stimuli have more mismatching features than the truly identical ones (i.e., both suffer from mismatches due to noise) but since all mismatches must be rechecked, it takes longer to process nonidentical forms than identical ones. Therein lies the resolution of the "paradox" and the advantage of Krueger's noisy operator model for modeling same–difference judgments.

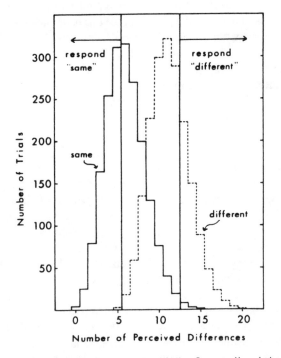

FIG. 4.9. The similarity between the "Noisy Operator" and signal detection theory is clearly illustrated in this model of the former (from Krueger, 1978).

One problem with Krueger's noisy operator theory is that it involves a "rechecking" procedure that is essentially sequential and dependent on earlier evaluations. It assumes, therefore, that a series of examinations is made by the visual system, a series that takes place over time, and that is based upon the presence or absence of mismatches that virtually have to be enumerated in each of many possible earlier steps in the sequence. Unfortunately, this is not in agreement with common experience; we have no sense of such a series of decision and reprocessing steps. There is, therefore, very much of a post hoc flavor to this hypothesized process that leaves much to be desired of Krueger's model.

Krueger and Chignell (1985) have gone on to prepare another updated generalization—the missing feature principle—that, in my opinion, removes them from the feature theorists and places them squarely among those who champion the precedence of holistic perception. They note that early in the perception of forms, local features have not emerged, and therefore some features are simply missing from the perceptual representation of, say, a letter. They go on to hypothesize that in those cases in which a feature may be missing from one of the pair of to-be-discriminated letters, a feature mismatch is simply ignored by the observer. Therefore, the observer is much more likely to falsely report that the letters are the same than to report that they are different.

Krueger and Chignell suggested that this phenomenon (which is essentially a reversal of the predictions for reaction times of the noisy operator theory described above) should occur when the observer is stressed by having to respond very quickly (or if a trailing mask is used). In these situations, the judgment would be made on the basis of the early global, but only partial, representation of the stimulus. If the observer is given sufficient time, then the availability of all of the features allow the expected preponderance of errors in which more false-different than false-same responses are made.

4. Proctor's Unified Theory of Matching Behavior

One recent effort that has been made to simplify the increasing number of phenomena and theoretical models in the field of discrimination research is to be found in the work of Robert Proctor (1981). Proctor notes that both in the case of the "paradoxical" advantage in reaction times of "same" stimuli (seen in the work of Nickerson and others) and in the case of the advantage of physical over verbal matches (seen in the work of Posner and others), explanatory models, whatever their details, have tended to concentrate on the early matching stages as the locus of the effects. In the case of the same-different advantage, Proctor points out that the theories generally attribute the phenomenon to either of two kinds of matching. In one kind of theory (e.g., Bamber, 1969), it is proposed that there are two different processes and the differences in reaction times are due simply to the time-constant characteristics intrinsic to the two processes. The other type of theory, exemplified by the work of Krueger (1978) that I have already discussed, suggests that there is only one process, but this process operates differently in the "same" and "different" stimuli. The observed differences in performance are due to noise effects or some other factor that would necessarily demand that the comparison be rechecked more often for different than same stimuli because there are more discrepant features in nonmatching stimuli than in matching ones. Proctor's summary of the basic hypothesis underlying this latter theoretical orientation is that it argues that noise "is more likely to result in spurious *mismatches* of features than in spurious *matches*" (p. 292). Despite the differences in detail, both theories localize the critical decision at which the match occurs at a relatively peripheral level.

In developing his alternative "unified" model, Proctor argues that because the two phenomena—the time advantage of "same" over "different" judgments and the abbreviated reaction times for physical matches—are so similar in their phenomenology, it is essential that some effort be made to explain them in a common context and within a common theoretical rubric. Indeed, he also links both of these phenomena to the data obtained when certain other experimental paradigms, namely *priming* and *repetition*[6] are carried out following up on a suggestion that seems to have been first made by Nickerson (1978).

Proctor suggests that there is a universal principle that brings together both of the matching phenomena, as well as the priming and repetition effects, under a common explanatory umbrella. That principle, he suggests (quite to the contrary of most of the other theoreticians who have worked in this arena) is not to be found in the matching process, but rather in the conditions that determine the rate of encoding of the stimuli. Proctor reports additional empirical research to justify this hypothesis, but because our concern here is mainly with theory, let us concentrate on the details of his model.

Proctor's version of an explanatory model is based upon three premises:

1. Several levels of processing occur. He refers to both passive physical or perceptual matching, on the one hand, and cognitive matching, which is linked to some aspect of memory or previous experience, on the other. This is very much in the vein of the preattentive–attentive dichotomy made by many contemporary investigators.

2. Repetition facilitates the process of stimulus encoding (i.e., when stimuli

---

[6] *Priming* (e.g., see Beller, 1970) refers to the fact that a response to a particular stimulus may be facilitated or enhanced if another stimulus, to which the observer need not respond, but which is in some way similar to the test stimulus, precedes the test stimulus. *Repetition* (e.g., see Kornblum, 1969) refers to the fact that in a sequence of reaction-time trials the reaction time will be shortened if the trial preceding the test one used the same stimulus. The differences between the two experimental designs are, obviously, quite small. One, repetition, uses whatever is the previous trial in the run of trials as the influential one; the other, priming, introduces a special stimulus as a precursor of the test stimulus as the influential one. It is not at all clear that two distinct processes are at work in this situation.

are transferred from some preattentive, physical code to some symbolic, cognitive representation the process will go faster if it has occurred previously).

3. When competing cognitive codes are activated they inhibit each other.

Thus, Proctor has three degrees of freedom to work with in his attempt to unify the explanation of all four perceptual processes he proposes to bring within the same theoretical structure. His argument goes on to assert that there is a major difference in how the visual system handles simultaneous and sequential physical matches. In the case of simultaneous (side-by-side) matches, his assertion is in agreement with most other theories that the advantage of the physical match occurs because a physical match is processed at a lower, simpler, and therefore faster level of processing. However, Proctor's approach does differ with some of the other theories in at least some ways; he deviates from the mainstream when he goes on to assert that in all cases in which sequential comparisons must be made, both the diminishing advantage of the physical match over a name match and the progressive increase in the reaction times to "same" responses as the temporal interval between the stimuli increases is due to a "facilitation through repetition" process.

Proctor's analysis thus incorporates many of the concepts of predecessor theories but brings them together by calling attention to the similarities among a number of different perceptual phenomena. This is a useful process, but by calling upon a triad of different processes (levels, facilitation, and inhibition) Proctor actually has not simplified the situation very much. Rather he has shown the existence of similarities and overlap, but from a formal point of view his model does not reduce the number of premises that must be involved to explain a multitude of different phenomena. There are, however, a few differences from the conventional perspective in his model that are novel contributions. Proctor does, for example, propose a totally different explanation of the sequential physical matching process than is typical and his analysis does add to the arguments for a clear-cut distinction between the preattentive and attentive that is often blurred in other discussions.

F. FORM MATCHING
WITH TRANSFORMATIONS

In the previous section, I considered many theories that have to do with form matching. This topic was characterized by sets of stimuli that were presented in pairs typically in some standard orientation and with some common size. Because of the relatively simple way in which these stimuli are arranged, there was a persistent theoretical focus on what appeared to be a rapid, automatic, preattentive processing relatively uninfluenced by attentive cognitive processes. In this section we consider a paradigm that is significantly different—before the stimuli can be compared, they must be transformed by what appears to be a very active cognitive process to a canonical orientation, position, or size. As we see, what seems at first to be only a slight design difference has major ramifications both empirically and theoretically. One effect, in particular, is that the topics we discuss cannot by any stretch of the theoretical imagination be considered independently of some relatively high-level attentive and cognitive mechanisms.

In all cases of this kind of experiment the observer must make a "conscious" and active effort to retransform the stimuli from their altered form into a standard form so that different items can be compared with each other. Whatever the nature of the comparison or matching process itself, it *must* be preceded by an attentive effort that takes this kind of matching process into what is now commonly referred to as the *cognitive domain*. There was, at least, a modicum of doubt about the issue of perceptual-versus-cognitive mechanisms for matching processes that occur without requiring such transformations. In this case, there is none.

The experimental paradigm in this new case—matching following a necessary transformation—is much the same as that simpler task described earlier. The observer is asked only to specify if a pair of objects is the "same" or "different." However, before this is done, it is assumed that the observer must scale, rotate, or fold the stimuli in his or her "mind" to get the to-be-compared objects into the appropriate and comparable configuration. Obviously, such a mental image transformation makes very substantial demands on cognitive abilities that are not activated when an observer is asked to make a texture discrimination or to compare two untransformed stimulus objects. Some memory or representation of the two stimuli must be established and processed (thus giving an entree into the nature of that memory itself). Some active mental manipulation or transformation of at least one of the images is required (thus making it possible to examine the characteristics of the process of mental manipulation itself). These new processes must be superimposed upon what are, at the very least, analogs of the matching processes invoked in the standard form-matching paradigm that are also still required to carry out the task. I use the word *analog* in this context because there is no way at this point to tell whether the process of matching two simultaneously presented, untransformed images is identical to the process of matching memorized images in this new situation.

The idea of comparing pairs of stimuli when one of them was transformed away from the canonical configuration of the other is an idea, as so many other in perceptual research, that has its origins well back in the classic literature. Ernst Mach (as cited in Shepard & Cooper, 1982) as early as 1886 had shown that pairs of random geometrical shapes were perceived as being identical more easily when they were in the same orientation than when one of them was rotated to some other orientation. The idea languished for many years, but it became an object of renewed interest to a number of investigators in the 1960s. One of the first modern studies on the mental rotation of geometrical forms was reported out by Boynton, Elworth, Onley, and Klingberg (1960). However, the names most often associated with this line of research today are that of Shepard, Metzler, and Cooper, as well as a number of their other colleagues who have worked with them over the years. Indeed, the technique of mental transformation has become the centerpiece of an extensive theoretical development in which this group has attempted to describe and explain the process underlying the mental representation of geometrical stimuli. It has also laid the basis for a renaissance of interest in mental imagery—a field that lay fallow for many years in want of a satisfactory experimental tool with which to probe and analyze what previously had been only introspective and anecdotal reports of mental imagery. Fortunately, for any one seriously interested in this topic, the evolution of this very important perceptual study has been reported in an anthology (Shepard & Cooper, 1982) of the key papers that have emerged in the previous 17 years from Shepard's group. This anthology of previously published papers has been annotated and commented to give us a very complete review of the development of these ideas and a deep insight into their theoretical approach.

Shepard recounts, in an anecdote characterized by extraordinary temporal precision, that he conceived the idea of combining mental rotation and paired comparison techniques "in a state of 'hyponopomic' (sic) suspension between sleep and wakening, in the early morning of November 16, 1968. Just before 6:00 A.M." (p. 7). Although this sudden-insight phenomenon would itself be worthy of considerable study [What had he been reading or talking or thinking about in the hours before sleep the previous night?] it was only 2 days after the "hyponopomic" event that Shepard set down on paper the details of the experimental procedure that had leapt so curiously into his early morning consciousness. This brief note constituted the program of research that was to occupy him and his colleagues for over 2 decades. In this document (Shepard, 1968) Shepard spells out the general framework of the technique that was to be so powerfully utilized in the years to come. The original stimuli proposed were pairs of block constructions, as shown in Fig. 4.10, which may or may not be the same object simply

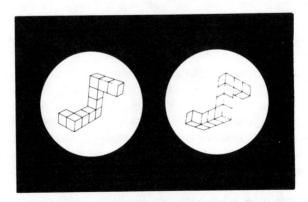

FIG. 4.10. The stimuli used by Shepard, Metzler, and Cooper in their experiments on mental rotation (from Shepard & Cooper, 1982).

rotated to a new orientation. The observer was to do exactly what the title of the work suggested, that is, rotate one of the two block objects in his or her imagination and as quickly as possible assert whether the two were identical or not. Frequently the objects were designed to appear to be three-dimensional (by the judicious choice of monocular cues), but in other cases they were two-dimensional forms that simply had to be rotated on the plane of the paper (i.e., about an invisible depth axis). The main independent variable was the difference in the initial degree of rotation between the two objects. The main dependent variable was the time it took to make this rotational transformation and respond that they were the same or different. This is, therefore, a chronometric experiment in the tradition of Donders, Sternberg, and Posner.

The first paper to grow from this fertile (and remarkably complete statement of the problem) was published by Shepard and Metzler (1971) and proved to be one of the most influential documents of its kind in perceptual psychology in this century. This brief *Science* article was then expanded with other experimental data and published by Metzler and Shepard (1974). In the expanded report, the tone for the program of research was set. The series of papers contained in Shepard and Cooper's anthology includes those by Shepard, Cooper, Metzler, Feng, Judd, Farrell, and others on mental rotations, paper folding, imagined construction, and apparent motion—each representing a creative and insightful experimental attack on a rich and diverse set of hitherto nonmanipulable perceptual phenomena. Among the many findings emanating from these studies were these:

1. The reaction time to tell if two objects are the same or different increases linearly as a function of the initial angular orientation differences between the two objects.

2. Mental rotation was typically carried out at less than 60 deg/sec.

3. Performance is only slightly degraded if the observers do not know in advance what the orientation of the presented objects is to be.

4. It does not matter to any significant degree whether the rotation is in the plane of the picture or, as indicated by monocular cues, to be in depth.

5. If a single character is presented at other than a vertical orientation, the time it takes to mentally rotate the character for recognition is not linear.

6. Imagined and real rotations are dealt with in virtually the same reaction times.

To what theoretical issues does this work speak? The prime problem to which the authors direct their theoretical analysis concerns our understanding of the nature of the mental representation of two- and three-dimensional forms. As I have noted earlier, a major debate has raced for years in the imagery field concerning whether or not the image is stored in a symbolic (or verbal or propositional) form as opposed to a pictorial (or analog) manner. We have already seen in the work of Posner that both answers may be correct in different situations; pictorial representations seem to be short-lived and transient, rapidly (in a second or two) being transformed into some kind of a verbal or symbolic code.

The work of Shepard, Metzler, and Cooler presents a vigorous case for the pictorial or analog representation theory. Their main point is that because the major result—the observed linearity of mental rotation speeds corresponds to the physics of a true physical rotation—the underlying process should also be occurring in the same continuous and analog manner. In their words ". . .intermediate stages in the (mental) process have a one-to-one correspondence with the intermediate stages in the external rotation of an object" (p. 185 in Shepard & Cooper, 1982). Furthermore, they argue, in the holistic Gestalt tradition, that this means that the overall organization of the stimulus is maintained, and that it is, therefore, likely that the representation is also dealt with as an integrated pictorial whole rather than a series of propositions or verbal codes.

It must be made explicit, however, that the analog representation to which Shepard and his colleagues allude is not a naive kind of "toy-in-the-head" model. They specifically eschew that sort of simplistic interpretation. Shepard goes out of his way to dismiss that notion and to substitute for it a notion of analog representation as a kind of mathematical isomorphism in which the representations of objects are related to, but not the same as, the attributes of the originally depicted object. In his model, there are one-to-one correspondences between objects and symbols, not dimensionally isomorphic physical maps.

As distinguished and influential as this work has been, it must also be appreciated that the model of analog representation presented by Shepard and his colleagues is not without its critics; their arguments are not considered to be unequivocal by all contemporary theoreticians in the field. A number of criticisms of the analog (as opposed to the propositional or symbolic) approach to representation of visual images have been made. Among the most influential of the critics is Pylyshyn (1979, 1981). Some of his arguments are based on philosophical criteria of logic and parsimony. For example, Pylyshyn has asked: Because there are such good data that a great deal of pictorial information is encoded propositionally, why should we have to make a special system to handle data of this kind? Other arguments forwarded by Pylyshyn are based upon the fact that the results can be influenced by the kinds of stimulus, the nature of instructions, and practice. Thus what seems to be an analog system is nothing more than another propositional system clothed in what must be considered to be a phenomenological disguise.

Another kind of counterargument to Shepard's notion of analog representation has already been mentioned. If it is true, as suggested by Moore (1956) that we cannot distinguish between alternative models on the basis of input–output relations alone, then there can be no resolution of the issue of what kind of internal representation is actually being used in any case no matter how high quality the empirical data. This argument has also been made by Anderson (1978), among others. I have more to say about this important point in the concluding chapter of this book.

5

THE RECOGNITION
OF VISUAL FORMS

A. INTRODUCTION

In a previous book (Uttal, 1978) I wrote about the neurophysiological bases of learning and memory. I spoke of a major conceptual peculiarity concerning the most commonly accepted theoretical explanations of these memorial processes. That peculiarity lay in the fact that the nearly universally accepted theory of the most probable neurophysiological mechanism of learning and memory (synaptic changes as a result of use) was not based on any substantial amount of direct empirical evidence, but rather upon the logical and plausible argument that synaptic plasticity is, in fact, virtually the only possible neuroreductionistic mechanism of behavioral change as a result of experience. Although many experiments have been carried out in search of what Lashley (1950) referred to as the *engram*—the biological correlate of memory—it is a truism that no psychobiologist has ever shown changes in any synaptic junctions that can be directly related to any particular behavioral changes in mammals.[1]

---

[1] There will probably be some argument about this assertion from biologists using simple invertebrate populations even if such an argument can easily be justified for vertebrates. Even in the case of those animals without spinal cords, I feel that the link between synaptic changes and learning (in the sense that we commonly think of learning is yet to be established. Whereas there is no question that simple behavioral changes analogous to vertebrate conditioning and habituation can be linked to certain neurophysiological events in invertebrates, the more elaborate kinds of learning in higher organisms still remain opaque to neurophysiological analysis.

The reader interested in pursuing the problem of the neurophysiological basis of memory would profit from a reading of Lynch's (1986) essay. Lynch presents an up-to-date review of the field, but also acknowledges how preliminary is our wisdom in this field—even his own model is "long on speculation and short on data" (p. 65).

Nevertheless, the hypothesis of synaptic conductivity changes, perhaps associated with actual physical growth and perhaps associated with more subtle biochemical changes in membrane that are also putatively driven by use, is virtually universal in its acceptance among psychobiological theorists as *the* explanation of most persistent kinds of learning. There are, of course, many unknown details—we do not know how the specific biochemical mechanisms of synaptic plasticity are altered, whether use leads to a reduction or an increase in the synaptic count, or even where in the brain the critical synaptic events underlying any particular engram may be located. Nevertheless, a consensus has emerged that seems to agree that it is at the junctions between nerves—the synapses—that the necessary macromolecular events must occur to account for the retention of the effects of previous experience. Some insights are emerging into the biochemistry that accompanies changes from short-term to long-term storage and of the growth and swelling of junctions; there are even some hints being uncovered as to some of the particular regions of the brain in which the salient plastic events either actually take place or from where they may be controlled: *There has, however, never been any experiment that directly establishes the necessity and sufficiency of these neuronal changes for some closely linked behavior.* For learning, as for all other cognitive processes, the leap from the discrete cellular mechanisms to the molar psychological phenomena has not yet been made. Anyone who disputes this point is living in a scientific fantasy world of connections unmade and of leaps unleapt. In spite of this unbridged conceptual gap, indirect arguments and simple logical necessity have made the synaptic hypothesis of learning among the most widely accepted of psychobiological theories.

In this chapter the reader observes a similar situation unfolding concerning contemporary theories of the process underlying form recognition. The contemporary consensus among theoreticians, if the literature is to be accepted at face value, is that recognition occurs as a result of the analysis of a form into local features. As I review the theoretical literature, it is shown that the problem of form recognition is nearly universally approached from a point of view that argues that the analysis of complex forms into their "parts," "features," or "components" is the initial information-processing step in classification and recognition. I believe, however, that a considerable body of evidence argues that there are global strategies at work in human form perception that have little to do with the feature-by-feature algorithms that currently are the most popular theories of form recognition. The analogy I have drawn here between synapses and learning on the one hand and features and form recognition on the other is far from complete, however. In the former case there is little inconsistency between theory and empirical data; in the latter case data clashes with theory, even if this is not generally appreciated to be the case.

There are many arguments why feature analysis can not be considered to be the main means by which the human being actually recognizes forms regardless of the ubiquitousness of this feature or elementalist approach in contemporary theory building. Indeed, most of the demonstrations (as opposed to parametric experiments) that represent the first-order evidence of how we recognize forms are largely ignored by researchers in this field when it comes to generating theory. This kind of phenomenology, as so eloquently pointed out by Pomerantz and Kubovy (1981) in the summary to their very important book (a work that may be a harbinger of the arousal of interest in the currently dormant global or Gestalt perspective) must not be underestimated in terms of its impact on psychological thinking in the last half century.

Demonstrations reflect the fundamental nature of perception in a direct and immediate fashion and should set the stage for research activities. Perceptual phenomena, therefore, must be, from one point of view, not only the initial guides to valid theories of perceptual reality, but the final arbiter in any dispute between a hypothetical mechanism and that perceptual reality. Simple demonstrations cannot be ignored in the search for reductionistic explanations solely because they urge a kind of theory for which we are not particularly well prepared by technique, tradition, or current approach. The psychophysical fact, the final result of a long series of processes and transformations, must be the ultimate authority in disputes of this kind. Phenomenology incorporates the influences of all of the previous stages. Therefore, whatever neural- and feature-oriented explanations or heuristics we may develop must be altered if they are in conflict with these phenomenological first approximations. The point is that it is the explanations and models that must be modified, not the implications of the phenomenal demonstrations. Indeed, controlled psychophysical experimentation, one must remember, is nothing more than another way of achieving a more quantitative or more precise definition of phenomena; demonstrations differ from the graphic or statistical results of an experiment only in the degree of quantification and not in quality. To reject a demonstration because "it is but an illusion" or "it is not sufficiently quantified" runs counter to the very concept of theory testing that has graced modern science. It is only in the rarest instances that a good mix of demonstration and more formal experimental data is produced. (One good recent example is Todd's, 1985, elegantly designed study of structure from motion.)

And yet, we seem so very frequently to ignore the message being sent by some first-approximation demonstrations in the field of form perception. Whereas phenomenology cries out a distinctly global, Gestalt, and holistic message, our theories are predominantly elementalistic and feature oriented.

Why should this be the case? I believe that the main arguments for the predominance of today's elementalistic theories are *expediency* and *availability*. These two reasons for the utter domination of feature analytic thinking in contemporary theory emerge from the successes of two powerful and influential bodies of knowledge—(a) modern studies of the discrete nature of the neuron and its responses and (b) the extraordinary engineering developments underlying the architecture and programming logic of the modern digital computer. These enormously exciting and fertile scientific traditions have been among the most effective intellectual forces constraining and guiding our theoretical structures in perception (as well as many other areas of science) in the past 40 years. The period of emergence of the new elementalistic form-recognition theories overlaps with the period in which both computer science and neurophysiological science have flourished. From an even broader perspective, and with the possible exception of macromolecular biochemistry, these two sciences have been the ones driving the current stage of human intellectual development in many of its different guises just as nuclear physics did in the era surrounding World War II.

Nevertheless this influence has not been without its costs. Just as computer science has been a powerful heuristic for theory building in perception, it has also circumscribed a very specific kind of theoretical thinking because of its own intrinsic limits. I am referring to a much more esoteric reason than the fact that computers are made of discrete parts for this pervasive elementalism in psychobiological thinking: The theory-driving force exerted by the *practical limits* of currently available computational algorithms and programming procedures.

We currently have available a broad array of programming algorithms and other analytic methods that can be used to dissect forms into their parts and features and an equally large armamentarium of techniques for looking at the resulting components or parts. Our mathematics is quite competent, in other words, as a means of *analyzing* complex structures into their components. This programming limitation arises out of a contemporary computer hardware technology that is mainly one of serial "von Neumann" machines. Devices of this sort are well suited to dealing with the sequential analysis of local features, but are not well designed for the parallel processing of spatially distributed arrays. It has only been in the last few years that attention has been directed towards the development of machines that are inherently global and distributed in their organization. It is only recently that parallel organized computers like the "Connection" machine produced by Thinking Machines, Inc. and the "Butterfly" machine produced by Bolt Berenek and Newman, Inc. (both stimulated by their close proximity to the covey of parallel-processing researchers at MIT in Cambridge, Massachusetts) and the N-Cube machine have become commercially available. It is yet to be seen if these new machines with their distinctly different philosophy of logical organization will successfully force our thinking and lead to holistic, rather than feature-oriented, theories as proposed by "connectionist" and "PDP" theorists.

It is not difficult to establish how deficient we currently are, on the other hand, in dealing with global form and the ensemble properties of complex structures. At the most fundamental level, there is yet no satisfactory means of even classifying and categorizing broad classes of geometrical forms. A few mathematical expressions can be used to define narrowly specified classes of forms (e.g., the polynomial that defines quadric and cubic surfaces in space), but as I have shown in chapter 1, a consensus does not even exist concerning what we verbally mean by geometrical "form." Much less is there a formal means of specifying form in a wider context so that it (form) could become grist for some kind of theoretical engine.

Similarly, however much we know about the physiology and information encoding and transmission properties of the individual neural components of the brain, there are few who can yet assert anything about the logical processes that are executed by arrays of neurons to instantiate even the simplest perceptual process. Beyond such stabilizing necessities as "lateral inhibitory interaction" and the logical necessity we can both deduct and observe for some kind of convergent and divergent mechanisms, there is a paucity of knowledge and even speculation about the kind of logical processes that neurons collectively carry out. The artifices of Artificial Intelligence such as list processing and the so-called expert systems (which seem to be nothing more than elaborate look-up tables based on elaborate sets of canned rules) are hardly likely to provide much insight into the mechanisms used by the brain to associate concepts that are similar only in meaning, but not in coded representation. Indeed, although it is understandable how these subtle brain processes may be obscured by their complexity even if we could localize them in the brain, it is also true that we do not know where to look: Where, indeed, is it in the brain that neural activity becomes perception or thought? What is the locus of psychoneural equivalence? In general? In particular? We have not the inkling of a clue to answers to these questions in spite of almost a century of attempts to answer them.

What the extirpation–behavioral analysis of classical physiological psychology has offered is still equivocal. We know of some regions that seem to be associated with sensory or motor processing or the control of memory. But, there is yet little insight into the locus of higher cognitive processes which, for that matter, may not be localized, or localizable, but, rather, distributed throughout the brain. Classic physiological psychology has thus generally failed to achieve its goals, based as it was on a premise of precise localizability. The extraordinary proliferation of visual areas (see especially the work of Kaas, 1978 and Van Essen, 1985) accentuates the problem, it does not ameliorate it, by raising the necessity for interaction over broad regions of the brain to accomplish something like vision.

The recent shift of attention from localization to the biochemistry of psychoactive drugs reflects this failure. This paradigm shift has brought us to the consideration of matters that are even less theoretical, less explanatory, and less enlightening vis-á-vis the questions of mentation than were the outcome of decades of tissue extirpation studies. Indeed, most neurochemical studies of behavior seem to be primarily concerned with the metabolic, rather than the information-processing aspects of the brain.

It must also be acknowledged that both contemporary perceptual psychology and computational science have only recently begun to develop algorithms and theories that would permit, as well as stimulate, us to examine the global attributes or Gestalt properties of a stimulus-form. Yet, if one considers the many prima facie pieces of evidence that characterize how recognition occurs, the a priori argument seems compelling that *people recognize forms not because of the nature of the parts but, rather, because of some attribute of arrangement of the parts.*

That is, I argue that the human perceptual system is, at its most fundamental level, holistic rather than elementalistic in the strategies it uses to carry out visual information-processing tasks. Other circumstantial and demonstrable evidence lies in the generalized ability of the human observer to (a) categorize objects under the same rubric even when constructed from many different kinds of features or in grossly degraded or reduced forms and (b) the ability of readers to virtually ignore the particular type font of printed words. There are many other similar demonstrations and arguments that can be made that our nervous system operates by holistic rules of logic in which *global arrangement is more important than local features*.

Yet, when most perceptual theorists go into the laboratory, or, worse, when they attempt to develop computational models or psychological theories of form perception, the contemporary zeitgeist is to look at features, to analyze features, to manipulate features, and generally to emphasize features as the putative means by which humans process forms. However satisfactory this approach may be for computer vision engineering development projects that are not deeply concerned with modeling the human perceptual mind, such a hyperelementalistic philosophy and predilection has been a major distraction leading us away from the development of what first-approximation demonstrations suggest is a more truly valid theory of human recognition processes. Contemporary theory and experimentation in neurophysiology, on the one hand, and computer vision technology, on the other, in their joint emphasis on local features seem therefore to be divergent and digressive from what seems a priori to a more plausible approach to understanding how people recognize forms in terms of their most fundamental premises.

Of course, there are many other contributing factors (e.g., both the difficulty in generating an arbitrary form and the difficulty in formally representing families of unrelated forms), but the main problem is that we do not yet have either a satisfactory holistic theory or an empirical methodology to provide the bases for a truly modern holistic theory of recognition based on the global rather than the local attributes. Any critic must acknowledge that even primitive holistic explanations are few and far between these days. But there are glimmerings, such as Hoffman's Lie Algebra approach, my own work with autocorrelation transforms, and some of the others emphasizing spatially distributed interactions.

It must also be acknowledged that the fact that current thinking is dominated by feature-oriented theories may be unavoidable. It may not be so much a criticism of current thinking to describe it as over- or hyperelementalistic as it is a historical description of a necessary evolutionary step in the natural development of the science toward a more valid theory of form perception. We may simply have to accept the fact that what we have today is a prerequisite step toward full understanding. But whether it be a misdirected conceptual deficiency or a primitive evolutionary step, the point I make here is that current theories probably are nothing but the most preliminary of expedients and crutches. Just as with the study of the neurophysiological basis of learning in which synaptic plasticity is accepted without substantiating evidence, logic and first order demonstrations argue that form perception is largely processed in terms of the global attributes of the organized stimuli.

The argument that most form-recognition paradigms involve feature-oriented, and not holistically oriented methods may not seem, at first glance, to be supportable when one leaves the field of perceptual science and looks at what has happened in recent attempts to develop mathematical theories of "pattern" recognition. There is at least the initial suggestion that some of these models are looking at the global, rather than local, attributes of forms. However, as we see when we examine the various taxonomies of recognition algorithms later in this chapter, this is not the case.

The purpose of this chapter is to review recognition theory. I present a review and analysis of a set of theories that, I believe, is based upon premises that, unfortunately, must be considered to be inaccurate, incomplete, and nonrepresentative of perceptual reality, as well as being patently misleading in that they are not even pointing in the right direction—that is, towards parallel and holistic mechanisms. It is an unfortunate state of affairs, but a necessary one in the absence of viable holistic theories and approaches to the problem of form recognition. My hope is that the reader, forewarned by the preceding paragraphs, will not assume (as so many of my colleagues seem to have) that the dominant elementalistic approach is anything other than a preliminary step toward understanding the psychology of human form perception. The repetitive recitation of a long series of what are essentially elementalistic theories, it is hoped, do not detract attention from the fact that, in fundamental principle, *people seem to see by virtue of the arrangement of the parts rather than by the nature of the parts.*

With this caveat in place (and by force of repetition, in the forefront of our thinking about this problem) we now turn to some of the other issues that concern the process of form recognition. It might be well to start out by reasserting what it is that is meant by recognition. Phenomenologically, it is the act of classifying, categorizing, or conceptualizing a stimulus object as a member of a class of which it is a member. It is, of course, possible for an object to be a member of many different classes and have many different names: It is either the natural context or the design of the recognition experiment that determines within which of these many possible alternative classes an object will be classified. A "woman walking down a street" may be Mrs. Smith, my wife, a living organism, or a potential threat, depending upon the situation and the observer; a wide variety of contextual cues will determine the response of the observer to the stimulus object so inadequately described in the few words "a woman walking down a street." In each case, there is much about the recognition process that transcends the requirements of the detection or discrimination processes. The question asked is always of the form: What, *specifically*, is the name of the stimulus object? or: To what group does this stimulus object belong? In the laboratory the experimenter is not simply structuring the procedure so that the observer can respond: "Is there anything there?'' or ''Are these two things the same?'' as characterized the processes described in previous two chapters, but is asking ''What is it?''

Recognition, therefore, is a process that requires more of the observer than simply answering questions of existence or similarity. It is also an act of conceptualizing or classifying that, without doubt, entails far more than just a straightforward tabulation of the specific features of the object. Just as discrimination subsumed detection, but added requirements of its own, so, too, does recognition require more information and more extensive information processing than did either detection and discrimination to be completely executed. Just as discrimination added a memorial requirement (the first stimulus, once having been attended to, must be remembered to be compared with the second one), recognition adds the further requirement that the characteristics of not just another single stimulus, but rather of a class (or several classes) of stimuli be recalled.

At the most a priori and primitive theoretical level, the information-processing requirements are increasing as we pass through this hierarchy of visual processing stages. Whereas it is certainly conceivable to think of form detection and discrimination as the outcome of a relatively simple and passive algorithmic process, the process of recognition conjures up a theoretical environment in which terms like *induction* and *logic* are more likely to be encountered. And, as we see, recognition also seems to reflect a far greater influence of cognitive processes than do the earlier and lower stages: Empirical evidence suggests that recognition is, to a substantial degree, much more *cognitively penetrable* than is either detection or discrimination.

Despite this a priori consideration of the increased complexities of the recognition process, it is the case that there is an enormous variety of recognition theories about, many of which assume some kind of a serial comparison or correlation process and most of which (if I may belabor a point) assume that some kind of a feature-by-feature sequential template-matching process occurs. Both logically and empirically, the sequential matching of an input stimulus with an array of comparison templates suggested by many of these theories seems implausible— our recognition processes do not seem to require more or less time to recognize a caricature than a photograph. Nor does it seem likely that an exhaustive series of templates are actually stored in our memory, each of which must be compared in turn with the stimulus object. The memory requirements of such a system would be enormous and the information processing inefficient.

Preliminary examination of the recognition process thus suggests that something quite different from template matching is going on in the visual system, something that occurs in parallel and that does not depend upon a serial search (unless the experiment is specifically designed to make this demand on the observer by asking him to search a list of many stimuli in sequence) or a sequential series of simple cross-correlations. The nature of the associations that are made between percepts and classes of percepts seem to be incompatible with such serial processes.

Another way to look at this problem is from the point of view of the logician.

Watanabe (1985), in the most recent of his distinguished series of works on pattern (i.e., form) recognition (to which we turn for wisdom and organization in the next section of this chapter), describes the process of recognition as one of induction; that is, of the creation of concepts and categories by generalization based on the examination of many different exemplars. He distinguishes induction from deduction by noting that deduction is the production of specific exemplars from a general rule. The categorization or inductive process, from this point of view, can be seen (and has been seen by Watanabe and others) as more descriptive of form recognition. This hypothesis, however, is not entirely satisfying. Whereas induction may be described as the generation of a class, category, or concept from the specific examples, that is not exactly what a recognizer is doing. Rather, this kind of visual process requires that the observer place a newly presented exemplar into one of a set of preexisting classes or categories.

Even though it does not seem, therefore, that we can confidently propose a pure identity of recognition and induction, the former process—recognition—clearly has much more of the flavor of the latter—induction—than it does of the passive, automatonlike, deductive mechanisms that characterize so many of the theories of form recognition currently in the theoretical literature. It may be that the "deduction–induction" dichotomy is just not adequate to describe these processes, but that we should more properly consider a trichotomy of deduction–induction–recognition to be more descriptive of the logical reality of the form-perception context. Their processes are separable enough to justify making this distinction among them.

There is another unique attribute of recognition that transcends those of detection and discrimination. That attribute is that the act of recognition requires, to a far greater degree than did either detection or recognition, the association of meaning to the stimulus object; that is, dealing with the stimulus as a symbol for something else. Recognition is intrinsically more cognitive and semantically "loaded" than the previous two stages of visual processing, a fact that the empirical data seems to substantiate. The detection process does not require any semantic processing of the kind. The prototypical question: Is there anything there? requires only a binary response that ignores the nature of the detected form or any meaning that it may convey. Similarly, form discrimination requires only that the observer distinguish between two forms, and in the typical visual-perception experiment it is possible to do so on the basis of partial mismatches of the geometry of the two stimuli while totally ignoring any semantic content it may contain. One can, to reiterate a previously made point, easily imagine an automaton performing either detectiom or discrimination perfectly well on the basis of the purely physical attributes of the stimuli. Detection and discrimination, therefore, may be considered to be purely syntactic, deductive (in a primitive sense), or even geometrical. It is these kinds of processes that computers simulate quite well with algorithms that imitate feature-sensitive and preattentive, automatic processes. It is likely that these are also the kinds of processes being carried out within the human brain when it performs detection or discrimination. It seems quite unlikely, however, that the same argument can be made for recognition.

I argue here that recognition is not simply syntactic in the same sense as detection or discrimination. Rather, this argument goes on, it is prototypically semantic; the act of classifying, or conceptualizing, or categorizing can be made dependent more on the meaning of the stimulus object than on its physical properties. This is true even when the forms are strictly geometrical in nature. A letter *a* can be readily recognized and categorized regardless of the font, exactly because the parts of the object letter possess certain relationships that transcend their local nature. Although the geometry of the font may perturb or modulate the recognition process,[2] it is not sufficient to define the process as it is in the detection and discrimination processes.

In short, the boundary between the passive, automatic, preattentive processes and the active, attentive, cognitive processes to which I alluded in chapter 1 may now be more specifically designated as the boundary between geometry-sensitive discrimination and meaning-loaded recognition. It is for this reason, among others, that I consider there to be an even smaller likelihood of help from neurophysiology in solving the problem of recognition mechanisms than in solving those of detection, for example. This is also the reason for the strong conjecture that the feature-sensitive and triggered neurons that have so often served as heuristic models (line detectors, etc.) for form-recognition processes are probably totally irrelevant in actual fact to this kind of visual process in particular. Rather the complexities of a recognition process, with its heavy superstructure of meaning and classification, involve neural mechanisms that are as far from the simple and complex cells of the identified visual areas of the cerebral cortex as they are from the retina. I believe that it will ultimately prove necessary to look elsewhere to find the psychoneural locus of recognition (if such a linkage can ever be established).

B. THEORIES OF RECOGNITION

The emphasis throughout this book has been to comsider theories of form perception as opposed to an exhaustive listing and discussion of the empirical data base. It is remarkable, in this context, that there are so many more theories of form *recognition* than of any other process within the form-*perception* domain. In fact, there may be more approaches to the problem of recognition than to all of the other processes put together. It is fortunate in such a situation in which there is such a plethora of models, theories, and approaches, that others have attempted to develop taxonomic systems that organize and classify these theories of

---

[2] Later in this chapter we see how the geometric form of a stimulus can produce modulations of results that appear to be the outcome of cognitive (categorical) influences when, in fact, they are not. These simulated cognitive influences must be distinguished from the true ones of the categorization process itself.

recognition. In the following section I have drawn upon the thoughts of several of the leaders in the field of form-recognition theory concerning the different approaches that are available and the ways in which the different theories can be categorized. Each provides a specific classification system of theories. Townsend and his collaborators Landon and Ashby are mathematical psychologists and approach their taxonomies from the point of view of the psychologically oriented theories. Watanabe is a distinguished physicist who has moved from the physics of matter to the physics of information oven the last four decades. He treats form-recognition theories from a completely different point of view—that of the physical and engineering sciences. Most of the models he treats are not explicitly theories of perception, but are techniques for accomplishing the categorization process by analytical means. Nevertheless, Watanabe's list includes many approaches that have interesting things to say about the human visual processes. Pinker represents a new group of computational vision theorists and discusses the interrelationships among these theories. The reader is likely to be astonished, as I was, just how nonoverlapping the three taxonomies are.

I.   Townsend, Landon, and Ashby's Taxonomy

The first part of our discussion introducing three taxonomies of recognition theories is based entirely on the astute analysis of models of form recognition published in a preliminary form by Townsend and Ashby (1982) and subsequently in a more complete form by Townsend and Landon (1983). All members of the four classes of models that these authors describe can be said to fall into the category of descriptive mathematics and statistics. There is, as there should not be, in my opinion, virtually no allusion to possible physiological or mechanical mechanisms; the emphasis is placed upon formal descriptions of the psychological processes that may be taking place in the observer when he recognizes a form. These processes are described in terms of their functions, not their physical instantiations.

Figure 5.1 presents Townsend and Landon's taxonomy of these mathematical form-recognition models. Two major subdivisions are indicated. The first includes

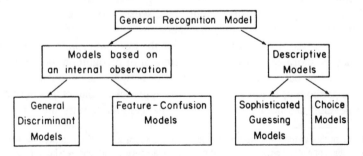

FIG. 5.1.   Townsend and Landon's taxonomy of theories of recognition (from Townsend & Landon, 1983).

those that are "based on an internal observation." Exemplars of this class of theories all suggest that each stimulus event is dealt with separately by the perceptual-processing system. The probability of a correct recognition (i.e., a response with the correct name of the stimulus or the name of the appropriate category), therefore, depends on the evaluation of that stimulus item by a set of internal rules and criteria in the immediate terms of that particular event. In this subdivision of their taxonomy Townsend and his colleagues mainly pay attention to the specific processes such as feature detection that are presumed to exist within the cognitive structure of the observer. The important generality is that theories of this class, whatever their details, are characterized by the fact that they deal with the properties of the individual stimulus event without recourse to other previous events or the current state of the observer.

The second major subdivision includes those theories that Townsend and Landon (1983) call "descriptive." In this case the role of the individual event is minimized. Instead, the process of recognition is modeled as a kind of guessing or choosing an item from a set of possible responses on the basis of probabilistic (or weighted probabilistic) rules involving context properties that go far beyond the characteristics of the immediate event. Rather than processing the attributes of a single stimulus, as did the internal-observation theories, models falling into this category merely use the stimulus as one of many influences leading to an appropriate guess or choice of the proper response by the observer.

The first major division—the "internal observation" category is further broken down into two other subdivisions by Townsend and Landon (1983)—the *general discriminant* models and the *feature confusion* models. General discriminant models are characterized by decision rules and procedures that evaluate the attributes of a particular stimulus and calculate a numeric value or discriminant for all possible responses that could conceivably be associated with that stimulus. This process thus produces, according to the premises of this kind of model, a set of numeric values associated with the possible responses or categories into which an item may be placed. Which response is chosen is determined in a very straightforward manner: The largest numeric value associated with any possible response becomes the selection criterion leading to the emission of that response. Examples cited by Townsend and Landon of discriminant-type theories include linear-discriminant models (see my discussion of the similarity models and the debate between Tversky, 1977, and Krumhansl, 1978, for a discussion of what are essentially alternative versions of linear-discriminant models), nonlinear-discriminant models, statistical decision theories (including the influential-signal-detection theory—see my discussion in Uttal, 1973b), template-matching models (as exemplified by Neisser, 1967), correlational models (including autocorrelation models), and feature-discriminant models. Other particular examples of each of these different theories are cited in Townsend and Landon's (1983) article.

A related discussion of discriminant-type theories (which he refers to as "decision-theoretic" approaches to pattern recognition) has been presented by

Fu (1982b). Fu considered the problem from the point of view of an engineer interested in computer-form recognition, but the methodology is virtually the same. In addition to the decision-theoretic category of recognizers, Fu also classifies another group of recognizers as "syntactic." These recognizers work on the basis of a kind of geometric structural analysis analogous to sentence parsing to divide a complex form into simpler components or features but in a way that preserves their spatial relationships. As I have noted and reiterate later, there is no necessary suggestion that these computer algorithms represent the way in which humans recognize patterns: Our internal logic may be, in fact probably is, quite different.

It is important to reiterate, if only in passing, an important point made by Townsend and Landon, Fu, and myself, among others. That is that virtually all of these theories that dote on the properties of the individual stimulus are feature theories. The word *feature* is not a sharply defined word, and there has been a great deal of debate concerning what is actually meant by a "feature." Nevertheless, there is a commonsense consensus concerning the meaning of the word in the computer form-recognition field as well as perceptual theory; it connotes a local attribute, region, or part; something that is less than the whole form. A ubiquitous theme in feature-analysis theory, therefore, is that a feature is some separable localized attribute of a form rather than an organizational property of the form.

With one exception all of the theories that fall into the "internal-observation" category of Townsend and Landon's taxonomy and all of Fu's decision theoretic and syntactic algorithms operate on the parts rather than the whole. Unfortunately, the exception is the one kind of theory that has been most criticized and least acceptable for combinatorial, intuitive, and logical reasons to the psychological community—the template-matching theory. Template matching refers to a physical "superimposition" of the stimulus and the various items of the potential response set. The response selected is the one that fits (or correlates with) the stimulus the best according to the template-matching theory. The implausibility of the existence of a huge set of templates, some of which may never have been experienced previously and the equally implausible nature of a exhaustive search through the library of templates have always provided strong conceptual arguments against the template hypothesis.

The second category of internal-observation-type theories—feature-confusion models—postulated by Townsend and Landon is characterized by a different criterion. Models falling into this category are purported to actually compute matrices of specific confusions among the set of possible responses. Theories of this genre use the confusion data as a means of determining the rules for generating a reduced set of possible responses from among which the response is finally selected (rather than from the full range of possible responses). The experimental paradigm generating appropriate data for the feature-confusion models must be designed so as to maintain a substantial error rate. An example of this approach is Appleman and Mayzner's (1982) model.

Descriptive theories—the second major heading of Townsend and Landon's taxonomy—are also divided into two subcategories. The first gathers under a single rubric called the "sophisticated guessing-type model," a number of different types of models including the *sophisticated guessing* models themselves, *all-or-none* models, *overlap* models, and *confusion-choice* models. The second category, which they designate the "choice category," includes but a single exemplar—the "similarity-choice" model.

For our present purposes it is important to note that the formal mathematical approach of the descriptive models represents a strictly macroscopic theoretical orientation. The mathematical formulae describe, in a formal way, processes that are, at best, only analogous to those presumably carried out in the perceptual nervous system. The variety of different assumptions about the nature of those processes is indicative of the fact that these models cannot, in fact, definitively resolve the matter of the specific nature of the internal mechanisms instantiating the form-recognition process any more than can psychophysics. Indeed, these models are typically statistical in nature and can be thought of as describing (rather than analyzing) the recognition processes. The degree to which each model fits the psychophysical data is only suggestive and can never unequivocally exclude, or include, any particular set of assumptions from a long list of possible and plausible statements about internal-processing mechanisms. It is also the case that many of these models, although classified in different parts of Townsend and Landon's taxonomy, may be very similar in fundamental principle, not only to each other, but also to several of the other theoretical approaches that have been and are discussed. It is often surprising to discover that models based on slightly different experimental domains and nomenclatures are, in fact, formally equivalent to each other.

Descriptive theories, thus, tend not to be reductionistic; rather they describe processes but make no definitive statement concerning the mechanisms by means of which they may be implemented. The processes are all described at a molar level and must, at best, be considered to be analogs of the actual underlying processes. Because, in general, they are all statistical rather than deterministic, they do not deal with individual cases of recognition or individual stimuli. Indeed, it must be remembered that all of these descriptive models are only descriptions of molar processes that are the behavioral analogs of human perceptual mechanisms and processes. There can be no conclusive proof, however, even when the fit between the model's prediction and psychophysical data is excellent, that, for example, such "processes" as "calculating discriminants" are actually going on inside the perceptual nervous system. Indeed, it seems unlikely that such a thing as this kind of numerical computation would be occurring. At best, the models relate to something that is comparable, analogous, and functionally similar, but probably not homologous or identical.

The two subcategories into which the descriptive category of Townsend and Landon's taxonomy are broken down—the "sophisticated guessing" models and the "choice" models—are both closely related and, indeed, given a few restrictions, turn out to make much the same predictions. The choice models are characterized by the work of Luce (1963). The sophisticated guessing models are much more varied and include an all-or-none model, an overlap model (as exemplified by the work of Townsend 1971a,b), an informed-guessing model, as exemplified by Pachella, Smith, and Stanovich (1978), and Smith's (1980) symmetric sophisticated guessing model.

Looking back over the two major classes of theories of recognition—the internal observation and descriptive categories—that have been suggested by Townsend and Landon, it is clear that they vary in one classic way that these authors did not emphasize. The internal-observation models are typically algorithmic interpretations of the characteristics of a single stimulus. They bring to mind mechanisms that could be constructed of relatively automatic computational engines that ignore both the immediate environment and the history of the recognizer previous to the stimulus event. They deal with the parts (with the exception of the unpalatable template-matching model) in a manner that is best characterized as empiricist in terms of the classification system offered in chapter 2 of this work.

On the other hand, the descriptive models all involve a kind of active decision making or choice behavior in which the observer's characteristics, history, and set can be thought of as specifying the nature of the response. In the classic taxonomy of chapter 2, this would be considered to be characteristic of a rationalist approach. The existence of these two themes in such a modern context (they become the bottom-up-vs.-top-down distinction in computational vision, for example) is evidence of the persistence of this controversy over the centuries.

2. Watanabe's Taxonomy

Another outstanding source in which a carefully constructed taxonomy of mathematical theories of form recognition has been provided was authored by Watanabe (1985). Watanabe does briefly consider human recognition in his extensive discussion of the field, but the main theme of his book is the recognition process as it is executed by the different kinds of mathematical methods used by computers to classify and categorize forms. The relevant portion of his taxonomy looks at recognition[3] as it may alternatively be considered to be a form of:

---

[3] One may argue that the use of the word *recognition* here is certainly not appropriate from a philosophical or psychological point of view. Machines, however good they may be at classifying and categorizing, are no more cognitive entities in the sense that the human is than is an amoeba. Machine classification is not a form of re-cognition or any other kind of cognition. It is, as I hope has been made clear in this chapter, the outcome of the evaluation of very precise rule-defined algorithms. The differences in logic that underlie machine "recognition" and human recognition are unknown. At the very least they differ vastly in their complexity: At the very most they are totally different entities. Therefore, the use of the word *recognition* is a shorthand that though useful is loaded with theoretical connotations that can lead us astray at other points this discussion. Be warned!

- Entropy minimization
- Covariance diagonalization
- Statistical decision making
- Mathematical discrimination
- Structure analysis

In addition to using his taxonomy to explicate the variety of mathematical techniques that are used by modern artificial intelligence and computer-vision researchers, I also want to use Watanabe's analysis to emphasize the conceptual theme that dominates this chapter—the predominance of local-feature approaches in the field of form recognition. At the outset, I reiterate a persistent difficulty that many of us who study form recognition (artificial or human) have alluded to in one way or another. That difficulty is based upon the fact that the word *feature* is so poorly defined. *Feature* is the equivalent in the world of form recognition, it seems, of the word *mind* in psychology, and indeed, is closely related to the difficulty in defining the word *form* itself.

Let us consider in each case why each of the underlying mathematical procedures described in Watanabe's taxonomy is actually an example of a feature-analysis approach and predominantly elementalistic, rather than holistic, in terms of its fundamental premises. The last of the five methods (structure analysis) in Watanabe's taxonomy is explicitly a local-feature-analysis procedure and can be dealt with briefly in making this point. Structure analysis explicitly deals with two-dimensional forms as combinations of local component features of prespecified types. That is, each stimulus object is defined as nothing more than a construction of, for example, vertical and horizontal straight lines, arches, and hooks. The task of the structural-analysis program is to take any stimulus form and specify from which of these component parts it has been constructed. In some algorithms, the order in which these parts have been assembled to produce the original figure can be determined, and this sequence information may also provide useful clues to the recognition of the form. A particular example in which assembly sequence may be critical is the recognition of handwriting.

Nowadays, with the powerful image-processing algorithms that computer science has made available to us, determining where various prespecified parts are in a complex figure is relatively easy. Each of the prespecified local features, for example, can be convolved with the entire object in turn. Convolution is a well-established mathematical routine that is simply implemented on even the relatively small personal computers currently available. The convolution of a set of prototypical features (again for clarity, these exemplars might be straight or curved lines) with a stimulus-form produces a set of derivative maps in which the location of each of the prototypical features is highlighted. Simple superimposition techniques may then permit even the order in which each of the parts has been combined to be determined.

As I noted, in the case of the various kinds of mathematical treatments that fall within the structure-analysis rubric in Watanabe's taxonomy, the feature-analytic orientation of the method is explicit, and the meaning of the term *feature* is clear; they are the local geometrical components or parts of the overall form. They are also the prototypes used in the convolution procedure. Two other categories of his taxonomy, the mathematical discrimination and statistical-decision-making methods, on the other hand, invoke feature analyses in a slightly more subtle manner. The objects dealt with by these two methods are typically defined, according to Watanabe, as a multidimensional set of "vectors." But, what are these vectors? Watanabe indicates that they are either "observations" (i.e., the result of different measurements) or the outcome of some kind of distillation procedure in which the number of measurements, dimensions, or descriptors of the original object is reduced. In any case, in an ideal mathematical world, each of these vectors would be orthogonal or independent of the others so that no information would be redundant and, therefore, no processing time would be wasted. Of course, the vectors may have a common causal basis and, therefore, be correlated to some degree (e.g., the height and weight of the members of a population are related), but at the least, each can be measured independently of the other.

Described in this way, it becomes clear that these decision-making techniques are also, at their foundation, feature analyzers and, for all practical purposes are equivalent to Fu's (1982a) decision theoretic classification. In this case, the features may be numeric rather than geometric as they were in the methods classified within the structural-analysis category, but they are, nevertheless, features in exactly the sense I have been using the term previously. To the mathematical engine, this difference is irrelevant: A vector, a feature, or a measurement representing a nongeometrical attribute (such as weight) would be treated identically—as a feature of the pattern that must be processed. For that matter, the "patterns" need not even be geometric forms but may be organized bodies of information of other kinds. The important fact is that these methods are just as much feature analyzers in terms of their fundamental approach as are the explicitly structural-analysis methods described earlier.

The general category of covariance diagonalization suggested by Watanabe includes a very large number of different methods that are very similar to each other in basic principle. Some of these methods are familiar to psychologists (who were among the leaders in developing them), whereas others are quite alien. Two that are familiar include diagonalization of the covariance matrix and factor analysis: Two that are not so familiar to psychologists are the Karhunen–Loeve expansion and self-featuring information compression (SELFIC). All of these methods, however, are characterized by attempts to draw out of a mass of data the major dimensions, vectors, or (one hopes without begging the question by a too-narrow definition) features that minimize the number of measurements that have to be made. In other words, all of these methods try to find some common measurement that is closely enough correlated with sets of features that it can be used in their place. The extraction of such new features or factors from the many measurements that may make up the raw data of a survey or experiment depends upon correlations among the various measurements, and like the multidimensional scaling techniques discussed in chapter 4, is a means of reducing information to a set of essential, nonredundant measurements.

The point to be made in the current context is that the inputs to these "diagonalization" procedures are nothing other than the kind of simple, measurable, and, when geometrical, usually local attributes we have called *features*. The outputs are not so simply categorized, but reflect the outcome of information-reducing processes that were fed by these features. To the extent that we feed local features into this mill, these methods too must be considered also to be exemplars of the feature approach.

Finally, let us consider the remaining method alluded to by Watanabe as being prototypical of the pattern-recognition process—entropy minimization. *Entropy* is defined as the degree of disorder or randomness in a system, and Watanabe (1985) has analogized the process of recognition or categorization as being equivalent to removing this disorder. Therefore, categorization is akin, in his thinking, to discovering the intrinsic order of a system. From another point of view, Watanabe also notes, recognition is analogous to organic growth wherein disordered components are organized in ordered forms or entities. In other words, recognition minimizes disorder (entropy) by organizing the system into ordered classes or categories.

Central to the analogy drawn between form recognition and entropy reduction, as it was to the covariance-diagonalization methods, is the concept of the reduction of dimensions so that the unimportant redundant dimensions can be ignored. This is the process by which order arises out of disorder. It is at exactly this point, however, that entropy reduction also can be seen to be currently nothing more than another feature-oriented approach, for the dimensions to be emphasized in reducing the entropy are the same measurable features or measurements that we have already considered. This state of affairs is, of course, due to today's nearly total deficiency of global descriptors of form. It must be acknowledged that the entropy-reduction technique does have a potential for a more global interpretation. If there are new developments in identifying holistic attributes, then this model or procedure may be transformable into a more holistic, arrangement-centered methodology.

In summary, we can see that virtually all of the pattern-recognition models that are proposed in the field of computer information processing are feature analytic in their fundamental approach. They prejudge the issue (of globality versus features) by their mechanics; they do not deal with overall structure, even though in principle it is probably more a matter of the paucity of global dimensions and descriptors that prevents them from doing so. As we see shortly, the generalization that these mathematical methods for categorizing forms are predominantly oriented toward manipulating the elements of a form rather than its global structure is also true of the majority of psychological theories of form perception.

In the case of the engineering goal, such artifices are acceptable. In the case of psychological theory, they are not acceptable because they mislead theory, drawing experiment and interpretation away from a valid model of human form perception.

The fact that these methods are all predominantly oriented toward feature analysis leaves in doubt the issue of whether or not they could ever be applicable to the problem of recognition and classification in humans should our object descriptions themselves begin to take on more global qualities. Some might argue that any new global properties might themselves become "features," however different in kind, and these mathematical methods might still be useful. It seems plausible, on the other hand, that the explicitly feature-oriented logic of these methods may, in fact, make them inappropriate as processors of truly global properties. Other methods, more in tune with the global and holistic attributes of a form, are likely to be required to validly model the human form-perception process. This is a problem for the future to test; I raise it here as a caveat, not in any attempt to resolve it one way or another at the present time.

The essential point I wish to make is that models of form recognition that are based on local features should, at best, only be considered to be superficial analogies of the logical methods that are being executed in the human brain. They are first approximations or analogies, but are probably not good homological explanations of the actual psychobiological mechanisms used to process forms. Despite the elaborate mathematical superstructure that surrounds these methods, the underlying mechanisms, logical processes, and implementations are most likely quite different from those utilized by organic form-recognition processes, particularly those of human vision. We can be sure of at least one thing: Modern computer and analytical methods, designed as they are to run on serial computers and to dote on local features, do not homologize the mechanisms of perceptual reality. That reality is much more likely to incorporate parallel processes that can treat global form holistically and act upon spatial relationships rather than local features. Most of what we know of perceptual phenomenology gently pushes our theories in that direction just as contemporary mathematical and computer models tend to push us toward thinking about features. Whatever the quality of the analogy between the feature-oriented models and human form perception, it must be appreciated that whatever is actually going on inside the brain remains as opaque nowadays as it did in a more philosophical and speculative age. To sum it all up in a single phrase, *the imitation of behavior is not tantamount to the understandinq of inner mechanisms*. This is another way to assert the black-box limitation originally alluded to in chapter 1. It is a fundamental limitation of mathematical models of any kind and a shadow lurking over the future of cognitive psychology as we know it today.

3. Pinker's Summary

Pinker (1985), reprinting a special issue of the journal *Cognition: International Journal of Cognitive Science*, has also summarized a group of other form-recognition theories that, though generally less formal and mathematical, are among the most popular and well-known approaches to explaining this process. His outline also serves us well in furthering our appreciation of the wide variety of different form-recognition theories that have been proposed.

Pinker points first to template matching. The basic idea behind this simple and oft-discussed model is essentially one of cross-correlation, as we have seen. That is, it assumed that recognition occurs when a fit between the stimulus object and one of a large set of different patterns or templates stored somewhere in the memory system is maximized. The "best fit" may be measured by one of the statistical or mathematical procedures already considered, but whatever measure of fit is used, the match is strictly determined on the basis of the congruence of the stimulus and members of the set of templates.

As I have already stressed, from its inception the template model has been beset with a number of obvious difficulties that have always made it unpalatable to theoreticians in this field. The number of templates that would be necessary to fit all possible retinal images of even a single three-dimensional object on a purely geometrical fit basis would be enormous. And, for the recognition of all possible stimulus objects in all possible orientations, projections, and magnifications, it seems that the set of necessary templates should approach a size that would overload even the 10^3 possible connections of any neuron to any one of the other 10^{13} neurons in the brain. The processing time required to carry out a search for a match between all possible templates and a single stimulus-form also strains credibility, even in the context of the parallel-processing milieu that now pervades computer theory. Pinker also points out that the template model is really only applicable to the recognition of single objects, and a far more complex kind of pattern recognition is typically at work in human visual perception in which complex scenes must not only be recognized but also analyzed into their component parts and the relationships among those parts established.

Pinker goes on to discuss a variety of different "feature"-analysis models, raising many of the same objections I have already discussed in previous sections. The main problem with models of this sort, he asserts, is the absence in most feature models of parameters that describe the relationship of the features that compose the stimulus object, that aspect that I have already called "arrangement." Next, he considers Fourier-analysis models and his criticisms in that case are also in agreement with those made elsewhere. Specifically, the transformation from the space domain into a frequency domain really does not solve the problem—it merely shifts it from how one processes patterns of lines to how one processes spatial frequencies. And, most distressing of all, from a philosophical point of view, there is just no similarity between the stimulus object and its Fourier representation in the two domains even though there is a formal/transformation from one to the other from a mathematical point of view.

All three of the theoretical approaches to which Pinker has pointed up to this point are dependent on the geometry either in its raw form or as transformed by some fixed algorithm like the Fourier-analysis procedures. The next category he identifies, however, is one in which *structural descriptions* are made of the form in a way that is not geometrical, but rather symbolic or propositional. Thus, for example, a theory of this sort might invoke a set of rules that describe the nature of the parts and the relationships between them either in words or in terms of some kind of a graphical structure. Pinker is somewhat more positive about this, noting that the putative advantages of the structural-description approach include the fact that they do not lose information (a point with which I do not agree) and that a complex recognition process can be broken up into smaller parts. However, he also indicates that, like Fourier analysis, this method really is not a theory of recognition but another means of describing and representing stimulus objects. Once described by a structural model, the stimulus object is no closer to being recognized or classified than before its description. Subsequent processing steps akin to cross-correlation (if one is a template theorist) must now be invoked to carry out the identification itself.

Of course, one step forward has been achieved after any transformation—the stimulus object is now represented in a format that may be simpler than the original spatial representation. It may be more precisely quantified or it may be symbolically denoted by structural relationships that bear a simpler kind of similarity to the set of object-classes within which it may be classified than it did when represented as a purely geometrical form.

Pinker (1985) also describes the Marr-Nishihara (Marr 1982; Marr & Nishihara, 1978) approach, which I discuss later in this chapter. His evaluation of their theory is that it is a far better way to proceed than the traditional approaches he previously summarized. It is important to point out in preview, however, that the work of Marr and Nishihara is very specific: Their theoretical treatment, and much of the other work in this field, is aimed at problems of precise definition (How do we reconstruct the third dimension from projective drawings, from disparity, from motion, etc?) They are not, in any sense of the word, general theories of form recognition. This is the source of both their great strength and their tightly constrained limits.

4. Other Taxonomies

Another older, much more formal, and very deep analysis of the pattern-recognition process has been presented by Duda and Hart (1973) in their classic textbook on the topic. This book represents what was perhaps the epitome of the pattern-recognition field in the mid-1970s. It is interesting to note that Duda and Hart separate their book into two parts: One deals exclusively with scene analysis and the representation of scenes. (Included in this section, incidentally, is a discussion of the spatial frequency or Fourier methods, which Duda and Hart correctly identify as a means of representing objects and scenes and not, as is so often done, as a form-recognition process itself.)

The other section of their book, on pattern classification, is a survey of a set of techniques for classifying stimulus objects into one or another category. It is fascinating to note that all of the methods they describe are essentially statistical and presume that one or more features or attributes have been measured. The task of the pattern recognizer is (sometimes not so simply) to determine into which category the set of features or attributes specifies that an object should be placed. There is, once again, a presumption here of local-feature analysis, of a set of separable measures of a form, that is sufficient to classify the object. All of these techniques, a number of which we have encountered before in this section and a few new ones (Bayes' decision theory, parameter estimation, nonparametric techniques, linear-discriminant functions, and clustering—all of which are also discussed in Fu, 1982a) are to be applied after the feature attributes of an object are measured and defined. The problem becomes akin to signal-detection theory, which itself can be considered to be a primitive form of a two-alternative (usually) classification or recognition system. The feature measures are assumed to be available, but the matter of what are the essential attributes of an object that should be fed into this statistical engine are finessed with only a few words in the introductory chapter of Duda and Hart's book.

The point I make is that if a theory of human form recognition is to be developed it must include far more than just the statistical-decision rules. The entire analysis presented by Duda and Hart (1973) ignores the issue of what attributes of global form and arrangement might be used as inputs to the statistical-decision engine. This distinguished book illustrates, once again, the utter domination of the field of form recognition by methods that are mainly dependent on localized features with little attention given to the global, molar, or organizational properties that seem to be used by humans in their visual processing of scenes and objects.

C. SPECIAL TOPICS

In the following sections I consider a number of special topics that characterize the contemporary work that is done in the field of human form recognition. In line with the emphasis on theory, as opposed to the empirical data, I stress in each of these special topics the nature of the ideas that have been invoked as explanations of form-recognition phenomena and the controversies that have erupted among these ideas.

1. Visual Search

As I mentioned in an earlier chapter, the language used by many perceptual psychologists in specifying exactly which process is under examination in an experiment is sometimes not as clear as it should be. One of the most confusing examples of such a misnomer occurs in the experiments that are designed to test an observer's ability to identify (i.e., recognize) a particular object when it is embedded in an ensemble of other objects. Although this paradigm is very often described as being an example of visual discrimination (between the target item and the nontarget items in the ensemble), in fact, a closer examination of this paradigm suggests that in many, if not most cases, the process being assayed in such "discrimination" experiments is, in reality, better considered to be an example of recognition performance. The critical test to distinguish which process is actually being assayed, I believe, is quite simple: Which of the three basic perceptual questions ("Is there anything there?" "Are these two things the same or different?" "What is [the name of] this thing?" is being asked? It seems to me that, in fact, the visual-search problem is associated most closely with the last of these three queries. When an observer is asked to go through a list and, for example, pick out a noun or an alphabetic character from a list of verbs or numerals, the observer is actually categorizing, (i.e., recognizing) each item in sequence. A major controversy revolves around whether several categorization processes of this sort can be handled simultaneously (in parallel) or whether they must be done in sequence (in serial order).

Another issue concerns the nature of the search. Is it exhaustive (i.e., are all or the items in a list examined?) or is it automatically terminated when the sought-for item is discovered? Most search experiments of this kind do show a characteristic response pattern when the material is more than just physically dissimilar. Phenomenologically, the observer reports attentive scrutinization of each item in the list, categorizing each according to the rules of the game defined by the experimenter, until one of the items fits the properties of the search item. This item-by-item serial search is terminated when the fit to some criteria (e.g., find the name of a mammal) occurs[4] and the length of time that is spent scanning the list is typically linearly related to the number of items that have been scanned. The process, if the material is sufficiently rich, is, therefore, intrinsically attentive: The observer's attention must be focused in sequence on each item in the ensemble until the search is completed.

The properties of the serial search process that I have just described characterize experiments in which the items differ according to some meaningful criteria. The evaluation of each item necessitates the effortful and attentive scrutiny of all of the items in the ensemble. The situation is quite different when the items in the ensemble differ in some manner that is not semantic, but physical: The search process does not work as described when there are geometric, chromatic, or temporal properties distinguishing between the searched-for item and the other nontarget items in the list. For example, if the irrelevant items in the list are all smaller than the target item, if they have a different color, if they have certain specific geometrical properties (akin to those defining Julesz's statistical moments, or tex-

---

[4] In some serial search experiments of this kind observers may be asked to find two such fits or even to find all such members of the set that fits the criterion. These represent perturbations on the basic theme; we consider for the moment only the simple prototypical experiment.

tons), or if they display different temporal properties than the target, the target will be more or less immediately *discriminated* from its neighbors by virtue of that physical difference.

I purposely emphasize the word *discriminate* in the previous sentence, because it seems more likely that in those cases of the kind of "physical" differences I have just described the process is distinctly different from those in which semantic or meaningful properties distinguish between targets and nontargets. In the physical-difference case, the experiments probably are assaying a preattentive discrimination process rather than an attentive recognition process. This conclusion flies in the face of the fact that the procedure of the experimental paradigms may be virtually identical in each case. It should be noted how very easy it is to completely change the context of an experiment and the mechanisms that are being assayed by a simple alteration of the nature of the stimulus material. It should also be noted how very difficult it often is to determine exactly which process one is actually examining in a given experiment. This is a pitfall that is evidenced throughout the literature of cognitive psychology; similar experimental designs often assay totally different underlying processes, much to the confusion of emerging theoretical explanations. And, vice versa, completely different experimental paradigms often turn out to be assaying the same underlying process.

The visual search processes with which we are concerned in this chapter, therefore, are assumed to exist because of the outcome of a contrived and restricted subset of all possible search paradigms. In general, it seems most appropriate to designate them as recognition processes by virtue of what seems to be their semantic content. (We see, however, how this assumption does not always hold and that some presumably semantic influences have turned out to be dominated by the physical aspects of the stimulus.) The desire to emphasize the semantic content has often dictated that word and alphabetic information be used. However, even when this was done, as we see, the "semantic" nature of the stimulus categories could not be guaranteed. For example, the shape of a word can be significant in its recognition. Work that deals with such "physical" stimulus parameters as color, size, or local texture shall be considered only in passing: Such physical differences produce results that are more comparable to the texture-discrimination experiments dealt with in the previous chapter. The influence of the physical attributes of a stimulus is suggested when the target form just "pops out" in the preattentive manner that was characterized by Triesman and by Julesz.

Thus constrained, what are the theoretical questions and problems that guide research in the field of visual search? One of the most important, to which I briefly alluded earlier, is: Under what conditions is recognition intrinsically a serial process, and under what conditions does it display parallel processing properties? This question is, in large part, one that can be attacked empirically and, indeed, there is a consensus supporting the conjecture that for the nonphysical, semantic type of search material, a serial sequence of selectively and individually attentive judgments must be made.

A corollary of the serial–parallel issue concerns whether a serial search is exhaustive (i.e., even though the search may be serial, are all items in a searched list evaluated before a decision is made?) or self-terminating (i.e., does the search process stop when the target item is located?). Although it might seem very inefficient to continue a search once the target is located there is, in fact, some evidence that exhaustive searching does occur in some situations. Sample evidence speaking to this point would be of the form of response times that do not vary as a function of the position of the target item in lists of constant length.

Another set of questions revolves around the matter of whether or not the items in the ensemble interact with each other. It seems clear that the interaction of an item with its neighbors, not in the simple sense of a spatial inhibition or the interaction among neural receptors that is so popular in the preattentive, passive models of lower level visual processes, but in the sense of interactions among semantic categories and classes, does occur. This is an issue of enormous complexity, for it involves interactions at high cognitive levels, not through passive processes sensitive to geometric shape or form, but through those sensitive to something as intangible as meaning. How, for example, would the outcome of a visual search for a word that was the name of a member of the cat family be affected if the nontarget words surrounding the target word were the names of other small mammals as opposed to the names of invertebrates? Experiments of this kind explore the impact of a kind of conceptual clustering, as opposed to simple geometrical propinquity, on recognition in the search paradigm.

Another important issue in visual search experiments concerns the impact of the degree of familiarity of a word on its recognizability. It is presumed that more familiar words are more likely to be recognized than less familiar words. Indeed, targets made up of strings of letters that are not words do seem to be harder to locate than those that do make up words.

Similarly, the nature of the categories or conceptual groups of the nontarget items may be important in determining the search time. Similarities and differences in semantic content, category, or some other meaningful attribute of the nontarget items in the search set have repeatedly been shown to interact with the target item in a way that modulates search times.

Another closely related question concerns whether or not the information about the category to which the items in the search array belong can be determined prior to their recognition. This would imply some kind of a cognitive evaluation of the items occurs prior to full-blown recognition. Such an outcome would be strong evidence that the search-and-recognition process for items differing only in semantic content is actually carried out in a series of stages—a possible finer taxonomy than has been proposed here or elsewhere.

Let us consider the current status of the answers to some of these issues. We begin with a discussion of the serial–parallel controversy. The issue of whether visual search takes place in parallel (i.e., all of the items in an ensemble are examined simultaneously—a process that may a priori seem unlikely but in the light of the work on visual textures seems more credible) or in serial order (each item in the ensemble is examined in sequence) was probably first raised to theoretical consciousness by another one of those seminal and classic experiments that historically have had such impact in psychological research. This classic experiment was carried out by Sternberg (1966, 1967) and reported in two relatively brief but extremely influential articles in the journals *Science* and *Perception & Psychophysics*.

Sternberg reasoned that if a search process of the kind we have described took place in serial order, that the larger the number the items in a limited set of alphabetic characters, the longer would be the reaction time to search through that set. If, on the other hand, the search process occurred in parallel, then the length of the list should not materially affect the reaction time. To carry out this experiment in a way that was free of many of the difficulties that exceptionally long lists would entail, Sternberg exposed relatively short lists of alphabetic characters to the observer in a tachistoscope. After the list was presented and, presumably, stored by the observer in some kind of short-term memory (the specific nature of which is not material at this point) a single probe character was presented. The observer's task was to specify whether or not the particular alphabetic character was in the list originally presented.

The results of Sternberg's experiment seemed very clear-cut. The reaction times measured were strong linear functions of the number of items in the list that had been presented to the observer and committed to short-term memory. The search process seemed, therefore, to be best characterized as being serial; it could also be characterized as being self-terminating because the process was completed when the target item was identified—reaction times were strong functions of where the item was positioned in the memorized list. That is, if the item occurred early in the list, then the reaction times were short; if later, they were longer.

There have been many others who followed in Sternberg's footsteps and have provided similar kinds of data supporting the contention that the search for a single-target alphabetic character is a self-terminating, serial process in which each character takes about 30 to 35 msec to process. However, others have argued that there is evidence that similar search processes are, quite to the contrary, carried out in parallel. The arguments for parallel processing are somewhat less direct and compelling, in my opinion, however.

One modestly strong argument for the existence of some kind of parallel processing is to be found in the observation that there are some kinds of categorical and contextual effects exhibited by the results of search experiments. If any interaction (as evidenced by the modulation of reaction times as a result of the relations between the semantic content of the items in the list) occurs between the items in a search, then it must be inferred that the examination of each item in the list is not entirely independent of the nature of the other items. This argument goes on to assert that such an interaction is tantamount to some kind of parallel interaction if not a patently simultaneous solution of all parts of the problem.

Another set of somewhat stronger, arguments for parallel-search processes has come from the work of Shiffrin and Schneider (1977) and Schneider and Shiffrin (1977). The experimental design they used differed from the Sternberg paradigm in several ways, but the critical difference between the two experimental procedures lay in the fact that the observer was required to search for any one of several different targets at a given time rather than for only one single target letter. The argument is that if the observer has to compare each item in the nontarget list with only one target, it should take less time than if he has to make the comparison for all of the possibilities of the alternative target list serially. And, indeed, this is what seemed to happen initially to their untrained observers; the response time to specify the presence of a target varied linearly, as in the Sternberg experiment, but in this case as a function of the number of possible target items. Serial processing was thus initially supported for this kind of experiment.

Shiffrin and Schneider's subsequent results, however, indicated that something quite different was occurring later when the observers were well trained: As long as the multiple target items and the nontarget items in the ensemble were always used in the same way (i.e., the target items were either all letters or all numerals and the nontarget items were always chosen from the other category—a condition referred to as "homogeneous") then there was little difference in the search times required for the observer to report whether or not any of the target items were present as a function of the number of possible alternative targets. There was only a slight degradation in the performance (i.e., elongated reaction times) of their well-trained observers when they were asked to look for six as opposed to one target letter. This result suggested the possibility of the conversion of a serial to a parallel process with experience.

In the context of our present discussion, these results were presented by Shiffrin and Schneider as a proof of the existence of parallel processing under at least certain conditions of stimuli and experience. Whether it be called "automatic" processing (as some researchers more interested in memory than perception are likely to do) or "parallel" processing (as students of perception are likely to do), the absence of a prolongation of response times with increasing difficulty of the task suggests that some mental processes may be occurring simultaneously. On the other hand, if the items of the same category could be used as both target or distractor (nontarget) items (a condition referred to as "heterogeneous") , then there was always nearly a linear increase in search times.

There is one strong argument that may refute the line of logic suggesting that observers in this experiment were converting from a serial to a parallel process with experience or vice versa when the experiment went from a homogeneous to a heterogeneous type. It is alternatively possible that the observers are not learning how to carry out a fixed set of underlying processes in parallel but have actually changed the nature of the task in some fundamental way. That is, as observers become well practiced, there is no assurance that they have changed the task from a letter-by-letter comparison to a multiple simultaneous comparison (this is a basic premise essential to the argument that parallel processing takes place) late in training. Perhaps all of the letters have become stimuli for a higher level of information encoding that now requires only a single comparison to be made where many were required previously. It is difficulties like this, the enormous adaptability of the human observer, that makes such external arguments or cognitive theories difficult, if not impossible, to test. The premises of the serial-parallel argument simply may no longer be valid: In such an inconsistent world, (see chapter 6 for an extended discussion of this issue of individual variability, strategy shifts, and elusive laws in psychophysics) it becomes difficult to provide a compelling argument for one side or the other of the controversy.

Another more immediate and direct difficulty with the argument that Shiffrin and Schneider's experimental design makes for parallel processing in at least some situations is that the two procedures, which use homogeneous and heterogeneous target and nontarget sets, respectively, are very different in terms of their respective levels of difficulty. In the first case, in which the targets are always from the same category and the nontargets are always from the other, the level of redundancy is very much higher than in the case in which the nontargets may be either alphabetic characters or numerals. In the latter case, the heterogeneous set of nontargets must be sorted in a more complex way than in the first, and the probability of the observer encountering a target on any given item is also much smaller. If the target is, for example, an alphabetic character, the observer is cued by the appearance of any alphabetic character that this item must be examined for a match whereas any numeral can be ignored. This difference in difficulty is further evidenced by the fact that observers made very few errors in the homogeneous case in which the target category items were never used as nontargets, but made many in the case in which heterogeneous items from the target category could be used as nontargets.

Shiffrin and Schneider's (1977) experiment is, therefore, likely to be tapping much more complicated perceptual processes than it may at first seem. From one point of view, the sometimes-parallel results (no change in response time as a function of the number of target items) and the sometimes-serial results (a linear increase in response times with an increase in the number of target items) may be considered to be only the end points of a continuum describing the behavior of observers when they are presented with tasks of various and varying levels of difficulty. When the task is relatively simple, then faster and less computationally demanding processes can be executed in what seems to be a parallel manner. The simplest condition of all exists when the stimuli are so distinctly different in a physical manner (color, shape, size, etc.) that the processing is so fast that the percept "pops out" in a virtually automatic and preattentive way reflecting a patently parallel discrimination rather than serial search or recognition processes.

There are other options that can simulate parallel processing, such as the substitution of one process for another that I mentioned earlier. More difficult tasks may not be so easily restructured as alternative tasks and may require more extensive, attentive effort: As the computational and analytic complexities increase, the observer must concentrate a limited supply of "attentive energy" on a more narrowly defined portion of the task at hand. As the observer concentrates and slows down, the underlying processes may simply be becoming more difficult and must increasingly be carried out in sequence; they thus appear to the experimenter in the guise that we have come to call "serial."

This line of thought suggests that the serial and parallel controversy may be a false dichotomy. Rather it may be that some kind of psychobiological reality exists in which there is a more or less constant amount of "mental processing capacity" (if I may use this phrase without being challenged to define it too precisely) that can be allocated either to single difficult tasks or to multiple easy tasks. This is exactly the theoretical theme proposed by the late Marilyn Shaw (whose tragic and premature death diminished the profession of psychology in many different ways) and her colleagues. Shaw (1978) was among the first to propose a formal model that emphasized that in addition to some limit on the amount of information that could be stored in the various memories of the observer, there was also a limit on the amount of processing capacity available. Depending on the nature and difficulty of the tasks with which the observer was confronted, various numbers of processes could be simultaneously executed.

More recently, Shaw joined with other colleagues (Harris, Shaw, & Altom, 1985; Harris, Shaw, & Bates, 1979) to expand this allocation-of-limited-store-of-attentive-energy theory in ways that are extremely germane to the present discussion. The original model (Shaw, 1978) was expanded in these two more recent papers from one purely dependent on limited capacity to one that stressed the overlapping of various subprocesses in the visual-search tasks with which we are now concerned. The term "overlapping", the essential idea in the Shaw et al. theory, is presented by them as an alternative hypothesis to an extreme serial-versus-parallel dichotomy. This new version of their theory proposes the existence of a "scanning" mechanism that, under certain conditions, is able to process more than one a item at a time. The process is sequential in terms of its information acquisition, but can operate on several items simultaneously. Thus, there is an overlap of the processing of items that entered previously, but that have not yet been completely processed, and those that enter later.

Accepting the idea from the work of Sperling (1963) that it takes about 10 msec to process a single character, Shaw and her colleagues proposed that the scanning mechanism stepped along from alphabetic character to alphabetic character sequentially entering a new item into the processing mechanism at this rate. However, the essentially new aspect of their model is the proposal that the processing need not be completed for any character in the 10-msec acquisition period. If the processing takes longer than that quantal period of time, several items may simultaneously be processed. The processing of several items thus overlaps in time: by one definition this is a partially parallel system. It is also, of course, from another point of view, a serial system, in that the items are accessed in serial order. In point of fact, it is neither a serial nor a parallel system, but an overlapping one that can simulate either at its extremes and also behave quite differently from either in intermediate conditions.

The amount of service that an item receives by the processing mechanism is a function of several factors, according to Shaw and her colleagues. First, it is a function of the number of items in the processor at any given time. Second, it depends to a different degree upon the number of items that entered the processor before the item being processed and the number of items that entered the processor after the item currently being processed. There is also a minimum amount of time within which any character can be processed, a value that for quite separate reasons the authors assumed was about 40 msec. But, for lists with multiple items, the factors mentioned above may prolong this processing time. Obviously, and this is the essence of the Shaw, et al. theory, if the minimum processing time for each item is 40 msec and the access time for each item is 10 msec, the processing of items must overlap.

The overlap theory is empirically quite effective in modeling a wide variety of data. In the last paper in this series (Harris, Shaw, & Altom, 1985), the authors note that most of the previous experimental attempts to distinguish between serial and parallel processes produced inconclusive results—results that neither completely reflected serial nor parallel mechanisms. The very inconclusivity of the data forthcoming from so many of these experiments is, itself, compelling evidence that something intermediate between the two must actually be occurring and that the serial–parallel dichotomy of the extremes is probably an inappropriate model of the actual mechanisms.

It must be appreciated, however, that the overlap model, as any other mathematical function, cannot establish beyond doubt anything specific about the nature of the underlying mechanisms. What it does do is establish an existence proof that something intermediate between the two extreme alternatives can and probably does exist. As such it transforms the serial–parallel question from one of great and enthusiastic absoluteness into a much less well-structured query about what was originally formulated as an unrealistic dichotomy.

The eventual resolution of such exclusive and extremist controversies as the parallel–serial argument in the form of some sort of an intermediate compromise represents a step forward in the annals of this science. It is also typical of the eventual outcome when dichotomous arguments of this kind occur in any science. Perhaps the best known analogy is from physics—the wave-and-quantum issue that divided physicists for so many years. But, there are other significant and important historical examples of the power of such theoretical compromise, not the least of which is the heredity–environment debate that ravished psychology and biology until it came to be appreciated that neither could fully explain the richness and variety of adult behavior. In the same way, the serial–parallel controversy seems to have been resolved by an outstanding act of theoretical insight—the overlap theory proposed by Shaw and her colleagues.

There is also other evidence that the extreme serial and parallel alternatives may not be quite as distinct as they may at first seem. Jordan (1986), for example, has developed a model of certain forms of serial behavior (specifically of coarticulation—the utterance of a series of overlapping sounds—and dual task execution—simultaneously carrying out two tasks) based upon a parallel-processing network. He shows that the apparent temporal sequencing of superficially serial behaviors can easily be generated from simple parallel networks if one introduces some kind of a feedback process either from the output of a unit in a network to earlier stages of that network or even from the unit emitting the output to itself. In the latter case, the feedback is referred to as being "recurrent."

The specific formal details of Jordan's model are not germane to the present context, but it is important to consider the possibility that mechanisms that seem to be behaving in one manner can actually be implemented by the mechanical structure of the other. Thus, mechanisms behaving according to principles that must certainly be considered to be parallel at the microscopic level, can, if properly interconnected, produce macroscopic behavior that is patently serial and vice versa. It is necessary, therefore, to make a clear distinction between behavior and mechanism. This is often not done in literature of this field. Psychologists typically use intermediate terms (e.g., *process*) in a way that is intrinsically ambiguous.

The strong evidence that some kind of overlapping must occur in the visual-search task that has been provided by Shaw and her colleagues, and the formal demonstration of the fact that parallel mechanisms can give rise to serial behavior (and vice versa; if the serial process is fast enough, apparently parallel system behavior emerges from the operation of a single, but very fast, serial mechanism), raise serious additional questions about the validity of the parallel-serial dichotomy. Confounding the difficulty of distinguishing between a serial and a parallel mechanism is the "black-box problem" to which I have repeatedly alluded earlier in this book. The theoretical limit to our ability to infer inner mechanism of the kind denoted by such words as *serial* and *parallel* from external behavior is another clue that the serial–parallel controversy invoked by cognitive psychologists may be a false one.

The next major theoretical issue in the visual-search domain concerns the nature of the interactions between different categories of stimulus materials. From the earliest period in which this problem had been studied, there have been repeated suggestions that the semantic, cognitive, or categorical nature of the material used as target and non target items affected search behavior. This specific issue has been rephrased in a number of different ways (e.g., Do we extract general categorical information before we classify the specific item?), but the fundamental issue remains the same. Over the last decade or so in which interest in this problem has been at a peak, theory has turned to shambles as some of the early ideas have been shown to be artifactual or incorrect. A brief history places the recent chaos in this field in an appropriate context.

The experimental paradigm in which the category task is assayed is a fairly straightforward modification of the basic search task utilized by Sternberg (1967) and, indeed, was prototyped in his experimental work. The significant modification from a pure and simple search task is that the target and nontarget items are chosen to come from different "categories"; for example, the target character may be a letter whereas the nontarget items might be numerals. One main control condition is the one in which the target and nontarget items are chosen from the safe category—either all numerals or all alphabetic characters.

When the target and nontargets came from different categories, the experiment is said to use a *between-category* design. When the target items and the nontarget items come from the same category, the experiment is referred to as one displaying a *within-category* design. (Be careful to note the differences between these two terms and the closely related use of *heterogeneous* and *homogeneous* defined earlier. They are not the same.) As we have seen in my earlier discussion of the Sternberg (1967) experiment, within-category experiments produce a very linear increasing slope for the reaction-time experiment; each character in the list took about 35 msec (as opposed to 25 msec in a subsequent study by Jonides & Gleitman, 1972). The original results of experiments purporting to show a category effect, however, indicated that in the between-category condition, the slope of the reaction-time function was much flatter, indeed, often approaching a perfectly flat function. In addition to Sternberg's work, this result was also forthcoming in studies by Brand (1971), Ingling (1972), Egeth, Jonides, and Wall (1972), and in the most extensive series of studies of the category effect by Jonides and Gleitman (1972, 1976) and Gleitman and Jonides (1976, 1978).

Jonides and Gleitman (1972), for example, reported, among many other strong effects of category, that ambiguous letters such as a O, which could be interpreted as either as the letter "oh" or the numeral "*zero*", would be dealt with quite differently, depending on whether observers were instructed to deal with them as either a between- or within-category item. That is, if in a list of alphabetic characters, the observers were told to search for an numerical "zero," search times would be much less than if they were asked to search for the same physical stimulus, but to deal with it as if it were an alphabetic "oh." The implication of this result was that the semantic category in which the item was placed determined how it would be processed and that, more generally, semantic category could be a powerful determinant of visual-search reaction times. This special and very dramatic case of the category effect captured an enormous amount of attention among cognitive psychologists at the time because it seemed to suggest a level of cognitive penetration of what hitherto had seemed to be very simple search tasks that was quite unexpected and, therefore, quite exciting.

However, several investigators have reexamined the evidence for the visual search categorization effects in the 1980s. It now appears, in the light of these new experiments, that much of that evidence for these pseudoexciting results is beginning to evaporate. Specifically, Duncan (1983) replicated as exactly as was possible the original Jonides and Gleitman (1972) "zero" and "oh" experiment, but did not find the reported results. In both the within- and between-category conditions, observers produced the same positive linear slopes for this ambiguous target. The different reaction times for the between- and within- categories that had been reported by Jonides and Gleitman were replicated in Duncan's experiments only when the targets *were not ambiguous*. But even in this latter case, Duncan points out, the results are equivocal, in that even in situations in which the putative "category" effects seem to be present, they can be eliminated if "the physical resemblance between targets and nontargets is controlled" (p. 231).

More specific refutation of the existence of the category effects has been forthcoming from Krueger (1984). To appreciate the impact of this important study, it must be remembered that if the target and nontarget stimuli varied in some salient physical dimension such as color or size, there was likely to be a preattentive "popout" of the target stimulus from what was essentially a different physical background. All of the characteristics of this kind of task suggest that performance in this case is preattentive and independent of the cognitive or semantic context of the stimuli. Upon close examination, this kind of task seems much closer to the texture-discrimination experiments and the experimental results that were discussed in the previous chapter on what might more appropriately be designated as a discrimination process.

Krueger specifically proposed and tested the hypothesis that the "semantic category effect," reported so frequently in the 1970s, was, in fact, a manifestation of just this kind of physical-stimulus difference. In other words, he suggested that there is some physical difference between the alphabetic characters and the numeric stimuli that would allow them to be distinguished in the same manner as would a group of red lights within a field of green lights, or as a group of curved lines would be discriminated from among a field of curved lines. In his experiments Krueger equated the letters and numerals in terms of their physical appearance: He controlled the local curves and lines from which the stimuli were constructed. Under these conditions of physically equivalent stimuli, the so-called cognitive-category effect disappeared. In other control experiments, Krueger found that if the local detailed microstructure of the alphabetic characters and numerals was not controlled, then a substantial "category" effect did appear.

The implication of these findings is that the category effect is not real; rather that it is due to an artifact of the simplest kind—the alphabetic characters and numerals are distinguished from each other by their physical properties. In a similar vein, Krueger went on to note that differential familiarity between characters and numerals, itself, might play a very important role in simulating an influence of category with characters and letters.

2. Object and Word Superiority

Closely related to the category effect is another phenomenon of form recognition that has been referred to as the *word-* and/or *object-superiority* effect. Briefly this effect can be observed in either the context of words constructed from alphabetic characters or diagrammatic objects. The effect, which was brought back into prominence by Reicher (1969) in another one of those fruitful and seminal experiments, was first reported by Cattell (1886), a century ago. Reicher showed again that the recognizability of individual alphabetic characters increased drastically when they were presented in the context of a meaningful word as opposed to when they were presented alone or in the context of a nonsense word. Reicher's experiment was carefully designed to overcome a number of difficulties with earlier work that had been contaminated by guessing behavior or sequential dependencies. The main control he used was to require the observer to choose between only two alternative alphabetic responses, either one of which might form a word or might be a part of a nonword. Thus there is one critical experimental condition—the character in a real word—and two control conditions—the character alone and the character in a nonword.

The general result of Reicher's (1969) experiment was that the letters that were embedded in real words were recognized much better than letters presented alone or in nonwords. The fact that the observers were required to choose between two letters (a two-alternative, forced-choice psychophysical procedure) guaranteed that the guessing behavior that had contaminated many previous experiments concerning word recognition would not be a problem. The stimuli were also masked by a pattern of visual "noise" presented a short time after their presentation. This kept the observer from repeatedly reexamining the visual icon (a form of very short-term storage) by "obliterating the stored image after a short period of observation time."

Reicher's experiment was particularly interesting to psychologists because it was another one of those linking experiments that tied together what had previously been considered to be two more or less independent mental activities—the recognition of visual form and the cognitive aspects of information acquisition and interpretation. For the meaning of a word or even the sequential dependencies between the letters of the alphabet to affect the recognition of a form was a result that cried out that the recognition process was not simply the results of some simplistic feature analysis or template fitting. Rather, it should be classified at a much higher level process involving meaning and information about the environment in which that form was embedded. This was an extraordinary result and immediately changed the way (or should have changed the way) in which letter-recognition experiments were interpreted. A full review of the literature of word-superiority effects has been given by Baron (1978), and I have more to say about theoretical analyses of this topic later, but for the moment, let us turn to a closely related topic—the object-superiority phenomena.

The object-superiority effects are of the same genre as the word-superiority effects but do not depend on the semantic content of words. Rather, they depend on the geometrical order of organized structures. The effects (in the paradigm I discuss here) were first demonstrated by Weisstein and Harris (1974). Once again, their work was reported in a brief article in the journal *Science* and further developed as a paradigm by Williams and Weisstein (1978) and Weisstein, Williams, and Harris (1982). Figure 5.2 shows the type of stimuli that were used in the experiment. The observer is asked to "identify" by naming (with a code such as an alphabetic character or by depressing one of several alternative keys) which one of several familiar test lines was present in each case. In some experiments a pre-or postmask might be used; in others no masking was utilized.

The general result obtained in these experiments was analogous to the general effects observed by Reicher (1969) in the word-superiority experiment. The stimulus lines were identified better when they had a "meaningful" (i.e., in this case, an organized geometrical structure) context surrounding them than when they were presented alone. The effect has been attributed to a variety of different causes (as comprehensively reviewed by Enns & Prinzmetal, 1984) including:

1. The apparent three-dimensionality (Lanze, Weisstein, & Harris, 1982) of the complex stimuli (reflecting the assumption that three-dimensional stimuli were processed better than two-dimensional ones).

2. The production of emergent features such as arrows and triangles in the more organized and complex figures (Lanze, Maguire, & Weisstein, 1985; Pomerantz, Sager, & Stoever, 1977).

3. The activation of additional global organization-processing mechanisms when organized figures are presented (Earhard, 1980).

4. The possibility that separate mechanisms are activated by straight lines and complex figures (therefore, placing a line in a structured context made it immune

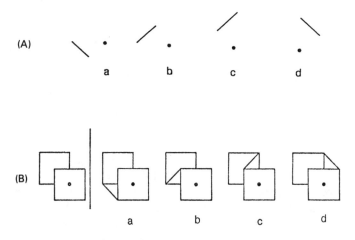

FIG.5.2   Stimuli used in Weisstein and Harris's work on the object superiority effect (from Weisstein & Harris, 1974).

to the masking by the set of disordered straight lines that is typically used as a mask in this type of experiment), an explanation proposed by McClelland (1978).

Enns and Prinzmetal (1984) have carried out several experiments concerning the object-superiority effect and have analyzed the problem from a somewhat different perspective. They point out that most of the previous research and explanatory models have failed to find any one or any group of the several variables that are known to influence the object-superiority effect to be sufficient to account for all of the various phenomena. One variable after another has been shown to influence the results of an experiment of this kind, but no unified principle emerges that can account for their collective influence. They propose, instead, that the results of the object-superiority effect can be totally accounted for by a process that I believe is also likely to explain the word-superiority effect discovered by Reicher.

Enns and Prinzmetal suggest that the object superiority effect occurs only when the ''object'' in which the target line is placed conveys redundant or additional information that is not conveyed by the line alone. That is, the context is not simply making the target line more detectable but is able, by virtue of its own structure, to convey information about which line should have been there *even if it (the target line) was not present*. The assertion they are making is that object superiority is not a perceptual phenomena, but one of inference and higher level cognitive processing. The structures in which the target line is embedded are not simply noninformational ''contexts'' but are themselves clues to the solution to the problem posed to the observer. Enns and Prinzmetal, therefore, make the point that all of the discussion concerning holistic processing mechanisms, emergent features, or depth are largely irrelevant. These perceptual attributes are correlated with the critical variable—the amount of redundant nongeometrical information available to supplement the geometrical information. This object-superiority effect is really an experiment on the meaning and interpretation of geometric forms and does not really assay the perceptual visibility of the stimuli: It is, in other words, an experiment of inference and not of feature recognition.

The word-superiority effect is also, I believe, of this same genre. Even though some attempt has traditionally been made to control for the sequential redundancy of the letters in the words, the observed effects are not so much associated with the increased visibility of the letters as they are of the structure of the English language. To talk of such processes as being inhibitory or excitatory may allow one to simulate the effects or act as an analogy, but the interactions between the letters in the word-superiority effect are, in my opinion, more likely to be associated with the sequential dependencies of letters in a language than with spatial interactions among the geometrical features of the letters.

The most extensive theoretical statement of the word-superiority effect was published by two groups at approximately the same time and with essentially the same point of view. McClelland and Rumelhart (1981) and Rumelhart and McClelland (1982), on the one hand, and Paap, Newsome, McDonald, and Schvaneveldt (1982), on the other, have proposed what essentially is a feature-oriented model of the word-superiority phenomenon. Their theories are based upon a set of concepts that clearly seem to have emerged by analogy from the neurophysiological laboratory. Although cloaked in psychological terminology and not associated with specific neurons per se or even anatomic loci by any of these authors, both groups have presented a model that asserts that there are "inhibitory" and "excitatory" interactions between "detectors" for features, letters, and words. The three kinds of detectors are presumed to lie at increasingly higher hierarchical levels within the perceptual nervous system, but no attempt is made to precisely define the absolute anatomy of this system other than to note that they become selectively more complex in their ability to deal with the units of the stimuli (local geometrical features, letters, and words). Each of these levels (and presumably others even higher in the hierarchy that we would otherwise refer to as cognitive processes) are able to influence those at lower levels. The process is interactive in the sense that high-level processes are influenced by lower level ones, as well as vice versa, and lateral inhibitions between comparabie detectors are also invoked. Indeed there can even be intersensory interactions with acoustic responses, and vice versa.

The basic idea in both of these models (as applied to the letter-identification situation) is that the perception of incompletely detected letters can be enhanced by the activation of possible words that might contain the letters. It is at this point that the metaphor introduced in this type of theory between perception and the putative "detectors" begins to strain plausibility. The kind of activation and interaction being discussed, which is claimed by theoreticians of this school of thought to be due to the interactions (inhibition and excitation of the several levels of their hypothetical "detectors"), becomes an untestable metaphor for the mechanisms actually underlying these processes. Indeed, the model at this level comes very close to being more parsimoniously explained in terms of the sequential dependencies of words in the English language than in terms of, for example, any inhibitory interactions between the putative feature or letter detectors. The metaphorical interaction between "detectors" that are proposed by these workers seems to be an oversimplification par excellence.

The point is that the simulations used by these authors are based upon mathematical equations that could as easily represent linguistic dependencies in the English language as they could hypothetical neural inhibitions and excitations. The analogy drawn between the detectors and sequential dependencies is useful in a mathematical sense, but it could as easily be supplanted by the language of the higher, linguistic level, which although less physiologically analyzable is equally well modeled by the chosen mathematics. The goodness of fit of the model to whatever data is available is virtually irrelevant in this case. It is the meaning of the factors in the formal equations that is the issue at hand and, as with so many other mathematical models, even a perfect fit of the model is not tantamount to the validation of the proposed mechanisms. The mathematical model is a description—a description that can be interpreted in terms of a number of different underlying implementations.

Another important feature of this kind of model is that all of these authors are very specifically suggesting an advantageous response accuracy when a letter is perceived embedded in a word. This is, to them, a perception model, and not one in which higher level interpretations allow the observer to *infer* the correct response. The observer, it is assumed, actually sees the letters in words even though the same letter may not be seen when it is presented in isolation. I, for one, do not believe this general approach to be correct. Word superiority, like object superiority, is an inferential, not a perceptual phenomenon.

3. Computational Reconstruction

One of the most influential of the new approaches to form recognition is the computational vision approach that was originally championed by the late David Marr and his colleagues and that has now become a major driving force of a substantial portion of contemporary research and theory in vision. The computational approach is based upon the idea that although we cannot currently (and may not ever) be able to understand the specific neurophysiology or the specific logical "language" that underlies any visual process, it is possible to look at the transformations that are carried out and to determine from them what functional processes *must* be executed to pass from the input form to the output form. Understanding, from the point of view of Marr and his followers, would then be achieved when a computational model carries out these processes in a way that simulates the transformations even though it may do so by logical rules and computational algorithms that are quite distinct from those actually used by the human visual system.

To make this point clear, for it is the essence of this school of thought, the investigator may wish to determine what has to be done to reconstruct a three-dimensional visual form from some attribute of the stimulus such as its motion or the disparities between the images in the two eyes. The tone of the research that is carried out by computational vision theorists is not, therefore, characterized by questions like: How do we recognize forms? but rather by very special queries such as: How do we imitate the processes that transform the invariances implicit in the slightly different images on the retina to information that is interpretable as three-dimensional structure?. In the sense that the observer is reconstructing form from something that is less than (that kind of) form, it is an act of classification and recognition that I think fits better in this context than in any other.

As an aside I should note that the perceptual tasks of reconstruction and recognition are psychophysically indistinguishable. In my laboratory the two tasks are procedurally identical; both require that the observer name the stimulus object.

The differences in the experiment turn out to be the nature of the stimulus itself. If one is asked to *reconstruct* something, fewer parts (or fewer parts in the appropriate order) are presented to the observer than when he or she is asked to *recognize* it. I believe that this would be the case with virtually all comparable tasks.

To return to the main point, the computational vision tradition that has emerged today is one in which the steps in going from one information base—the input form—to another—the output form—(which is presumed to be implicit in the first) are extracted, identified, and then simulated. There is seemingly little interest in carrying out the steps, so identified, by necessarily using the same logical rules the observer does. In fact, there seems to be an implicit acceptance of the idea that we cannot, in principle, know the exact way in which these steps are carried out by the different logical mechanisms of the brain even if lip-service is often given to an opposite point of view. The emphasis, to the contrary, is on the steps that "must" be taken to make the transformation from the form of the information in the stimulus to the form of the information in the response. We "must," for example, be able to specify which points in one eye's view correspond to which points in the other eye's view (the correspondence problem) if we are to determine (by other steps of similar complexity) what the three-dimensional shape is of the dichoptically presented object. The main intellectual goal of this kind of theory, therefore, becomes the determination of the necessary processing steps: The development of analogous and efficient, if not biologically homologous, mathematical algorithms to implement the identified steps becomes a mere technical tour de force, which, though impressive, is not at the heart of the theoretical problem stressed by students of human perceptions: What do people do when they recognize forms?

It cannot be overstressed that although the steps may be intended to have biological, as well as logical, significance, there is really nothing about the specific mathematical algorithms that need necessarily be linked to the underlying biology. I doubt if any of the leaders in this field would argue that a Laplacian operator, for example, is actually executed in the brain in the same way as the algorithm is executed in the computer. Rather, there is a processing step, or a function that has to be carried out—edge enhancement—and one way to do so is by use of this particular mathematical tool. But that same processing step may be executed by totally different algorithms within the brain.

The summary point of this brief introduction to computational vision is that the practical success of a particular algorithm in carrying out some information-processing step is not a proof that the particular algorithm is being executed in the head. There may be literally an infinite number of analogous procedures that would do as well.

Thus, Marr's computational approach, and that of all of those whom he has influenced, is fundamentally intended to concentrate on the information-processing aspects of the transformations that are presumed to underlie visual perception independently of the neurophysiological and logical processes of the brain that are (for reasons of complexity) largely invisible to the experimenter or theoretician. It is my opinion that, in large part, the emergence of this brand of computational theory was a reaction to the failures of both the single-cell neurophysiological approach to carry on beyond the enormous progress in understanding individual neurons to the level at which the essence of the neural problem must lie—the interactive relationships between neurons—and the failure of psychological theory to be validated. Coupled with the combinatorial barrier—too many neurons interacting to be computed—is the fundamental difficulty with psychophysics—the "black-box" limitation—that is, its inability to say anything definitive about the underlying mechanisms.

It must also be appreciated that Marr's ideas, as expressed in his important 1982 book, also transcended the specifics of the computer program itself by concentrating on the information-processing aspects of the problem. In the case of the kinds of problems he and his followers have worked on, the term *information* is very precisely defined. Marr was trying to determine what logical transformations "must" be carried out to enable the perceiver to transform the properties of the stimulus pattern into those of the psychological experience. To the extent that these information transformations could be identified, then, the visual process was "understood" in Marr's view, even though it was not possible to know much about the specific neural mechanisms or the (quite possibly very different than those used in the computer program) computational algorithms actually carried out in the nervous system. In Marr's (1982) words:

> The message was plain. There must exist an additional level of understanding at which the character of the information-processing tasks carried out during perception are analyzed and understood in a way that is independent of the particular mechanisms and structures that implement them in our heads. This was what was missing—the analysis of the problem as an information-processing task. Such analysis does not usurp an understanding at the other levels—of neurons or of computer programs—but it is a necessary complement to them, since without it there can be no real understanding of the function of all those neurons. (p. 19)

Marr then notes that there are three levels of this task with which the computational theorists must be concerned. First the theorist must be concerned with the logic and goals of the transformation from input to output. It must be appreciated what it is that the program must do and what strategies are suitable, if not biologically relevant, for achieving these intended goals. This level of analysis is a conceptual one and involves none of the technical details of the procedures or algorithms of the computer or the neural logic of the brain.

Detailing the program is the essence of the next level. The theorist must then, according to Marr, commit himself to specifying the exact information processes to be simulated and the ways in which the images will be encoded or represented in order to be so processed. The specific algorithms necessary to carry out the transformation from the raw input to the processed output must be established.

Finally, at the third level, the theorist must be concerned about the ways in which these algorithms can be implemented physically. (I should note some disagreement on my part with this assertion.) In fact, this third level has to be divided into two separate sublevels. First, one should be concerned with the physical implementation of the information-processing algorithms as theoretical tools. What kind of computational mechanisms can execute these processes and make the necessary transformations? This is a sublevel that is certainly achievable. However, the second sublevel of this third level of Marr's analysis implies that one must also attempt to define the actual physiological implementation in the nervous system of these processes, and it is this kind of analysis that, as I have already noted, may not be achievable.

What Marr was seeking, I believe, is a statement of the information processes that must be executed to transform stimuli to percepts on the one hand and some speculation concerning plausible mechanisms on the other. I do not, however, believe that it is possible, or that it will ever be possible, to definitively assert which of the many plausible mechanisms that might be conjured up are indeed the physiologically real ones because of the essential indeterminacy of the mathematical and input–output approaches with regard to internal structures. This is the essence of Moore's automaton theories, to which I have referred several times earlier.

It is in the specifications of the information processes that ''must'' be executed, as opposed to either elegant computation algorithms or wilder speculations concerning the specific neural mechanisms that Marr's (1982) work makes its most significant contribution. In particular, he and his colleagues have made great strides in understanding the nature of the computations that ''must'' be carried out to derive three-dimensional shape information from the two dimensional projective images formed on the retina. Marr suggests that there are four sequential processing steps required to make this transformation. The four levels of processing are:

1. The representation
2. The primal sketch
3. The 21/2-D sketch
4. The 3-D model representation

Table 5.1 (from Marr, 1982) describes the purpose of each of these steps and the primitives (or parameters of the representation) at each stage that must be manipulated to accomplish the task at each level.

Marr's work obviously ranges over a very wide prospect. But in terms of general approach, it is mainly concerned with how a system *might* implement the transformations that it *must* go through to arrive at a stage at which recognition or classification of the solid objects derived from the 2-D representation can be made. Grimson's (1981) computational approach is in the same vein and con-

TABLE 5.1
The Marr Theory of the Transformation Steps Involved in Stereoscopic
Depth Perception (from Marr, 1982)

Name	Purpose	Primitives
Image(s)	Represents intensity.	Intensity value at each point in the image.
Primal sketch	Makes explicit important information about the two-dimensional image, primarily the intensity changes there and their geometrical distribution and organization.	Zero-crossings Blobs Termination and discontinuities Edge segments Virtual lines Groups Curvilinear organization Boundaries
2½-D sketch	Makes explicit the orientation and rough depth of the visible surfaces, and contours of discontinuities in these quantities in a viewer-centered coordinate frame.	Local surface orientation (the "needles" primitives) Distance from viewer Discontinuities in depth Discontinuities in surface orientation
3-D model representation	Describes shapes and their spatial organization in an object-centered coordinate frame, using a modular hierarchical representation that includes volumetric primitives (i.e., primitives that represent the volume of space that a shape occupies) as well as surface primitives.	3-D models arranged hierarchically, each one based on a spatial configuration of a few sticks or axes, to which volumetric or surface shape primitives are attached

centrates on the disparity aspects of the stereopsis problem. Grimson's version of a computational model is illustrated in Fig. 5.3.

From the same group at MIT has come the closely related computational theory of Ullman (1979), dealing with the manner in which the three-dimensional structure of an object can be reconstructed from knowledge about the relative motions of its parts in a two-dimensional projection. Ullman concentrates on how we can use such cues as relative motion as a cue to the three-dimensional organization of a form (structure from motion) just as Marr and Grimson emphasized disparity-type computations. Work in this field has progressed rapidly in the last few years mainly because of the very well-defined nature of the problem of how structure can be retrieved from motion.

How precisely formulated this issue has become is evidenced by the very specific question motivating current research in this field: Given certain constraints, how many points and how many views does it take to define a sampled three-dimensional form when the relative two-dimensional motion of the dots of which

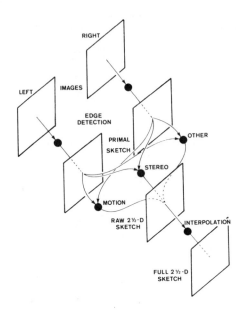

FIG. 5.3. A model of stereoscopic visual perception (from Grimson, 1981).

it is composed is the only cue? Investigators have presented stimuli to observers as a means of psychophysically answering this question, but mathematicians have also attacked it analytically. A comparison of the two approaches is most informative because it allows us to determine how close the human observer comes to being an ideal observer—the later state being defined by the mathematics simulating the situation. It is fascinating to observe that the mathematics answering the question How many views of how many points does one need to recover the three-dimensional shape of an object from the relative positions of the points in sequential views? is very well developed. Indeed, the question has been answered for several of the constraints that can limit the possible family of three-dimensional shapes. The work has been done mainly by Ullman (1979) for the case in which structural rigidity of the three-dimensional object is assumed and by Hoffman and his colleagues and others for a number of other situations in which planar motion, constant velocity, or fixed-axis constraints apply. In general this table indicates that as additional constraints are imposed a smaller number of views and points is required to reconstruct the visual form. Similarly, increasing the number of dots will reduce the number of views, and increasing the number of views will reduce the number of dots theoretically necessary to reconstruct a form under any of these conditions. Table 5.2 summarizes the various answers to the question How many views of how many points are necessary to reconstruct? for a number of these constraining conditions.

Intuitive predictions for the extreme conditions in which a very large number

TABLE 5.2
Sufficient Conditions (How Many Views and How Many Dots are Required)
for Recovery of Three-Dimensional Structure from Moving Sets of Points
for Various Constraints
From Braunstein, Hoffman, Shapiro, Andersen, and Bennet, 1986

	Number of points		
	2	*3*	*4*
2		Pairwise-rigid and planar motion[a]	
3	Rigid planar motion[a] Rigid fixed axis motion parallel to image plane constant angular velocity[b]	Rigid fixed axis motion[b]	Rigid motion[c] Nonrigid fixed axis motion[d]
4	Nonrigid fixed axis motion[d] Rigid fixed axis motion, constant angular velocity[e]		
5	Rigid fixed axis motion[e]		

Number of Distinct Views (row axis label)

[a]Hoffman & Flinchbaugh, 1982; [b]Hoffman & Bennett, 1986; [c]Ullman, 1979; [d]Bennett & Hoffman, 1985; [e]Hoffman & Bennett, 1986.

of dots or a very large number of views are available have been confirmed psychophysically by Lappin, Doner, and Kottas (1980) and Lappin and Fuqua (1983). The former paper showed that very large numbers of dots (i.e., 512) allowed the observer to perceive a sphere when only two different views were presented. Conversely if the the observer could see only three dots, it was still possible to reconstruct depth when a large number of views was allowed even if each view was as far apart as 120 deg of rotation of the represented three-dimensional sphere.

The work of Lappin and his colleagues, however, did not look at the minimum conditions that were formally specified in Table 5.2. These conditions are at the opposite end of the continuum—the smallest number of combined dots and views that are necessary to reconstruct the form. Braunstein, Hoffman, Shapiro, Andersen, and Bennett (1986) have attacked this problem psychophysically by presenting dot stimuli that simultaneously contained small numbers of dots and small numbers of views. The objects used as stimuli were also constructed from samples of the dots on a sphere, but with few dots, they actually could represent simpler structures. Observers were asked to make a discriminative judgment of "same" or "different" of two presentations that differed in the position of only one dot. To make the task reasonably difficult, the stimuli were rotated with respect to each other so that the two stimulus presentations were not identical even when the forms were the same. The main variable in the experiment was the degree of constraint placed on the figures. The stimuli could be constrained to be either (a) a rigid body, (b) a rigid body rotating around a fixed axis, or (c) a rigid body rotating around a fixed axis at a constant velocity. In additional trials, motion was eliminated and only two points used.

The results of this experiment were extraordinary—Braunstein and his colleagues determined that their observers seemed actually to be performing better than the predictions of a theoretical model suggested that they should. Subservient to the assumption of rigidity, the model predicted, for example, that three views of four points should be necessary to recover three-dimensional structure. However, for some of the tested conditions they discovered that their observers were able to discriminate shape at better than chance levels and thus beyond the predictions of the models when only two points were presented. At first glance this suggests that the human visual system is able to perform better than does the theoretically ideal observer, but this dreadful impossibility can be exorcised if, as the authors of this study correctly noted, other constraints, redundancies, or information are available to the observer that were not incorporated in the mathematical model. Three additional pieces of information that Braunstein and his colleagues suggest may have been operating in this situation to allow the human to surpass the model were:

1. Observers may have assumed that distances in the two-dimensional projection and the three-dimensional object were related by a constant. This constraint, they believe is the principal one in explaining the high level of performance vis-à-vis theory.

2. Observers may have noted the lack of movement of the center of rotation of the stimuli.

3. Observers may have noted the limited range of the velocity and axis movements in those cases in which these parameters did vary.

Each of these constraints,[5] possibly available to the observer but not to the theoretical model, would have made it understandable how the observer's performance could exceed that predicted by the model without any assumption that

---

[5] It is, of course, the essence of the psychological problem how and which of these constraints are imposed by the observer. By applying constraints (or, as some might call them, *prejudices*), the human observer surpasses the currently available "ideal" mathematical observer by simplifying the task. Thus the definition of the ideal-observer model usually follows the psychophysical data because the ideal observer is not likely to be as fully constrained as the human observer. Simply put, we do not have ideal modelers supplying ideal constraints to ideal observers.

the human observer was performing ''better'' than some full-blown ideal would allow. The problem lies, of course, with the model of the ideal. It, quite simply, was not specific, complete, or constrained enough. The psychophysical data, therefore, showed that the model must be refined to truly represent the visual process.

Surprisingly, the general prediction that increasing the number of dots should decrease the number of views and generally increase performance did not hold up in these experiments either. In the low-dot-numerosity range in which they worked, Braunstein and colleagues discovered that adding dots actually reduced performance on the task in certain conditions. They attributed this unpredictable outcome to the increasing complexity of the spatial interactions between the dots in the sequential views. Obviously, the trend of this function must reverse when the number of dots becomes so large that they were dealt with more holistically as shown in the Lappin, Doner, and Kottas (1980) study.

An important point to be extracted from this discussion is that any model contains but a subset of the total information contained in the entity or process being modeled. Thus, predictions made by the model may not incorporate all of the aspects and constraints of the real entity. Therefore, when a conflict occurs between a model and a psychophysical experiment, barring some rare artifact, it is virtually always necessary to modify the model to meet the results of the experiment rather than to doubt the phenomena. This holds true if the model is either mathematical or neural. The final authority in any conflict between theory and experiment, as occurred here, must ultimately be the perceptual phenomenon.

Another instance in which performance exceeded theory is to be found in my own work. In my studies (Uttal, 1975, 1983, 1985, 1987) I have been studying the perception of dotted forms when they are embedded in random noise (as described in chapter 3). In its most ''recent incarnation (Uttal, Davis, Welke, & Kakarala, in press) this work has evolved to include the processes of discrimination and recognition. In particular, my colleagues, Ramakrishna Kakarala, Nancy Davis, and Cynthia Welke, and I have recently been working on the problem of the reconstruction of single-valued, geometrical surfaces, such as those shown in Fig.3.1 when only very sparse samples (i.e., dots) are presented. The question asked in this case was: How many dots (samples) of a surface must be presented to an observer to permit recognition of which one of a set of surfaces had been sampled? The question is analogous to the one asked by Ullman, Braunstein, and the others who were interested in how many dots and how many views of a moving object were necessary to reconstruct its shape. In our case, only a single view of a certain number of dots was presented; the critical information necessary to accomplish the task being presented in the form of *binocular disparity* rather than motion, the cue used in the previously mentioned ''structure from motion'' studies.

The answer to the question of how many dots arenecessary for reconstruction of a stationary object was quite straightforward mathematically. It was determined, using a two-dimensional polynomial curve-fitting procedure, that if the sampled surfaces were generated from a polynomial expression that was of the second order—a quadric—it required at least five dots for mathematical reconstruction. If, on the other hand, the surface was generated from a third-order equation—a cubic—then it took at least seven sample dots for the mathematical model to correctly reconstruct the form from which the dots were sampled.

In corresponding psychophysical experiments, we were also astonished to discover that our observers' performance, as indicated by his or her accuracy at recognizing and naming the forms from those very sparsely sampled stimuli, also exceeded the predictions of the curve-fitting model! There was a better than 50% accuracy of recognition with as few as six dots. Furthermore, even surfaces sampled with as few as two or three dots were recognized at better than chance levels, far better than the predicted mathematical model. Almost certainly this level of performance occurred because our observers used information not available to the model in the simple form in which it was initially programmed.

For example, the observer could use the information that a pair of dots can, in some cases, distinguish between two groups of the forms—the flatter and the more convex ones. Furthermore, our observers were only required to select one from among eight forms, whereas the mathematical model must select one from among virtually an infinitude of possible cubic or quadric forms.

Nevertheless, and in spite of this discrepancy between data and theory, it is important to note that both the model and our observers require very few sampled dots to reconstruct these shapes. As an answer to the twin question (How many dots for reconstruction? Mathematically? Perceptually?), the number is considerably lower than initially projected.

Reconstruction is a more general problem than I have indicated here so far. Not only can motion and disparity be used to specify the shape of an object, but the human has a powerful ability to recognize a complex scene consisting of many objects. Each demonstration of the power of the human visual system to reconstruct form from one or another partial cue is another illustration of how far we have to go in understanding how the observer carries out these functions. There are certainly many other constraints and cues to reconstruction yet to be discovered.

With the continuing evolution of computerized robotics, a vigorous cottage industry of computer-vision techniques has grown up, all of which attempt to simulate the reconstructive power of the visual system and all of which provide hints about potential reconstruction cues to the perceptual theoretician. Stevens (1983 , 1984, 1986), for example, has studied the reconstruction of forms from the slant of surface contour maps and gradients of texture. We have already spoken of the reconstruction of three-dimensional forms from the cue that is implicit in the invariances of disparity in a stereoscopic picture, and Horn (1975) discusses the way in which the shading of an object can be used to specify the shape of a solid but differentially reflecting object. Horn (1983) has also proposed using unit surface perpendiculars—the Needle Map—to generate a function known as an extended Gaussian image of a surface. A wonderful property of the Gaussian image is that no two convex objects can have the same form of this expression, and it, therefore, is a formidable mathematical representation of functionally discriminable forms.

I am sure that many other cues that I have not mentioned have been suggested as a means to recognize or reconstruct surfaces and shapes. The main point is that the visual system of organisms like the human seems to be able to take advantage of a wide variety of different cues as it recognizes visual scenes.

Grimson (1984) makes some especially interesting points in an insightful discussion of the way brightness cues are used in the reconstruction of surfaces. Among his most important points are the ideas that a comparison is often needed between two or more views (either the object moves, the head moves, or the two eyes receive not-quite-duplicate images). (See the comparable discussion of relational Level IV processes in my earlier work [Uttal, 1981] for another expression of the importance of relative comparisons in vision.) In addition Grimson also notes that in most visual situations there are far more reconstructions possible than the one that finally is perceived by the observer. To reduce the possible number, the observer must "assume" certain constraints, a process that vastly exceeds current computer capabilities. Both mathematics and perception become plausible in light of the inferred constrained possibilities. Some we have already discussed—for example, the rigidity constraint that Ullman, Braunstein, and other workers in the field of structure through motion, impose upon their mathematical models. Apparently, similar constraints are imposed by the human observer as the prompt awareness of three-dimensional form is created from a stimulus as impoverished as a few briefly exposed, slightly translated dots.

In summary, the ability of human observers to reconstruct visual images from grossly degraded images is outstandingly good. In several cases we have seen that the human equals or even exceeds the performance of what must frankly be considered to be relatively primitive mathematical models designed to simulate the visual process. We do not know exactly what logical mechanisms are used inside the human perceptual system to accomplish these computational feats, but it is clear that the models that have been developed by computational theorists, are, at best, only remote approximations to completely reductive and biologically valid explanations of the wonders of the human vision. It seems quite unlikely, considering the combinatorics of the situation, that we will be able to unravel the intricate network details of the neurophysiological basis of form perception. Without that information, it becomes problematic exactly how far we can go in understanding the logical mechanisms that underlie the extraordinarily powerful ability of the the human to recognize forms. The newly emerging fact of the cognitive penetrability of recognition processes, in particular, further argues that the neural processes involved are probably far more complicated than those underlying detection and discrimination. Theories to explain human form recognition may be among the most refractory ever attempted by scholars in any field of psychology, in spite of considerable progress in comparable fields of computer vision.

Ullman, as did Marr and the others of this emerging new school of computational vision research, also notes his negative reaction to the neuroreductionistic theoretical approach and expresses his view that we must turn to more abstract computational theories to understand form recognition. I cannot overemphasize the importance of this point of view. Marr, Ullman, Braunstein, Hoffman, Grimson, and the others are to a significant degree also asserting (as I do) in one context or another that the neuroreductionistic approach is not going to succeed for reasons of deep principle, not just because of current technological limitations. We all agree that the best possible progress toward understanding the complex mental process called form recognition requires extensive computational simulations of the informational processes and interactions more than it requires further study of individual neurons.

What computational-vision theorists have done is to provide an organized and powerful research paradigm. In such elementary ways as their insistence on precise definition of what it is that is intended to be modeled, they have made an important contribution. So much of the psychological literature of the last few decades has described, analyzed, or modeled processes that are very poorly defined, and fuzziness of explanations has followed fuzziness of definition. Recognition is a much coarser concept than is edge detection or three-dimensional reconstruction from sampled motion. Very often in the earlier psychological literature, the definition of the visual process under investigation was defined by nothing more than the task presented to the observer. This led to enormous difficulty in relating the results of different experiments or the outcomes of different theories to each other. Computational theory provides a precise statement of the specific processes and, perhaps even more fundamentally, represents an easy step to a taxonomy of the processing steps involved in complex acts of visual perception. There is much yet to be learned about the actual homologous processing steps, as opposed to the analogies that have been put forward, but without question the requirement that computer programs make for precision of definition is a superb contribution by itself. Our science is much better off than it was previously now that we are asking such questions as: How are contours intensified? How do we segment a complex scene into its constituent surfaces? How do we reconstruct a three-dimensional object from disparity, motion, texture, lighting, or some other of the many cues to solidity? Even if we cannot currently answer these questions fully, we are moving forward.

There is another critical interpretive point concerning computational models of vision that should be made at this point in our discussions. Many computational vision projects are specifically intended to be models of human vision. This, however, is not always the case in the more applied realms of the AI field where computer techniques are purposely being developed to perform practical functions such as image classification and recognition, but without any specific intent to simulate the actual processes and logic by which humans perceive form. There is a host of methods and algorithms being developed today that are all but free of psychological theoretical overtones. These methods are intended only to allow engineers to carry out certain useful and necessary tasks. Even though the mathematics in these cases may develop its own theoretical superstructure and even be useful and germane as heuristics leading to the kinds of theories that might be developed to study human form perception, understanding human psychological properties is not the main goal of this field of endeavor.

4. The Recognition of Individual Forms

This chapter would be incomplete if we did not deal with the very specific problem of how we recognize single geometric forms. The problem is the classic one in form perception: How do we know what a face, or an alphabetic character, or, for that matter, any other circumscribed stimulus-object is when, at best, we are presented with a two-dimensional, projective retinal mapping of the object? In terms of alphabetic characters (which have enormous advantages as stimuli because of the substantial degree to which they have been overlearned and the fact that they represent such a well-defined and limited set of stimulus-objects): How can we distinguish that an A is what it is and that it is not a B, or, at a more subtle level, that a C is not a U (more subtle because both share the same topology)? Or in terms of a more complex, but more natural, set of stimulus objects—human faces: How does one recognize a particular face as that of his wife and not that of the gas station attendant or some other individual?

As simple as it is to pose these questions, perceptual psychologists must admit that they are among the most refractory faced by science. After many decades, if not centuries, of research on the problem of alphabetic character and face recognition, we still know precious little about the nature of the information processes that allow us to effortlessly and preattentively carry out these deceptively simple tasks. The most modern research gives us only the slightest amount of information concerning the extraordinary mechanisms that must underlie our powerful recognition ability. For example, it was only recently established that low frequencies seem to convey less information in a face-recognition task than do the high frequencies. In other words, we now have confirmed a fact that should have been a priori obvious, namely that outlines or contours seem to be more important than the slowly changing and, therefore, redundant regions of a face in determining recognition.

Nevertheless, and in spite of a rather meager psychophysica data base, innumerable pattern recognition theories and algorithms have been suggested. Most, however, seem to be based upon what is arguably an erroneous assumption—that the visual system performs a detailed analysis of the objects from its global form into the local features of which it is constructed. I have already presented arguments that should have made my opposition to this point of view clear, but another "argu-

FIG. 5.4. Kolers's "random forms" (from Kolers, 1970).

ment" that is also effective is the collection of "random" objects shown in Fig. 5.4. It takes no sophisticated psychophysical test to determine that all of these objects fall into the same perceptual category—chair—even though they share virtually no local feature communalities. The same point is made by Fig. 5.5, in which a group of alphabetic characters of widely differing fonts can easily be recognized or classified into the same name category in spite of the fact that they, similarly, share virtually no common local features.

The point to be driven home once again by these demonstrations of first-order phenomena is that it is probably not the local features of a stimulus-object that dominate the recognition process, but rather the *arrangement of the parts*. The parts from which a picture is constructed can be totally irrelevant or have their own symbolic load, and yet we still see the intended global form if they are properly arranged.

There is also a number of more formal empirical studies that argue against the feature analytical approach. In general these experiments either show the precedence of the global form over the local feature or illustrate the bizarre nature of features. Let us consider the latter data first. One of the most interesting

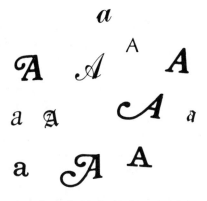

FIG. 5.5.   A compendium of alphabetic characters from different fonts.

phenomena of recent years has been the newly discovered subjective contour illusion (e.g., Kanisza, 1974. See also Petry & Meyer, 1986, for a summary of much recent work). As illustrated in Fig. 5.6, the subjective contours are suggested by the arrangement of the parts of the stimuli. The germane aspect of these phenomena in the present context is that these contours are powerfully perceived even though they do not physically exist! They represent forms that are perceived because of the *arrangement* of the elements of the stimulus.

The point is that perception is a process in which different rules apply from those in physics. Percepts, unlike energy or matter, can be created and destroyed by suggestion—without the necessity of their antecedents being present in an energetic or material sense. What we are discussing in this case is *information* and its corollary *arrangement* and not matter or potential—a distinction often overlooked by theoreticians in this field. Theories of illusion and perception that attempt to fill in the blanks by showing how the energy or matter is actually created or moved from one part of the image to another (e.g., Ginsburg's, 1983, argument that the subjective contours were produced by band-pass filtering of the image or that they are produced by partial activation of neural line detectors) typically do not generalize beyond the specific situations for which the putative energy-related analogy was suggested. It is far more likely that the percept, be

FIG. 5.6.   A Kanizsa triangle (courtesy of Dr. Gaefano Kanizsa of the University of Trieste).

it subjective contour or otherwise, is created from a processing of the information, or arrangement, or significance, or invariances that exist in the stimulus-form rather than by any manipulation of the distribution of physical energy incident on the retina or passing along the visual pathway.

An even more immediately compelling argument against energy-dependent perception can be seen in some data obtained by Townsend and Ashby (1982) in a study in which their main goal was, in fact, to compare various alternative feature-analysis models. One unusual aspect of the Townsend and Ashby experiment was that they asked their observers to specifically report what features they "saw"—an analytical step beyond simply naming the alphabetic characters that were presented. The astonishing and disconcerting result was that their observers reported the presence of features (i.e., component lines of a limited set of alphabetic characters) even when the features were not present in the original stimulus! Thus, the feature seems in this case to be an attribute created by the observer from interpretation of the global shape. This is in sharp opposition to its putative role as the driving force that creates the perception of the global form. Townsend and Ashby refer to the visible, but nonexistent, parts as "ghost features." The analogy between their result and the letter-in-word and object-superiority phenomena is immediate and direct. It seems, perhaps, that one could reasonably extrapolate this finding to call all local features "ghosts" and feature theories of form recognition "ghost" theories. It seems more likely that they are processed well after the global attributes and arrangements have been processed and only in those situations in which very specific focal attention is directed at the details of the stimulus form. This assertion is essentially identical to the proposal of global precedence made by Navon (1977) and others discussed previously and formulated from another point of view.

Other support for global precedence has been provided by Lupker (1979) in a study in which he examined the confusions among a small set of alphabetic characters. Acknowledging that the contemporary theoretical scene emphasizes the features of a form (specifically, the temporal precedence of features rather than global wholes), Lupker determined that the error matrices emerging from his experiment reflected confusions among a particular set of alphabetic and quasi-alphabetic characters that depended more upon their global form than on their shared constituent features. Similar results had been obtained by Bouma (1971) earlier but explained in a way that was criticized by Lupker as being inadequately justified, although in the latter's opinion quite correct.

In spite of an array of empirical arguments for global influences in form perception, virtually every psychological theory of visual form recognition that I now consider conceptualizes the task of form recognition to be one of analysis into parts, of feature detection, or of local attribute processing. I have already alluded to the reasons for this misdirection: The limits on our mathematical skills in dealing with global arrangement, the influence of the findings from the single-cell neurophysiological laboratory, and the discrete nature of computer hardware and software technology.

Clearly, the redirection of our theoretical energies toward a more holistic point of view is not going to be easy. We need an increased mass of psychophysical data, like those of the studies of Bouma (1971), Navon (1977), and Lupker (1979), that strengthen the argument for the perceptual influence of the global arrangement of the features of stimulus-objects. We need new and more powerful mathematical and computational algorithms that measure and are sensitive to the arrangement of these parts and features. Most of all, however, we need a new perspective on the problem that will guide us to emphasize the holistic attributes of stimulus-forms rather than localized ones—a perspective that can come only from an appreciation that a misdirected trend in the current theoretical zeitgeist has led us to ignore the basic demonstrations and the empirical data supporting global influences. It is a remarkable fact how effective the zeitgeist has been in guiding our thinking. Feature-oriented theories are so elegant, so efficient, and so contextually consistent with the findings of other sciences that workers in this field have virtually ignored the data that many Gestalt psychologists argued decades ago to be the empirical facts of the matter.

With this preamble in place, let us consider some of the theories of form perception that have been specifically offered as explanations of how we see specific forms. We will not consider in this section any further details of the wide range of computational vision "engines" that have been designed to mimic, without deep explanation or theoretical validity, human visual recognition processes. Though these practical engineering efforts have their own charm and utility and often can feed back heuristics to the theoretical effort, they are, in the main, unconcerned with the problem that is our main focus here—the recognition of forms by the brains of humans and other organisms.

One of the earliest (post-World War II) approaches to form recognition was a relatively naive and implausible *template* theory. Template theories, although primitively holistic, can be quickly disposed of logically if not empirically. I have already introduced the basic idea that a cross-correlation is carried out between the input stimulus-form and an enormous set of templates or prerecorded images that were supposed to have been previously stored in some kind of visual memory. Carrying out this set of cross-correlations between the input stimulus and the set of "templates," according to the tenets of this hypothetical model, would eventually produce one maximum correlation between the input and a particular one of the very large number of templates. That maximum correlation acts as the decision criterion for the choice of a response. The arguments against template theory should be familiar now. Considering how good humans are at recognizing objects that are magnified, translated, or rotated, and the specifically spatial-correlation process implied by this theoretical approach, it is obvious that an implausibly large number of templates would be required to permit this system to work. The vast number of templates is perhaps the most damning criticism of this approach, but explaining how the enormous number of cross-correlations could be carried out in the brief period of time required for recognition to occur is certainly another.

An interesting sidelight of the template-matching theory is that it probably cannot be invalidated empirically. That is, if one accepts the premise that there is a set of templates recorded in the brain, the theory obviously could work. All one has to do to account for recognition is to propose more and more templates. Because we cannot neurophysiologically identify a template (because it is likely to be too complex for neurophysiological analysis), we cannot reject its existence a priori, and the system could, in principle, operate in the way suggested. Similarly, some kind of a parallel correlational system, implausible but possible, cannot be rejected out of hand. The arguments against the template theory, therefore, mainly have to be made in terms of the logical and logistical demands made by the necessary processing and memory requirements, that is, by the combinatorics of the situation. Simply put, it seems that the template idea is just too much of a hammer-and-tongs approach, too gross, and too unsophisticated to be the process of choice of organic evolution. Admittedly, this is a matter of taste and not a rigorous argument, but it is compelling, at least to this reader of the theoretical scene.

Another set of contemporary theories of form recognition, as noted, typically concentrates on the identification of the local features and assumes that at some higher level these elements interact with each other to produce a classificatory response. Although there were many early steps in the sequence of ideas that led to this general approach to form perception, the most influential prototypes of this general class of theories was the work done in the 1950s and 1960s on neural-network models. Most of these early network models had a common architecture regardless of the details of the information processing proposed by their formulators. At the lowest level a map of the stimulus is projected on a series of receptors; the output of these receptors is then fed into a some kind of a local feature-processing network that analyzes the image into a collection of narrowly defined local features such as angles or straight lines. The outputs of this stage of processing are then fed into another level of processing where they influence the choice of an output by virtue of some interactive concatenation of their outputs. These theories have the advantage of not requiring an extensive set of templates; the processing acts algorithmically upon the attributes of the stimulus to make a decision from among a prestored set of responses. Responses, we are assured, can be stored far more economically than are the putative templates of that even more primitive type of theory.

One, of the most influential early theories (Selfridge, 1959) of this genre can be considered to be prototypical in that its operation was dependent upon features, but not upon templates. Selfridge proposed a multilayer system in which the raw sensory input was fed to a system of feature detectors. These specialized elements were activated by the presence of stimuli that matched their specific preset sensitivities. Thus a vertical line in the stimulus would activate a vertical line detector that would then proceed to signal its activation by increasing its level of activity—a simple geometrical-straight-line-to-frequency-of-response (i.e., a spatial to temporal) conversion. All of the other feature-detecting elements in the system would do the same when selectively activated by their respective trigger feature. The result was that there was a pattern of greater or lesser amounts of activity spread across the simulated array of feature detectors. At this point there was no special order to the outputs, only a variable amount of activity being differentially signaled by the detectors. Selfridge referred to this state of affairs as a *pandemonium*, and the name has stuck to this kind of model.

The second stage of this type of system typically consisted of a set of integrators, each of which was tuned to a particular pattern of activity in the pandemonium of signals being sent up from the feature detectors. If a particular pattern of detector outputs appeared in the barrage of signals, certain elements of this second level of integrators were selectively and differentially activated. Thus a second level of pandemonium (in which the features triggering these units were patterns of activity from the receptors rather than the geometric features of the stimulus form) was established with each of these second-tier detectors activated to the extent that its specific input trigger pattern was present in the first level.

A final decision level was then proposed by Selfridge. At this level a single mechanism capable of isolating the most active of the second-tier detectors selected the particular output response of the system. Recognition had been achieved because the appropriate response was made to an input three levels away.

Selfridge's system depended on built-in feature detectors at several levels responding to different kinds of features. It was unspecific enough to have had a monumental influence in establishing the idea that feature detection by an interconnected network of receptors lay at the heart of the recognition problem. This idea has been persistent throughout the history of form-perception research, as we shall see here even though it was not possible to practically implement these ideas until the recent arrival of parallel computers.

Another important influence on theoretical thinking in the form-recognition field was Rosenblatt's (1958) perceptron model, an attempt to build a network-type recognition machine that learned by appropriate "reinforcements" of the sequential stages of information processing. We saw in chapter 2 that Rosenblatt's perceptron consisted of a mesh of receptors randomly connected through a network of interconnections to a group of output devices. Rosenblatt had proposed that a random network of this kind would "learn" to recognize particular input stimuli if appropriately "reinforced" by strengthening signals sent to particular interconnections in the network when an appropriate connection between one of the inputs and one of the outputs was established. Thus, the system would increasingly tend to respond with a correct response (i.e., the correct "recognition" or classification of the input pattern) as a result of experience. Rosenblatt's ideas had recently been challenged in the sense that there were thought to be severe constraints on the learned behavior of such a random network. Only certain types of network arrangements are capable of adapting in the sense he proposed, according to Minsky and Papert (1969), and, therefore, only certain ones would in principle be capable of becoming recognition-type engines.

It is now thought, however, that some of Minsky and Papert's criticism may have been too severe and there is a resurgence in interest in this approach. Newly emerging parallel processor technology, in particular, has allowed actual testing of some of these older ideas. A whole new field of "neural computers" purportedly modeled on them has suddenly exploded onto the scene. *Neural* is probably a misnomer in this case (no neuron-like elements are used in most of the neural computers); rather, the term has been rather loosely employed to describe the new generation of massively parallel computers. Some of these new machines are currently beginning to be used to simulate the kind of connected networks that Rosenblatt and Selfridge had so insightfully conceived years ago with considerable success. However, the field of parallel processing is so new and so little is known about the programming of these incredible machines (some are capable of 2 to 3 billion instructions per second) that it will probably be a prolonged time before we understand what their impact will be on form recognition theory in the future.

Even though all of the details of Rosenblatt's perceptron theory with its randomly connected and unspecialized elements do not stand unqualified, the notion of a network of interacting neuronlike elements coupled with the feature detectors of the Selfridge system to produce recognitionlike behavior became a main theme of contemporary recognition theory.

We have already seen how this approach influenced the work of McClelland and Rumelhart (1986) and Papp and his colleagues (1982). Though there were many intervening steps, a review of the most recent form-recognition models reflects the fact that this basic idea of analysis-into-features is still the predominant premise of form-recognition theory.

For example, one of the most interesting recognition theories of recent years (Bennett & Hoffman, 1985b; Hoffman & Richards, 1984) explicitly bases its "decomposition-into-parts" approach on the premises that we: (a) "must recognize an object from only partial information"; (b) that "decomposing such objects into appropriate parts, thereby decoupling configuration from other aspects of their shapes, can make easier their recognition"; and (c) that "a classification or description of parts . . . is likely to be simpler than a classification of arbitrary shapes" (Bennett & Hoffman, 1985b). Arguments such as these, however, do not necessarily reflect the biological reality of the human visual system; they read very much like a recipe for the simplest possible computer-vision system. The work of Hoffman, Richards, and Bennett is extraordinarily sophisticated in a mathematical and a philosophical sense. One wonders, however, how relevant it is to psychophysical reality.

There are many other examples of feature-oriented perceptual theories, of course. Many are straightforward applications of the pattern-recognition theories that were summarized from Watanabe's taxonomy discussed earlier in this chapter. However, there are also many others that are intended to be specific models of psychological processes. We have already mentioned some of the most notable of these, including that of McClelland and Rumelhart (1981) and Rumelhart and McClelland (1982). Others include the hypotheses governing the experiments of Geyer and DeWald (1973) and Biederman's (1987) work.

Some recent developments, however, do seem to be steps in the direction I am advocating; that is, toward an increased emphasis on the global aspects of the form in the recognition process. Kahn and Foster (1981) and Foster and Kahn (1985) have proposed a scheme in which the spatial relations among a constellation of dots are used to explain discrimination performance in experiments in which observers are asked to assert whether two dot patterns are the same or different. Individual dots are categorized in terms of their spatial relations to all other dots of the constellation. Patterns are, according to this theory, represented in the visual system not by specific features but, rather, by neuromathematical-like expressions describing the spatial relationships among the systems of dots. Although this model is certainly incomplete and was developed in the context of a discrimination-type model, it is a step forward from the naive feature-oriented model so prevalent in today's literature. It is also, if I may note, very similar in principle to my own autocorrelation theory (Uttal, 1975), which also deals with multiple and global interdot relationships.

Foster (1984) has gone on in an excellent review of the form-perception problem to note some of the other higher order global relationships that may be important other than the simple spatial relationships of the individual dots. For example, symmetry and the orientation between an object-based frame of reference and some independent frame of reference also may be salient aspects of global form perception. As an example, Foster points out, the orientation of a letter or a face is extremely important in its recognition by the human observer.[6]

Modern theories that are specifically oriented towards the global organization of the stimulus-form are less frequently published these days than are feature theories for the reasons I have already mentioned. Others that tend in that direction, however, include Lockhead's (1970) work on blob perception, discussed in chapter 4 and Hoffman's (1966, 1980) theory discussed in chapter 2. Others certainly will appear in the future and are eagerly awaited.

---

[6] Another aspect of this very interesting paper by Foster is his powerful critique of the spatial-frequency "channel" model of form perception. It is a must-read item for everyone interested in visual perception and the rise and fall in recent years of this particular theoretical orientation. It should also not go unmentioned that although the Fourier model of visual perception is essentially a global one, it does not serve the need for a universal global model, for the reasons identified by Foster.

6

A CRITIQUE
OF CONTEMPORARY
APPROACHES TO
FORM-PERCEPTION THEORY

Mathematics is too powerful to provide constraints on information; it models truth and drivel with equal felicity.

—Cutting, 1986, p. xi

A. INTRODUCTION

This book has been written to review and evaluate the state of the psychological sciences in the 1980s with regard to our understanding of how people see forms. I have sought to develop a minitaxonomy of the various stages of visual information processing—detection, discrimination, and recognition—that I believe represents the core of the visual-perception problem. These processes can generally be considered to be somewhat "higher level" than most of the visual processes discussed in my earlier works (Uttal, 1973b, 1978, 1981), in that they more likely than not involve neural networks for their execution that are more central and more complex than the primarily transductive, communicative, or initial encoding mechanisms previously emphasized.

Somewhere within the sequence of processes that I have discussed here there is a transition from what many of us now believe is a kind of more or less preattentive perception to a kind that is generally agreed to require effortful attention. It is my judgment based on a somewhat modest amount of evidence that this occurs at the interface between discrimination and recognition as I have specifically defined them in chapter 1.

This book, as a conscious effort toward the development of some order in what otherwise often appears to be a disorganized collection of raw empirical data and isolated microtheories, should be considered to be a continuation and culmination of the train of thought that has developed during the course of preparing this tetralogy. In this series of books I can see how my personal reductionistic approach has evolved from one stressing explanations that were patently and exclusively neurophysiological to one reflecting an equal commitment to psychological, descriptive, phenomenological, mathematical, and even philosophical interpretations. My perspective is now largely based upon the premise that perceptual processes may, in principle, be immune to a purely neuroreductionistic explanation. Furthermore, I now suspect that they may, indeed, even be beyond any reduction to either process or mechanical implementation.

The outcomes of this evolution of personal theory, admittedly, may place me perilously far from the current consensus with regard to how we believe we see forms (a consensus that is dominated by direct, unmediated, algorithmic, elementalistic, empiricistic, and both mathematical and neuroreductionistic thinking), but I do see the dim outline of an emerging change in that consensus as reflected in the contemporary literature of perceptual theory. In an increasing number of instances it seems to me that some of my colleagues are beginning to be concerned about today's zeitgeist and are expressing an awareness that most interesting perceptual processes are not instantiated in simple and automatic mechanisms. There is a new realization of the enormous complexity of human perceptual processes and of the holistic, approximate, and indirect ways in which perceptual information is processed. The story has not yet fully unfolded; there are many conceptual and technical barriers yet to be overcome, but there are a few theorists (e.g., Teller, 1984) who are also currently expressing these new points of view.

One of the disappointing developments associated with this new enlightenment, however valid it may be, is that we are now beginning to see some signs of limits or constraints on what we may hope to accomplish even in the ultimate future. These limits may be fundamental and may inhibit us from achieving some of the more or less naive goals set by cognitive, computational, and physiological psychologies in recent years. Upon reflection, the hubris that characterizes some of the goals set by students of perception for themselves is astonishing. That hubris is often compounded by a lack of awareness of the constraints imposed on theory building in this field by mathematical and logical principles that are much more directly applicable to perceptual research than many perceptual psychologists and other cognitive psychologists yet acknowledge.

In pursuing this project I have sought to step outside the system sufficiently to at least permit myself to maintain the pretense that I am not championing a vested theoretical interest or grinding a personal ax. Not having been a top-down, cognitively oriented psychologist in the past has helped me to maintain that personal illusion. From this somewhat detached position I have assumed the roles of gadfly and critic. My hope is that this book, which has turned out to be much more of a critique of the field of perceptual theory than the synoptic review I had originally intended, is neither unfair nor abrasive, but constructive and positive. I remain a true believer in this science and am convinced that even those approaches of explanation I have criticized can be either beautiful or useful, or both, in their own right. Whatever I say in this chapter about the validity of neurophysiology, Artificial Intelligence, or mathematics as models of form perception should not be misinterpreted to mean that I think these fields of endeavor should be abandoned. They have interest, utility, elegance, and beauty sufficient to stand on their own and do not require perceptual theory to be sustained. I am only concerned here with the linkages that are made between them and the *truth* about perception.

Having assumed the role of a critic, it would be unfair for me not to further acknowledge at the outset that the current state of theoretical affairs in perceptual psychology may be as good as it can possibly be given the intellectual forces acting on it—forces that come both from the nature of the material and the quality of the tools available from other closely related sciences. Some of the powerful intellectuals who have contributed to this field may be incorrect in their interpretations, from my point of view, but neither I nor anyone else could have reacted to these invalid (in my judgment) interpretations without the pioneering contributions of those colleagues and predecessors. It is their thoughts, right or wrong, that represent the foundation on which future understanding will be built. Sometimes progress is enhanced because of a mistake or misinterpretation that highlights some conceptual confusion.

My goal has been to concentrate on form perception theory in this book. I was correct that it would have been both impossible and wasteful to try to review all of the empirical evidence for all related perceptual phenomena. Theory is, first of all, why we are at work—theory in the most positive sense of integrative understanding and explanation. Theory is an important digester and summarizer of what sometimes may seem to be a tangle of trivial and irrelevant experiments. It is a truism, but a necessary one to assert, that it is only to the extent that an experiment contributes to integrative theory that it is worthwhile.

B. SOME SOURCES OF DIFFICULTY

When I began this book it was with a deep fascination with the wondrous accomplishments of perceptual theory. At the conclusion of this project I find myself much less sanguine about the state of integrative thought in this field, for several reasons, each of which can be traced to a particular source.

1. First, much of what passes for explanatory theory these days has been misdirected by the accidents of what statistical, mathematical, or computational tools are fortuitously available. In particular, there is an enormous gap between the kind of mathematical processes that are necessary to describe the logic of the human visual system and currently available formal systems. Some tools (e.g., Fourier transformations) have quite correctly gained wide acceptance as convenient nomenclatural or descriptive systems, but quite incorrectly have been ex-

tended to incorporate superfluous and interpretive pseudoreductionistic baggage that could easily be and should better have been kept separate.

2. Second, it seems to me as a result of my studies that there has been a paucity of thinking about fundamentals. What is it that we are trying to do? What do other sciences and methodologies, such as combinatorial mathematics, chaos theory, and automata theory (to highlight only three particularly salient examples), have to say about the strategies with which such goals can be approached? To assert that such matters are just "philosophical" (a word read by many as being synonymous with "frivolous") excursions misses the point that formal logic, mathematics, and epistemology have always acted and must continue to act as guides and constraints to speculation concerning the study of mental processes, just as the laws of physics have constrained what might be ill-posed efforts in applied engineering. Most practitioners of the physical arts and sciences know that it would be a wasted effort to attempt to do something (e.g., develop a perpetual-motion machine or build a faster-than-light space ship) that is formally excluded by those laws. Sometimes, however, it seems that many of my perceptual colleagues attempt to achieve goals that should have been similarly excluded by analogous constraints and fundamental principles. Sometimes this is due to the fact that they are not familiar with the caveats of mathematics or physics. Sometimes it seems that it is because they ignore these principles even though they are familiar with them. Frankly, I am at a loss to explain these logical lacunae.

There are important limits and constraints that must be attended to by perceptual theoreticians. One of the most important is the mathematical fact expressed by Stockmeyer and Chandra (1979) that "some kinds of combinatorial problems require for their solution a computer as large as the universe running for at least as long as the age of the universe" (p. 140) in spite of the fact that they are not infinite and are "solvable in principle." The germane fact for perceptual and other kinds of reductionistically oriented cognitive scientists is that such "intractable problems" include systems as simple as a checkerboard (and the rules of checkers or chess). It seems that given the intractability of this simple problem it world be well for us to consider the discrepancy between the magnitude of the connectivity of the checkerboard and that of the brain before we somewhat overambitiously attempt to analyze the cognitive functions of the brain from the same elemental level.

There are several misperceptions at work here. One is that if a computer program simulates to some degree some perceptual process, it is akin to an explanation of that process. In fact, such a simulation is virtually always at the level of the molar *process* or *function* of the simulated system; it is an extrapolation of the most fundamental tenet of analog theory that the instantiated mechanism by which a given algorithm works can often be completely different from the mechanism by which the brain works, and yet both may be explained by the same formulae. For another, consider the relationship between the measurement of pressure in a container and the properties of the ensemble of the gaseous molecules within that container. The overall measure—pressure—although directly related to the concatenation of the microscopic details of molecular position and dynamics tells us nothing about the behavior of the molecules. There is no way to go backwards from the global to the locally discrete. Yet, reductionistically oriented psychologists quite commonly assert that we can adduce something about the behavior of individual neurons from the molar phenomenology of the perceiver. On the other side of the coin, although it is possible in principle, it is in practice very difficult to go from the discrete to the global even when the number of elements is not very large. A bit of thinking about fundamentals seems to be in order here.

Considering the number of neurons, the combinatorics of the human brain become formidable indeed. Although there is no universally agreed measure of complexity, one can get a feeling for the magnitude of the problem by appreciating that there are something like 10^{10} (or, as some would assert, 10^{13} if all of-the-very small cells of the cerebellum are counted) neurons and that each neuron may be connected to as many as 10^3 other neurons. Considering that comparably huge numbers of cerebral neurons may be involved in even the most simple percept, thought, or cognition, but without the regularity that permitted some early stabs at network simulations (e.g., in the retina or cerebellum), this is all too likely to be an intractable problem in the way identified by Stockmeyer and Chandra (1979). This is some checkerboard, indeed!

The perceptual theorizer is often misled by an uncritical acceptance of the degree of accomplishment of simple network simulations of some perceptual process. In fact, no network model has ever produced behavior of the complexity of the simplest organism with, perhaps, only one area of exception—those situations in which the outcome is due to the function of highly repetitive, almost quasi-crystalline kinds of structures such as has occurred in the modeling of the Mach band by lateral inhibitory interactions in the retina and some interesting analyses of the equally highly regular cerebellar network. But the irregular network of even a small portion of the central nervous system of a vertebrate has never been analyzed, much less simulated in a computer program. Models that purport to do so are often very simple networks of a few cells that analogize simple forms of molar behavior. Thus, simple networks of a few neurons (such as those found in invertebrate nervous systems) can be used to produce behavior that is comparable to that produced by a much more complicated vertebrate organism. Here, too, there is ample opportunity for a fallacious leap from the minimal model to the full-blown network of the more complicated brain because of analogous behavior, when, in fact, the actual processes and mechanisms in model and organism are probably totally different.

3. A third cause of my concern about the state of integrative thought in the field of perceptual theory is that perceptual psychologists seem to be all too easily attracted to distinguished accomplishments in other sciences as putative models even when those data are demonstrably invalid in the context of cognition and

mental processes. It is an oft-told aphorism that experimental psychologists really want to be physicists. To the extent that this means that they should introduce quantitative procedures and precise measurements into well-controlled experiments, this is all to the good. To the extent that they assume that the same kind of simple, monodimensional, functional relationships that characterize the study of physical entities are characteristic of what is intrinsically a multidimensional perceptual universe, this is probably a mistake.

Many other psychologists seem to have an inexorable desire to be neurophysiologists and to study neurons rather than mental phenomena. Although the study of individual neurons is exciting in its own right and has proven to be a seductive heuristic for perceptual theory, it is important to appreciate that the outstanding intellectual achievements that have resulted from the invention of the microelectrode by Ling and Gerard (1949) may be totally irrelevant to perception or cognition. Most of what we have learned from this powerful tool deals with the metabolism and function of *individual* neurons. We also have a good idea of the function of isolated synaptic junctions between pairs of neurons, but we have very limited knowledge of the nature of the realistically complicated networks into which they are connected. Nevertheless, this missing information is the only kind that is really relevant to developing a sound neuroreductionistic theory of perceptual processes. It seems far more likely that perception is the outcome of the *interaction* of myriad neurons and not the *action* of a single cell. In spite of this clash between levels of discourse and a substantial amount of data to the contrary, single-cell hypotheses purporting to explain perceptual processes still hold wide sway among perceptual theorists.

Similarly, many psychologists seem to want to be computer experts in contemporary science. Although the computer is the closest analog to the brain our technology has yet produced, these two distinctly different kinds of information processors are almost certainly organized internally in accord with fundamentally different principles and operate according to totally different rules and logics. Nevertheless, the computer metaphor of perceptual processes is also widely accepted, particularly among cognitive psychologists with what seems to be a minimum of critical examination of the fundamental issues raised and without careful attention to the formal rules that constrain achievement of their often ill-defined goals. In retrospect, it seems that we have been all too willing to let the conveniences of the computer model distract us from the principles of perceptual organization that are clearly expressed in observed phenomenology.

4. Another concern I have is that perceptual psychologists are all too prone to inadequately define the entities and concepts that they study. We all acknowledge how intrinsically difficult it is to define mental terms; even such basic operational terms as *detection* or *discrimination* are used in a variety of different and often conflicting ways in various experimental reports. For example, we have seen in chapter 5 how the word *discrimination* (in the context of visual search) is often used to describe what is clearly a recognition process. In other instances

discrimination has been used to define the task in what clearly seem to be detection experiments. The lack of precise operational definitions of many of the most fundamental ideas of perceptual psychology often leads to a situation in which contradictory findings are ignored or false controversies engendered.

A further definitional difficulty is often produced when the same word is used to denote two quite different processes that share some superficial functional similarities. Is, for example, the dishabituation of the response to a touch to the mantle observed in the Aplysia a reflection of the same kind of neural mechanism as that underlying human adaptation to seeing the same movie three or four times? Are we using words that are merely metaphors or analogs of each other to incorrectly identify distinctly different structural entities as homologs of each other?

5. Perceptual theorists also tend to both ignore the first-order demonstrations that should set the context and limit the data base to which they apply their models. In a previous chapter I discussed the role of demonstrations and how important they are to establishing the basic premises (e.g. , recognition is locally or globally precedent) of the intellectual domain of perceptual theory even when they are not sufficient by themselves to authenticate a perceptual theory (see following). All too often the message being broadcast by these important pieces of first-order data is ignored. It seems to me, for example, that many of these demonstrations, if not most, argue that we should pursue a global, interpretive theoretical approach. To the contrary, however, much of contemporary perceptual theory seems to be more influenced by the available computational technology than by these phenomena in its initial choice of the strategy by means of which a theoretical attack will be made. Not unexpectedly, artificial controversies sometime occur between theories that are based on what appear to be totally different premises concerning the nature of psychobiological reality. But even worse, theoretical traditions sometimes tend to perpetuate themselves and to be reinforced by analogies and metaphors even though they are not speaking to the true mechanisms by means of which perceptual processes are carried out.

6. Further, psychologists, particularly those involved in the development of theories of vision, have often not heeded the empirical facts of modern cognitive psychology. They still tend to assume that passive and automatic processes account for most perceptual phenomena when, in fact, there is an emerging feeling that perception is far more a matter of interpretation and active reconstruction than of "hard-wired," automatic, and algorithmic calculations. Bruce Bridgeman (1987) summed it up well in the introduction to a recent book review when he asserted: "A specter is haunting neuroscience. It is the specter of cognition, of higher level influences that can no longer be ignored" (p. 373). Bridgeman asserts that this is "motivating systematic attempts at interaction between neurobiologists and cognitive psychologists." But, there is another possibility, namely that active, cognitive processes can not be modeled by simulations of neural networks for the reasons I have considered earlier and will summarize later in this chapter. Perhaps the message of modern cognitive psychology's empirical research

program—that perception is far more complicated than it previously seemed, and higher level effects penetrate down far lower than we had thought—is also being ignored.

7. Another cause for concern is that very grand perceptual theories are often based on astonishingly slight amounts of data: A single type of experimental result or even the outcome of a single experiment or demonstration has often been used to justify the most sweeping generalizations concerning how people see forms. Given the very low level of validity testing, virtually any microtheory can be supported simply because there is always some microscopic phenomena that can be found that can be made to appear to be relevant. However, because of the enormous variability of human perceptual and cognitive skills, it is often the case that vastly different conclusions can emerge from what are thought to be nearly identical experiments. Fit with a single experimental datum should not be allowed to validate any theory. It is easy to find a formula to describe individual phenomena, but theories of worth should describe broad classes of data.

I have criticized the Artificial Intelligence movement for developing programs that are not generalizable and thus cannot be considered to be intelligent in the sense applied to organic reasoning. But psychologists should be aware that many of our theories also do not generalize beyond the immediate empirical environment in which they were created. Those that do not are terribly vulnerable to repudiation.

8. Further, there is a desperate shortage of mathematical techniques and algorithms that are appropriate for the study of complex, interacting systems in which the global structure or arrangement of parts is more important than the nature of the local features. Perceptual and other kinds of cognitive psychology are very much in need of something that can play a role analogous to that played by the noneuclidean mathematics of Lobachevsky and Riemann in relativistic physics. Those mathematical developments allowed physics to take its giant leap forward early in this century. We might not recognize it when it comes along, but one hopes someone will perform the essential Einsteinean task of linking a truly applicable and relevant mathematics to a truly valid theory of perceptual and other cognitive phenomena. Bennett, Hoffman, and Prakesh's (1988) *Observer Theory* is a recent attempt to provide such a mathematical foundation, but the mathematics is extremely difficult, the conceptual structure subtle and cryptic, and it may be some time before this work becomes accessible to and understandable by other perceptual theorists.

One of the most glaring lacuna in this regard must be filled by some novel mathematics that will help us to understand how the molar phenomenological properties of perception can emerge from the concatenated action of a host of discrete neurons. Though there are very few insights in the way in which this may occur, one possible line of thought has been stimulated by Hoffman's (1966, 1980) application of the Lie algebra to perception (see chapter 2). But there are also some other obvious leads that must be followed up. It is, of course, possible that there will never be a completely satisfactory mathematics (mathematics as we know it may not be adequate to model mind), but until we can establish such a dismal fact beyond a reasonable doubt it would be foolhardy to abort our efforts in that direction.

Neurobiological networks, of course, do produce intelligent behavior (any intellectual accomplishment and any cognitive process stands as an existence proof of that fundamental truth), but there is a great need for research and development of more appropriate kinds of mathematics to represent the particular kind of computational engine—the brain—with which we are concerned. The necessity for establishing this foundation of understanding of how neural networks compute and the logic they use is very great. We must not deceive ourselves, however; this task will certainly be very difficult and may be impossible. Along with this search must go a substantial effort to determine what are the limits of analysis of such problems.

9. The final source of my concern is that the very empirical data upon which we perceptionists base our theories are often embarrassingly transient. We have seen throughout this book many instances in which some observation has drifted away like a smoke ring when attempts are made at replication. I argue that this paucity of reliable data is, at the most fundamental level, a result of the multivariate complexity of most psychological functions and the adaptive power of the cognitive system rather than any deficiency of control in a given experimental design. Nevertheless, the fragility of even the data base upon which we base our theories is a signal of the extreme care that must be taken in such complex situations to guarantee data validity.

In short, because of the plasticity and adaptability of the organic mind-brain, perceptual research is a far more treacherous universe for the theoretician or empirical researcher than the much simpler worlds of basic particle or cosmological physics. Later in this concluding chapter I shall consider the widespread problem of the enormous changes in findings that can result from the slightest changes in experimental design, as well as the surprising absence of general rules able to describe reasonably broad ranges of psychological phenomena.

C. SOME THEORETICAL MISJUDGMENTS

What are the misjudgments that we have collectively made with regard to current perceptual theory as a result of these forces?

1. My discussion of major misjudgments begins with the fact that there has been much too great an emphasis on local-feature-oriented models of perception rather than theories accentuating the global, Gestalt, holistic attributes of stimulus-forms. In my judgment, all too many perceptual theorists have currently fallen victim to the elementalist technological zeitgeist established by neurophysiology and computer science. Although disappointing, this is not surprising, because

it is exactly comparable to the way in which theoreticians in this field have been influenced by the pneumatic, hydraulic, horological, and telephonic analogies that have sequentially characterized theories of perception and mind over the last two millennia.

In spite of this fallacious tendency toward features, a considerable body of evidence, only some of which has been surveyed in this volume, suggests that in fact we see holistically, that is, that there is a primary global precedence in human perception. We can, of course, direct our attention and scrutiny to the details of a picture, but we are as often ready to perceptually create details on the basis of some inference as to be influenced by the presence of the real physical details of the stimulus. First-order demonstrations, usually ignored but always compelling, urge us to consider the global aspects of a form, whereas one has to carefully construct an experimental situation to tease out some semblance of local precedence. In retrospect, we can now appreciate that classic Gestalt psychology set a tone that was fundamentally correct in spite of the fact that they were no better at explaining phenomena than we are today; and many well-controlled contemporary experimental studies also suggest a global precedence in our perception of the world around us. We have not listened to these messages.

2. Further, there has been much too much emphasis on theories that are essentially empiricist rather than rationalist. We tend to develop models of recognition in particular, that depend upon a passive transformation of the geometry of the stimulus-form by algorithms that are supposed to be directly sensitive to the details of the local geometry of the stimulus. In fact, it seems far more likely that the level of cognitive penetrability of perceptual processes is far greater than is generally accepted today within the empiricist tradition. What I am suggesting here is that, in psychophysical reality, there is a much more adaptive and interpretive processing of the symbolic content of the coded stimulus information transmitted along the peripheral sensory pathways than is generally appreciated. These codes, the media for the communicated information, are not the essential input for some kind of passive processing, but rather are only cues and hints that are used by more complex and higher level (i.e., more central) systems that very quickly throw out the specifics of the stimulus geometry. The meaningful messages—the relationships and salient relevancies—conveyed by those ''media''—the neural signals and codes—are then processed in what can best be called a symbolic manner that has little to do with the physics or geometry of the stimulus or the dimensions of the neural codes by which the information was transmitted to the central nervous system.

A corollary of this misinterpretation of perceptual reality, in which a valid rationalism has been supplanted by a superficially easy but spurious empiricism, is evidenced in the many models (of what are almost certainly very complicated, high-level perceptual processes) that are erroneously based on known peripheral neural mechanisms. This tendency to descend to the periphery for explanations is a miscalculation of the same order as the tendency toward deterministic, passive-process models—in other words, those that I have classified as empiricistic. At some later time, I am convinced that we shall come to agree that more symbolically representative and computationally active processes—those that I have classified as rationalistic—are actually at work here.

In short, there is an ubiquitous fuzziness in the selection of the point of demarcation between the strictly deterministic, passive, and preattentive processes of the peripheral nervous system, on the one hand, and the active, symbol-processing, attentive visual processes on the other. It appears that cognitive penetration can be discerned in recognition behavior but much less so in the lower levels of visual processing. My own research on the perception of dotted, stereoscopic forms, as well as many conversations with others who also work with stereoscopic stimuli, suggest to me that the cognitive penetration of which I speak is especially salient in studies involving actual three-dimensional stimuli or equivalent virtual objects inferred from two-dimensional invariances.

3. Another misjudgment has been a profound unwillingness to accept the seemingly obvious fact that perceptual processes are immensely more complex in terms of the numbers of involved variables, neurons, mechanisms, and processes than hitherto believed. A corollary of this misunderstanding is the general lack of appreciation of how sensitive most perceptual data are to relatively trivial changes in experimental design. To put it most directly, we have neither appreciated how complex even the simplest appearing perceptual process actually is nor how adaptive the human is.

4. For another misjudgment, we perceptionists exhibit a bizarre tendency to become involved in controversies between nonexclusive alternatives or dichotomies that actually represent only the end points of a continuum. As is typical of all of the sciences, usually both extreme points of view have some support and eventually both are reconciled in terms of some compromise theory.

5. And another: The descriptive powers of mathematical models are often not distinguished from the many alternative physiological or physical instantiations that can be modeled by any single one of those formularizations. The possibility of analogous processes, describable with a common mathematics but implemented by totally nonhomologous mechanisms, is all too often ignored in perceptual theory.

6. Further, we tend not to be appreciative of the constraints and limits imposed upon the analysis of internal structure by behavioral methods. Moore's (1956) second theorem, the "black-box" limit from engineering, and simple combinatorics all argue that in principle some of the goals of perceptual theorists, particularly those of the "cognitive" persuasion, in which attempts are made to determine the inner mechanisms or processes underlying some observed or inferred mental states, are spurious and overly ambitious.

It is worthwhile to restate Moore's (1956) theorem, which is so central to this argument: "Given any machine S and any multiple experiment performed on S, there exist other machines experimentally distinguishable from S for which the original experiments would have had the same outcome'' (p. 140). In other words, no experimental tests of a completely unknown and closed automaton can by themselves ever distinguish between two alternative hypotheses that both adequately predict or explain the internal workings of the machine.

There are, indisputably, many ways in which to challenge the relevancy of Moore's theorem to perceptual science: Is the brain an automaton in the strict sense of the term? Are there other ways to restrict the number of alternatives and thus to converge on a valid understanding of inner mechanisms? Is the theorem even true? However, in the absence of proven alternatives and equally formal disproofs, it seems appropriate to accept this proof and to acknowledge the fact that there may be, *in principle*, limits on how far we can go in searching for a structural explanation or analysis of the kind of closed and complex system exemplified by the human mind-brain.

To make this point clear, let me suggest that although it is very easy to specify that $2 + 2 = 4$, it is impossible, given only the outcome of some such calculation (e.g., 4) to establish what the algorithm or process was that led to that particular number. It might have been $5 - 1$, $3 + 1$, 2^2, or any of an infinite number of computational pathways leading to 4. Even though it is possible to eliminate certain hypotheses, especially in a simple numeric system such as the one exemplified here, there will always be a very large number, perhaps an infinite number of possible alternatives remaining.

A closely related argument expressing the difficulty of understanding complex systems even when they are open to internal examination has been made by Crutchfield, Farmer, Packard, and Shaw (1986) in their important and clear discussion of chaos theory—a significant new development in mathematics. These authors point out that seemingly random behavior can be generated by the concatenation of very simple deterministic systems.[1] The apparent "chaos" of a plume of smoke, for example, unanalyzable back to its origins, results from the amplification of small uncertainties by even very simple interactions in systems of many constituent components and repeated processing steps.

If one interprets random states as being, by definition, irreducible to regular, periodic, or lawful forcing functions, then the implication of this new development is that even though simple rules and processes may be involved at some primitive elemental level, it may be impossible to go backwards from the resulting chaotic or random state (for example, the details of the neural activity of the brain underlying some mental act) to understand the steps by means of which the outcome was achieved. This is a handicap added to the difficulty of going from the answer 4 to the problem that generated that particular number. 4 is not reversible to $2 + 2$ because there are so many routes along which one can pass to get to 4. Chaos is not reversible no matter how precise our knowledge of the details

---

[1] Though Crutchfield and his colleagues assert that this is a "striking" and novel development, the same point was made by Cox and Smith (1954) over 30 years ago and was well known among some statisticians.

of the processes that led to it, because the paths have been obscured by the "magnification of small uncertainties." If both correct and applicable, this theorem essentially challenges the top-down approach of reductionist-oriented psychologists.

Similarly, the goal of realistically synthesizing complex behavior from the bottom up (by means of neural-net models) is also challenged. If concatenations of even modest numbers of real or modeled neurons quickly produce apparently chaotic behavior, we will never be able to distinguish one of those neural chaoses from another: two "random" systems of this kind would look very much alike (in that both are "random") even if they are actually performing very different perceptual functions. Thus, *brain* (read that word as "complex neural network") states would be indiscriminable, regardless of how well the mental states can be distinguished. Brain-mind associations at the network level would, therefore, be impossible.

Crutchfield and his colleagues (1986) go on to explicitly make the same point I wish to make here. According to them, chaos "implies new fundamental limits on the ability to make predictions." I assert, in addition, that chaos theory also implies new and fundamental limits on our ability to disassemble complex behavior into its neural, cellular constituents. Although these authors go on to assert that some classes of random processes may actually be opened to analysis using the mathematics of chaos theory, their argument mainly can be read as implying that there will be fundamental limits emerging from this analysis that will constrain our ability to understand the breakup of smoke, the weather, the erratics of fluid motion, or the operation of a very large number of neurons in some perceptual process. In all of these cases, the strong implication is that it is unlikely that we will ever be able to go backward or down from the concatenated outcome to the rules of the individual elements. In each of these cases, the output is so complicated that it must essentially be considered to be random—thus precluding reductionistic analysis. Although it is possible to demonstrate some global measure that may satisfactorily summarize these random states in some statistical manner (e.g., pressure, the ratio of turbulent to laminar flow, or perceptual phenomenology), reduction to the behavior of individual elements is impossible in *principle as well as in practice* according to chaos theory!

In short, the important conclusion is that where such a constraint had previously been considered to be one of simple complexity and *in practice* limits on computability, chaos theory now suggests that there may be *in principle* limits. These systems are not just complex and multivariate, they produce random—that is, intrinsically unanalyzable—behavior.

Crutchfield, Farmer, Packard, and Shaw (1986) also note that extreme numerosity of interacting components is not necessary for a chaotic situation to occur—chaos can arise out of the uncertainty that is inherent in repetitive processes of interaction among a few components as well as from a large number of components. They allude to such "simple" systems as the collision of a few billiard balls as potentially evidencing chaotic behavior in very short periods of time. The reason is that at the microscopic level, even the billiard table and balls turn out not to be a simple system—at each collision there is enormous uncertainty about the points of curvature at which the balls will collide, and as each ball travels across the table it is undergoing serial interactions each of which inserts its own microscopic portion of uncertainty into the quickly emerging chaotic behavior of the balls.

Crutchfield, Farmer, Packard, and Shaw's (1986) discussion of chaos is not just mathematical esoterica—it is directly relevant and specifically damning to the neuroreductionistic strategies and theories that I have challenged here. This relevance can be made most clear by letting them speak for themselves, as follows:

> Chaos brings a new challenge to the reductionist view that a system can be understood by breaking it down and studying each piece. This view has been prevalent in science in part because there are so many systems for which the behavior of the whole is the sum of its parts. Chaos demonstrates, however, that a system can have complicated behavior that emerges as a consequence of simple, nonlinear interaction of only a few components.
>
> The problem is becoming acute in a wide range of scientific disciplines, from describing microscopic physics to modeling macroscopic behavior of biological organisms. The ability to obtain detailed knowledge of a system's structure has undergone a tremendous advance in recent years, but the ability to integrate this knowledge has been stymied by the lack of a proper conceptual framework within which to describe qualitative behavior. *For example, even with a complete map of the nervous system of a simple organism, such as the nematode studied by Sidney Brenner of the University of Cambridge, the organism's behavior cannot be deduced.* Similarly, the hope that physics could be complete with an increasingly detailed understanding of fundamental physical forces and constituents is unfounded. *The interaction of components on one scale can lead to complex global behavior on a larger scale that in general cannot be deduced from knowledge of the individual components.* (p. 56; italics added)

The relevance of these comments also can be discerned with regard to the hierarchical model of perceptual processes (i.e., detection, discrimination, and recognition) that I have proposed in this book. Specifically, is this type of analysis of perception into a set of subprocesses appropriate? Or, are the subprocesses so entangled by the complexity of the even lesser neural mechanisms that the simplicity that seemed to have been achieved by applying the method of detail in this case is only illusory? Did we lose the "baby" when we abstracted out manipulable components from the "bath water" and segmented perception into its microgenetic subprocesses? Is some of the transitoriness and fragility of our data due to this kind of perceptual chaos? These questions are not answerable at this time, but they must be asked and seriously considered if the course of our science is to be a sound one.

7. Another misjudgment is that perceptual theorists display a terrible weakness for deifying the concepts that they originally invoked merely as useful heuristics

or metaphors with which to think about some of these terribly difficult problems or as computational analogs with which to describe them. Just as we have progressed to a point in our scientific knowledge of brain and behavior at which no one should now think that there is a homunculus in our head, neither should any reasonable student of cognition now accept the existence of any "list processor" or anything like an "expert system" between our ears. Furthermore, based on what we know about the limits of the neuroreductionistic strategy, perhaps not even the apparent successes of the simplistic, quasi-crystalline type of nerve-net models (the regularity of which is their sine qua non) should be allowed to influence our thinking about perceptual systems. The tools of the simulation trade are not a priori good theories of how the mind works, and to go backwards from even excellent imitations of real cognition to detailed, unique conclusions concerning internal structure and logic in the perceiving brain is patently absurd.

8. Finally, there is a pervasive tendency throughout our profession *not* to accept three fundamental facts concerning that which modern science has *not* yet accomplished.

a. First, we still have not the slightest inkling of how we bridge the gap from the action of discrete neurons to the molar mental processes that are indisputably the outcome of the interaction of vast networks of these same neurons. Chaos theory and simple combinatorics suggest that such a goal may not be ultimately achievable; even given that any conclusion about the state of the science in the distant future may be arguable, certainly we have not yet achieved any such bridging hypothesis or explanation inn our current psychobiological science.

b. Second, we still have virtually no information about the kind of logic and logical processes that are executed by the brain in carrying out perceptual processes at more molar levels. The best nonneural, process-oriented analogies, those proposed by modern computational-vision experts, have no better justification than some of the other more primitive metaphors proposed as verbal or statistical models by earlier cognitive psychologists. The computational models, as David Marr—the late founding father of the field—so correctly asserted, only describe and simulate the transformations that "must" be made to go from an input to an output; but they, like all mathematical models, are essentially indeterminate with regard to the particular neural mechanism by which each step in the transformation is made. To assume that we can take a pair of two-dimensional images and extract invariant information concerning depth from them is a totally reasonable behavioral description of a visual process. To assume that contour enhancement takes place somewhere in this process is a plausible hypothesis. However, to specifically assume that there is a Laplacian operator in the brain is an unwarranted extrapolation from those reasonable assumptions. The point is that even the best fitting mathematical description is not tantamount to a unique definition of internal mechanisms. There are many different sequences of processes that will lead to the same transformation between input and output.

c. Third, in this same vein, my retrospective examination of the discussions in earlier chapters of this book suggests that there is currently precious little data to vigorously support any "cognitive-type" model of internal process. Controversy, disagreement, and conflict seem to be more characteristic of what we think we know about internal processes than is consensus. This ongoing inability to achieve closure in cognitive studies may itself once again reflect the fact, as I argue, that the exposition of internal mechanisms by behavioral techniques may be *in principle* an unsolvable problem.

I must stress that it is totally inappropriate to consider any of the major theoretical transgressions in perceptual theory as the product of an "incompetent" group of perceptual scientists. This is not the case. The real source of these difficulties with contemporary theory is the terrible task that psychologists, in general, and perceptual theoreticians, in particular, have set for themselves. We are not dealing with simple, single-valued functions, but with an active, adaptive, interpreting, responding, self-modifying mechanism—the human brain—that often changes the rules of the perceptual game in midstream. How often has an experiment "failed" because the observers "played a different game" than the one the experimenter tried to define by the experimental protocol? How varied is our repertoire of illusions[2]—the common discrepancies between the message of the physical stimulus and the perceptual responses? The perceiving brain does not slavishly respond to stimuli but *acts* upon them. While the experimenter tries hard to devise a clever task to get at an underlying process, the observer in the experiment is working equally hard to devise a clever process to adapt to the needs of the task.

Thus, cognitive penetration seems to reach deep into the visual process, into processes that at first glance seem to happen almost automatically, but which, in fact, on close analysis reflect more of Helmholtz's unconscious inference than it is popular to admit these days. The "cognitive specter," to which Bridgeman alludes, does more than simply haunt the neurosciences—it demonically possesses it!

D. DO LAWS OF PERCEPTION EXIST?

The adaptability of the human visual system is so great that it is almost as if a universal rule is operative that prohibits universal rules. We might call this *the Rule of Multiple Rules: Slight changes in procedure, stimulus material, or methodology often produce dramatic changes in the rules of perception.*[3] One

---

[2] From one point of view, illusions may be thought of as making the opposite arguments. In spite of repeated demonstrations that a line is straight, or two objects are the same size, or that a spiral is standing still, we still "see" these discrepancies with physical reality. However, I believe that this reflects the prepotency of the implied meaning of the stimulus over these other objective measures. Both meaning and secondary measures are examples of cognitive penetration; one merely dominates the other.

[3] Some of the material in the following discussion of the Rule of Multiple Rules has been revised and edited from another of my works (Uttal, 1987) but is considered to be so germane to the current discussion that I have included it here in an edited and updated form.

implication of this generalization is that the perceptual system must now be thought of as operating in a highly active way on any stimulus input rather than in a highly passive and automatic manner. Such a property, along with complexity and multivariateness per se, makes prediction of experimental outcomes and generalization to other experimental situations extremely difficult.

That this generalization should emerge after a century or more of experimental work based on the hope and premise of unification and simplification is unfortunately perplexing, counterintuitive, somewhat distressing, and certainly surprising. It has been virtually axiomatic in psychophysical research that, if we are diligent in our collection of descriptions of the phenomena of vision, in the long run general principles of perception should emerge that will unify the outcomes of what often seems to be, at best, a random assortment of the results of small-scale and isolated experiments.

As successful as the proposition of ultimate generalization has been in other scientific enterprises, *the analogous hypothesis that psychophysical phenomena can also be so unified remains unproven and, astonishingly, largely untested.* Perceptual psychology currently remains a collection of small and seemingly unrelated empirical thrusts. Certainly, it is only in the rarest cases that psychophysical data obtained from different paradigms and under different conditions have even been compared. Perceptual psychophysics has long been characterized by experiments specific to a microscopically oriented theory and by theories that either deal with a narrowly defined data set at one extreme or, to the contrary, a global breadth that is so great that data are virtually irrelevant to their construction. Theories of this kind are more points of view than analyses.

The question posed now is: Is the lack of unification and the absence of truly comprehensive theoretical simplifications (i.e., generalizations), which is apparent in contemporary psychophysical science, a result of the youth of the science, or, to the contrary, does it reflect in some fundamental way the actual biological reality of perceptual processes? Though the latter alternative is anathema to both experimental and theoretical psychologists and, from some points of view, a depressing prospect, it can not be rejected out of hand. It is at least conceivable that the perceptual brain-mind operates by means of subprocesses that are more independent and noninteracting than we had anticipated or hoped. It is entirely possible that superficially similar visual processes may be mediated by quite different underlying mechanisms. There have been so few instances in which a sufficiently wide range of experimental conditions has been explored within the context of a single paradigm that there is actually little support for the antithesis—the idea that unification is, in fact, possible (regardless of how much such an outcome would have pleased us or satisfied William of Ockham or Lloyd Morgan).

A closely related idea is that all perception is entirely uncodifiable and enormously adaptive inference; a necessary consequence is that because the sensory channels are so heavily coded, the observer can never know the world with certainty. Perception, after all, exists for the survival of the organism, not for the convenience of the theorist. The concept of rigid laws or rules may be another one of those inapplicable ideas uncritically transposed from physics to psychology.

Furthermore, it must not be overlooked that there is also a possibility that the difficulty in identifying universal laws is also caused by differences in the perceptual strategies of individual observers. Evidence that individual differences are larger than we had thought even in carefully controlled and contrived experimental situations can be found in the work of Ward (1985) at even such a relatively early level of processing as that of defining whether stimulus dimensions will be integral or separable in Shepard's (1964) and Garner's (1974) sense. Intraobserver experimental designs (i.e., using the same observer, to the extent possible, for all conditions of an experiment that are to be compared) are absolutely necessary, if it turns out that in fact different rules are applied by different observers. Even such designs are not foolproof, however. Shifting relationships among stimuli and alternatively selected responses may result in strategies that vary from task to task even for the same observer.

The evidence for independence of processes, however strongly they may interact, rather than generality is prevalent in the findings of perceptual psychophysics once one begins to look for it. As one goes from one laboratory to another, or from one research problem to another, there is rarely any linkage between the various outcomes. Furthermore, as we survey the history of psychophysical research, how often we notice that the classic summary statements are clusters of almost independent rules (e.g., Korte's, 1915, laws of apparent movement; Wertheimer's, 1923, enunciation of the Gestalt Rules of Grouping; Grassman's, 1853, laws of color mixture; etc.) rather than a single unified conclusion or formula tying together the separate results of experiments carried out in different settings.

Many other psychologists have also noted the absence of universal principles in perception. Hurvich, Jameson, and Krantz (1965) have suggested that this is the case in their insightful comment: "The reader familiar with the visual literature knows that this is an area of many laws and little order" (p.101).

Ramachandran (1985) phrased it neatly when he raised the possibility that vision is characterized more as a perceptual "bag of tricks" (p. 101) than by great universal principles. Of course, in any theoretical endeavor everything looks like a "bag of tricks" early in the game before the unifying principles become evident. Nevertheless, an increasingly large number of observers of this field agree with the conjecture that a widely diverse set of mathematical models may be necessary to describe what are best viewed as a set of nearly independent visual processes. Grossberg (1983) makes the same point by listing the numerous different mathematical models that are now used to describe visual processes of which seems to be applicable to another. He also alludes to a comment by Sperling (1981) concerning the necessity of multiple formal models (and thus multiple, and presumably independent, internal mechanisms).

A specific instance in which this same sort of idiosyncratic perceptual behavior is rampant has been noted by Grossberg and Mingolla (1985). Pointing out that the way texture segregation occurs depends more on the "emergent perceptual units" than on the "local features" of the stimulus, they warn that this "raises the possibility of scientific chaos." In their words:

> If every scene can define its own context-sensitive units, then perhaps object perception can only be described in terms of an unwieldy taxonomy of scenes and their unique perceptual units. One of the great accomplishments of the Gestaltists was to suggest a short list of rules for perceptual grouping that helped to organize many interesting examples. As is often the case in pioneering work, the rules were neither always obeyed nor exhaustive. No justification for the rules was given other than their evident plausibility. More seriously for practical applications, no effective computational algorithms were given to instantiate the rules. (p. 142)

It should not go unmentioned, however, that Grossberg and Mingolla provide in this article what they believe to be a step forward from the "scientific chaos" that they perceive as such a danger. Their model is based upon a set of analytic expressions that are collectively called the "Boundary Contour System Equations." In their 1985 paper, Grossberg and Mingolla do apply the model to a number of more or less well-known perceptual phenomena with a substantial amount of success. These phenomena include certain textural discriminations (Beck, Prazdny, & Rosenfeld, 1983); the neon spreading illusion (Van Tuijl, 1975); the Glass Moire patterns (Glass & Switkes, 1976); and the Cafe Wall illusion (Gregory & Heard, 1979). In doing so, they have linked several visual phenomena to a common mechanism and may have taken a step forward from the "scientific chaos" they have viewed with such alarm.

However, Grossberg and Mingolla do stray from their goal of finding universal mechanisms in a way that suggests that they are still suffering along with the rest of us from the problem of idiosyncratic rules. In analyzing Beck's data, they point to a "remarkable aspect" of perceptual grouping due to colinearity. They ask: "Why do we continue to see a series of short lines if long lines are the emergent feature that control perceptual grouping?" (p. 150). Their response to this question is to invoke at least two separate and distinct perceptual "outputs" from the boundary-contrast system; one of which is terminator sensitive and one of which is not. Both, however, influence the perceptual outcome of the stimulus. Unfortunately, this invocation of multiple mechanisms appears to me to be conceptually identical to the "idiosyncratic rules" solution to the scientific-chaos problems in visual psychology about which they and others have complained. The invocation of multiple mechanisms is identical, in principle, to permitting additional degrees of freedom in an increasingly flexible model within which a wider variety of functions can be fit.

The situation seems the same even when we are dealing with as specific and fundamental a problem as the search for a putative universal metric of visual space. How does the visual system distort or transform physical space as it views it with its "cyclopean eye"—an "eye" influenced by many monocular and dichoptic cues? Wagner (1985), in the very act of presenting a new metric for the transformations assayed by his experimental procedure, came to the conclusion: "In sum, this multiplicity of well-supported theories indicates that no single geometry can adequately describe visual space under all conditions. Instead the geometry of visual space itself appears to be a function of stimulus conditions" (p. 493). And, I might add, of procedure as well.

Haig (1985) alludes to the same limitations on the search for generalities with regard to face recognition when he notes: "Individual differences (in recognition strategy) are strong, however, and the variations are such that the uncritical application of generalized-feature-salience lists is neither useful nor appropriate" (p. 601). Haig also explains that different stimulus-faces seem to evoke different recognition strategies, thus further complicating the search for simple rules of face perception in particular and form perception in general.

It is possible that we simply do not yet perceive the grand scheme because our experiments have been too spotty and disorganized. The unfortunate conclusion is that whatever the youth of this science, the current state of theory is one that seems to support the unhappy conclusion that separation and independence of the constituent processes of perception and idiosyncratic behavior may be real and not artifacts of an inadequate experimental technology.

It should also be noted, lest one incorrectly concludes that the absence of general rules is unique to vision, that the underlying separateness of function seems also to be typical of many other cognitive processes. Indeed, in a recent report, Hammond, Hamm, and Grassia (1986) summed up the general problem in the following way:

> Doubts about the generality of results produced by psychological research have been expressed with increasing frequency since Koch (1959) observed, after a monumental review of scientific psychology in 1959, that there is 'a stubborn refusal of psychological findings to yield to empirical generalization' (pp. 729–788). Brunswik (1952, 1956), Campbell and Stanley (1966), Cronbach (1975), Epstein (1979, 1980), Einhorn and Hogarth (1981), Greenwald (1975, 1976), Hammond (1966), Meehl (1978), and Simon (1979), among others, have also called attention to this situation. Jenkins (1974), warned that 'a whole theory of an experiment can be elaborated without contributing in an important way to the science because the situation is artificial and *nonrepresentative*' [italics added] (p. 794). Tulving (1979) makes the startling observation that 'after 100 years of laboratory-based study of memory, we still do not seem to possess any concepts that the majority of workers would consider necessary or important.' (p. 3)

Hammond, Hamm, and Grassia (1986) argue that at least in the fields that they have surveyed this situation is caused not by the nature of human biology, but, rather, by the absence of an appropriate analytic methodology. They propose a technique they suggest would help to alleviate the lack of generality in studies of cognitive judgment—their field of interest. It is not possible for me to judge if their technique is suitable for the kind of perceptual separateness observed in the perceptual domain—the reader will have to refer to their work for details; here I merely raise the issue for other students of cognitive psychology to ponder.

The list of other distinguished psychologists who have made the same point includes Ulrich Neisser (1976). He also noted the absence of generality and of the limits of psychological facts to the specific experiments that originally elucidated them in the field of cognitive psychology.

In summary, a considerable body of theoretical and empirical research, therefore, does seem to currently support the argument that the perceptual system is a constellation of relatively idiosyncratic and independent information-processing engines. Furthermore, analyses of a variety of higher level cognitive approaches also suggest that narrowness, specificity, and a lack of generality characterize work in that domain.

We should make no mistake about this point: However abstract and esoteric it may seem, however remotely ''philosophical,'' the issue raised is fundamental. Have we missed the generalities (assuming they are there in some true biological sense) because of the method of detail that we must use for practical, paradigmatic reasons? Or, to the contrary, has our ''hope'' that these generalities exist blinded us to a very important, although contradictory, generality in its own right—namely, that because of the enormous adaptability of the human cognitive system (i.e., the mind), there are few perceptual generalities beyond the most global or the most trivial to be discovered concerning visual perception?

To conclude this discussion, it may be more positively hypothesized that perhaps the elusive laws and aggravating variability observed in human form perception are but other arguments for the deep cognitive penetration of our visual processes. Perhaps we will have to accommodate ourselves to the performance of a system that itself is so adaptive that it permits strategy shifts in what are ostensibly the most well-controlled experiments, and that allows wide-ranging individual differences to influence data. That system may operate, in general, more by what has classically been called *rationalistic* than by *empiricistic* principles.

E. A SUMMARY AND A PRESCRIPTION FOR THE FUTURE

In summary, my review of the data and theories of visual form perception in the preparation of this volume has left me with two very different views of the nature of psychobiological reality in this science—what the science is at present, and what it should be in the future. Clearly we are in a phase of the study of form perception that is characterized by the terms: *elementalistic*, *empiricistic*, and *reductionistic*.

Elementalistic Form Perception. There is a pervasive local-feature orientation in modern theory, perhaps due to the absence of good tools to study overall organization. This is in contrast to the demonstrations and formal data that seem to support a holistic, Gestalt, global kind of thinking emphasizing the arrangement of the parts rather than the nature of the parts.

Empiricistic Form Perception. The vast amount of contemporary theory in form perception assumes that the perceiving organism operates on the basis of passive, automatic, algorithmic interpretations of those local features by what are essentially rigid and mechanical computational engines. This is in contrast to a vast amount of phenomenal evidence that form perception is so adaptive and interpretive, and is so influenced by the meaning of the stimulus, that it would be better to classify it as rationalistic.

Reductionistic Form Perception. There is an enormous contemporary confidence that form recognition can be analyzed into the underlying constituent mechanisms and processes in the not-too-distant future. This philosophy operates at two levels. First, it is assumed that neurophysiological findings can be used as a model of form perception in spite of the arguments from chaos, automata, and combinatorial considerations that such a reductionism is, in principle, not to be realized. Second, it is also assumed that perception can be reduced to units of cognitive process, which themselves may or may not be reducible to neurophysiological terms. Such a conviction, however, also flies in the face of the arguments that "black boxes" cannot have their internal mechanisms uniquely defined by input–output methods alone and that for combinatorial reasons, neither can the cellularly oriented neurophysiologist neurosurgeon open the "black box."

What major guidelines should direct perceptual research in the immediate and long-term future? Here are my suggestions.

1. First, it must be recognized that the many applied computer-vision and Artificial Intelligence models of human form perception, however useful they may be and however well they mimic the properties of human vision, are not necessarily valid explanations or theories of human vision. Indeed, it can be argued that some models (such as the "expert system") are a complete surrender of the hope that we can really model human mental processes. These table-lookup operations clearly do not model the way human associative thinking works, but simulate the behavior by logics and mechanisms that are beyond a doubt entirely different than those used in human cognition. To put it bluntly, "expert systems" may be the unacknowledged swan song of a dying belief—that natural intelligence can be realistically modeled on computers. It is essential that the relationship between an imitation by an analogy and the elucidation of a homologous logical mechanism must be clarified and understood. Even though we can admire and respect the practical and useful accomplishments of this field of engineering application and development (i.e., AI), we must rid ourselves of any misconception that such

engineering tools are any more likely than any other type of model to be valid theories of human perception.

Computational modeling of visual processes represents a special case and is an especially seductive quasi-theory, but it must also fall victim to this same criticism in the final analysis. Computational models are designed to simulate the transformations that *must* be executed to go from the informational state defined by the stimulus input to the state described by the perceptual phenomenology. As such, they are also process analogs and may plausibly invoke any useful (and available) mathematical or computational process to accomplish the transformation. Although this is an extremely useful approach to understanding some of the transforming steps, it does nothing to tell us which of the many possible alternative machanisms or logics within the visual system is the one that actually carries out these transformations. Indeed, the steps need not even be computationally defined in the sense demanded by Marr and his collaborators. The human brain may use approximate processes quite unlike the Marrian algorithms. These approximations may depend upon linkages of meaning and global organization rather than upon numerical or algebraic transformations of local attributes. These processes (or combinations of processes) may produce solutions to perceptual tasks that are totally adequate, even though not satisfying the criteria of the computational theorists as a good model. In short, computational modeling is also subject to the limits imposed by the Moore theorem and the fundamental indeterminacy of mathematical descriptions or input–out analysis with regard to internal structure.

2. My second proposed guideline requires acknowledgment that human visual perception is mainly holistic in its operation. The Gestalt psychologists understood and correctly taught this principle, but their wisdom was not influential because the computational and mathematical technology that was needed to pursue the holistic strategy was not then and is not now, for all practical purposes, available. We have an enormous obligation to convince mathematicians to develop techniques better suited to studying arrangement than parts. A major effort is necessary to develop the appropriate mathematics in order that some future equivalent of a noneuclidean mathematics can be utilized by some future equivalent of an Einstein to make the much-needed breakthrough in visual theory, so that our science can enjoy the same kind of growth in understanding. This breakthrough may not be in the form of general principles, but perhaps a softer kind of mathematics, able to handle different kinds of relationships beyond added to, subtracted from, and multiplied or divided by.

3. Next, we must determine what limits apply to the goals of visual theory buidling. There is an urgent need for additional efforts to determine what constraints are operating on this science so that we can avoid a naive and enormous waste of impossible theory-building energy. That there should be limits is in no sense a condemnation of perceptual psychologists or psychology any more than acceptance of the limits on perpetual motion or speed of light are of physics. It is clear, however, that perceptual science can be correctly and justifiably criti-

cized for not paying sufficient attention to the fundamentals before going off ill-prepared and overconfident into the heady world of neurophysiological or cognitive process reductionism. I am convinced that a few more skeptical combinatorial, automata, or chaos theorists interested in the problems raised by perceptual psychology would do more for the future progress of our science than an army of "true believers" in the ultimate solvability of all our problems.

4. Another guideline stresses that the empirical psychophysical approach, in which the phenomena are sought, discovered, and described, must be the center-piece of any new development in this science. This empirical effort, however, should be redirected to emphasize the global or holistic properties of stimuli rather than the local ones currently in vogue. This is the most effective means of divert-ing the zeitgeist from what it is to what it should be.

5. Further, we must develop mathematical models that concentrate on quan-tifying, formalizing, and describing reported perceptual phenomena. But not just any models: It is mandatory that there be a conscious effort to develop techni-ques that emphasize the global and organizational attributes of a stimulus-form. It is also mandatory that we understand the intrinsically nonreductive nature of mathematics in this kind of theory building.

6. Reluctantly, given my personal scientific background, I think that we are going to have to abandon the idea that perceptual processes can be reduced to neurophysiological terms. This romantic notion, this will-of-the-wisp, this dream, is almost certainly unobtainable in principle as well as in practice if combinatorial and chaos theory do turn out to be applicable to this domain of inquiry. What we know about the metabolism and physiological functioning of individual neurons, though a distinguished intellectual and scientific accomplishment in its own right, can probably never be transformed into knowledge of how they operate collectively in the enormous networks of the brain to produce molar behavior.

7. Equally reluctantly, I believe an appreciation must emerge that the major goal of cognitive psychology—to determine the functional processes that are car-ried out by the nervous system in form perception or, for that matter, in any other kind of mental activity—will always be equivocal. Not only have the data been inconsistent, but so too have been the conclusions drawn. These outcomes reflect the enormous adaptability of the perceiver on the one hand, and the fundamental indeterminateness of any theory of the processes going on within what is, for any conceivable future, a closed system.

8. We will also have to come to appreciate that the study of perception, as all of the other cognitive processes, is an information-processing science, and not an energy- or matter-processing one. The nature of internal codes and represen-tations, therefore, is far more arbitrary and complex, and the laws describing operations are necessarily going to appear to be far less rigid than those emerg-ing from the study of simple physical systems. Indeed, there is even a question whether or not the general concept that "laws" exist that are operative in the energy/matter dominated fields of science may be transferable to this much more

multivariate domain of perceptual processes. I argue that stimuli do not lead inexorably to responses by simple switching circuitlike behavior. Rather, it seems that there is a rational, meaningful, adaptive, utilitarian, and active construction of percepts and responses by mechanisms that depend more upon the meaning of a message than its temporal or spatial geometry. In the perceptual world, information, unlike matter or energy in the physical world, can actually be created and destroyed.

9. We are going to have to accept the reality of mental processes, and the fact that these processes are the result of ultra-complex neurophysiological mechanisms. The basic principle of psychobiological monism asserts that there is nothing supernatural, extranatural, or even separate at work in mental activity—it is nothing more or less than one of the processes of neural activity. But we do have to appreciate that complexity and numerosity themselves can exert influences that come perilously close to producing exactly the same kind of mysteries that would appear if there were unnatural forces at work. Thus, we must at once reaffirm our commitment to psychobiological monism (without which any scientific study of the mind would certainly perish) and at the same time acknowledge that the gap between the two levels of discourse—neuronal network state and mental phenomenon—may never be crossed. This requires an epistemological or methodological behaviorism in practice and a metaphysical neuroreductionism in principle. The intrapersonal privacy of perception may also require some compromises in that it, too, forces us to simultaneously function as behaviorists and introspective mentalists. Nevertheless, we must accept the facts that mind, in general, and perceptual experience, in particular, exist, that they are unobservable directly, and that they can at best only be inferred from behavioral responses by observers. The interpersonal privacy of a percept may be as much a barrier to analysis as is the combinatorial limit or the "black-box" constraint.

10. Finally, we are going to have accept the primacy of the phenomena in any controversy between different points of view or theories in perceptual science. That is, the final arbiter of any explanatory disagreement or controversy must be the reported nature of the perceptual experience. Neurophysiology, mathematics, parsimony, and even some kind of simplistic plausibility are all secondary and incomplete criteria for resolving such disputes. The perceptual experience is the final outcome of a concatenation of processes and is complete in the sense that it reflects all of the relevant previous steps. Anything—idea, theory, formal model, or verbal explanation—that is in conflict with the perceptual phenomenon, in principle, requires modification or rejection. This does not mean that the percept can define everything or even indicate to us what the underlying processing steps were, but rather that in those cases where a conflict between observation and explanation does occur, the former must be definitive. At a qualitative level the perceptual phenomenon is also a good source of heuristics for theory building in this science simply because it is the stuff of this science: Perceptual psychologists are primarily in business to describe and explain the psychobiological reality we

call *perceptual experience*, not to exercise computers or to speculate about uses for the increasingly large number of anatomically or physiologically specialized neurons that are appearing at the tips of our microelectrodes.

In short, what I am proposing is a *mathematically descriptive, nonreductionistic, holistic, rationalistic, mentalistic, neobehaviorism* that is guided more by the relevant phenomena than by available analytic tools—a neobehaviorism ambitious to solve the classic problems of perceptual psychology, but modest in avoiding recourse to strategies that are patently beyond the limits of this or any other science. All too much of our effort has been spent on unattainable goals in the past few decades. I believe such a strategy would be a step toward a realistic and mature scientific approach to understanding how people see forms.

REFERENCES

Abadi, R. V. (1976). Induction masking—a study of some inhibitory interactions during dichoptic viewing. *Vision Research, 16*, 269–275.

Abelson, R. P. (1973). The structure of belief systems. In R. C. Schank & K. M. Colby (Eds.), *Computer models of thought and language.* San Francisco: Freeman.

Abu-Mostafa, Y. S., & Psaltis, D. (1987). Optical neural computers. *Scientific American, 256*, 88–95.

Adelson, E. H., & Bergen, J. R. (1984). Motion channels based on spatiotemporal energy. *Investigative Ophthalmological Visual Science Supplement, 25*, 14.

Aiba, T. S., & Granger, G. W. (1983). Colour and position processing mechanisms in human vision. *Hokkaido Behavioral Science Report*, Series P, No. 12.

Alpern, M. (1953). Metacontrast. *Journal of the Optical Society of America, 43*, 648–657.

Anderson, J. R. (1978). Arguments concerning representations for mental imagery. *Psychological Review, 85*, 249–277.

Andreassi, J. L., Mayzner, M. S., Beyda, D., & Waxman, J. (1970). Sequential blanking: A U-shaped function. *Psychonomic Science, 18*, 319–321.

Andrews, H. C. (1970). *Computer Techniques in Image Processing.* New York: Academic Press.

Andrews, H. C., & Hunt, B. R. (1977). *Digital image restoration.* Englewood Cliffs, NJ: Prentice-Hall.

Appleman, J. B., & Mayzner, M. S. (1982). Application of geometric models to letter recognition: Distance and density. *Journal of Experimental Psychology: General, 111*, 60–100.

Arbib, M. A. (1975). Parallelism, slides, schema, and frames. In M. A. Arbib (Ed.), *Two papers on schema and frames* (COINS Technical Report 75C-9). Amherst, MA: Department of Computer and Information Sciences, University of Massachusetts.

Armstrong, D. M. (1960). *Berkeley's theory of vision.* Melbourne: Melbourne University Press.

Arnheim, R. (1974). *Art and visual perception: A psychology of the creative eye, the new version.* Irvine: University of California Press.

Attneave, F. (1950). Dimensions of similarity. *American Journal of Psychology, 3*, 516–556.

Attneave, F., & Arnoult, M. D. (1956). The quantitative study of shape and pattern perception. *Psychological Bulletin, 53*, 452–471.

Auslander, L., & Mackenzie, R. E. (1963). *Introduction to differentiable manifolds.* New York: McGraw-Hill.

Bachmann, T. (1980). Genesis of subjective image: *Acta et Commentatione. Universitat Tancuensis #522 Problems of Cognitive Psychology*. 102–126 Tartu Estonia, USSR.

Bachmann, T., & Allik, J. (1976). Integration and interruption in the masking of form by form. *Perception*, 5, 79–97

Bamber, D.(1969). Reaction times and error rates for "same"–"different" judgments of multidimensional stimuli. *Perception and Psychophysics*, 6, 169–174.

Banks, W. P., Bodinger, D., & Illige, M. (1974). Visual detection accuracy and target noise proximity. *Bulletin of the Psychonomic Society*, 2, 411–414.

Banks, W. P., & Prinzmetal, W. (1976). Configuration of effects in visual information processing. *Perception and Psychophysics*, 19, 361–367.

Barlow, H. B. (1972). Single units and sensation: A neuron doctrine for perceptual psychology. *Perception*, 1, 371–394.

Barlow, H. B. (1978). The efficiency of detecting changes of density in random dot patterns. *Vision Research*, 18, 637–650.

Barlow, H. B. (1982). The past, present and future of feature detectors. In S. Levin (Ed.), Lecture notes in biomathematics, Vol. 44 of Duane G. Albrecht (Ed.), *Recognition of pattern and form*. Berlin: Springer-Verlag.

Barlow, H. B., & Levick, W. R. (1965). The mechanism of directionality selective units in the rabbit's retina. *Journal of Physiology*, 178, 477–504.

Barlow, H. B., & Mollon, J. D. (1982). *The senses*. Cambridge: Cambridge University Press.

Barlow, H. B., & Reeves, B. C. (1979). The versatility and absolute efficiency of detecting mirror symmetry in random dot displays. *Vision Research*, 19, 783–793.

Baron, J. (1978). The word-superiority effect: Perceptual learning from reading. In W. K. Estes (Ed.), *Handbook of learning and cognitive processes*. (Vol. VI). Hillsdale, NJ: Lawrence Erlbaum Associates.

Beck, J. (1966). Perceptual grouping produced by change in orientation and shape. *Science*, 154, 538–540.

Beck, J. (1972). *Surface color perception*. Ithaca, NY: Cornell University Press, 1972.

Beck, J. (1982). Textural segmentation. In J. Beck (Ed.), *Organization and representation in perception* (pp. 285–317). Hillsdale, NJ: Lawrence Erlbaum Associates.

Beck, J. (1983). Textural segmentation, second-order statistics, and textural elements. *Biological Cybernetics*, 48, 125–130.

Beck, J., Prazdny, K., & Rosenfeld, A. (1983). A theory of textural segmentation. In J. Beck, B. Hope, & A. Rosenfeld (Eds.), *Human and machine vision*. New York: Academic Press.

Beller, H. K. (1970). Parallel and serial stages in matching. *Journal of Experimental Psychology*, 84, 213–219.

Bennett, B. M., & Hoffman, D. D. (1985a). The computation of structure from fixed axis motion: Nonrigid structures. *Biological Cybernetics*, 51, 293–300.

Bennett, B. M., & Hoffman, D. D. (1985b). Shape decompositions for visual shape recognition: The role of transversality. In W. A. Richards (Ed.), *Image understanding: 1985*. Norwood, NJ: Ablex.

Bennett, B. M., Hoffman, D. D., & Prakash, C. (1988). *Observer mechanics*.

Bergen, J. R., & Julesz, B. (1983). Parallel versus serial processing in rapid pattern discrimination. *Nature*, 303, 696–698.

Berkeley, G. (1954). *An essay towards a new theory of vision and other writings*. New York: Dutton. (Originally published as *An Essay Towards a New Theory of Vision*, 1709)

Bernstein, I. H., Proctor, R. W., & Schurman, D. L. (1973). Metacontrast and brightness discrimination. *Perception and Psychophysics*, 14, 293–297.

Biederman, I. (1987). Recognition-by-components: A theory of human image understanding. *Psychological Review*, 94, 115–147.

Bjork, E. L., & Murray, J. T. (1977). On the nature of input channels in visual processing. *Psychological Review*, 84, 472–484.

Blakemore, C., & Campbell, F. W. (1969). On the existence of neurons in the human visual system selectively sensitive to the orientation and size of retinal images. *Journal of Physiology, 203*, 237–260.

Blank, A. A. (1959). The Luneberg theory of binocular space perception. In S. Koch (Ed.), *Psychology: A study of a science* (Vol. 1). New York: McGraw-Hill.

Bouma, H. (1971). Visual recognition of isolated lower-case letters. *Vision Research, 11*, 459–474.

Boynton, R. M. (1972). Discrimination of homogeneous double pulses of light. In D. Jameson & L. M. Hurvich (Eds.), *Handbook of sensory physiology; Visual psychophysics* (Vol. VII/4), pp. 202–232 New York: Springer-Verlag.

Boynton, R. M., Elworth, C. L., Onley, J. W., & Klingberg, C. L. (1960). *Form discrimination as predicted by overlap and area* (Report RADC-TR: 60-158). Rome, NY Rome Air Development Center, Air Research and Development Command. Brand, J. (1971). Classification without identification in visual search. *Quarterly Journal of Experimental Psychology, 23*, 178–186.

Braunstein, M. L. (1976). *Depth perception through motion*. New York: Academic Press.

Braunstein, M. L. (1983). Contrasts between human and machine vision: Should technology recapitulate phylogeny? In J. Beck, B. Hope, & A. Rosenfeld (Eds.), *Human and machine vision*. New York: Academic Press.

Braunstein, M. L., Hoffman, D. D., Shapiro, L. R., Andersen, G. J., & Bennett, B. M. (1986). Minimum points and views for the recovery of three-dimensional structure. In *Studies in the cognitive sciences* (No. 41). Irvine, CA: School of Social Sciences, University of California.

Breitmeyer, B. G. (1984). *Visual masking: An integrative approach*. New York: Oxford University Press.

Breitmeyer, B. G., & Ganz, L. (1976). Implications of sustained and transient channels for theories of visual pattern masking, saccadic suppression, and information processing. *Psychological Review, 83*, 1–36.

Brick, D. B. (1969). Pattern recognition: The challenge, are we meeting it? In N. S. Watanabe (Ed.), *Methodologies of pattern recognition*. New York: Academic Press.

Bridgeman, B. (1971). Metacontrast and lateral inhibition. *Psychological Review, 78*, 528–539.

Bridgeman, B. (1987). Psychology and neuroscience. Review of mind and brain: Dialogs in cognitive neuroscience. *Science, 235*, 373–374.

Broadbent, D. (1977). The hidden preattentive process. *American Psychologist, 32*, 109–118.

Brown, D. R., & Owen, D. H. (1967). The metrics of visual form: methodological dyspepsia. *Psychological Bulletin, 68*, 243–259.

Bruner, J. S., & Postman, L. (1947). Perception, cognition, and behavior. *Journal of Personality, 16*, 69–77.

Bruner, J. S., & Postman, L. (1949). Perception, cognition, and behavior. *Journal of Personality, 18*, 14–31.

Brunswik, E. (1939). The conceptual focus of some psychological systems. *Journal of Unified Science*, 36–49.

Brunswik, E. (1952). The conceptual framework of psychology. In *International encyclopedia of unified science* (Vol. 1; No. 10). Chicago: University of Chicago Press.

Brunswik, E. (1955). Representative design and probabilistic theory in a functional psychology. *Psychological Review, 62*, 193–217.

Brunswik, E. (1956). *Perception and the representative design of psychological experiments* (2nd ed.). Berkeley: University of California Press.

Bunge, M. (1980). *The mind–body problem: A psychobiological approach*. Oxford: Pergamon Press.

Burgess, A. E., & Barlow, H. B. (1983). The precision of numerosity discrimination in arrays of random dots. *Vision Research, 23*, 811–820.

Burgess, A. E., Jennings, R. J., & Wagner, R. F. (1982). Statistical efficiency: A measure of human visual signal-detection performance. *Journal of Applied Photographic Engineering, 8*, 76–78.

Burgess, A. E., Wagner, R. F., Jennings, R. J., & Barlow, H. B. (1981). Efficiency of human visual signal discrimination. *Science, 214*, 93–94.

Burks, A. W. (1974, April). *Who invented the general-purpose electronic computer?* Lecture at The University of Michigan. Ann Arbor, MI.

Burks, A. W., & Burks, A. (1981). The ENIAC: First general-purpose electronic computer. *Annals of the History of Computing, 3,* 310–399.

Burks, A. W., Goldstine, H. H., & von Neumann, J. (1947). *Preliminary discussion of the logical design of an electronic computing instrument.* (Part I, Vol. I). Princeton, NJ: Institute for Advanced Study.

Caelli, T. M. (1980). Facilitive and inhibitory factors in visual texture discriminations. *Biological Cybernetics, 39,* 21–26.

Caelli, T. M. (1981a). Some psychophysical determinants of discrete Moire patterns. *Biological Cybernetics, 39,* 97–103.

Caelli, T. M. (1981b). *Visual perception theory and practice.* Oxford: Pergamon Press.

Caelli, T. M. (1982). On discriminating visual textures and images. *Perception and Psychophysics, 31,* 149–159.

Caelli, T. M. (1985). Three processing characteristics of visual texture segmentation. *Spatial Vision, 1,* 19–30.

Caelli, T. M. (1987, January). Lecture at Naval Ocean Systems Center—Hawaii Laboratory, Kailua, HI.

Caelli, T. M., & Dodwell, P. C. (1980). On the contours of apparent motions: A new perspective on visual space-time. *Biological Cybernetics, 39,* 27–35.

Caelli, T. M., & Julesz, B. (1978). On perceptual analyzers underlying visual texture discrimination: Part I. *Biological Cybernetics, 28,* 167–175.

Caelli, T. M., Julesz, B., & Gilbert, E. (1978). On perceptual analyzers underlying visual texture discrimination: Part II. *Biological Cybernetics, 29,* 201–214.

Caelli, T. M., & Yuzyk, J. (1985). What is perceived when two images are combined? *Perception, 14,* 41–48.

Campbell, D. T., & Stanley, J. (1966). *Experimental and quasi-experimental designs for research.* Chicago: Rand-McNally.

Campbell, F. W., .& Robson, J. G. (1968). An application of Fourier analysis to the visibility of gratings. *Journal of Physiology, 197,* 551–566.

Cannon, T. M., & Hunt, B. R. (1981). Image processing by computer. *Scientific American, 245,* 214–225.

Cattell, J. M. (1886). The time taken by cerebral operation. *Mind, 11,* 220–242.

Cheatham, P. G. (1952). Visual perceptual latency as a function of stimulus brightness and contour shape. *Journal of Experimental Psychology, 43,* 369–380.

Cheeseman, J., & Merikle, P. M. (1984). Priming with and without awareness. *Perception & Psychophysics, 36,* 387–395.

Cherry, C. (1957). *On human communication.* New York: The Technology Press of Massachusetts Institute of Technology and Wiley.

Chomsky, N. (1981). A naturalistic approach to language and cognition. *Cognition and Brain Theory, 4*(1), 3–22.

Coffin, S. (1978). Spatial frequency analysis of block letters does not predict experimental confusions. *Perception and Psychophysics, 23,* 69–74.

Cohen, P. R., & Feigenbaum, E. A. (1982). *The handbook of artificial intelligence* (Vol. 3). Los Altos, CA: William Kaufmann.

Cohn, P. M. (1957). *Lie groups.* London: Cambridge University Press.

Coren, S., & Girgus, J. S. (1978). *Seeing is deceiving: The psychology of visual illusions.* Hillsdale, NJ: Lawrence Erlbaum Associates.

Cormack, R., & Blake, R. (1980). Do the two eyes constitute separate visual channels? *Science, 207,* 1100–1101.

Cox, D. R., & Smith, W. L. (1954). On the superposition of renewal processes. *Biometrika, 41,* 91–99.

Crawford, B. H. (1947). Visual adaptation in relation to brief conditioning stimuli. *Proceedings of the Royal Society of London, 134,* 283–302.

Cronbach, L. J. (1975). Beyond the two disciplines of scientific psychology. *American Psychologist, 30*(2), 116–127.

Crutchfield, J. P., Farmer, J. D., Packard, N. H., & Shaw, R. S. (1986). Chaos. *Scientific American, 256*(6), 46.

Cutting, J. E. (1986). *Perception with an eye for motion.* Cambridge, MA: MIT Press.

Dalcq, A. M. (1951). *Form and modern embryology.* In L. L. Whyte (Ed.), *Aspects of form.* New York: Pellegrini & Cudahy.

Daugman, J. G. (1984). Spatial visual channels in the Fourier plane. *Vision Research, 24,* 891–910.

Davis, E. T. (1981). Allocation of attention: Uncertainty effects when monitoring one or two visual gratings of noncontinuous spatial frequencies. *Perception and Psychophysics, 29,* 618–622.

Davis, E. T., Kramer, P., & Graham, N. (1983). Uncertainty about spatial frequency, spatial position, or contrast of visual patterns. *Perception and Psychophysics, 33*(1), 20–28.

d'Espagnet, B. (1979). The quantum theory and reality. *Scientific American, 241*(5) 158–181.

DeValois, R. L., Albrecht, P. G., & Thorell, L. G. (1982). Spatial frequency selectivity of cells in macaque visual cortex. *Vision Research, 22,* 545–559.

Diener, D. (1981). On the relationship between detection and recognition. *Perception and Psychophysics, 30*(3), 237–246.

Dodwell, P. C. (1970). *Visual Pattern Recognition.* New York: Holt, Rhinehart & Winston.

Doehrman, S. (1974). The effect of visual orientation uncertainty in a simultaneous detection recognition task. *Perception & Psychophysics, 15,* 519–523.

Donders, F. C. (1868). On the speed of mental processes. (W. G. Koster, Trans). In W. G. Koster (Ed.), *Attention and performance II. Acta Psychologica,* 1969, *30,* 412–431.

Dreyfus, H. L. (1979). *What computers can't do: The limits of artificial intelligence* (rev. ed.). New York: Harper & Row.

Duda, R. O., & Hart, P. E. (1973). *Pattern classification and scene analysis.* New York: Wiley.

Duff, M. J. B. (1969). Pattern computation in pattern recognition. In S. Watanabe (Ed.), *Methodologies of Pattern Recognition* (pp. 133–140). New York: Academic Press.

Duncan, J. (1983). Category effects in visual search: A failure to replicate the "oh-zero" phenomenon. *Perception & Psychophysics, 34,* 221–232.

Earhard, B. (1980).The line in object superiority effect in perception: It depends on where you fix your eyes and what is located at the point of fixation. *Perception & Psychophysics, 28,* 9–l8.

Eccles, J. C. (1979). *The human mystery.* Berlin: Springer-Verlag.

Egeth, H., & Blecker, D. (1971). Differential effects of familiarity on judgments of sameness and difference. *Perception & Psychophysics, 9,* 321–326.

Egeth, H. E., Jonides, J., & Wall, S. (1972). Parallel processing of multi-element arrays. *Cognitive Psychology, 3,* 674–698.

Einhorn, H.J,, & Hogarth, R. M. (1981). Behavioral decision theory: Processes of judgment and choice. *Annual Review of Psychology, 32,* 53–88.

Emerson, P. L. (1979). Necker cube: Duration of preexposure of an unambiguous form. *Bulletin of the Psychonomic Society, 14,* 397–400.

Encyclopedia of philosophy (1967). New York and London: Macmillan and Collier.

Enns, J. T., & Prinzmetal, W. (1984). The role of redundancy in the object-line effect. *Perception and Psychophysics, 35,* 22–32.

Enroth–Cugell, C., & Robson, J. G. (1966). The contrast sensitivity of retinal ganglion cells of the cat. *Journal of Physiology, 187,* 517–552.

Epstein, S. (1979). The stability of behavior: I. On predicting most of the people much of the time. *Journal of Personality and Social Psychology, 37,* 1097–1126.

Epstein, S. (1980). The stability of behavior: II. Implications for psychological research. *American Psychologist, 35,* 790–806.

Eriksen, C. W. (1960). Discrimination and learning without awareness: A methodological survey and evaluation. *Psychological Review, 67,* 279–300.

Eriksen, C. W., Becker, B. B., & Hoffman, J. E. (1970). Safari to masking land: A hunt for the elusive U. *Perception and Psychophysics, 8,* 245–250.

Eriksen, C. W., & Hoffman, M. (1963). Form recognition as a function of adapting field and interval between stimulation. *Journal of Experimental Psychology, 66,* 485–499.

Eriksen, C. W., & Lappin, J. S. (1964). Luminance summation-contrast reduction as a basis for certain forward and backward masking effects. *Psychonomic Science, 1,* 313–314.

Eriksen, C. W., & Lappin, J. S. (1967). Independence in the perception of simultaneously presented forms of brief duration. *Journal of Experimental Psychology, 73,* 468–472.

Eriksen, C. W., & Marshall, P. H. (1969). Failure to replicate a reported U-shaped visual masking function. *Psychonomic Science, 15,* 195–196.

Estes, W. K. (1972). Interactions of signal and background variables in visual processing. *Perception & Psychophysics, 12,* 278–286.

Estes, W. K. (1974). Redundancy of noise elements and signals in the visual detection of letters. *Perception and Psychophysics, 16,* 53–60.

Falzett, M., & Lappin, J. S. (1983). Detection of visual forms in space and time. *Vision Research, 23,* 181–189.

Fitts, P. M., & Leonard, J. A. (1957). *Stimulus correlates of usual pattern perception: A probability approach.* Columbus: Ohio State University, Aviation Psychology Laboratory.

Fodor, J. A. (1978). Tom Swift and his procedural grandmother. *Cognition, 6,* 229–247.

Foster, D. H. (1979). Discrete internal pattern representations and visual detection of small changes in pattern shape. *Perception & Psychophysics, 26,* 459–468.

Foster, D. H. (1984). Local and global computational factors in visual pattern recognition. In P. C. Dodwell & T. Caelli (Eds.), *Figural synthesis.* Hillsdale, NJ: Lawrence Erlbaum Associates.

Foster, D. H., & Kahn, J. I. (1985). Internal representations and operations in the visual comparison of transformed patterns: Effects of pattern point-inversion, positional symmetry, and separation. *Biological Cybernetics, 51,* 305–312.

Freeman, W. J. (1981). A physiological hypothesis of perception. *Perception in Biology and Medicine, 24,* 561–592.

Freeman, W. J. (1983). The physiological basis of mental images. *Biological Psychiatry 10,* 1107–1125.

French, R. S. (1954). Pattern recognition in the presence of visual noise. *Journal of Experimental Psychology, 47,* 27–31.

Fu, K. S. (1982a). *Applications of Pattern Recognition.* Boca Raton, FL: CRC Press.

Fu, K. S. (1982b). *Syntactic pattern recognition and applications.* Englewood Cliffs, NJ: Prentice-Hall.

Fukushima, K. (1970). A feature extractor for curvilinear patterns: A design suggested by the mammalian visual system. *Kybernetik, 7,* 153–160.

Fukushima, K. (1975). Cognitron: A self-organizing multilayered neural network. *Biological Cybernetics, 20,* 121–136.

Fukushima, K., & Miyake, S. (1982). Neocognition: A new algorithm for pattern recognition tolerant of deformations and shifts in position. *Pattern Recognition, 15,* 455–469.

Furcher, C. S., Thomas, J. P., & Campbell, F. W. (1977). Detection and discrimination of simple and complex patterns at low spatial frequencies. *Vision Research, 17,* 827–836.

Ganz, L. (1966). Mechanism of the figural aftereffect. *Psychological Review, 73,* 128–150.

Gardner, E. P., & Spencer, W. A. (1972a). Sensory funneling. I.: Psychophysical observations of human subjects and responses of cutaneous mechanoreceptive afferents in the cat to patterned skin stimuli. *Journal of Neurophysiology, 35,* 925–953.

Gardner, E. P., & Spencer, W. A. (1972b). Sensory funneling. II.: Cortical neuronal representation of patterned cutaneous stimuli. *Journal of Neurophysiology, 35,* 954–977.

Gardner, G. T. (1973). Evidence for independent parallel channels in tachistoscopic perception. *Cognitive Psychology, 4,* 130–155.

Garner, W. R. (1974). *The processing of information and structure.* Hillsdale, NJ: Lawrence Erlbaum Associates.

Garner, W. R. (1978). Aspects of a stimulus: Features, dimensions, and configurations. In E. Rosch & B. B. Lloyd (Eds.), *Cognition and categorization.* Hillsdale, NJ: Lawrence Erlbaum Associates.

Garner, W. R., & Clement, D. E. (1963). Goodness of pattern and pattern uncertainty. *Journal of Verbal Hearing and Verbal Behavior, 2,* 446–452.

Garner, W. R., & Felfoldy, G. L. (1970). Integrality of stimulus dimensions in various types of information processing. *Cognitive Psychology*, *1*, 225–241.

Geiger, G., & Lettvin, J. Y. (1986). Enhancing the perception of form in peripheral vision. *Perception*, *15*, 119–130.

Geyer, L. H., & DeWald, C. G. (1973). Feature lists and confusion matrices. *Perception & Psychophysics*, *14*, 471–482.

Gibson, J. J. (1950). *The perception of the visual world*. Boston: Houghton Mifflin.

Gibson, J. J. (1966). *The senses considered as perceptual systems*. Boston: Houghton Mifflin.

Gibson, J. J. (1979). *The ecological approach to visual perception*. Boston: Houghton Mifflin.

Ginsburg, A. P. (1983). Visual form perception based on biological filtering. In L. Spillmann & B. R. Wooten (Eds.), *Sensory experience, adaptation and perception: Festschrift for Ivo Kohler*. Hillsdale, NJ: Lawrence Erlbaum Associates.

Glass, A. L., Holyoak, K. J., & Santa, J. L. (1979). *Cognition*. Reading, MA: Addison-Wesley.

Glass, L., & Switkes, E. (1976). Pattern recognition in humans: Correlations which cannot be perceived. *Perception*, *5*, 67–72.

Gleitman, H., & Jonides, J. (1976). The cost of categorization in visual search: Incomplete processing of target and field items. *Perception and Psychophysics*, *20*, 281–288.

Gleitman, H., & Jonides, J. (1978). The effect of set on categorization in visual search. *Perception and Psychophysics*, *24*, 361–368.

Goldmeier, E. (1965). Limits of visibility of bronchogenic carcinoma. *The American Review of Respiratory Diseases*, *91*(2), 232–239.

Goldmeier, E. (1972). Similarity in visually perceived forms. *Psychological Issues, 8* (Whole #29). (Originally published 1936)

Goldmeier, E. (1982). *The memory trace: Its formation and its fate*. Hillsdale, NJ: Lawrence Erlbaum Associates.

Graham, N. (1977). Visual detection of a periodic spatial stimuli by probability summation among narrow-band channels. *Vision Research*, *17*, 637–652.

Graham, N. (1980). Spatial frequency channels in human vision: Detecting edges without edge detectors. In C. S. Harris (Ed.), *Visual coding and adaptability*. Hillsdale, NJ: Lawrence Erlbaum Associates.

Graham, N., & Nachmias, J. (1971). Detection of grating patterns containing two spatial frequencies: A comparison of single channel and multichannel models. *Vision Research*, *11*, 251–259.

Graham, N., Robson, J. G., & Nachmias, J. (1978). Grating summation in fovea and periphery. *Vision Research*, *18*, 815–826.

Grassman, H. (1854). On the theory of compound colours. *Philosophical Magazine*, *7*, 254–264.

Green, D. M., & Birdsall, T. G. (1978). Detection and recognition. *Psychological Review*, *85*, 192–205.

Green, D. M., & Swets, J. A. (1966). *Signal detection theory and psychophysics*. New York: Wiley.

Greenspon, T. S., & Eriksen, C. W. (1968). Interocular nonindependence. *Perception and Psychophysics*, *3*, 93–96.

Greenwald, A. G. (1975). Significance, nonsignificance, and interpretation of an ESP experiment. *Journal of Experimental Social Psychology*, *11*, 180–191.

Greenwald, A. G. (1976). Within-subjects design: To use or not to use? *Psychological Bulletin*, *83*, 314–320.

Gregory, R. L. (1970). *The intelligent eye*. London and New York: Weidenfeld.

Gregory, R. L. (1974). Choosing a paradigm for perception. In E. C. Carterette & M. P. Friedman (Eds.), *Handbook of perception; Historical and philosophical roots of perception* (Vol. I). New York: Academic Press.

Gregory, R. L., & Heard, P. (1979). Border locking and Café Wall illusion. *Perception*, *8*, 365–380.

Grice, G. R., Canham, L., & Boroughs, J. M. (1983). Forest before trees? It depends where you look. *Perception and Psychophysics*, *33*, 121–128.

Grimson, W. E. L. (1981). *From images to surfaces: A computational study of the human early visual system*. Cambridge, MA: MIT Press.

Grimson, W. E. L. (1984). On the reconstruction of visible surfaces. In S. Ullman & W. Richards (Ed.), *Image Understanding*, Norwood, NJ: Ablex Publishing Corporation.

Grossberg, S. (1983). The quantized geometry of visual space: The coherent computation of depth, form, and lightness. *The Behavioral and Brain Sciences*, *6*, 625–692.

Grossberg, S., & Mingolla, E. (1985). Neural dynamics of perceptual groupings: Textures, boundaries, and emergent segmentations. *Perception and Psychophysics*, *38*(2), 141–171.

Haber, R. N. (1966). Nature of the effect of set on perception. *Psychological Review*, *73*, 335–351.

Haber, R. N. (1969). Repetition, visual persistence, visual noise, and information processing. In K. N. Leibovic (Ed.), *Information processing in the nervous system*. New York: Springer-Verlag.

Haig, N. D. (1985). How faces differ—A new comparative technique. *Perception*, *14*, 601–615.

Hammond, K. R. (1966). *The psychology of Egon Brunswik*. New York: Holt, Rhinehart, & Winston.

Hammond, K. R., Hamm, R. M., & Grassia, J. (1986). Generalizing over conditions by combining the multitrait multimethod matrix and the representative design of experiments. *Psychological Bulletin*, *100*(27), 257–269.

Harris, C. S. (1980). *Visual coding and adaptability*. Hillsdale, NJ: Lawrence Erlbaum Associates.

Harris, J. R., Shaw, M. L., & Altom, M. J. (1985). Serial position curves for reaction time and accuracy in visual search: Tests of a model of overlapping processing. *Perception and Psychophysics*, *38*, 178–187.

Harris, J. R., Shaw, M. L., & Bates, M. (1979). Visual search in multicharacter arrays with and without gaps. *Perception and Psychophysics*, *26*, 69–84.

Hartline, H. K., & Ratliff, F. (1957). Inhibitory interaction of receptor units in the eye of Limulus. *Journal of General Physiology*, *40*, 357–376.

Hebb, D. O. (1949). *The organization of behavior*. New York: Wiley.

Hecht, S., Shaler, S., & Pirenne, M. H. (1942). Energy, quanta, and vision. *Journal of General Physiology*, *25*, 819–840.

Helmholtz, H. von (1948). *On the sensations of tone as a physiological basis for the theory of music*. (A. J. Ellis Trans.). New York: (Originally published 1863).

Helmholtz, H. von (1968). An address delivered on Founder's Day at Berlin University, August 3, 1878. In R. M. Warren & R. P. Warren (Eds.), *Helmholtz on perception: Its physiology and development*. New York: Wiley.

Helmholtz, H. von (1968). Excerpts from Treatise on Physiological Optics (3rd ed.). In R. M. Warren & R. P. Warren (Eds.), *Helmholtz on perception; Its physiology and development*. New York: Wiley.

Helson, H. H. & Fehrer, E. (1932). The role of form in perception. *American Journal of Psychology*, *44*, 79–102.

Hernandez, L. L., & Lefton, L. A. (1977). Metacontrast as measured under a signal detection method. *Perception*, *6*, 695–702.

Hinton, G. E., & Anderson, J. A. (1981). *Parallel models of associative memory*. Hillsdale, NJ: Lawrence Erlbaum Associates.

Hobbes, T. (1665). *De Corpore*. In W. Molesworth (Ed.), *English Works of Thomas Hobbes*. Oxford: Reprinted, 1961.

Hochberg, J. E., & Peterson, M. A. (1985) *Perceptual couples as measures of the role of local cues and intention in form perception*. Unpublished manuscript.

Hochberg, J. E., & McAlister, E. (1953). A quantitative approach to figural "goodness." *Journal of Experimental Psychology*, *46*, 361–364.

Hoffman, D. D., & Bennett, B. (1985). Inferring the relative 3-D positions of two moving points. *Journal of the Optical Society of America*, *75*, 530–533.

Hoffmann, D. D., & Bennett, B. (1986). The computation of structure from fixed axis motion: Rigid Structures. *Biological Cybernetics*, *54*, 1–13.

Hoffmann, D. D., & Finchbaugh, B. (1982). The interpretation of biological motion. *Biological Cybernetics*, *42*, 197–204.

Hoffman, D. D., & Richards, W. A. (1984). Parts of recognition. *Cognition, 18,* 65–96.

Hoffman, J. (1980). Interactions between global and local levels of form. *Journal of Experimental Psychology: Human Perception & Performance, 6,* 222–234.

Hoffman, W. C. (1966). The Lie algebra of visual perception. *Journal of Mathematical Psychology, 3,* 65–98.

Hoffman, W. C. (1970). Higher visual perception as prolongation of the basic Lie transformation group. *Mathematical Biosciences, 6,* 437–471.

Hoffman, W. C. (1971). Visual illusions of angle as an application of Lie transformation groups. *Society for Industrial and Applied Mathematics, 13,* 169–184.

Hoffman, W. C. (1978). The Lie transformation group approach to visual neuropsychology. In E. L. J. Leeuwenberg & H. Buffart (Eds.), *Formal theories of visual perception.* Chichester, England: Halsted.

Hoffman, W. C. (1980). Subjective geometry and geometric psychology. *Mathematical Modeling, 1,* 349–367.

Hoffman, W. C. (1985). Some reasons why algebraic topology is important in neuropsychology: Perceptual and cognitive systems as fibration. *International Journal of Man Machine Studies, 22,* 613–650.

Hogben, J. H. (1972). *Perception of visual pattern with components distributed in time.* Unpublished doctoral dissertation, University of Western Australia.

Horn, B. K. P. (1975). Obtaining shape from shading information. In P. H. Winston (Ed.), *The psychology of computer vision.* New York: McGraw-Hill.

Horn, B. K. P. (1983). Extended gaussian images. *MIT Artificial Intelligence Laboratory Memo No. 740,* Cambridge, MA.

Hubel, D. H. (1978). Vision and the brain. *Bulletin of the American Academy of Arts and Sciences, 31,* 17–28.

Hubel, D. H., & Wiesel, T. N. (1959). Receptive fields of single neurons in the cat's striate cortex. *Journal of Physiology, 148,* 574–591.

Hubel, D. H., & Wiesel, T. N. (1962). Receptive fields, binocular interaction, and functional architecture in the cat's visual cortex. *Journal of Physiology, 160,* 106–154.

Hubel, D. H., & Wiesel, T. N. (1965). Receptive fields of and functional architecture in two nonstriate visual areas (18 and 19) of the cat. *Journal of Neurophysiology, 28,* 229–289.

Hughes, H. C. (1982). Search for the neural mechanisms essential to basic figural synthesis in the cat. In D. J. Ingle, M. A. Foodale, & R. J. W. Mansfield (Eds.), *Analysis of visual behavior.* Cambridge, MA: MIT Press.

Hughes, H. C., Layton, W. M., Baird, J. C., & Lester L. S. (1984). Global precedence in visual pattern recognition. *Perception and Psychophysics, 35,* 361–371.

Hume, D. (1941). *A treatise on human nature* (L. Selby-Bigge, Ed.). New York: Oxford University Press. (Originally published 1739)

Hume, D. (1966). *Enquiry concerning human understanding* (2nd edition; T. J. McCormack & M. W. Calkins, Eds.). LaSalle, IL: Open Court Publishing. (Originally published 1748)

Humphreys-Owens, S. P. F. (1951). Physical principle underlying inorganic form. In L. L. Whyte (Ed.), *Aspects of form.* New York: Pellegrini & Cudahy.

Hurvich, L. M., Jameson, D., & Krantz, D. H. (1965). Theoretical treatments of selected visual problems. In R. D. Luce, R. R. Bush, & E. Galanter (Eds.), *Handbook of mathematics psychology* (Vol. III). New York: Wiley.

Ingling, N. W. (1972). Categorization; A mechanism for rapid information processing. *Journal of Experimental Psychology, 94,* 239–243.

Ittleson, W. H. (1952). *The Ames demonstrations in perception.* Princeton: Princeton University Press.

James, W. (1950). *The principles of psychology.* New York: Dover. (Originally published, 1890).

Jameson, D., & Hurvich, L. M. (1972). *Handbook of sensory physiology: Visual psychophysics* (Vol. VII/4). Berlin: Springer-Verlag.

Jenkins, B. (1982). Redundancy in the perception of bilateral symmetry in dot textures. *Perception and Psychophysics*, *32*, 171–177.

Jenkins, B. (1983a). Temporal limits to the detections of correlation in transpositionally symmetric textures. *Perception and Psychophysics*, *33*, 79–84.

Jenkins, B. (1983b). Component processes in the perception of bilaterally symmetric dot textures. *Perception and Psychophysics*, *34*(5), 433–440.

Jenkins, B. (1983c). Spatial limits to the detection of transpositional symmetry in dynamic dot textures. *Journal of Experimental Psychology: Human Perception and Performance*, *9*, 258–269.

Jenkins, J. (1974). Remember that old theory of memory? Well, forget it! *American Psychologist*, *29*, 785–795.

Jonides, J., & Gleitman, H. (1972). A conceptual category search in visual search: O as letter or as digit. *Perception & Psychophysics*, *12*, 457–460.

Jonides, J., & Gleitman, H. (1976). The benefit of categorization in visual search: Target location without identification. *Perception & Psychophysics*, *20*, 289–298.

Jordan, M. I. (1986). Serial order: *A parallel distributed processing approach* (ICS Report 8604). San Diego, CA: Institute for Cognitive Science, University of California at San Diego.

Julesz, B. (1962). Visual pattern discrimination. *Institute of Radio Engineers Transactions on Information Theory*, *IT-8*, 84–92.

Julesz, B. (1971). *Foundations of cyclopean perception*. Chicago: The University of Chicago Press.

Julesz, B. (1975). Experiments in the visual perception of texture. *Scientific American*, *232*(4), 34–43.

Julesz, B. (1978). Perceptual limits of texture discrimination and their implications to figure-ground separation. In E. L. J. Leeuwenberg & H. F. J. M. Buffart (Eds.), *Formal theories of visual perception*, New York: Wiley.

Julesz, B. (1981). Textons, the elements of texture perception and their interactions. *Nature*, *290*, 91–97.

Julesz, B. (1983a). Textons, the fundamental elements in preattentive vision and perception of textures. *Bell System Technical Journal*, *62*, 1619–1645.

Julesz, B. (1983b). Adaptation in a peephole: A texton theory of preattentive vision. In L. Spillmann & B. R. Wooten (Eds.), *Sensory experience, adaptation, and perception*. Hillsdale, NJ: Lawrence Erlbaum Associates.

Julesz, B. (1984). A brief outline of the texton theory of human vision. *Trends in Neurosciences*, *7*, 41–45.

Julesz, B., & Bergen, J. (1983). Textons, the fundamental elements in preattentive vision and perception of texture. *Bell System Technical Journal*, *62*, 1619–1645.

Julesz, B., Gilbert, E. N., Shepp, L. A., & Frisch, H. L. (1973). Inability of humans to discriminate between visual textures that agree in second order statistics—revised. *Perception*, *2*, 391–405.

Julesz, B., & Schumer, R. A. (1981). Early visual perception. *Annual Review of Psychology*, *32*, 575–627.

Kaas, J. H. (1978). The organization of visual cortex in primates. In C. Noback (Ed.), *Sensory systems of primates*. New York: Plenum Press.

Kahn, J. I., & Foster, D. H. (1981). Visual comparison of rotated and reflected random-dot patterns as a function of their positional uncertainty and separation in the field. *Quarterly Journal of Experimental Psychology*, *33A*, 155–166.

Kahneman, D. (1968). Metacontrast: Method, findings, and theory in studies of visual masking. *Psychological Bulletin*, *70*, 404–425.

Kahneman, D., & Triesman, A. (1984). Changing views of attention and automaticity. In R. A. Parasuraman & D. R. Davies (Eds.), *Varieties of attention*. Orlando, FL: Academic Press.

Kanizsa, G. (1974). Contours without gradients or cognitive contours. *Italian Journal of Psychology*, *1*, 93–112.

Kanizsa, G. (1976). Subjective contours. *Scientific American*, *234*(4), 48–52.

Kanizsa, G. & Luccio, R. (1987). Pragnanz and its ambiguities. (Personal Correspondence).

Kant, I. (1781). *Critique of Pure Reason*. Riga.

Kaufman, L. (1974). *Sight and mind: An introduction to visual perception*. New York: Oxford University Press.

Kawabata, N., Yamagami, K., & Noaki, M. (1978). Visual fixation points and depth perception. *Visual Research, 18*, 853–854.

Kelly, D. H. (1972). Flicker. In D. Jameson & L. M. Hurvich (Eds.), *Handbook of sensory physiology: Visual* psychophysics (Vol. VII/4). New York: Springer-Verlag.

Kendrick, K. M., & Baldwin, B. A. (1987). Cells in temporal cortex of conscious sheep can respond preferentially to the sight of faces. *Science, 236*, 448–450.

Kidder, T. (1982). *The soul of a new machine.* New York: Avon.

Kinchla, R. A. (1974). Detecting target elements in multi-element arrays: A confusibility model. *Perception and Psychophysics*, 1974, *15*, 410–419.

Kinchla, R. A., Solis-Macias, V., & Hoffman, J. (1983). Attending to different levels of structure in a visual image. *Perception and Psychophysics, 33*, 1–10.

Kinchla, R. A., & Wolfe, J. (1979). The order of visual processing: "Top-down," "bottom-up," or "middle-out." *Perception and Psychophysics, 25*, 225–230.

Kinsbourne, M., & Warrington, E. K. (1962). The effect of an after-coming random pattern on the perception of brief visual stimuli. *The Quarterly Journal of Experimental Psychology, 14*, 223–234.

Klein, R. M., & Barresi, J. (1985). Perceptual salience of form versus material as a function of variation in spacing and number of elements. *Perception and Psychophysics, 37*, 440–446.

Knuth, D. E. (1976). Mathematics and computer science: Coping with finiteness. *Science, 194*, 1235–1242.

Koch, S. (1959). Epilogue. In S. Koch (Ed.), *Psychology: A study of a science* (Vol. 3). New York: McGraw-Hill.

Koffka, K. (1935). *Principles of Gestalt psychology*. New York: Harcourt, Brace.

Köhler, W. (1947). *Gestalt psychology: An introduction to the new concepts in modern psychology*. New York: Liverright. (Originally published, 1929)

Kolers, P. A. (1968). Some psychological aspects of pattern recognition. In P. A. Kolers & M. Eden (Eds.), *Recognizing patterns*. Cambridge, MA: MIT Press.

Kolers, P. A. (1970). The role of shape and geometry in picture recognition. In B. S. Lipkin & A. Rosenfeld (Eds.), *Picture processing and psychopictorics*. New York: Academic Press.

Kolers, P. A., & Rosner, B. S. (1960). On visual masking (metacontrast): Dichoptic observation. *American Journal of Psychology, 73*, 2–21.

Konorski, J. (1967). *Integrative activity of the brain*. Chicago: University of Chicago Press.

Kornblum, S. (1969). Sequential determinants of information processing in serial and discrete choice reaction time. *Psychological Review, 76*, 113–131.

Korte, A. (1915). Kinematoskopische untersuchungen. *Zeitschrift fur Psychologie, 72*, 193–296.

Krueger, L. E. (1978). A theory of perceptual matching. *Psychological Review, 85*, 278–304.

Krueger, L. E. (1984). The category effect in visual search depends on physical rather than conceptual differences. *Perception and Psychophysics, 35*, 558–564.

Krueger, L. E., & Chignell, M. H. (1985). Same-different judgements under high speed stress: Missing-feature principle predominates in early processing. *Perception and Psychophysics, 38*(2), 188–193.

Krumhansl, C. L. (1978). Concerning the applicability of geometric models to similarity data: The interrelationship between similarity and spatial density. *Psychological Review, 85*, 445–463.

Krumhansl, C. L. Independent processing of visual forms and motion. *Perception*, 1984, *13*, 535–546.

Kubovy, M., & Pomerantz, J. R. (1981). *Perceptual organization*. Hillsdale, NJ: Lawrence Erlbaum Associates.

Land, E. H. (1977). The retina theory of color vision. *Scientific American, 237*, 108–128.

Land, E. H. (1983). Recent advances in retinex theory and some implications for cortical computations: Color vision and the natural image. *Proceedings of the National Academy of Science* (USA), *80*, 5163–5169.

Land, E. H., & McCann, J. J. (1971). Lightness and retinex theory, *Journal of the Optical Society of America, 61*, 1–11.

Lanze, M., Maguire, W., & Weisstein, N. (1985). Emergent features: A new factor in the object-superiority effect. *Perception and Psychophysics, 38*, 438–442.

Lanze, M., Weisstein, N., & Harris, C. S. (1982). Perceived depth versus structural relevance in the object-superiority effect. *Perception & Psychophysics, 31*, 376–382.

Lappin, J. S., Doner, J. F., & Kottas, B. (1980). Minimal conditions for the visual detection of structure and motion in three dimensions. *Science, 209*, 717–719.

Lappin, J. S., & Fuqua, M. A. (1983). Accurate visual measurement of three-dimensional moving patterns. *Science, 221*, 480–482.

Lappin, J. S., & Uttal, W. R. (1976). Does prior knowledge facilitate the detection of visual targets in random noise? *Perception & Psychophysics, 20*, 367–374.

Lashley, K. S. (1942). The problem of cerebral organization in vision. *Biological Symposium, 7*, 301–322.

Lashley, K. S. (1950). In search of the engram. *Society of Experimental Biology Symposium, No. 4. Physiological Mechanisms of Behavior*, 454–482.

Lashley, K. S., Chow, K. L., & Semmes, J. (1951). An examination of the electrical field theory of cerebral integration. *Psychological Review, 58*, 123–136.

Lawden, M. C. (1983). An investigation of the ability of the human visual system to encode spatial phase relationships. *Vision Research, 12*, 1451–1463.

Lawton, T. B. (1984). The effect of phase structures on spatial phase discrimination. *Vision Research, 24*, 137–148.

Leeuwenberg, E. (1971). A perceptual coding language for visual and auditory patterns. *American Journal of Psychology, 84*, 307–349.

Lefton, L. (1973). Metacontrast: A review. *Perception and Psychophysics, 13*(1B), 161–171.

Liam, A. (1973). *Obiect and perceptual identity: Erroneous presuppositions in psychological studies of colour and space perception.* Olso: University of Olso.

Lindberg, D. C. (1976). *Theories of vision from Al-Kindi to Kepler.* Chicago: University of Chicago Press.

Ling, G., & Gerard, R. W. (1949). The normal membrane potential of frog sartorius fibers. *Journal of Cellular and Comparative Physiology, 34*, 383–385.

Locke, J. (1975). An essay concerning human understanding. In P. H. Nidditch (Ed.), *Clarendon edition of the works of John Locke.* Oxford: Oxford University Press. (Originally published 1690)

Lockhead, G. R. (1966). Effects of dimensional redundancy on visual discrimination. *Journal of Experimental Psychology, 72*, 95–104.

Lockhead, G. R. (1970). Identification and the form of multidimensional discrimination space. *Journal of Experimental Psychology, 85*, 1–10.

Lockhead, G. R. (1972). Processing dimensional stimuli: A note. *Psychological Review, 79*, 410–419.

Lowry, E. M., & De Palma, J. J. (1961). Sine-wave response of the visual system: I. The Mach phenomenon. *Journal of the Optical Society of America. 51*, 740–746.

Luce, R. D. (1963). Detection and recognition. In R. D. Luce, R. Bush, & E. Galanter, (Eds.), *Handbook of mathematical psychology* (Vol. 1). New York: Wiley.

Luckiesh, M. (1965). *Visual illusions.* New York: Dover.

Luneberg, R. K. (1950). The metric of binocular visual space. *Journal of the Optical Society of America, 40*, 627.

Lupker, S. J. (1979). On the nature of perceptual information during letter perception. *Perception & Psychophysics, 25*, 303–312.

Lynch, G. (1986). *Synapses, circuits, and the beginnings of memory.* Cambridge, MA: MIT Press.

Mach, E. (1959). *The analysis of sensations* (C. M. Williams Trans.). New York: Dover.

MacLeod, I. D. G., & Rosenfeld, A. (1972a). *The visibility of gratings: a space domain model.* (Tech. Rep. No. 205). College Park, MD: University of Maryland.

MacLeod, I. D. G., & Rosenfeld, A. (1972b). *The visibility of periodic bar patterns: Prediction of a space domain model.* (Tech. Rep. No. 209). College Park, MD: University of Maryland.

Mandelbrot, B. B. (1983).*The fractal geometry of nature.* New York: Freeman.

Marks, L. E. (1987). On cross-modal similarity: Auditory-visual interactions in speeded discrimination. *Journal of Experimental Psychology: Human Perception & Performance, 13*, 384–394.

Marr, D. (1982). *Vision: A computational investigation into the human representation and processing of visual information*. San Francisco: Freeman.

Marr, D., & Nishihara, H. K. (1978). Representation and recognition of the spatial organization of three-dimensional shapes. *Proceedings of the Royal Society of London, 200*, 269–294.

Marx, M. H., Hillix, W. A. (1973). *Systems and theories in psychology*. New York: McGraw-Hill.

McClelland, J. L. (1978). Perception and masking of wholes and parts. *Journal of Experimental Psychology: Human Perception & Performance, 4*, 210–223.

McClelland, J. L., Rumelhart, D. E., and the PDP research group. (1981). An interactive activation model of context effects in letter perception; Part 1. An account of Basic findings, *Psychological Review, 88*, 375–407.

McClelland, J. L., Rumelhart, D. E., and the PDP research group. (1986) *Parallel distributed processing: Explorations in the microstructure of cognition. Vol. 2: Psychological and biological models*. Cambridge, MA: MIT Press.

McCulloch, W. S., & Pitts, W. A. (1943). A logical calculus of the ideas immanent in nervous activity. *Bulletin of Mathematical Biophysics, 5*, 115–123.

McFarland, J. H. (1965). Sequential part presentation: A method of studying visual form perception. *British Journal of Psychology, 56*, 439–446.

McFarland, J. H., & Prete, M. (1969). The effect of visual context on perception of a form's parts as successive. *Vision Research, 9*, 923–933.

Meehl, P. E. (1978). Theoretical risks and tabular asterisks: Sir Karl, Sir Ronald, and the slow process of soft psychology. *Journal of Consulting and Clinical Psychology, 46*, 806–834.

Meisel, W. S. (1972). Computer oriented approaches to pattern recognition. In *Mathematics in science and engineering*. New York: Academic Press.

Metzler, J., & Shepard, R. N. (1971, April). *Mental correlates of the rotation of three-dimensional objects*. Paper presented at the Annual Meeting of the Western Psychological Association, San Francisco, CA.

Metzler, J., & Shepard, R. N. (1974). Transformational studies of the internal representation of three-dimensional objects. In R. L. Solso, (Ed.), *Theories of cognitive psychology: The Loyola Symposium*. Hillside, NJ: Lawrence Erlbaum Associates.

Miller, G. A., Galanter E., & Pribram, K. N. (1960). *Plans and the structure of behavior*. New York: Henry Holt.

Miller, J. (1981). Global precedence in attention and decision. *Journal of Experimental Psychology, 7*, 1161–1174.

Minsky, M., & Papert, S. (1969). *Perceptions: An introduction to computational geometry*. Cambridge, MA: MIT Press.

Monahan, J. S. & Lockhead, G. R. (1977). Identification of integral stimuli. *Journal of Experimental Psychology: General, 106*, 94–110.

Moore, E. F. (1956). Gedanken-experiments on sequential machines. In C. E. Shannon & J. McCarthy (Eds.), *Automata studies* (pp. 129–153). Princeton, NJ: Princeton University Press.

Morotomi, T. (1981). Selective reduction in visibility of a post target by an identical pre target masked by noise. *Perception and Psychophysics, 30*, 594–598.

Mostow, G. D. (1950). The extensibility of local Lie groups of transformations and groups on surfaces. *Annals of Mathematics, 52*, 606–636.

Mountcastle, V. B., Lynch, J. C., Georopoulos, A., Sakata, H., & Acuna, C. (1975). Posterior parietal association cortex of the monkey: Command functions for operations within extrapersonal space. *Journal of Neurophysiology, 38*, 871–908.

Nachmias, J., & Rogowitz, B. E. (1983). Masking by spatially-modulated gratings. *Vision Research, 23*, 1621–1629.

Nachmias, J.. & Weber, A. (1975). Discrimination of simple and complex gratings. *Vision Research, 15*, 217–222.

Nachmias, J., & Webster, A. (1983). Discrimination of simple and complex gratings. *Vision Research,* *23,* 1621–1629.

Nagano, T., & Fujiwara, M. (1979). A neural network model for the development of direction selectivity in the visual cortex. *Biological Cybernetics, 32,* 1–8.

Nakatani, K. (1980). A model of pattern recognition by binary orthogonal transformation. *Behaviormetrika, 2,* 47–59.

Navon, D. (1977). Forest before trees: The precedence of global features in visual perception. *Cognitive Psychology, 9,* 353–383.

Necker, L. A. (1832). On an apparent change of position in a drawing of engraved figure of a crystal. *Philosophical Magazine, 1.*

Neisser, U. (1967). *Cognitive pschology,* New York: Appleton–Century–Crofts.

Neisser, U. (1976). *Cognition and reality.* San Francisco: Freeman.

Nickerson, R. S. (1965). Response times for "same"-"different judgments. *Perceptual and Motor Skills, 20,* 15–18.

Nickerson, R. S. (1968). Note on "same"-"different" response times. *Perceptual and Motor Skills, 27,* 565–566.

Nickerson, R. S. (1969). "Same"-"different" response times: A model and a preliminary test. In W. G. Koster (Ed.), *Attention and performance II.* New York: Academic Press.

Nickerson, R. S. (1972). Binary classification reaction time: A review of some studies of human information processing capabilities. *Psychonomic Monograph Supplements, (Whole No. 65),* 275–318.

Nickerson, R. S. (1973). Frequency, recency, and repetition effects on same and different response times. *Journal of Experimental Psvchology, 101,* 330–336.

Nickerson, R. S. (1975). Effects of correlated and uncorrelated noise on visual pattern matching. In P. Rabbit & S. Dornic (Eds.), *Attention and Performance V.* New York: Academic Press.

Nickerson, R. S. (1976). Short-term retention of visually presented stimuli: Some evidence of visual encoding. *Acta Psychologica, 40,* 153–162.

Nickerson, R. S. (1978). On the time it takes to tell things apart. In J. Requin (Ed.), *Attention and Performance VII.* Hillsdale, NJ: Lawrence Erlbaum Associates, 77–88.

Nosofsky, R. (1985). Overall similarity and the identification of separable dimension stimuli: A choice model analysis. *Perception and Psychophysics, 38,* 415–432.

Ohzu, H., & Enoch, J. M. (1972). Optical modulation by the isolated human fovea. *Vision Research, 12,* 245–251.

Olson, C. X., & Boynton, R. M. (1984). Dichoptic metacontrast masking reveals a central basis for monoptic chromatic induction. *Perception & Psychophysics, 35*(4), 295–300.

Olton, D. S., Branch, M., & Best, P. J. (1978). Spatial correlates of hippocampal unit activity. *Experimental Neurology, 58,* 387–409.

Osgood, C. E. (1957). Motivational dynamics of language behavior. In M. R. Jones (Ed.), *Nebraska symposium on motivation.* Lincoln: University of Nebraska Press.

Oyama, T., & Watanabe, T.(1983). Effect of test-mask similarity on forward and backward masking of patterns by patterns. *Psychological Research. 45,* 303–313.

Paap, K. R., Newsome, S. L., McDonald, J. E., & Schvaneveldt, R. W. (1982). An activation-verification model for letter and word recognition: The word-superiority effect. *Psychological Review, 89,* 573–594.

Pachella, R. G., Smith, J. E. K., & Stanovich, K. E. (1978). Qualitative error analysis and speed classification. In N. J. Castellan & F. Restle (Eds.), *Cognitive theory* (Vol. 3). Hillsdale, NJ: Lawrence Erlbaum Associates.

Palmer, S. E. (1975). Visual perception and world knowledge: Notes on a model of sensory-cognitive interaction. In D. A. Norman & D. E. Rumelhart (Eds.), *Explorations in cognition.* San Francisco: Freeman.

Pavio, A. (1978). The relationship between verbal and perceptual codes. In E. C. Carterette & M. P. Friedman (Eds.), *Handbook of perception, Vol. III: Perceptual coding* (pp. 376–397). New York: Academic Press.

Perrett, D. I., Rolls, E. T., & Caan, W. (1982). Visual neurones responsive to faces in the monkey temporal cortex. *Experimental Brain Research, 47*, 329–342.

Peterson, M. A. (1986). Illusory concomitant motion in ambiguous stereograms: Evidence for nonstimulus contributions to perceptual organization. *Journal of Experimental Psychology: Human Perception and Performance, 12*, 50–60.

Petry, S., & Meyer, G. E. (1986). Adelphi international conference on illusory contours: A report on the conference. *Perception and Psychophysics, 39*(3), 210–221.

Piaget, J. (1969). *The mechanisms of perception.* (G. N. Seagrim Trans.). New York: Basic Books.

Pieron, H. (1935). Le processus de metacontraste. *Journal de Psychologie Normale et Pathologique, 32*, 5–24.

Pinker, S. (1985). *Visual cognition.* Cambridge, MA: MIT Press.

Pippenger, N. (1978). Complexity theory. *Scientific American, 238*(6), 140–159.

Pitts, W., & McCulloch, W. S. (1947). How we know universals: The perception of auditory and visual forms. *Bulletin of Mathematical Biophysics, 9*, 127–147.

Pollack, I. (1971). Perception of two-dimensional Markov constraints within visual displays. *Perception and Psychophysics, 9*, 461–464.

Pollack, I. (1972). Visual discrimination of "unseen" objects: Forced choice testing of Mayzner–Tresselt sequential blanking effects. *Perception and Psychophysics, 11*, 121–128.

Pollack, I. (1973). Discrimination of third-order Markov constraints within visual displays. *Perception and Psychophysics, 13*, 276–280.

Pomerantz, J. R., & Kubovy, M. (1981). *Perceptual Organization.* Hillsdale, NJ: Lawrence Erlbaum Associates.

Pomerantz, J. R., Sager, C. S., & Stoever, R. J. (1977). Perception of wholes and of their component parts: Some configural superiority effects. *Journal of Experimental Psychology: Human Perception & Performance, 3*, 422–435.

Popper, K. R., & Eccles, J. C. (1977). *The self and its brain.* New York: Springer-Verlag.

Posner, M. I. (1969). Abstraction and the process of recognition. In G. Bower & J. T. Spence (Eds.), *Psychology of learning and motivation* (Vol. 3). New York: Academic Press.

Posner, M. I. (1978). *Chronometric explorations of mind.* Hillsdale, NJ: Lawrence Erlbaum Associates.

Posner, M. I., & Mitchell, R. F. (1967). Chronometric analysis of classification. *Psychological Review, 74*, 392–409.

Posner, M. I., Boies, S. J., Eichelman, W. H., & Taylor, R. L. (1969). Retention of visual and name codes of single letters. *Journal of Experimental Psychology, 79*, 1–16.

Posner, M. I., Snyder, C. R. R., & Davidson, B. J. (1980). Attention and the detection of signals. *Journal of Experimental Psychology: General, 109*, 160–174.

Pratt, W. K. (1978). *Digital image processing.* New York: Wiley.

Pribram, K. H., Nuwer, M., & Baron, R. J. (1974). The holographic hypothesis of memory structure in brain function and perception. In D. H. Krantz (Ed.), *Contemporary developments in mathematical psychology* (Vol. II). San Francisco: Freeman.

Price, H. H. (1940). *Hume's theory of the external world.* Oxford: Clarendon Press.

Prinzmetal, W., & Banks, W. P. (1977). Good continuation affects visual detection. *Perception and Psychophysics, 21*, 389–395.

Proctor, R. W. (1981). A unified theory for matching-task phenomena. *Psychological Review, 88*, 291–326.

Proctor, R. W., & Rao, K. V. (1981). On the "misguided" use of reaction time differences: A discussion of Ratcliff & Hacker (1981). *Perception & Psychophysics, 31*, 601–602.

Pylyshyn, Z. W. (1979). Validating computational models: A critique of Anderson's indeterminacy of representation claim. *Psychological Review, 86*, 383–394.

Pylyshyn, Z. W. (1981). The imagery debate: Analogue media versus tactic knowledge. *Psychological Review, 87*, 16–45.

Raab, D. (1963). Backward masking. *Psychological Bulletin, 60*, 118–129.

Ramachandran, V. S. (1985). The neurobiology of perception. *Perception, 14*, 97–103.

Ranck, J. (1973). Studies on single neurons in dorsal hippocampal formation and septum in unrestrained rats. Part 1. Behavior correlates and firing repertoires. *Experimental Neurology, 41,* 461–531.

Ratcliff, R. (1981). A theory of order relations in perceptual matching. *Psychological Review, 88,* 552–572.

Ratcliff, R., & Hacker, M. J. (1981a). Speed and accuracy of same and different responses in perceptual matching. *Perception & Psychophysics, 30,* 303–307.

Ratcliff, R., & Hacker, M. J. (1981b). On the misguided use of reaction time differences: A reply to Proctor & Rao. *Perception & Psychophysics, 31,* 603–604.

Ratcliff, R., & Hacker, M. J. (1982). On the misguided use of reaction-time differences: A reply to Proctor and Rao (1982). *Perception & Psychophysics, 31,* 603–604.

Ratliff, F. (1965). *Mach bands: Quantitative studies on neural networks in the retina.* San Francisco: Holden-Day.

Ratliff, F., & Hartline, H. K. (1959). The responses of Limulus optic nerve fibers to patterns of illumination on the receptor mosaic. *Journal of General Physiology, 42,* 1241–1255.

Reicher, G. M. (1969). Perceptual recognition as a function of the meaningfulness of stimulus material. *Journal of Experimental Psychology, 81,* 274–280.

Reicher, G. M., & Wheeler, D. D. (1970). Processes in word recognition. *Cognitive Psychology, 1,* 59–85.

Restle, F. A. (1961). *Psychology of judgment and choice.* New York: Wiley.

Robinson, D. N. (1966). Disinhibition of visually masked stimuli. *Science, 154.* 157–158.

Robinson, D. N. (1968). Visual disinhibition with binocular and interoculat presentation. *Journal of the Optical Society of America, 58,* 254–257.

Robinson, J. O. (1972). *The Psychology of visual illusion.* London: Hutchinson University Library.

Robson, J. G. (1983). Frequency domain visual processing. In O. J. Braddick & A. C. Sleigh (Eds.), *Physical and biological processing of images.* Berlin: Springer-Verlag.

Rock, I. (1975). *An introduction to perception.* New York: MacMillan.

Rock, I. (1983). *The logic of perception.* Cambridge, MA: MIT Press.

Rogers, T. D., & Trofanenko, S. C. (1979). On the measurement of shape. *Bulletin of Mathematical Biology, 41,* 238–304.

Rosch, E. (1975). Cognitive representations of sematic categories. *Journal of Experimental Psychology: General, 104,* 192–233.

Rosenblatt, F. (1958). The perceptron: A probabilistic model for information storage and organization in the brain. *Psychological Review, 65,* 386–408.

Rosenblatt, F. (1962). *Principles of neurodynamics.* Washington, DC: Spartan Books.

Rosenfeld, A. (1969). *Picture processing by computer.* New York: Academic Press.

Rosenfeld, A., & Kac, A. C. (1982). *Digital picture processing* (Vols. 1 & 2). Orlando, FL: Academic Press.

Royce, J. R. (1974). Cognition and knowledge: Psychological epistemology. In E. C. Carterette & M. P. Friedman (Eds.), *Handbook of perception, Vol. I: Historical and philosophical roots of perception* (pp. 149–176). New York: Academic Press.

Rumelhart, D. E. (1977). *Introduction to human information processing.* New York: Wiley.

Rumelhart, D. E., & McClelland, J. L. (1982). An interactive activation model of context effects in letter perception: Part 2. The contextual enhancement effect and some tests and extension of the model. *Psychological Review, 89,* 60–94.

Rumelhart, D. E., McClelland, J. L., and the PDP research group. (1986). *Parallel distributed processing: Explorations in the microstructure of cognition. Vol. 1: Foundations.* Cambridge, MA: MIT Press.

Ryle, G. (1949). *The concept of mind.* New York: Barnes & Noble.

Sachs, M. B., Nachmias, J., & Robson, J. G. (1971). Spatial frequency channels in human vision. *Journal of the Optical Society of America, 61,* 1176–1186.

Sagi, D., & Hochstein, S. (1983). Discriminability of suprathreshold compound spatial frequency gratings. *Vision Research, 12,* 1595–1606.

Sakitt, B. (1972). Counting every quantum. *Journal of Physiology, 223,* 131–150.

Santee, J. L., & Egeth, H. E. (1982). Independence versus interference in the perceptual processing of letters. *Perception & Psychophysics, 31,* 101–116.

Schade, O. H. (1956). Optical and photoelectric analog of the eye. *Journal of the Optical Society of America, 46,* 721–739.

Scheerer, E. (1973). Integration, interruption, and processing rate in visual backward masking: 1, Review. *Psychologische Forschung, 36,* 71–93.

Schiller, P. H., & Smith, M. C. (1966). Detection in metacontrast. *Journal of Experimental Psychology, 71,* 32–39.

Schneider, W. (1987). Session I—Presidential Address. Connectionism: Is it a paradigm shift for psychology? *Behavior Research Methods, Instruments, & Computers, 19*(2), 73–83.

Schneider, W., & Shiffrin, R. M. (1977). Controlled and automatic human information processing. I. Detection, search, and attention. *Psychological Review, 84,* 1–66.

Schonemann, P. H., Dorcey, T., & Kienapple, K. (1985). Subadditive concatenation in dissimilarity judgments. *Perception & Psychophysics, 38,* 1–17.

Schwartz, E. L. (1977). Afferent geometry in the primate visual cortex and the generation of neuronal trigger features. *Biological Cybernetics, 28,* 1–14.

Schwartz, E. L. (1980). Computational anatomy and functional architecture of striate cortex: A spatial mapping approach to perceptual coding. *Vision Research, 20,* 645–669.

Selfridge, O. (1959). *Pandemonium: A paradigm for learning. In Symposium on the mechanization of thought processes.* London: HM Stationary Office.

Selwyn, E. W. H. (1948). *Photographic Journal,* Sec. B., 88B.

Shaw, M. L. (1978). A capacity allocation model for reaction time. *Journal of Experimental Psychology: Human Perception & Performance, 4,* 586–598.

Shaw, R., & Bransford, J. (1977). *Perceiving, acting, and knowing: Towards an ecological psychology.* Hillsdale, NJ: Lawrence Erlbaum Associates.

Shaw, R. E., & Turvey, M. T. (1981). Coalitions as models for ecosystems: A realist perspective on perceptual organization. In M. Kubovy & J. R. Pomerantz (Eds.), *Perceptual organization* (pp. 343–415). Hillsdale, NJ: Lawrence Erlbaum Associates.

Shepard, R. N. (1957). Stimulus and response generalization: A stochastic model relating generalization to distance in a psychological space. *Psychometrika, 22,* 325–345.

Shepard, R. N. (1962). The analysis of proximities: Multidimensional scaling with unknown distances. Part I. *Psychometrika, 27,* 125–140.

Shepard, R. N. (1964). Attention and the metric structure of the stimulus space. *Journal of Mathematical Psychology, 1,* 54–87.

Shepard, R. N. (1968). *On turning something over in one's mind.* Unpublished manuscript, Stanford University.

Shepard, R. N. (1978). Externalization of mental images and the act of creation. In B. S. Randhawa & W. E. Coffman (Eds.), *Visual learning, thinking, and communication.* New York: Academic Press.

Shepard, R. N. (1981). Psychophysical complementarity. In M. Kubovy & J. R. Pomerantz (Eds.), *Perceptual organization* (pp. 279–341). Hillsdale, NJ: Lawrence Erlbaum Associates.

Shepard, R. N., & Cooper, L. A. (1982). *Mental images and their transformations.* Cambridge, MA: MIT Press.

Shepard, R. N., & Metzler, J. (1971). Mental rotation of three-dimensional objects. *Science, 171,* 701–703.

Shiffrin, R. M., & Schneider, W. (1977). Controlled and automatic human information processing. II. Perceptual learning, automatic attending, and a general theory. *Psychological Review, 84,* 127–190.

Shor, R. (1971). Symbol processing speed differences and symbol interference effects in a variety of concept domains. *Journal of General Psychology, 85,* 187–205.

Simon, H. A. (1979). *Models of thought.* New Haven: Yale University Press.

Smith, J. E. K. (1980). Models of identification. In R. S. Nickerson (Ed.), *Attention and Performance Vol. VIII.* Hillsdale, NJ: Lawrence Erlbaum Associates.

Smith, M. C., & Schiller, P. H. (1966). Forward and backward masking: A comparison. *Canadian Journal of Psychology, 20,* 191–197.

Sneddon, I. N. (1976). *Encyclopaedic dictionary of mathematics for engineers and applied scientists.* Oxford: Permagon.

Snodgrass, J. G., & Townsend, J. T. (1980). Comparing parallel and serial models: Theory and implementation. *Journal of Experimental Psychology: Human Perception and Performance, 6,* 330–354.

Snyder, C. R. R. (1972). Selection, inspection and naming in visual research. *Journal of Experimental Psychology, 92,* 428–431.

Sperling, G. (1960). The information available in brief visual presentations. *Psychological Monographs: General and Applied, 74,* 1–29.

Sperling, G. (1963). A model for visual memory tasks. *Human Factors, 5,* 19–31.

Sperling, G. (1981). Mathematical models of binocular vision. In S. Grosberg (Ed.), *Mathematical psychology and psychophysiology.* Providence, RI: American Mathematical Society.

Sperry, R. W., Miner, R., & Meyers, R. E. (1955). Visual pattern perception following subpail slicing and tantalum wire implantations in the visual cortex. *Journal of Comparative and Physiological Psychology, 48,* 50–58.

Staller, J. D., & Lappin, J. S. (1981). The visual detection of multi-letter patterns. *Journal of Experimental Psychology: Human Perception and Performance, 7,* 1258–1272.

Sternberg, S. (1966). High speed scanning in human memory. *Science, 153,* 652–654.

Sternberg, S. (1967). Two operations in character recognition. Some evidence from reaction time experiments. *Perception & Psychophysics, 2,* 45–53.

Stevens, K. A. (1983). Slant-Tilt: The visual encoding of surface orientation. *Biological Cybernetics, 46,* 183–195.

Stevens, K. A. (1984). On gradients and texture gradients. *Journal of Experimental Psychology: General, 113,* 17–220.

Stevens, K. A. (1986). Inferring shape from contours across surfaces. In A. P. Pentland (Ed.), *From pixels to predicates.* Norwood, NJ: Ablex.

Stevens, S. S. (1951). Mathematics, measurement, and psychophysics. In S. S. Stevens (Ed.), *Handbook of experimental psychology.* New York: Wiley.

Stigler, R. (1910). Chronophotische studien uber den umgebungs kontrast. *Pfluuger's Archiv fur die Gesante Physiologie des Menschen und der Tiere, 134,* 365–435.

Stockmeyer, L. J., & Chandra, A. K. (1979). Intrinsically difficult problems. *Scientific American, 240,* 140–159.

Stroop, J. R. (1935). Studies of interference in serial verbal reactions. *Journal of Experimental Psychology, 18,* 643–662.

Swenson, R. G., & Judy, P. F. (1981). Detection of noisy visual targets: Models for the effects of spatial uncertainty and signal to noise ration. *Perception & Psychophysics, 29,* 521–534.

Teller, D. Y. (1984). Linking propositions. *Vision Research, 24,* 1233–1246.

Thomas, J. (1978). Binocular rivalry: The effects of orientation and pattern color arrangement. *Perception & Psychophysics, 23,* 360–362.

Thomas, J. P., Gille, J., & Barker, R. A. (1982). Simultaneous visual detection and identification: Theory and data. *Journal of the Ophthalmology Society of America, 72*(12), 1642–1650.

Thompson, D. W. (1917). *On Growth and Form.* Cambridge: Cambridge, University Press.

Titchener, E. B. (1896). *An outline of psychology.* New York: MacMillan.

Todd, J. T. (1985). Perception of structure from motion. Is projective correspondence of moving elements a necessary condition. *Journal of Experimental Psychology: Human Perception and Performance, 11,* 689–710.

Tolansky, F. R. S. (1964). *Optical illusions.* Oxford: Pergamon Press.

Torgenson, W. S. (1958). *Theory and methods of scaling.* New York: Wiley.

Torgenson, W. S. (1965). Multidimensional scaling of similarity. *Psychometrika, 30,* 379–393.

Townsend, J. T. (1971a). Theoretical analysis of an alphabetic confusion matrix. *Perception & Psychophysics, 9,* 40–50.

Townsend, J. T. (1971b). Alphabetic confusion: A test of models for individuals. *Perception & Psychophysics, 9,* 449–454.

Townsend, J. T., & Ashby, F. G. (1982). Experimental test of contemporary mathematical models of visual letter recognition. *Journal of Experimental Psychology: Human Perception and Performance, 8,* 834–864.

Townsend, J. T., & Landon, D. E. (1983). Mathematical models of recognition and confusion in psychology. *Mathematical Social Sciences, 4,* 25–71.

Trevarthen, C. B. (1968). Two mechanisms of vision in primates. *Psychologische Forschung, 31,* 299–337.

Triesman, A. (1986). Features and objects in visual processing. *Scientific American, 255,* 114B–126.

Triesman, A., & Gelade, G. (1980). A feature integration theory of attention. *Cognitive Psychology, 12,* 97–136.

Triesman, A., & Patterson, R. (1984). Emergent features, attention, and object perception, *Journal of Experimental Psychology: Human Perception and Performance. 10,* 12–31.

Triesman, A., & Schmidt, H. (1982). Illusory conjunctions in the perception of objects. *Cognitive Psychology, 14,* 107–141.

Triesman, A., & Souther, J. (1985). Search Assymetry: A diagnostic for preattentive processing of separable features. *Journal of Experimental Psychology: General, 114*(3), 285–310.

Triesman, A., Sykes, M., & Gelade, G. (1977). Selective attention and stimulus integration. In S. Dornic (Ed.), *Attention and performance, VI.* Hillsdale, NJ: Lawrence Erlbaum Associates.

Tulving, E. (1979). Memory research: What kind of progress? In L. G. Nilsson (Ed.), *Perspectives in memory research.* Hillsdale, NJ: Lawrence Erlbaum Associates.

Turing, A. M. (1936). On computable numbers with an application to the entscheidungs problem. *Proceedings of the London Mathematical Society* (series 2), *42,* 230–265.

Turvey, M. T. (1973). On peripheral and central processes in vision information processing analysis of masking with patterned stimuli. *Psychological Review, 80,* 1–52.

Turvey, M. T. (1977). Contrasting orientations to the theory of visual information processing. *Psychological Review, 84,* 67–88.

Turvey, M. T., & Shaw, R. E. (1979). The primacy of perceiving: An ecological reformulation of perception for understanding memory. In L. G. Nilsson (Ed.), *Perspectives on memory research: essays in honor of Uppsala University's 500th anniversary.* Hillsdale, NJ: Lawrence Erlbaum Associates.

Turvey, M. T., Shaw, R. E., & Mace, W. (1978). Issues in the theory of action: Degrees of freedom, coordinative structures, and coalitions. In J. Requin (Ed.), *Attention and performance, VII.* Hillsdale, NJ: Lawrence Erlbaum Associates.

Tversky, A. (1977). Features of Similarity. *Psychological Review, 84,* 327–352.

Tversky, A., & Gati, I. (1982). Similarity, separability, and the triangle inequality. *Psychological Review, 89,* 123–154.

Tversky, A.. & Hutchinson, J. W. (1986). Nearest neighbor analysis of psychological spaces. *Psychological Review, 93,* 3–22.

Ullman, S. (1979). *The interpretation of visual motion.* Cambridge, MA: MIT Press.

Uttal, W. R. (1969a). Masking of alphabetic character recognition by dynamic visual noise (DVN). *Perception & Psychophysics, 6,* 121–128.

Uttal, W. R. (1969b).The character in the hole experiment: Interaction of forward and backward masking of alphabetic character recognition by dynamic visual noise (DVN). *Perception & Psychophysics, 6,* 177–181.

Uttal, W. R. (1970a). Masking of alphabetic character recognition by ultrahigh-density dynamic visual noise. *Perception & Psychophysics, 7,* 19–22.

Uttal, W. R. (1970b). Violations of visual simultaneity. *Perception & Psychophysics, 7,* 133–136.

Uttal, W. R. (1970c). On the physiological basis of masking with dotted visual noise. *Perception & Psychophysics, 7,* 321–327.

Uttal, W. R. (1970d). A masking approach to the problem of form perception. *Perception & Psychophysics, 9,* 296–298.

Uttal, W. R. (1973a). The effect of deviations from linearity on the detection of dotted line patterns. *Vision Research, 13,* 2155–2163.

Uttal, W. R. (1973b). *The psychobiology of sensory coding.* New York: Harper Row.

Uttal, W. R. (1975). *An autocorrelation theory of form detection.* Hillsdale, NJ: Lawrence Erlbaum Associates.

Uttal, W. R. (1976). Visual spatial interactions between dotted line segments. *Vision Research, 16,* 581–586.

Uttal, W. R. (1977). Complexity effects in form detection. *Vision Research, 17,* 359–365.

Uttal, W. R. (1978). *The psychobiology of mind.* Hillsdale, NJ: Lawrence Erlbaum Associates.

Uttal, W. R. (1981). *A taxonomy of visual processes.* Hillsdale, NJ: Lawrence Erlbaum Associates.

Uttal, W. R. (1983). *Visual form detection in 3-dimensional space.* Hillsdale, NJ: Lawrence Erlbaum Associates.

Uttal, W. R. (1985). *The detection of nonplanar surfaces in visual space.* Hillsdale, NJ.: Lawrence Erlbaum Associates.

Uttal, W. R. (1987). *The perception of dotted forms.* Hillsdale, NJ: Lawrence Erlbaum Associates.

Uttal, W. R., Bunnell, L. M., & Corwin, S. (1970). On the detectability of straight lines in visual noise: An extension of French's paradigm into the millisecond domain. *Perception & Psychophysics, 8,* 385–388.

Uttal, W. R., Davis, N. S., Welke, C. L., & Kakarala, R. (in press). The reconstruction of static visual forms from sparse dotted samples. *Perception and Psychophysics.*

Uttal, W.R,. & Hieronymous, R. (1970). Spatio-temporal effects in visual gap detection. *Perception & Psychophysics, 8,* 321–325.

Van Essen, D. C. (1985). Functional organization of primate visual cortex. *Cerebral Cortex, 3,* 259–329.

van Meeteren, A., & Barlow, H. B. (1981). The statistical efficiency for detecting sinusoidal modulation of average dot density in random figures. *Vision Research, 21,* 765–777.

von Neumann, J. (1951). The general and logical theory of automata. In L. A. Jeffries (Ed.), *Cerebral mechanisms in behavior: The Hixon symposium.* New York: Wiley.

Van Tuijl, H. F. J. M. (1975). A new visual illusion: Neonlike color spreading and complementary color induction between subjective contours. *Acta Psychologica Amsterdamn, 39,* 441–445.

Wade, N. J. (1978). Why do patterned afterimages fluctuate in visibility? *Psychological Bulletin, 85,* 238–352.

Wagner, M. (1985). The metric of visual space. *Perception & Psychophysics, 38*(6), 483–495.

Wallach, H. (1939). On constancy of visual speed. *Psychological Review, 46,* 541–552.

Wallach, H. (1948). Brightness constancy and the nature of achromatic colors. *Journal ᵕᶠExperimental Psychology, 38,* 310–324.

Ward, I. (1985). Individual differences in processing stimulus dimensions: Relation to selective processing abilities. *Perceptual & Psychophysics, 37,* 471–482.

Warren, R. M., & Warren, R. P. (1968). *Helmholtz on perception: Its physiology and development.* New York: Wiley.

Watanabe, S. (1985). *Pattern recognition: Human and mechanical.* New York: Wiley.

Watson, A. B. (1982). Summation of grating patches indicate many types of detector at one retinal location. *Vision Research, 22,* 17–25.

Watson, A. B. (1983). Detection and recognition of simple spatial forms. In O. J. Braddick & A. C. Sleigh (Eds.), *Physical and biological processing of images.* Berlin: Springer-Verlag.

Watson, A. B., & Ahumada, A. J. (1985). Model of human visual-motion sensing. *Journal of the Optical Society of America, 2,* 322–341.

Webster's new world dictionary. (1976). (2d college ed. D. B. Gwalink, Editor-in-Chief). Cleveland: William Collins & World Publishing.

Weisstein, N. (1972). Metacontrast. In D. Jameson & L. M. Hurvich (Eds.), *Handbook of sensory physiology: Visual psychophysics* (Vol. VII/4). New York: Springer-Verlag.

Weisstein, N. (1980). The joy of Fourier analysis. In C. S. Harris (Ed.), *Visual coding and adaptability* (pp. 365–380). Hillsdale, NJ: Lawrence Erlbaum Associates.

Weisstein, N., & Harris, C. S. (1974). Visual detection of line segments: An object-superiority effect. *Science, 186,* 752–755.

Weisstein, N., & Harris, C. S. (1980). Masking and the unmasking of distributed representations in the visual system. In C. S. Harris (Ed.), *Visual coding and adaptability* (pp. 317–364). Hillsdale, NJ: Lawrence Erlbaum Associates.

Weisstein, N., Jurkens, T., & Ondersin, T. (1970). Effect of forced choice vs. magnitude-estimation measures on the waveform of metacontrast type functions. *Journal of the Optical Society of America, 60,* 978–980.

Weisstein, N., Williams, M. C., & Harris, C. S. (1982). Depth, connectedness, and structural relevance in the object superiority effect: Line segments are harder to see in flatter patterns. *Perception, 11,* 5–17.

Werner, H. (1935). Studies on contour: I. Qualitative analysis. *American Journal of Psychology, 47,* 40–64.

Werner, H., & Wapner, S. (1952). Towards a general theory of perception. *Psychological Review, 59,* 324–338.

Wertheimer, M. (1923). Unterchungen zur Lehre von der Gestalt, II. *Psychologische Forschung, 4,* 301–350.

Wheeler, D. D. (1970). Processes in word recognition. *Cognitive Psychology, 1,* 59–85.

Whorf, B. L. (1956). *Language, thought, and reality.* Cambridge, MA: Technology Press.

Whyte, L. L. (1951). Aspects of Form. New York: Pellegrini & Cudahy.

Williams, A., & Weisstein, N. (1978). Line segments are perceived better in coherent context than alone: An object-line effect. *Memory and Cognition, 6,* 85–90.

Wolford, G. (1975). Perturbation model for letter identification. *Psychological Review, 82,* 84–199.

Yang, H. S., & Kac, A. C. (1986). Determination of the identity, position, and orientation of the topmost object in a pile. *Computer Vision, Graphics and Image Processing, 36,* 229–255.

Young, M. J. (1985). *Detection of dotted forms in a structured visual noise environment.* Unpublished master's thesis, University of Michigan.

Zusne, L. (1970). *Visual perception of form.* New York: Academic Press.

Zusne, L. (1975). Form perception bibliography 1968–1973. *JSAS Catalog of Selected Documents in Psychology, 5,* 272.

Zusne, L, (1981). Form perception bibliography 1974–1978. *JSAS Catalog of Selected Documents in Psychology, 11,* 48–49.

AUTHOR INDEX

Numbers in italics *denote reference citations.*

A

Abadi, R. V. 78, *300*
Ableson, R. P. 106, *300*
Abu-Mostafa, Y. S. 38, *300*
Acuna, C. 32, *312*
Adelson, E. H. 90, *300*
Ahumada, A. J. 90, *319*
Aiba, T. S. 43, *300*
Albrecht, P. G. 117, *304*
Allik, J. 158, *301*
Altom, M. J. 244, 245, *307*
Alpern, M. 158, *300*
Andersen, G. J. 259, *302*
Anderson, J. A. 35, 94, 215, *307*
Anderson, J. R. 35, 94, 215, *300*
Andreassi, J. L. 158, *300*
Andrews, H. C. 84, *300*
Appleman, J. B. 228, *300*
Arbib, M. A. 106, *300*
Armstrong, D. M. 67, *300*
Arnheim, R. 20, *300*
Arnoult, M. D. 21, *300*
Ashby, F. G. 226, 268, *318*
Attneave, F. 21, 179, *300*
Auslander, L. 91, *300*

B

Bachmann, T. 46, 158, *301*
Baird, J. C. 172, *308*
Baldwin, B. A. 79, *310*
Bamber, D. 209, *301*
Banks, W. P. 145, 155, 156, *301, 314*
Barker, R. A. 165, *317*
Barlow, H. B. 78, 90, 122, 143, 144, 188, 191, *301, 302, 303, 319*
Baron, R. J. 38, 82, 249, *301, 314*
Barresi, J. 168, *310*
Bates, M. 244, *307*
Beck, J. 153, 188, 196, 292, *301*
Becker, B. B. 158
Beller, H. K. 210, *301*
Bennett, B. M. 57, 68, 259, 272, 281, *301, 302, 307*
Bergen, J. R. 45, 90, 196, 197, *300, 301, 309*
Berkeley, G. 39, 67, *301*
Bernstein, I. H. 158, *301*
Best, P. J. 32, *313*
Beyda, D. 158, *300*
Biederman, I. 273, *301*
Birdsall, T. G. 165, *306*
Bjork, E. L. 44, 155, 156, *302*

321

SUBJECT INDEX